THE WISDOM OF THE SCOTS

THE WISDOM
OF THE SCOTS

A Choice and a Comment by
MORAY McLAREN

LONDON
MICHAEL JOSEPH

First published by
MICHAEL JOSEPH LTD
26 Bloomsbury Street
London, W.C.1
1961

Set and printed in Great Britain by Unwin Brothers Limited
at the Gresham Press, Woking, in Plantin type, ten-point,
leaded, on paper made by Henry Bruce at Currie, Midlothian,
and bound by James Burn at Esher.

CAROLINAE

PUELLAE PRUDENTISSIMAE
PULCHERRIMAE
ANGLORUMQUE VEL ANGELORUM
SAPIENTIA
IAM PRAEDITAE
HUNC LIBRUM

D.D.D.

EDITOR

Contents

Acknowledgments

I wish to thank:

Messrs. Thos. Nelson & Sons Ltd., Edinburgh, for the right to reproduce Lord Cooper's translation of 'The Declaration of Arbroath' and the extract from his 'The Declaration of Arbroath Revisited.'

Messrs. John Murray Ltd. for the right to reproduce the definitive version of Montrose's *To His Mistress*.

Admiral Cunninghame Graham for the right to reproduce an extract from *Success*, by R. B. Cunninghame Graham.

Messrs. Wm. Blackwood, Messrs. Methuen & Co. and Messrs. Wm. MacLellan for the rights to reproduce from the poetry of Hugh MacDiarmid (C. M. Grieve).

I would also like to thank Sir Compton Mackenzie for his permission to use extracts from his Rectorial Address to the students of Glasgow University.

As always I have received the greatest courtesy and help from the Librarians. In particular I thank the National Library of Scotland and the Keepers of the Reference Room of the Edinburgh Public Library.

An Apologia

When Messrs. Michael Joseph asked me to contribute to their 'Wisdom' series and suggested that, in one round, I should take on all Scotland, I at first declined: I didn't believe that there was, or ever had been, a coherent body of ideas or opinion that could be labelled 'the wisdom of the Scots'; nor, even if such a thing did remotely exist, could I see myself presenting it.

If I was uncertain about the general wisdom of the Scots, I never doubted their capacity for sardonic or unspoken disapproval. There might be some among the more thick-skinned of my compatriot professional writers who could face the obloquy or silent contempt of nearly all Scots who saw a book on 'the wisdom of the Scots' by another Scot: I did not think I could endure it. Nor did the unworthy and passing thought that the book might be meant for export only console me. I did not relish the role of an intellectual Harry Lauder rolling my cerebral R's across the Border or conveying highbrow equivalents of pawky, dour or sentimental sagacity overseas to the English-speaking world. However, I replied, giving my first objection about the lack of coherent Scottish wisdom:—

There is scarcely a belief, opinion or piece of wisdom which Scotsmen have held, uttered, fought or died for, which other Scots have not flatly and Scottishly denied. This is true of both high and trivial things. The Scots Shorter Catechism opens by stating that 'Man's chief end is to glorify God and enjoy Him for ever,' and this noble sentence has resounded down the centuries; but there have always been Scots who have, with a strong national note in their voices, dismissed it as empty rhetoric. Many others have equally characteristically denied it in their demeanour, in their grim unsmiling faces and in their behaviour. They don't propose to enjoy Him or anything else for ever—or possibly at all. Again there are others who propose to enjoy everything, even the most trivial things, all at once, all the time and, if their beliefs allow them, for ever, with an open gusto which more temperate or more compromising peoples find offensive.

Then what about the great and famous? Is the wisdom of the Scots to be found in Duns Scotus or in David Hume, in John Knox's blasts against women or idolatry or in Queen Mary's replies, in the countless Scots writers who have supported Knox or in the numerous historians and polemical authors who argue for Mary? Is one to find the true

Scottish wisdom amongst the common-sense philosophers and econo-
mists of Edinburgh's 'Golden Age,' the eighteenth century, or, still
within the extent of those hundred significant years, in the beliefs for
which many men (humble as well as famous) died—Jacobitism? And
what about Robert Burns and Walter Scott, who, while the same
Golden Age of Reason was being at its most reasonable in Edinburgh,
Glasgow, Aberdeen and many Scottish country places, were giving a
very different view of Scotland to the world? And what about Carlyle
and R. L. S.? And what about the inspired lunacy of McGonagall?
And what about some moderns? And so on. . . .

But a nation's wisdom, you could say, is found not only in its
literature but in the sayings, proverbs, folk-tales, folk-poetry and
behaviour of its ordinary people. Maybe, but I could point out that
the 'wisdom of the Scots' is just as difficult and elusive in the popular
mouth. Do you find it in the partly humorous, denigratory wise-saws
of the men of Aberdeenshire and the Lowlands, those men whom one
must describe by the unavoidable *cliché* of 'hard-headed'? Isn't the
torrent of Gaelic impetuosity equally (see the definition of 'Scot' in
the Oxford Dictionary) Scottish? Haven't we often been assured in
the Gaelic tongue that the world is well lost for love, honour, or other
immaterial things? And how the Lowland farmer of tradition would
laugh at such notions!

And there are divisions within the divisions. The 'cautious Low-
lander,' the enemy of poetry, the progenitor of the 'saxpence-banging,'
whisky-swilling, bawbie-hoarding Scot of the comic postcard was
after all the man who dreamed into immortal traditional words the
Border Ballads. The Celtic Highlander when the mood is on him can
produce remarks of bleaching understatement which have joined the
body of 'Scotch story,' and which, for sheer power to deflate enthusiasm, can rival the utterances of any Lowland East-coaster. But where
does the 'wisdom of the Scots' lie?

I wrote to the publishers in this way, and was taken aback to receive
a warmly welcoming letter from them. Yes, they knew that an anthology
on the 'wisdom of the Scots' would be an impossible task; but the
very eloquence (their word) which I had used convinced them that I
was the man to attempt that impossibility.[1] Their letter was so friendly
that I hadn't the heart to tell them of my second objection—that I
funked facing my compatriots.

I went to my learned friend Mr. R. L. C. Lorimer for support in
my intended, yet not completely decided, refusal. To my dismay he

[1] See the last words of this book.

let me down. 'Of course you must do it,' he told me at once. I still objected and only paused when he interrupted in a bell-like monitory tone: 'If you don't do it, just think *who will*. Just think of. . . . ' This was indeed a solemn and depressing thought: I began to waver.

Observing this, Mr. Lorimer returned to the word 'complementary' which he had used when I complained of the divisions in the so-called Scottish wisdom. 'Out of these complementary divisions,' he argued, 'you could make a duologue which would display a kind of wisdom that is all our own.' And, as we began tentatively to talk about a possible book, I saw his point. Wisdom revealed itself as we began to make tentative selections. It became apparent to us that there was, even in the most differing passages, a Scottish idea of wisdom.

Briefly, it is polarised between two contradictory principles, namely (1) the stern paternalism of the Old Testament School and the tradition of the Scottish warriors of old, and (2) the enthronement of the feminine ideal, notably as in the ballad of Thomas the Rhymer, which has run through the course of Scottish thought down to the present day and can be discovered too in the eighteenth century even in David Hume. In the conflict of these two ideas is something that shows the way Scottish people think and express themselves—something that one might fairly call the 'wisdom of the Scots.'

Conflict. From another point of view the word is as significant as 'complementary.' The Scots, as is well known, detest, or used to detest, compromise. They also claim to love liberty and freedom. They have certainly combined in the past to defend the freedom of their country— do they still ? At any rate, whether freedom-loving or semi-subservient (as both Mr. Lorimer and I are inclined to consider our country now to be) the Scot has shown what remains of his hatred of compromise within Scotland by looking on freedom as the liberty to knock the other fellow down for disagreeing with him. Out of this passion for knocking each other down which both the paternalists and the feminists possess doesn't a kind of wisdom born of conflict emerge ? Perhaps ?

It was in the exchange during discussion of such sophistries, as some would call them, or at least such characteristically Scottish abstractions, that I was persuaded and began to persuade myself that such a thing as the 'wisdom of the Scots' exists. Fighting a rearguard action, I then put it to my friend that I hadn't the temerity to place my name on an anthology impartially representing the 'wisdom of the Scots.' 'It would be all very well,' I added, 'just putting forward my own views. I can stand up to the knocks against them. But when it comes to what other people said and . . .'

'But,' he interrupted, 'that's just what you *must* do! Put forward your own views on what other people have said. Any elaborate attempt at fairness would just make the book dull, and wouldn't placate any true Scot. All anthologies annoy as many as they please; well, then, just make up your mind that you'll have to annoy people who don't agree with you. Put in what you want because it pleases you or goes with the flow of your thoughts. Leave out what you want just because it doesn't please you or because it bores you or because you just don't know enough about it.' Seeing my expression as he uttered these last words, he added kindly, if over-hastily, 'No one can know all about everything.'

It was this last which decided me. 'All right,' I said, 'I'll do it if you come in on it and help me.'

A word about Mr. Lorimer. If it had not been for him I would not have begun this book, nor, I think, could I ever have finished it. He is a professional publisher's editor in Scotland with a wide know-ledge of our country. Perhaps there were some things about Scotland I knew which he did not know at the beginning of our association; he knows them now. There were other things he knew which I did not; some of them I know now. There are, too, some views on Scotland in which we differ; these differences are not antagonistic but complementary. He said he would 'come in' on the book with me.

'Splendid!' I agreed. 'Then at least it will please two people, two people entirely, which is exactly one more than most other anthologies do. Let's start with the important thing, let's start at once deciding what things we shall leave out.' We started.

It will, to the reader well versed in Scottish history and literature, be only too apparent how much I have left out. (Some of the names, for instance, which I have already mentioned do not occur at all.) Even those who are not specialists in such matters may notice a tendency to avoid the obvious and the well-known pieces which are to be found in so many other anthologies. I do not intend to draw attention in this place to such omissions (though I shall mention one or two later on) nor to apologise for them. Still less do I intend to apologise for those inclusions which may seem to some to have little connection with wisdom in its more owlish connotation or to have been capriciously chosen. This book represents an individual view on the 'wisdom of the Scots,' and pretends to be no more. This view will appear in the manner of selection and in the annotations to those selections as the book goes along. It goes along, by the way, chronologically. I have not subdivided the themes. They succeed, follow each other and recur only in order of time.

I ought to say how this book formed itself, and how we grew to agree that I should present it. Save in one thing at bottom, Mr. Lorimer and I are not similar Scots; we do not inhabit adjacent pigeon-holes in the many and diversely pigeon-holed doocot of Scotland where even now uniformity is still bravely if a trifle defiantly kept at bay. I do not intend to describe or dwell upon these differences; they have been quite inumbrated by one fact; neither of us knows of any blood in him that is not Scottish. After all that I have implied about our native contentiousness it may seem odd then that here and there in our collaboration we have actually agreed to differ, but so it has been. This may be the first time such a thing has ever happened in Scotland.

Our agreement on what we should include, reject or glide over has been almost complete. We agreed too on the language in which Early and Middle Scots should appear. Neither of us has any taste for the emasculate and often misleading versions in which extracts from these periods of Scottish literature are all too often presented.

The use of a uniform spelling and the compilation of the running-glossary (possibly the first time that phrase has been used) in the margins have been entirely in Mr. Lorimer's hands. If my grateful submission to his expert knowledge and experience in this can be called agreement, we have agreed. He will explain his principles at the end of my introduction to the text and notes for Part I.

But one thing I must make quite clear: I have been entirely responsible for the annotation preceding and interpolated in our various choices. Even when I have used the editorial 'we,' its style is in my hand alone *and* the views expressed in it, though tempered by discussion between us, are mine. Even where I say 'we' I mean I. Sometimes maybe he has leaned one way, I the other, but we have always kept hold of each other. Where he has found it impossible to agree entirely and where I have been obdurate, where it has been a case of pull Devil, pull Lorimer, without result, he has gracefully given way.

The idea of making these notes in their present varied form (sometimes long, sometimes short, sometimes discursive) arose while we made our selection and while we talked. As the author of these notes I present this *apologia* for them. Having given the reader a 'running-glossary' I could not resist allowing myself a running-annotation as the book and our conversations about it ran their course. We did not believe, naturally, that all the 'wisdom of the Scots' had been expressed or written by the time I sat down to this task. It had been, was, and

B

still is, after a fashion, going on all the time. Clearly it was impossible for us to keep abreast of all this and use it. I decided, then, to provide our own contemporary brand of Scottish wisdom. The reader is assured that it is right up to date and that, we being who we are, it is Scottish. The proof of the latter claim will be found in the fact that nearly all our compatriots will disagree with every point of view or word that we have agreed upon between us.

But, in fairness to my friend's invaluable help, I must state that we have not agreed on everything. I accept full responsibility for the purpose, shape, style and contents of the book.

It is in two parts. This is no arbitrary choice, but is dictated by hard and inescapable facts in the history of Scotland or rather in the story of our decline as a nation. The first part, of necessity, requires from the modern reader a little more sympathy in understanding than the second; but it contains the purer matter of the book, the more purely Scottish, more purely wise. We have done our best in presentation, 'running-glossing' and 'running-comment' to make it as easy as possible to read without offending against our principles on the purity of Scottish style. My introduction to this first part follows, and is in turn followed by a note on the language and spelling by Mr. Lorimer.

All authors and sources, as well as minor headings of subject matter and title, are given in the contents. There is, therefore, no index.

MORAY McLAREN

PART ONE

An Introduction

The first part of this book is drawn from a period beginning about nine hundred years ago and ending in the first decade of the seventeenth century. It is a period which saw the founding and rise of the nation of Scotland our forefathers knew. It ends with the start of the gradual but, in the circumstances, inevitable decline of that nation. This decline, after so brave a beginning, had its origins in three things—internal weakness and corruption in government, Church and nobility, the implacable pressure of a stronger neighbour and the accident of dynastic succession. Nevertheless it is in the remote ambience of that first period (though we are scarcely aware of it) that we still move and, after a fashion, breathe, sucking in the inspiration of certain Scottish wisdom from our past.

This is no place for an historical exposition. Let it be enough to say that when the sixteenth century dawned Scotland was recognised as a completely independent kingdom within the framework of a united western Christendom. She had her own monarch whom she shared with none other, her own rights of war, peace and alliance with other countries and her own language. By language I mean the Lowland Scots tongue of the Court spoken by kings, courtiers, clergy and commonalty alike. (Mr. Lorimer will touch upon the Gaelic tongue briefly and later in his notes on 'language and spelling.') Three years after the century had ended, and when James VI of Scotland had gone to London to become James I of England by succession, she had lost her court and was compelled to share her sovereign with a much stronger neighbour who had for centuries struggled to gain possession over her. She had officially adopted the Protestant Faith which, though different from the English form, was sufficiently akin to it to make her more a part of the Protestant island of Britain than a free unit of Christendom. Finally she was losing her language.

The ending of this period, then, makes a watershed in Scottish affairs more potent to separate the past from the present than is any historical division you can think of in almost any other country in Europe. The watershed is there, whether you approve of its having raised itself up as an inevitable and healthy development in the growth of Britain, or whether, as a Scot, you regret it as something that has all but destroyed your nation. Whatever your political opinion, creed or class, it is, if you are a Scot, extraordinarily difficult for you to imagine what Scotland was like on the other side of the water-shed.

No matter whether you are (to take two differing but character-istically Scottish examples) an ardently practising member of the Protestant and Presbyterian majority or an equally faithful member of the indigenous West Highland and Hebridean Catholic minority with centuries of Celtic Catholicism in your blood and bones it will be difficult for you to imagine a Scotland of your own forefathers in which everyone was Roman Catholic. It is equally difficult for anyone who in Scotland is a member of that large group that is indifferent to religion. Indeed it would be with surprise that such would learn (were they to hear it at all) that the country was Roman Catholic for a longer period than she has been Protestant. Scotland has been officially, consistently, positively and without compromise Protestant for four hundred years, and that is that. You cannot ask the average modern man to stretch his historical imagination beyond four centuries.

In the same way, no matter whether you are an ardent Home-Ruler, extreme Scottish Nationalist or a respectable Conservative Unionist thinking of (though never quite calling) Scotland North Britain, it will be difficult for you to envisage a time when for centuries your country was as independent as Portugal or Holland is today.

Finally there is language. The ancient Lowland Scottish tongue in a debased form is spoken and understood in various modes in various parts of the country. Save for a literary group who have already made their mark and who have been endeavouring through serious poetry to restore its status, it has been degraded to a dialect. Not even the genius of Burns, still so vociferously lauded two hundred years after his birth, has been able to rescue it from that.

Not even the most practised orator apostrophising the haggis in Burns's own Scottish words, or reciting *Tam o' Shanter* faultlessly at a Burns supper or addressing a mouse or a daisy or a lassie or, in greater privacy, repeating some less well-known, less generally acceptable lines, can easily recall the beginnings and the adult state of the language he is using. Not even he, amidst the imagination-provoking fumes of Scotch whisky and the equally undoubtedly 'Scotch' noises uttered or flatulently emitted by his swollen and flushed compatriots gathered round the festive board, can easily imagine a time when the Scots language was the normal intercourse between kings, queens, courtiers, clerics, learned men and poets, as well as being the speech of the commonalty.

This watershed in the story of Scotland then exists. But, no matter how difficult it may be for us to imagine what it was like on the other side of it, a large part of the wisdom of the Scots lies upon that side. I would claim that it is not only a large part but a fundamental part. From it springs the most part and the most purely Scottish part of wisdom that exists among the Scots today. It is from the other side of that watershed, concluding with the works of a Scottish poet who died about 1611, that I have chosen the contents of the first part of this book.

Perhaps this is the place to refer to what may seem some of the more obvious omissions in Part I, especially of those whose names were mentioned earlier. Duns Scotus is left out, not because of his international sources, nor because he is lamentably referred to in the Gregorian lectures at Rome as a *monachus Anglicus*, but because there is no reason to claim his theology as Scottish. Indeed, save where it touches upon human behaviour, I have, after some thought, avoided theology and the rhetoric of religious dispute in Part I. It is for this reason that I have passed over the dispute between Knox and Mary Stuart. There are other eminent authors, such as Pitscottie and Buchanan, who were rejected in favour of those who could be quoted in the direct context of 'wisdom.'

I ask the reader to make the slight effort of sympathy necessary to follow the text in the manner we have presented it. If, as he reads, he does no more than glance at the marginal glosses, he will find the page swimming up into clarity like a developing negative; and only some of the text needs this assistance. But this is to trespass upon the textual footnote of my friend which is to follow. To him also will I leave the task of explaining why we have put in no Gaelic nor translations from the Gaelic.

M. McL.

The Language and Spelling

Whether Scots and English should properly be regarded as two different languages, or as two dialects of the same dead language, Insular West Teutonic—and for most practical purposes, I should be inclined to adopt a definition of 'language' from which it follows that they should be regarded as two different languages and as dialects of I.W.T.—there is no doubt that they have always been quite differently pronounced. From our present point of view this is very important, because in all Scots poetry, and most Scots prose, sound, tone, word-music have always, in themselves, been so highly valued that nobody can achieve anything approaching full enjoyment of any Scots text that he may read unless he has at least a working knowledge of the correct Scots pronunciation of all the words that it contains.

Till towards the end of the sixteenth century—or, in other words, till towards the end of the period that we have covered in Part I of this anthology—Scots had its own system of spelling. In most respects this traditional Scottish way of spelling Scots was very different from the English way of spelling English, which most foreigners find so confusing. Once one becomes sufficiently familiar with it, this traditional Scottish spelling gives a remarkably precise indication of how every syllable in any Early or Middle Scots text was meant to be pronounced. In certain small details it varies, however, a great deal from one manuscript or early printed edition to another. As a result, one of the most difficult questions confronting anybody who sets out to compile an anthology like this is what principles to go upon in standardising—as he must—the spelling of all Early and Middle Scots prose and poetry that he selects.

The method which, in practice, most previous anthologists have followed has been: (1) that all words which have the same (or roughly the same) pronunciation in Scots and English are respelt as in modern English; (2) that, of the remainder, some are respelt as in the kind of Scots written by modern writers like Allan Ramsay, Burns and C. M. Grieve, and others are left unaltered. Thus words like *quhen*, *quhat*, etc., are respelt *when* and *what*, with the result that the much harsher sound represented by *quh* is apt to be misinterpreted, by Scottish readers, as *hw* and by English readers as *w*; *deip*, *keip*, *sleip*, etc., become *deep*, *keep*, *sleep*, etc., which seems quite sensible, till we come up against such much less familiar words as *repreif*, *remeid*, and cannot quite be sure whether to pronounce them as in English if spelt *reprife* or *repreef*, *remide* or *remeed*; and *scheip* becomes *sheep*, but the much less familiar *schein* (usually) remains *schein*, and consequently takes on the appearance of a merely perverse or whimsical 'Scotch barbarism.'

In the early stages of editing Early and Middle Scots which Mr. McLaren and I provisionally selected for inclusion in Part I of this anthology, I soon came to the conclusion that these most undesirable consequences could not possibly be avoided unless I adopted the unorthodox policy of unifying the spelling in conformity with a purely Scottish set of orthographical standards. Robert Henryson, one of the greatest Makars, was also a schoolmaster. Perhaps because he was forced, therefore, to think out the problems of Scottish spelling much more thoroughly than any other Scottish writer of his period, the Scots spelling used in the best early texts of his poetry is by far the simplest, the most consistent and the most accurate that has yet been invented. With a few minor and quite unimportant modifications, then, I have used, throughout the whole of Part I, substantially the same Scots spelling as he did.

For all practical purposes, the reader, therefore, may take it that, throughout this part of the book, *ei* should always be pronounced like *ee* in *sheep*; that *ow* should almost always be pronounced as in Scots *grow* (i.e. approximately as in English *now*), and *ou* as in Scots *nou* (i.e. approximately, but only approximately, as in English *you*), that *eu* may be pronounced either like *yu* in *yum-yum* or the first syllable in *Europe*; that *sch* is always pronounced *sh* in any modern English word in which it occurs; that *quh* is pronounced rather like *wh* in *when*, *what*, etc., as still usually pronounced in English by most Scottish speakers and some of the best English actors—but much harsher, almost as if the words in question were spelt *khwen*, *khwat*, etc.

Those of our readers who are already familiar with the vocabulary of Early and Middle Scots may consider that I have glossed these texts too liberally. If so, I can only say that Mr. McLaren and I, and our publishers, all hope that the book will reach the much larger circle of readers who may be interested in Scottish wisdom, but have no previous acquaintance with any form of Scots; and that all words which might, perhaps, cause such specially well-deserving readers more than a moment's hesitation have, therefore, been glossed.

Mr. McLaren has left it to me to explain why we have not interpreted our remit as applying to Scottish Gaelic as well as Lowland Scots wisdom. One of my earliest recollections is of my nurse, herself the daughter of an Ayrshire coalminer, the widow of a sergeant in the

Black Watch, one of the very wisest Scots I have ever known, explaining to me the meaning of the proverb, 'It's ill taking the breeks aff a Hielanman.' I strongly suspect that Mr. McLaren left this task to me because he did not wish to be dirked in his ancestral countryside of Balquhidder—or lose his own breeks. All that I wish to say in explanation of this decision of ours is that Scottish Gaelic wisdom belongs to the same Q-Celtic tradition as Manx and Irish Gaelic wisdom, and should, in our opinion, be dealt with in the same volume as them.

R. L. C. L.

Thomas the Rhymer

'What is truth?' asked Pilate, and did not jest. Eighteen centuries later an English poet, John Keats, replied by saying that 'Beauty is truth, truth beauty—that is all ye know on Earth and all ye need to know.' Between Pilate and Keats, somewhere about the end of the thirteenth century, a shadowy Scottish figure, Thomas of Ercildoun, propounded one Scottish view of truth which has run through Scottish poetry and Scottish thought ever since. Briefly it may be said that he recounted the story of a vision of beauty in the form of a supernatural woman of great loveliness. By surrendering himself to her and her service he is endowed with the power of imagination and the power to express his imagination—the truth of what he sees. The belief in the value and the gifts of such a surrender to the truth of beauty is one strong element in the wisdom of the Scots.

Later these stanzas of Thomas of Ercildoun were manipulated into the well-known Ballad of Thomas the Rhymer—*True Thomas lay on Huntly Bank*—and acquired various religious and *ex post facto* prophetic accretions. The import of Ercildoun's message remained, however, undamaged, though it is to be heard in its purest form in the verses printed here.

He who surrenders himself to the truth of beauty must pay the price. He can never rest. He must be like the falcon whose nest is not in a stationary earth-bound tree but in the free air of heaven in which he flies. There is the nearest he can ever get to rest—there to float upon the morning wind with wings outstretched. His reward is the perpetual bird's-eye view of the truth of beauty. But there is another price he must pay for this heaven-borne vision of truth—the price of danger. In calling upon the vision of beauty to surrender to him he is surrendering himself to her. He is casting himself utterly upon the unknown as well as on to the mercies of the beautiful. But who, in the face of such beauty, would not take the risk? This wisdom is discovered in the concluding stanzas of the poem here printed.

It is a form of wisdom which has haunted the Scottish soul since Scotland began to be. It is a form of wisdom that has been denied and derided by many Scots throughout the centuries. It is in particular held in great contempt by most Scottish business men and politicians today.

But let Thomas of Ercildoun speak first.

THOMAS OF ERCILDOUN

^aAls I me went this ^bendris day,   ^aas ^bother
   Full fast in mind makkand my moan,
In a merry morning of May
   By Huntly Bankis myself alone,

I heard the jay and the ^athrostell,   ^athrush
 The ^amavis ^bmenied of hir sang,   ^asong-thrush ^blamented
The ^awoodwale ^bberied als a bell,   ^a(?) woodlark ^bsang
 That all the wood about me rang.

Alone in longing, thus als I lay,
 Underneith a seemly tree,
Saw I quhare a lady gay
 Came ridand ^aower a ^blang lee.   ^aover ^blong grassland

If I suld sit to Doomisday
 With my tongue to ^awrob and ^bwrye,   ^awarble ^btwist
Certainly that lady gay
 Never ^abese scho ascried for me.   ^ashall she be described

Hir palfray was a dapple gray;
 ^aSwilk ane ne saw I never ^bnane: ^asuch ^bnone
Als does the sun on summer's day,
 That fair lady hirself ^ascho ^bschane.   ^ashe ^bshone

Her ^aselle it was of ^broelle-bane,   ^asaddle ^bbone
 Full seemly was that sicht to see!
Stiffly set with precious stane,
 And compasst all with ^acrapotie.   ^atoadstone

Stanis of Orient, great plentie;
 Hir hair about hir ^aheid it hang;   ^ahead
Scho rode ower that lang lee,
 A while scho blew, another scho sang. . . .

Scho led three greyhoundis in a leish;
 And seven ^arachis by hir feet ^brone;   ^ascenting-dogs ^bran
Scho bare a horn about hir ^ahalse;   ^aneck, throat
 And under hir belt full mony a ^aflone.   ^aarrow

Thomas lay and saw that sicht,
 Underneith ane seemly tree;
He said, 'Yon is Mary, ^amost of micht,   ^amost powerful
 That bare that Child that died for me.

'*a*But I speik with yon lady bricht,   *a*unless
    I *a*hope mine hert will *b*brist in three;   *a*expect *b*burst
Now sall I go with all my micht,
    Hir for to meet at Eildon Tree.'

Thomas *a*rathely up he *b*rase   *a*promptly *b*rose
    And he ran ower that mountain *a*hie: *a*high
*a*Giff it be als the story says,   *a*if
    He hir met at Eildon Tree.

He kneelit doun upon his knee,
    Underneith that greenwood spray,
And said: 'Lufely lady, rue on me,
    Queen of Hevin, als thou *a*weill may!'   *a*well

*a*Than spak that lady mild of *b*thocht: *a*then *b*thought
    'Thomas, *a*lat swilk wordis be!   *a*let
Queen of Hevin am I *a*nocht,   *a*not
    For I tuik never so *a*heich degree.   *a*high

'Bot I am of another countrie,
    If I be *a*parellit *b*most of price: *a*apparelled *b*most richly
I ride *a*eftir this wild *b*fee,   *a*after *b*cattle (i.e. deer)
    My rachis *a*rinnis at my *b*device.'   *a*run *b*will, pleasure

'If thou be parellit most of price,
    And here ridis thus in thy folly,[1]
Of *a*lufe, lady, als thou art *b*wyis,   *a*love *b*wise
    Thou giff me leave to ly thee by.

Scho said: 'Thou man, that *were* folly:
    I pray thee, Thomas, thou lat me be;
For I say thee full *a*siccarly   *a*assuredly
    That sin will *a*for-do all my beauty.'   *a*destroy

'Now, lufely lady, rue on me,
    And I will evermore with thee dwell:
Here my troth I plicht to thee,
    Quhether thou will, in Hevin or Hell!'

---

[1] More probably 'in thy balye,' i.e. 'in thine own control.'

'Man of mould, thou will me ^amerre,   ^amar
  But yit thou sall have all thy will;
And, ^atrow it weill, thou ^bcheivis the werre, ^abelieve ^bcomest off
  For all my beauty will thou ^aspill.'   ^aspoil

Doun than ^alichtit that lady bricht,   ^aalighted
  Underneith that greenwood spray;
And, als the story tellis full richt,
  ^aSevin sythis by hir he lay.   ^aseven times

Scho said: 'Man, thou likis thy play:
  What ^abird in ^bbouer may dwell with thee? ^awoman ^bbower
Thou ^amerris me all this lang day;   ^amarrest
  I pray thee, Thomas, lat me be!'

Thomas stude up in that ^asteid,   ^aplace
  And he beheld that lady gay;
Hir hair it hang all ower hir heid,
  Hir ^aeen seemit out, that ere were gray. ^aeyes

And all the rich clothing was away
  That he before saw in that steid;
Hir ^aae schank black, hir uther gray,   ^aone shank
  And all hir body like the ^aleid.   ^alead

Than said Thomas: 'Allace! allace!
  In faith this is a duleful sicht:
How art thou faidit thus in the face,
  That ^aschane before als the sun sa bricht!' ^ashone

Scho said: 'Thomas, tak leive at Sun and Moon,
  And als at ^aleif that growis on tree;   ^aleaf
This twelmonth sall thou with me gone,
  And Middle Earth thou sall none see.'

He kneelit doun upon his knee,
  To Mary mild he made his moan:
'Lady, ^abut thou rue on me,   ^aunless
  All my gamis fro me are gone!

'Allace!' he said, 'and ^awa is me,   ^awoe
    I ^atrow my deedis will wirk me ^bcair;   ^abelieve ^bcare
My saul, Jesu, ^abeteich I Thee,   ^aentrust
    Quhithersome that ever my ^abanis sall fare!'   ^abones

Scho led him in at Eildon ^aBirk,   ^abirch-tree
    Underneith a ^adernie-lee;   ^ahidden-lea
Quhare it was derk als midnicht mirk,
    And ever the water ^atill his knee.   ^ato

The ^amontenance of dayis three,   ^aamount
    He heard bot ^aswoching of the flude;   ^arushing
'At the last,' he said, 'full wa is me—
    ^aAlmaist I die, for ^bfaut of fude!'   ^aalmost ^bwant

Scho led him ^aintill a fair ^bherbere,   ^ainto ^bgarden
    Whare fruit was growing, great plenty:
Pear and apple, both ripe thay were,
    The date, and ^aals the ^bdamasee. . . .   ^aalso ^bdamson plum

He ^apressit to pull the fruit with his hand;   ^atried
    Als man for fude that was ^aneir faint.   ^anear
Scho said: 'Thomas, thou lat thame stand,
    Or else the Feind thee will attaint!

'If thou it plock, ^asuthly to say,   ^atruly
    Thy saul goes to the fire of Hell;
It cummis never out ^aor Doomisday,   ^auntil
    Bot there in pain ay for to dwell.

'Thomas, suthly I thee ^ahicht,   ^apromise
    Come ^aligg thine heid doun on my knee,   ^alay
And thou sall see the fairest sicht
    That ever saw man of thy country.'

He did ^ain hy als scho him bade,   ^aimmediately
    Upon hir knee his heid he laid,
For hir to ^apay he was full glaid,   ^aplease, satisfy
    And ^athan that lady to him said: ^athen

'Seeis thou nou yon fair way,
 That ^aliggis ower yon heich mountain? ^alies
Yon is the way to Hevin for aye,
 Quhen sinful saulis have durit thair pain.

'Seeis thou nou yon other way,
 That liggis ^alaw beneith yon rise? ^alow
Yon is the way, the suth to say,
 Unto the joy of Paradise.

'Seeis thou yit yon ^athrid way, ^athird
 That liggis under yon green plain?
Yon is the way, with ^atein and ^btray, ^ainjury ^bvexation
 Quhare sinful saulis sufferis thair pain.

'Bot seeis thou now yon ^aferd way, ^afourth
 That liggis ower yon deep dell?
Yon is the way, the suth to say,
 Unto the ^abrennand fire[1] of Hell. ^aburning

'Sees thou yit yon fair castell,
 That standis upon yon heich hill?
Of toun and touer it ^abeiris the bell; ^ais pre-eminent
 In Middle Earth is nane like there-till.

'Forsuth, Thomas, yon is mine ^aawin, ^aown
 And the Kingis of this country:
Bot ^ame were leiver hangit and drawin, ^aI would rather be
 ^aOr that he wist thou lay by me. ^athan

'Quhen thou cummis to yon castel gay,
 I pray thee ^acourtas man to be; ^acourteous
And quhatso ony man to thee say,
 ^aLuik thou answer nane bot me. ^alook

'My lord is servit at ilka ^ameis ^acourse (of meal)
 With ^athritty knichtis fair and free; ^athirty
I sall say, sittand at the ^adeis, ^adais
 I tuik thy speich beyond the sea.'

---

[1] 'The burning fire': this phrase is still used colloquially in Scots euphemism for Hell.

Thomas still als stane he stude,
  And he beheld that lady gay;
Scho ^acome again als fair and gude,   ^abecame
  And als so rich on hir palfray:

Hir greyhoundis filled with deer-blude,
  Hir rachis couplit, by my ^afay;   ^afaith
Scho blew hir horn with main and ^amude   ^aspirit
  Unto the castel scho tuik the way.

Into the hall, suthly, scho went;
  Thomas followit at hir hand;
Than ladies come baith fair and gent,
  With courtesy to hir kneeland.

Harp and ^afethill both thay fand,   ^afiddle
  ^aGettern and als so the ^bsawtry;   ^astringed instrument ^bpsaltery
Lute and ^arybybe both ^bgangand,   ^astringed instrument ^bgoing
  And all manner of minstrelsy.

The most mervell that Thomas thocht,
  Quhen that he stude upon the floor:
For fefty ^ahertis in were brocht,   ^aharts
  That were both large, great, and ^astoor. ^abig

Rachis lay lappand in the blude,
  Cookis come with dressing-knife;
They ^abrittened thame als thay were ^bwood; ^acut up ^bmad
  Revel amangis thame was full rife.

Knichtis danced by three and three,
  There was revel, ^agamen, and play,   ^asport
Lufely ladies fair and free,
  That sat and sang on rich array.

Thomas dwelled in that solace,
  More than I ^ayou say, perdie;   ^ato you
Till on a day, so have I grace,
  My lufely lady said to me:

c

'Do ^abusk thee, Thomas, for thou must gone,   ^aget ready
  For thou may here no langer be;
Hie thee fast with ^amude and mone;   ^aspirit
  I sall thee bring till Eildon Tree.'

Thomas said ^athan with heavy cheer: ^athen
  'Lufely lady, now lat me be;
For certis, lady, I have been here
  Bot the space of dayis three.'

'Forsuth, Thomas, als I thee tell,
  Thou has been here sevin yeir and more;
Bot langer here thou may nocht dwell,
  The ^askill I sall thee tell quharefore.   ^areason

'To-morn of Hell the foul Feind
  Amang this folk will seik his fee;
And thou art ^ameikle man and ^bhend;   ^agreat ^bnoble
  I trou full weill he wald chuse thee.

'For all the gold that ever may be,
  Fro ^ahethin unto the worldis end,   ^ahence
Thou bese never betrayit for me;
  Tharefore with me I ^arede thou ^bwend.'   ^aadvise ^bgo

Scho brocht him again to Eildon Tree,
  Underneith the greenwood spray,
In Huntly Bankis is merry to be,
  Quhare foulis sing baith nicht and day.

'Far out ower yon mountain gray,
  Thomas, a ^afaucon ^bbiggis a nest: ^afalcon ^bbuilds
A faucon is an ^aernis prey,   ^aeagle's
  ^aFor-thy in na place may he rest. . . .   ^atherefore

'Fare-weill, Thomas, I wend my way;
  I may no langer stand with thee.'
'Give me a tokening, lady gay,
  That I may say I spak with thee!'

'To harp or ^acarp, quhare-so thou goes,   ^atell tales
  Thomas, thou sall have the ^achose, suthly.'   ^achoice
And he said: 'Harping keip I none,
  For tongue is chief of minstrelsy.'

'If thou will spell, or talis tell,
  Thomas, thou sall never ^aleising lie: ^atell lies
Quharever thou fare, by frith or fell,
  I pray thee, speik none ill of me.

'Fare-weill, Thomas, withouten guile,
  I may no langer dwell with thee.'
'Lufely lady, abide a while,
  And tell thou me of some ^aferly!'   ^awonder

'Thomas, hearken what I thee say:
  Quhen that a tree-rute is ^adeid,   ^adead
The ^aleivis fall and ^bwyce away;   ^aleaves ^bshrivel
  And fruit it beiris neither quhite ne ^areid.   ^ared

'Of the Balliolis blude so sall it fall,
  It sall be like a rotten tree:
The Comynis and the ^aBarlayis alle,   ^a (?) Burleighs
  The Russellis, and the ^aFresellis free.   ^aFrasers

'All sall thay faid and wyce away;
  Na wonder if the rute sall ^adrie: ^adry up
And meikle bale sall after ^aspray,   ^aspring up
  Quhare joy and bliss was wont to be. . . .'

Then Thomas a ^asairy man was he,   ^asorry
  The ^ateiris ran out of his een gray: ^atears
'Lufely lady, yet tell to me,
  If we shall part for ever and aye?'

'Nay, quhen thou sittis at Ercildoun,
  To Huntly Bankis tak thy way,
Thair sall I ^asiccarly be ^bboun,   ^aassuredly ^bbound
  To meet thee, Thomas, if that I may. . . .'

She blew hir horn on hir palfray,
  And left Thomas at Eildon Tree;
Till Helmisdale scho tuik the way,
  And thus ^adepertit scho and he.   ^aparted

John Barbour

I. FREEDOM

In Scotland we are fond of communicating wisdom by the telling of stories. Thomas of Ercildoun told us the story of his vision; and centuries later we have not quite lost the gleams from that vision, even now, even amidst all our laborious and much-vaunted accumulation of material prosperity. We trail our clouds of glory yet—but only just. They are becoming rather tattered and difficult to perceive.

A part of our glory (perhaps less difficult to apprehend than Ercildoun's vision) has been our ineradicable love of freedom. Though the Scots had, in a sense, always been free, it was not until they lost their freedom under the English Edward I that they learned how much more valuable it was to them than anything else. As all the world knows, we regained that freedom for some centuries by the efforts of that extraordinary man and converted patriot, Robert the Bruce. The world primarily knows the details of this recapturing of freedom through John Barbour's compiled chronicle *The Bruce*. Harry the Minstrel's historical romance on the immortal Wallace was composed in the middle of the fifteenth century well after the earlier events.

Barbour (*c.* 1320–95) was Archdeacon of Aberdeen. He made his compilation in the early years of the reign of Bruce's grandson, Robert II, the first Stewart to become King of Scotland. Robert II may indeed have commissioned Barbour to do the job. Barbour probably got most of the stories in his poem from two main streams of oral tradition, the first of which (the Bruce–Stewart one) was centred mainly on Bruce himself and probably came from Bruce–Stewart household tradition. The second source (the Douglas tradition) concerned itself exclusively with the deeds of Bruce's great captain, Sir James Douglas, and passed through the Douglas family. It is entirely the product of Douglas family tradition fostered to keep alive the courageous virtues of Douglas youth.

The poem is firstly of interest because it presents straight from the source the Scots military tradition as shaped by Bruce and his captains to train their men in the Wars of Independence. The presentation of this tradition in the poetic-story style passes on Scots *wisdom* in its barest and most essential form. Embedded in the straightforward tale, however, are sentiments spoken by the heroes of the tale. Printed immediately below are Barbour's most famous lines,[1] containing the famous apostrophe 'Ah! freedom is a noble thing!' They, or something like them, may well have been spoken by Bruce at the time of his rising in 1306. Only a generation had passed since these events. Men were living who had heard Bruce speak. These may be *ipsissima verba*. Though

---

[1] I. 219 ff. This and all further references under Barbour are to his *Bruce*.

not in their order in the poem, these lines are printed here first because
they are famous and because they are continually relevant to the Scottish
situation. At the time of writing, the Church of Scotland is speaking
these sentiments on behalf of the African people of Nyasaland.

After 'freedom is a noble thing' there follow various extracts from
Barbour's *Bruce* with notes before them.

Alas! that folk, that ever wes free,
And in freedom wont for to be,
Throu thar great mischance and folly,
War treatit *a*than sa wickitly,   *a*then
That thar *a*faeis thar judgis *b*war: *a*foes *b*were
Quhat wretchitness may man have *a*mar?   *a*more

Ah! freedom is a noble thing!
Freedom *a*mays man to haiff liking;   *a*makes
Freedom all solace to man giffis:
He *a*levis at ease that freely levis.   *a*lives
A noble hart may haiff nane *a*eis,   *a*ease
*a*Na ellis nocht that may him pleis,   *a*nor anything else
*a*Giff freedom faill: for free liking   *a*if
Is yarnit *a*owre all other thing.   *a*over, above
Na he that ay has levit free
May nocht knaw weill the property,
The anger, na the wretchit doom
That is couplit to foul *a*thirldom.   *a*thraldom

Bot giff he had *a*assayit it,   *a*experienced it ('thirldom')
Than all *a*perquer he suld it *b*wit;   *a*par cœur *b*know
And suld think freedom *a*mar to prize   *a*more
Than all the gold in warld that is. . . .

And thirldom is weill *a*wer than *b*deid;   *a*worse *b*death
For *a*quhill a *b*threll his life may *c*leid,   *a*while *b*thrall *c*load
It *a*merris him, body and *b*banis;   *a*mars *b*bones
And *a*deid annoyis him bot *b*anis.   *a*death *b*once
Schortly to say, is nane can tell
The *a*haill conditioun of a threll.   *a*whole

II. 'STORIES THAT SUTHFAST WER. . . .'

We return now to the Preface to the poem, in which we take up the theme of wisdom being communicated by story-telling: and in the following lines[1] Barbour tells us that it is chiefly to preserve true stories of Bruce and Douglas that he has decided to write them down. The wisdom in these stories is implicit not explicit. There is no moralising. The stories are merely intended to stimulate those who hear them and to shape their characters without their being aware of it. These stories are very much not 'art for art's sake' but art for glory's sake and for the sake of wisdom.

Stories to reid are delytable,	
Suppose that thay be nocht bot fable:	
*a*Than suld stories that *b*suthfast wer,	*a*then *b*true
*a*And thay *b*war said on gude manner,	*a*if *b*were
Have double pleasance in *a*heiring.	*a*hearing
The first pleasance is the *a*carping	*a*story-telling
And the tothir the suthfastness	
That *a*schawis the thing richt as it wes. . . .	*a*shows
Tharfore I wald fain set my will,	
Giff my wit micht suffice thartill,	
To put in write a suthfast story,	
That it lest ay furth in memory,	
*a*Swa that na time of lenth it *b*let,[2]	*a*so *b*prevent
Na *a*ger it *b*hailly be forget.	*a*cause . . . to
For auld stories that men reidis	*b*wholly
Representis to thame the deedis	
Of stalwart folk that *a*levit *b*ar,	*a*lived *b*formerly
*a*Richt as thay than in presence war.	*a*just as if
And certis, thay suld weill have *a*price	*a*esteem
That in thar time war *a*wicht and *b*wyis,	*a*strong *b*wise
And led thar life in great travaill,	
And oft, in hard *a*stour of bataill,	*a*blown dust
*a*Wan richt great price of chivalry,	*a*won
And war *a*voidit of cowardy.	*a*devoid
As wes King Robert of Scotland,	
That hardy wes of hart and hand;	

---

[1] I. 1 ff.
[2] i.e. 'Prevent it from having length (of life).'

And gude Schir ^aJames of Douglas   ^apron. Jamès
That in his time sa worthy was
That of his price and his ^abounty,   ^agoodness
In far landis renownit wes he.
Of thame I think this buke to ^ama: ^amake
Now God giff grace that I may ^aswa   ^aso
Treat it, and bring it till ending
That I say nocht bot suthfast thing!

III. THE SCOTTISH BARONS SHOW NO WISDOM

It is a frequent temptation for the Scots, which they do not always resist, to let things be decided for them in England. In 1290, when Queen Margaret died, John Balliol (whose family name is commemorated in England at that Oxford College where Scots still congregate), Robert Bruce, grandfather of Robert I, John Comyn and others claimed the throne of Scotland. The Barons of the country, having characteristically failed Scotland by being unable to come to an agreement amongst themselves, decided on the foolish step of asking Edward I of England to act as an arbitrator. In the next extract,[1] Barbour reproaches them for this.

This ordinance ^athame thocht the best,   ^ato them seemed
For at that time wes peace and rest
Betwix Scotland and Ingland baith;
And thay couth nocht ^apersave the ^bskaith   ^aperceive ^bharm
That towart thame wes ^aappeirand;   ^aappearing
For-that ^aat the King of Ingland   ^athat
Held ^aswilk friendschip and cumpany   ^asuch
To thar King, that wes ^aswa worthy,   ^aso
Thay ^atrowit that he, as gude ^bnichtbour,   ^abelieved ^bneighbour
And as freindsome ^acompositour,   ^aarbitrator
Wald have judgit in ^alawty: ^afairness
Bot other wayis all ^ayeid the ^bglee.   ^awent ^bgame

Ah! blind folk full of all folly!
Had ye ^aumbethocht you ^benkrely,   ^abethought ^bearnestly
Quhat peril to you micht appeir,
Ye had nocht wrocht on that manner:
Had ye ^atane keip ^bhow-at that King   ^ataken heed ^bhow-that
Alwayis, ^aforouten sojourning,   ^awithout

[1] I. 74 ff.

Travaillyit for to win [a]seignoury,	[a]sovereignty
And, through his micht, [a]till occupy	[a]to
Landis that war till him [a]marchand,	[a]adjoining
As Walis was, and [a]als Ireland. . . .	[a]also
Ye micht see he suld occupy	
Throu slicht that he ne micht throu [a]maistry.[1]	[a]power
Had ye tane kep [a]quhat was [b]thrillage,	[a]what [b]thraldom
And had considerit his usage	
That grippit ay, [a]but gain-geving,	[a]without giving in return
Ye suld, [a]forouten his [b]deeming,	[a]without [b]arbitration
Haiff chosen you a king that micht	
Have halden weill the land in richt.	
Walis ensample micht have been	
To you, had ye it [a]forow seen.	[a]before
And wyis men sayis he is happy	
That [a]be other will him [b]chasty.	[a]by other [b]chasten
For unfair thingis may fall, perfay,	
Als weill to-morn as yesterday.	

IV. MANLINESS

Here is a revealing character sketch[2] of 'The Good Sir James,' who never let anything prevent him from achieving his purpose. It was probably derived from Douglas family tradition, and all young Douglases were no doubt brought up in the simple ideal of manliness which it expresses. But it was not only the young Douglases who were the heirs of this tradition. We see here the wisdom of that pertinacity which is so famous a part of the Scottish character. It is character supported by wisdom—the wisdom to go on and on in pursuit of your object. We refrain from recounting the international rather than Scottish legend of Bruce and the spider, which does not figure in Barbour's poem.

Bot wonderly hard thingis fell	
[a]Till him, [b]or he till state wes [c]brocht.	[a]to [b]ere [c]brought
Thair wes nane [a]aventure that [b]mocht	[a]chance [b]might
Stunnay his hart, na [a]ger him let	[a]prevent him
To do the thing he wes on set;	
For he thocht ay [a]encrely	[a]earnestly
To do his deed [a]avysily.	[a]advisedly

[1] lit. 'Through cunning that which he might not by mastery.'
[2] I. 296 ff.

He thocht weill he wes worth na ^aseil	^agood

He thocht weill he wes worth na *a*seil   *a*good
That micht of nane anoyis *a*feel   *a*suffer
And *a*als for till *b*escheive great thingis   *a*also *b*achieve
And hard travaillyis and *a*bargainingis,   *a*encounters
That suld *a*ger his price doublit be.   *a*cause . . . to
Quharfore, in all his live-time, he
Wes in great pain, and great travaill;
And never wald for *a*mischeiff faill,   *a*misfortune
Bot drive the thing richt to the end,
And tak the *a*hour that God wald send.   *a*fortune

V. LEALTY

Scotland was and still is an intensely clannish country. Amongst Scots, loyalty to clan or cause has always been regarded as perhaps the supreme moral requirement, without which no other virtue, or combination of virtues, is of much practical significance. This may or may not be looked upon by the world as a wise thing in the long run; but it has certainly had a long run in Scotland, and will run for a long time yet. Dr. Samuel Johnson found the clannishness of the Scots in England odious, and the ghetto-like conglobulation of Scots in London as distasteful as it is today. His generous heart, however, warmed to true Scots clannishness when, in 1773, he saw it upon its native heath in the Highlands. This, in general, is the more generous English attitude towards Scots clannishness. Scots accept it, for good or ill, as an ineradicable part of their nature. At any rate, it is a part of Scottish wisdom: and, as the following passage[1] shows, Barbour thought so, too.[2]

*a*Leawty to lufe is greatumly;[3]   *a*loyalty
Through leawty levis men *a*richtwissly. . . .   *a*righteously
And *a*but leawty may nane haiff *b*price,   *a*without *b*esteem
Quhether he be wicht, or he be *a*wyis;   *a*wise
For *a*quhar it faillyis na virtue   *a*where
May be of price na of value,
To mak a man sa gude that he
May simply callit 'gude man' be.

[1] I. 365 ff.: perhaps also derived from Douglas family tradition. Cp. below, pp. 45, 46.
[2] '*Optimi corruptio.*' Scots clannishness can turn upon itself and reverse itself into a passion for dissension. When Scots lose their loyalty there are no traitors like them. See the eloquent distress of the author of the Complaint of Scotland below, p. 99.
[3] 'Loyalty is greatly to be loved.'

VI. ALLEGIANCE

After the Battle of Methven (1306) Bruce took to the hills and the
common people once more submitted to Edward I. Barbour, however,
does not blame them for this.[1] From a clannish point of view, no man
can be expected to place his strength and services at the disposal of any
chief who does not genuinely pursue the interests of his clanfolk, or
who cannot effectively protect them against their enemies. Despite the
emphasis that they have placed on loyalty, the Scots have never been
inclined to make a *mystique* of political allegiance.

He durst nocht to the plainis *a*ga,	*a*go
For all the commounis went him *a*fra;	*a*from
That for thar *a*lifis war full fain	*a*lives
To pass to the Inglis peace again.	
*a*Sa fairis it ay commouly;	*a*so goes it
In commounis may nane *a*affy,	*a*rely on
Bot he that may thar *a*warrand be.	*a*guarantor, protector
Sa *a*fure thay then with him; for he	*a*fared, went
Thame fra thar *a*faeis micht nocht *b*warrand:	*a*foes *b*protect
Thay turnit to the tother hand.	
Bot *a*threlldom, that men *b*gert thame feel,	*a*thraldom
Gert thame ay yarn that he fure weill.	*b*caused . . . to

VII. 'KEIPIS YOW FRA DESPAIRING. . . .'

One of Bruce's chief problems was that the Scots were so heavily out-
numbered by the English, and, if he had not constantly done all that
he could to raise their morale, Scotland could not possibly have regained
her independence. The 'auld stories' that he read to his followers in
their bivouacs during the autumn that followed his defeat at Dalry
(1306) gave them much encouragement. Barbour recounts this.[2] If all
Scottish children today were encouraged to read Barbour's *Bruce* at
school, the morale of the Scottish nation might be much higher than it is.

The King that nicht his watchis set,	
And *a*gert ordain that thay micht eat;	*a*made it be arranged
And bade thame comfort to thame tak,	
And *a*at thar michtis merry mak.	*a*as best they could
'For discomfort,' as then said he,	
'Is the werst thing that may be.	

[1] II. 496 ff.   [2] III. 187 ff.

For throu meikle discomforting
Men fallis oft into despairing.
And ^afra a man despairit be,   ^afrom (the time when)
Then utterly ^avencusit is he.   ^adefeated
And fra the hart be discomfite
The body is nocht worth a mite.
Tharfore,' he said, 'out-owre all thing,
^aKeipis yow fra despairing: ^akeep yourselves
And think, thouch we now harmis feel,
That God may ^ayeit relieve us weill.   ^ayet
Men reidis of mony men that war
Far harder ^astad than we yet are;   ^abeset
And ^asyne our Lord ^bsic grace thame lent,   ^alater ^bsuch
That thay come weill ^atill thair intent. ^ato
Tharfore men that ^awerrayand are   ^acampaigning
Suld set thair ^aettling evermar   ^aendeavouring
To stand again thar ^afaeis micht,   ^afoes'
^aUmquhile with strenth, and ^aquhile with   ^asometimes
    slicht;
And ay think to cum to purpose
And ^agiff that thame war set in chose,   ^agiven the choice
To die, or to ^aleiff cowartly,   ^alive
Thay suld ^aerer die chivalrously.'   ^asooner

Thusgate thame confortit the King;
And, to confort thame, ^agan inbring   ^abrought in
Auld storyis of men that wer
Set ^aintill hard ^bassayis ^cser,   ^ainto ^btrials ^cseveral
And that fortoun contraryit fast,
And ^acome to purpose at the last.   ^acame

VIII. THE LOVE OF WOMEN

Even Barbour, the exponent of the arduous Scots military tradition, admits that, without the comfort that women can give, men cannot achieve all that is required of them.

For ^alufe is of sa ^bmeikle micht,   ^alove ^bgreat power
That it all painis makis licht. . . .

In wemen ^ameikle comfort lyis;   ^amuch
And great solace on mony wise.[1]

[1] II. 520 ff.

IX. SCOTTISH SCEPTICISM

The scepticism with which Barbour,[1] unlike most of his contemporaries, regards astrology, is characteristically Scottish; the profound irony of tone in which he says what he thinks about it is really rather a remarkable anticipation of David Hume. This refusal to accept what is generally believed is often cropping up in the records of Scottish wisdom. It can, of course, easily deteriorate into a mean-minded denigration of anything noble. The comments of a large part of the citizens of the capital of Scotland upon the bold and imaginative project which brought the Edinburgh Festival into being in 1947 are typical of this petty attitude. '*Optimi corruptio*' again. 'Fairest lilies when they fester smell far worse than weeds.'

Bot me-think it war great [a]maistry	[a]skill
[a]Till ony [b]astrolog to say	[a]to [b]astrologer
'This sall [a]fall here, and on this day.'	[a]happen
For thouch a man [a]his life [b]hailly	[a]all his life [b]wholly
Studyit [a]swa in astrology,	[a]so
That on the [a]sternis his [b]heid he brak,	[a]stars [b]head
Wyis men sayis he suld nocht [a]mak,	[a]make
His lifetime, certain [a]doomis three;	[a]judgments (i.e. predictions)
And yeit suld he ay dout [a]quhill he	[a]until
Saw how that it [a]come [b]till ending:	[a]came [b]to
[a]Than is thar na certain [a]deeming. . . .	[a]judging
And [a]sen thay are in sic weening,	[a]since
[a]Fourouten certain [b]witting,	[a]without [b]knowing
Me-think, [a]quha sayis he knawis thingis	[a]who
To cum, he makis great [a]gabbingis.	[a]meaningless utterances

X. LEADERSHIP

The following three extracts[2] throw further light upon Bruce's character as a leader and also upon his wisdom. The first is a comment on clan morality. There is always, of course, a sharp distinction between leaders and followers. *But* all who belong to the clan must meet on a footing of equality. The chief is not there to impose the will of a ruling class, but (theoretically at least) to elicit a sense of common interest and purpose. Bruce is depicted in this extract and throughout the rest of the poem as one who had the virtues that Scottish clan morality demands

[1] IV. 706 ff.   [2] VIII. 375 ff.; IX. 63 ff., 632 ff.

of a great leader. He is polite, cheerful, always joking, yet stout in battle, wise and circumspect. His people have good cause to be happy.

In the second extract 'For folk forouten capitain' Bruce appears as the traditional 'Good Captain,' one whose example raises his followers' morale. The point is that Bruce had been ill, but he never showed it. He knew that his demeanour was all-important for the morale of his army. The wisdom of the imperturbable leader.

The four lines of the third extract speak for themselves. They are from Douglas family tradition. *Immediate* bold action often achieves surprisingly successful results. 'Oh for one hour of Dundee!' cried an old campaigner, exasperated by the indecision of the Jacobite leaders at Sheriffmuir. Bruce was an even greater leader than Dundee.

The Gude King Robert

Syne with prisoners that thay had ^atane,	^ataken
Thay are towart thair ^ainnis gane	^aquarters
Fast ^alowand God of thair weillfare.	^apraising
Men micht haiff seen, ^aquha had been there,	^awho
A folk that merry ^awar and glad	^awere
For thair ^avictour; and als thay had	^avictory
A lord so sweet and debonair,	
So courtas, and of ^asa fair effer,	^asuch fair manner
So blyith ^aals, and so weill ^bbowrdand,	^aalso ^bjesting
And in battail so ^astyith to stand,	^astout
So wyis, and richt swa ^aavysy	^awell advised
That thay had great cause blyith to be.	

The Gude Capitain

For folk ^aforouten capitain,	^awithout
^aBot thay the bettir be ^ba-pane,	^aunless ^bsomewhat
Sall nocht be all so gude indeed	
^aAs thay ane lord had thame to ^bleid	^aas (if) ^blead
That daur put him in ^aaventure,	^a(lit.) chance
^aBut abasing, to tak the ^bhour	^aunabashed ^bopportunity
That God will send: for ^aquhen that he	^awhen
Is of ^asic will and sic ^bbounty,	^asuch ^bgoodness
That he daur put him ^atill assay,	^ato (the) test
His folk sall tak ^aensample ay	^aexample
Of his gude deed and his bounty,	
^aThat ane of thame sall be worth three	^aso that

Of thame that wickit chieftain has;
His wretchitness so ^ain thame gais,   ^ainto
That thay thair manliness sall ^atyne   ^alose
Throu wretchitness of his ^acovyne. . . .   ^aassociation (with them)
Bot he that, throu his great ^anobillay,   ^anobleness
To perillis ^ahim abandounis ay   ^aexposes himself
For to reconfort his ^amenyie,   ^afollowers
^aGerris thame be of so great bounty   ^ainduces . . . to
That mony time unlikely thing
Thay bring richt weill to gude ending.

Hardiment

Lo! how ^ahardiment ^btane suddenly,   ^ahardihood ^btaken
And driven ^asyne till end scharply,   ^athereafter
May ^ager ^boft-syis unlikely thingis   ^acause . . . to ^boften
Cum to richt fair and gude endingis!

XI. MAN PROPONIS

Here[1] the narrator comments on Edward II's arrogant over-confidence before Bannockburn. In the second extract, 'Howis in Haill Claith,' the wisdom is seen in the shrewd Scottish comment on the folly of counting your chickens before they are hatched: 'I always count my chickens before they are hatched,' said a well-known wit, 'they run about so much afterwards.' Edward's chickens, in the form of his troops, certainly ran about a lot after Bannockburn.

God disponis

Bot oft faillyis the fulis thocht;
And wyis ^amennis ^bettling ^ccumis nocht   ^amen's ^bendeavouring ^ccome
^aTill ^bsic end as thay ween alwayis.   ^ato ^bsuch
A litill ^astane oft, as men sayis,   ^astone
May ^ager welter a meikle wain.   ^acause to wobble
Na ^amannis micht may stand ^bagane   ^aman's ^bagainst
The grace of God, that all thing steeris;
He ^awat ^bquhat-to all thing ^ceffeiris,   ^aknows ^bto what ^cappertains
And disponis at His liking,
^aEfter His ordinance, all thing.   ^aafter

[1] XI. 21 ff., 140 ff.

Howis in Haill Claith

And quhen the King[1] his host has seen
So gret, so gud men and so *a*clein   *a*clean
He wes richt joyful in his thocht
And weill presumit thar wes nocht
In warld a king micht him withstand;
Him thoucht all wonnin *a*till his hand.   *a*to
And largely amang his men
The landis of Scotland dealt he than.
Of other mennis landis large wes he;
And thay that war of his *a*menyie   *a*men
Menaucit the Scottis men *a*haillily   *a*wholly
With gret wordis: bot, nocht-for-thy,
*a*Or thay cum all to thair intent,   *a*ere
*a*Howis in *b*haill claith sall be rent!   *a*holes *b*whole cloth

XII. MORALE: BANNOCKBURN

The last three extracts from Barbour all show how Bruce finally raised
Scottish morale to the requisite pitch. In the first,[2] he reviews the
Scottish host as it assembles in the Tor Wood; and before finally making
his battle-plan, he closely observes the state of morale. The men
appreciate his interest in them, and this in itself raises their morale.

Then follows Barbour's account[3] of a famous incident highly characteristic of Scottish wisdom. Before finally committing his men to
action Bruce appeals to the 'Volunteer Spirit' by proclaiming that
anybody who isn't sure of his own courage can leave before it is too
late. Of course nobody does so, but everybody feels that everybody
else is in good spirits and morale rises. The result is mutual confidence
between commander and followers. This was the practical result of an
appeal which would have had its effect on any body of patriotic soldiers,
but which was of particular value when addressed to highly individual-
istic Scots.

In the last of these three passages,[4] Bruce once more shows his
supreme military wisdom by the manner in which he brings morale
to its highest pitch. After the inconclusive skirmish which took place
on the first day of the battle, he puts it to his followers whether on the
next day to stand and fight (it is to be remembered that they were out-
numbered three to one) or retreat and fight another day on possibly
more favourable ground. All, however, agree that 'Now's the day, and
now the hour.' As a result all are fully committed.

These last extracts show how wisely Bruce handled the morale of his

[1] Edward II.   [2] XI. 240 ff.   [3] XI. 396 ff.   [4] XII. 189 ff.

Scottish troops. He understood them and their nature. Without their morale Scotland could not possibly have conquered on the next day and won one of the 'decisive battles of history.'

The English are often tolerantly amused at the way we 'won't forget Bannockburn.' We refuse to forget it because it reminds us of what we can achieve against odds when we are *united* and well led.

The Host

^aOwre all the host ^bthan yeid the King,	^aover ^bthen went
And beheld to thair ^aconteining,	^abearing
And saw thame of full fair ^aeffer;	^aappearance
Of hardy countenance thay were,	
^aBe likelyness the ^bmais cowart	^aby appearance ^bmost
Seemit ^atill do richt weill his part.	^ato
The King has seen all thair ^ahaving,	^abehaviour
That knew him weill ^ainto sic thing,	^ain
And saw thame all commouly	
Of ^asiccar countenance and hardy,	^asure
^aForouten effray or abasing.	^aunafraid and unabashed
In his hert had he great liking.	
And thocht that men of sa great will,	
^aGiff thay wald set thair micht ^bthairtill,	^aif ^bthereto
Suld be full hard ^atill win, perfay!	^ato overcome
Ay as he met thame in the way,	
He welcummit thame with gladsome fare,	
Speikand gude wordis here and thair.	
And thay, that thar lord so meekly	
Saw welcum thame, and so hamely,	
Joyful thay war, and thocht ^aat thay	^athat
Micht weill put thame ^aintill assay	^ato (the) test
Of hard fechting in stalwart ^astour,	^adust (of battle)
For ^atill mainteym weill his honour.	^ato maintain

Let him Bide wi' me !

He ^agert array thame for the ficht,	^acaused . . . to
And ^asyne owre all gert cry ^bon hicht,	^athen ^bon high
That ^aquhat-sa-ever he ^bwar that ^cfand	^awhatsoever ^bwere ^cfound
His hert nocht ^asiccar for ^btill stand	^asure ^bto
To win all or die with honour,	
For to ^amainteym that stalward ^bstour,	^akeep up ^bdust (of battle)

That he betime suld tak his way;
And nane suld dwell with him bot thay
That wald stand with him to the end,
And tak the *a*hour that God wald send.   *a*fortune
Then all answerd with *a*a cry,   *a*one
And with *a*a voce said generally   *a*one
That nane for *a*dout of deid suld faill,   *a*fear of death
*a*Quhill discumfite war the *b*battaill.   *a*until *b*whole battle-unit
Quhen the gude King had heard his men
Sa hardily him answer then,
Sayand that *a*nouthir deid no dreid   *a*neither death nor dread
*a*Till sic discomfort suld thame *b*leid   *a*to *b*lead
That thay suld eschew the fechting,
In hert he had great rejoicing.
For him thocht men *a*of sic covyne,   *a*so well knit together
So gude, so hardy and so fine,
Suld weill in battaill hald thair richt
Agane men of full meikle micht.

In Yow sall all be

'Tharfore I *a*trow that gude ending   *a*believe
Sall follow *a*till our beginning.   *a*to
The-quhether I say nocht this yow till,[1]
*a*For-that ye suld follow *my* will   *a*so that
To ficht, for in *yow* sall all be.
For *a*gif ye think *b*speedful that we   *a*if *b*expedient
Ficht, we sall ficht; and gif ye will,
We *a*leiff, your liking to fulfil.   *a*leave, withdraw
I shall consent *a*on alkyn wise   *a*in every kind of way
Till do *a*richt as ye will devise;   *a*just
Tharfore *a*sayis on your will plainly.'   *a*speak (imp.)
Than with ane voce all *a*can thay cry;   *a*did
'Gude King, *a*forouten mair delay,   *a*without more
To-morn *a*als soyn as ye see day,   *a*as soon
Ordain yow *a*haill for the battaill.   *a*altogether
For doubt of deid we sall nocht faill;
*a*Na nane pain sall refusit be   *a*nor shall any. . . .
*a*Quhill we have made our country free!'   *a*till

------

[1] 'However, I don't say this to you. . . .'

D

The Declaration of Arbroath

In 1320, six years after Bannockburn, the Scottish nobles, assembling at Arbroath, sent to Pope John XXII in Avignon a declaration of Scottish national freedom. Its words, sentiment and wisdom are as celebrated as those of Magna Carta. It is frequently quoted today by many Scots who think nothing of papal authority and who may never even have heard the name of the exiled fourteenth-century Pontiff.

It is easy to misinterpret the Declaration as an erratic anticipation of nineteenth-century nationalism *à la* Mazzini. It is in fact the perfect, polished and consummate expression of a tradition of freedom which already was more than a thousand years old. It went back to a tradition from our ancestors—Caledonian, Gael and others who all came here because they did not want to be subjects of the Roman Empire whatever its advantages. Cp. Calgacus the Caledonian leader as reported by Tacitus: *Auferre trucidare rapere falsis nominibus imperium atque ubi solitudinem faciunt pacem appellant,* and also the sentence in which he says: *Nos integri et indomiti . . . primo statim congressu ostendamus quos sibi Caledonia viros seposuerit.*[1] Calgacus was beaten, but his spirit still lives, however deeply buried in the Scottish heart. It certainly lived and found immortal expression at Arbroath in 1320.

I have tended in this anthology to avoid the more famous passages in Scottish literature and eloquence. I do this, I hope, not from a laboured desire to shun the obvious but because I believe such passages are already well known; some, however, are imperative. Such a one is that part of the Declaration of Arbroath containing the words '*Non enim propter gloriam, divitias aut honores pugnamus sed propter libertatem solummodo. . . .*' ('It is not for glory or riches or honours that we fight, but only for liberty.')

Having decided to put this in I was regretful to take the usual course followed in most Scottish anthologies of removing it from its context. The passage proceeds from excellent argument and eloquence before it and leads on to an excellent conclusion. The Declaration of Arbroath may show various facets of the Scottish wisdom in freedom, but in expression and form it is a closely-knit unit. I therefore, and with pleasure,

[1] Cp. also Neil Ross, in *Heroic Poetry from the Book of the Dean of Lismore,* ed. Neil Ross, S.G.T.S., p. xvii:

'The older portions of the [Red Branch] saga in Ireland make frequent reference to Fian Alban and Fian Breatan [i.e. the Fenians or warrior-bands of Alba and Britain]. Alba is the region north of the Forth, and Breatain is the territory that has its seat at Dun Breatan [Dumbarton]. The heroism of Fian Alban and Fian Breatan is not an assertion of their own bards—it is a persistent Irish eulogy. The fight with the Romans had left a tradition of hardihood among the Caledonians [cp. Barbour on Douglas]. It was not by weaklings that the Roman legions were held day and night on their wall for thirty-eight years. So the heroic spirit lived on.'

decided to include 'the lot.' It is only some 1,500 words. And, in Latin, what words! I regret that there is no space to print that Latin.

The English version of this much-translated document which we have chosen is by the late Lord Cooper of Culross (1892–1955), Lord President of the Court of Session, and, as is statutory these days, Lord Justice General, one of the wisest and certainly one of the most patriotic of those who have ever held the highest office in the Scottish legal system. One thinks of Lord President Forbes of Culloden, Lord President Inglis of Glencorse and of Lord President Cooper of Culross, and one does not need to think of another.

We have chosen Lord Cooper's translation partly because of an admiration for this scholarly and patriotic Scottish Judge and partly because it is, in our opinion, the best one extant that is published. With the deepest respect, however, we have here and there in footnotes ventured to differ from or enlarge upon *minutiae* in his Lordship's rendering. To put it more happily, we have tenderly stressed a few meanings, nuances of meaning or implications in the Latin over which it had seemed to us that the Lord President had glided perhaps imperceptibly— imperceptibly, that is, for those who might not be familiar with the text in its relation to the story of Scotland at that time.

Having chosen Lord Cooper's version we turned to the essay 'The Declaration of Arbroath Revisited' with which in 1950 he had introduced his translation. For a time we trembled upon the brink of a decision to include the whole of this notable example of modern Scottish wisdom and scholarship in this the first part of our book. Regretfully we drew back from that brink.

We drew back because a large part of the late Lord President's fascinating analysis of this great document and of what might be called his detective work on the problem of its authorship depends upon his examination of the structure of its rhetorical Latin prose. This, we thought, might be too much to impose upon our readers.

Briefly, Lord Cooper's points are these. With the aid of much quotation he draws attention to the fact that the Declaration is 'a practically faultless specimen of the *ars dictaminis* of the thirteenth century.' He adds 'If you compare the Declaration as a piece of rhetorical Latin prose with the surviving records of the period in the charters and state papers of Scotland and England you will find extraordinarily little worthy of comparison with it.' It was, then, the work of a churchman of wide culture and exceptional skill. Only such a one could have composed a Declaration of this kind, a Declaration speaking not only from the heart of Scotland but designed by the melody and majesty of its style to sound sweetly and potently in the Papal ears at far-off Avignon.

Who was this Scottish patriot and prose poet? Lord Cooper persuasively argues that he was Bernard de Linton, Abbot of Arbroath, who held the office of Chancellor of Scotland and King's Secretary of State from 1308 to 1328. (Lord Cooper gives us a résumé of what we know of this man and some fruitful speculations on him.) He proceeds to deal with the troubled history of the copy of the Declaration which we possess and establishes clearly that what we might call the 'top-copy' did indubitably reach John XXII. He makes his point by much internal evidence as convincing as it is fascinating. It is evidence drawn from Papal records as well as from our own.

He concludes with an eloquent peroration based upon this evidence and interpreting the meaning and cause of a much discussed passage in which 'the Barons assert that, if Bruce weakened in his resolution, they would drive him from his throne and choose another king.'[1] This peroration we have printed here. It is a wise modern judgment upon a wise Scottish decision nobly expressed over six hundred years ago. In reproducing this passage in this the first part of the book we bring down the bird of Scottish wisdom hit in both wings (the past and the present) from one barrel.

Printed below then are (1) the final paragraphs from Lord Cooper's *The Declaration of Arbroath Revisited*; (2) the Declaration itself in Lord Cooper's translation; and (3) our footnotes upon the text and translation.

LORD COOPER OF CULROSS

Conclusion to 'The Declaration of Arbroath Revisited'

. . . These papal records deserve more study than they have received. We get the names of the two envoys who carried the letter—Edward de Mambuisson and Adam de Gordon—and we find that they were more than postmen, for they were charged with oral messages to the Pope and had several audiences with him. Moreover the Declaration of Arbroath was not the only letter which they carried, for there was also a private letter from Bruce. That letter has not (so far as I know) been preserved, but by great good fortune we can reconstruct its contents from two letters in reply which the Pope dispatched to Bruce, and from a further letter to Edward II which he wrote to report all that had happened. That is just as well, for this reason. There were 'Men of Vichy' at Arbroath on that fateful day when the Declaration was sealed, and the strange passage in the Declaration by which the Barons assert that, if Bruce weakened in his resolution, they would drive him from his throne and choose another king, creates a faint suspicion that Bruce himself was suspected of designs to make peace. The private letter thus becomes very important for the purpose of discovering where exactly Bruce stood. Happily its reconstructed contents refute this suspicion. What did Bruce write? He raised the question of the vacant Bishopric of Glasgow. He asked the Pope to

[1] The King or Queen 'of Scots' has usually been known by that title and not by 'of Scotland': an important distinction.

secure the pardon of certain ecclesiastics who were imprisoned, pre-sumably in England. And he made a spirited protest against the Pope's practice of refusing to give him his title of King of Scots. That was all. There is no hint or trace of weakening; and by the time we reach September Bruce comes out of that correspondence with much greater credit that John XXII.

And so we may conclude that when Bernard inserted that odd passage in the Declaration, he was not covertly hitting at Bruce, who, by the way, was not the kind of man to tolerate insinuations of that sort. So to read the passage is to miss the point. The draftsman— consummate artist as he was—was working up to his dramatic peroration in which he spoke of the one hundred Scots who might still be left alive; and his point was that the Pope had to reckon not with one man but with a nation; that Bruce was no more than the instrument of the people's will; and that, if Bruce vanished or had to be liquidated, the iron resolution of a nation would remain unbroken and unshaken. Any ruler who betrayed his trust forfeited his position. Bruce, I have little doubt, listened to that passage when it was read at Arbroath Abbey, not with a guilty conscience nor with resentment at any supposed innuendo, but with admiration for its rhetorical skill.

There is still much to be learned from that remarkable manifesto. Read it again, and judge for yourselves whether it does not deserve on its merits to be ranked as one of the masterpieces of political rhetoric of all time.

THE DECLARATION OF ARBROATH IN ENGLISH

Unto the Most Holy Father in Christ and the Lord, JOHN, by the Providence of God Supreme Pontiff of the Holy Roman Church Universal, Duncan, Earl of Fife [here follow thirty-nine names and designations] and the other Barons and Freeholders and the whole community of the Scottish realm offer all filial reverence with devout kisses to his blessed feet.

We know, Most Holy Father and Lord, and we find it written in the records and histories of the ancients, that amongst other peoples of renown our Scottish nation has been distinguished by many tributes to their fame. We passed over from Greater Scythia across the Tyrrhen-ian Sea and beyond the Pillars of Hercules, and sojourned for many a year amid the most savage races of Spain; but nowhere could any people, however barbarous, reduce us to subjection. From there, twelve hundred years after the Departure of the Children of Israel, we came to our abode in the West where we now dwell. The Britons were driven out; the Picts were utterly destroyed; we were assailed again and again by Norse, Angle and Dane: but by many a victory and with endless toil we established ourselves here, and, as the historians of old bear witness, we have ever held our land free from servitude of every kind. Within this our realm there have reigned one hundred and thirteen Kings of our native royal dynasty, and not one of alien birth. If proof be needed of the quality and worth of our people, it shines forth for all to see in this that the King of Kings, our Lord Jesus Christ, after His Passion and Resurrection, chose us as almost the first to be called to His most holy faith, though we dwelt in the uttermost parts of the earth, and He would not that we should be confirmed therein by anyone except the first of His Apostles by calling, though the second or third in rank, Andrew the Meek, the brother of blessed Peter, whom He appointed to be our leader and patron Saint for ever.

It was after pondering all these things in their minds that the Most Holy Fathers, your predecessors, fortified our realm and people, as the peculiar possession of the brother of blessed Peter, with many favours and countless privileges.[1] So it came about that under their protection our nation lived in freedom and in peace, until that august prince, Edward, King of England, the father of the present King, finding our realm without a king, and our people innocent of evil intent and still unused to the assaults of war, came to us in the guise of a friend and ally and then made a hostile attack upon us. As for the wrongs he inflicted upon us—the slaughter, violence, pillage, conflagration, prelates imprisoned, monasteries burned down and their inmates robbed and slain, and all the other outrages which he perpetrated on our people, sparing neither age nor sex nor religious order—none could describe nor even conceive these things unless he had actually experienced them.

From these innumerable evils, with the aid of Him who woundeth and His hands make whole, we have been delivered by our most valiant Prince and King, Robert[2]; who, that he might free his people and heritage from the hands of the enemy, rose like another Joshua or Maccabeus, and cheerfully endured toil and weariness, hunger and peril. He it is that by the providence of God we have made our Prince

[1] Literally: 'and privileges.' Ed.
[2] Literally: 'the Lord Robert. . . .' Ed.

and King, not only by right of succession according to our laws and customs, which we are resolved to maintain unto the death, but also with the due consent and assent of us all.[1] Unto him, by whom salvation has been wrought unto our people,[2] we are bound for the preservation of our liberties, both by force of law and out of gratitude for all he has done; and unto him we are determined in all things to adhere. But were he to abandon the task to which he has set his hand or to show any disposition to subject us or our realm to the King of England or the English, we would instantly strive to expel him as our enemy and the betrayer of his own rights and ours, and we would choose another King to rule over us who would be equal to the task of our defence.

For so long as one hundred men remain alive, we shall never under any conditions submit[3] to the domination of the English. It is not for glory or riches or honours that we fight, but only for liberty, which no good man will consent to lose but with his life.

For these reasons, revered Father and Lord, we most earnestly pray and from our hearts beseech your Holiness that in all sincerity and piety you will call to mind that with Him, whose earthly vicegerent you are, there is no respect of persons and neither Jew nor Greek, Scot nor English. We entreat you to look with a father's eye upon the tribulations and distress which the English have brought upon us and upon the Church of God: and we ask that you will be pleased to admonish and exhort the King of England (who should rest content with what he has seeing that it was enough to satisfy[4] at least seven kings), urging him to leave us in peace in our poor Scotland, where we live on the uttermost bounds of human habitation and covet nothing but our own. To secure such a peace we are willing in very deed to do anything in our power saving all these our vital interests. So to do, Holy Father, is a matter of real concern for yourself; for you see how the heathen rage against the Christians through the fault of the Christians, and how the boundaries of Christendom are being narrowed every day. See to it that your good name does not suffer if—which God forbid—the Church in any place suffers eclipse or offence while you

[1] Or, more literally: 'He it is whom the Providence of God, and (in accordance with our laws and customs, which we are resolved till death to maintain) both rightful succession and the due consent and assent of us all, have made our Prince and King.' The signatories are not suggesting that more of the credit is due to themselves than to the Divine Providence. Ed.

[2] Or, more literally: 'Unto him—as unto him by whom salvation hath been wrought among the people—. . . .' Ed.

[3] Literally: 'never, to any extent, submit. . . .' Ed.

[4] Literally: 'since it used to be enough for. . . .' Ed.

are Pope! Make an appeal therefore to the Christian princes who are alleging as false pretexts for their inability to go on a crusade to the Holy Land that they are at war with their neighbours—the truth being that they consider it more profitable and less dangerous to vanquish their weaker neighbours than to go on a crusade.[1] But if only the King of England would leave us in peace, He from whom no secrets are hid well knows how joyfully we and our King would go to the Holy Land; and this pledge we declare and testify to you as the Vicar of Christ and to the whole of Christendom.

But if your Holiness will not place reliance on these our assurances, preferring to lend too credulous an ear to the allegations of the English and continuing to show favour to them to our discomfiture, rest assured[2] that the destruction of life, the perdition of souls and all the other evils which will ensue and which we shall inflict on the English and they on us, will be laid by the Most High to your account!

Wherefore we are and ever shall be, as in duty bound, prepared as obedient children to do your good pleasure as His Vicar. And unto Him, the King and Judge most high, we commit our cause, casting all our care upon Him, and steadfastly trusting that He will endue us with courage and bring our enemies to nought.

May the Most High preserve your Holiness in health and strength for the service of His Holy Church to length of days.

Executed at the Monastery of Arbroath in Scotland on the Sixth day of April, in the year of Grace One thousand three hundred and twenty and in the Fifteenth year of the Reign of our said King.

[1] Or: 'that the advantage that they may gain by making war on their minor neighbours is more immediate—and the resistance weaker.' Ed.
[2] Literally: 'We believe that. . . .' A phrase which, though sufficiently polite, seems much more direct than the late Lord President's rendering. Ed.

Robert Henryson

A few years before the Polish cleric Copernicus had established the, humanly speaking, unimportant fact that the sun is the centre of our system, there lived a Scottish schoolmaster at Dunfermline. Robert Henryson in his wise, ironical, shrewd poetry based his philosophy on the more practical hypothesis that Dunfermline in the fifteenth century was for him, and his fellow-citizens, the centre of the universe. In that little flax-making Fife town, with all its historical and ecclesiastical associations, there lay all that needed to concern these people in their brief passage through the mortality of the flesh. How Scottish! How wise! Yet how hauntingly he evokes this theme!

But Henryson was no provincial hay-seed. This schoolmaster (a mediaeval forerunner of that admirable and famous type, now all but extinct—the Scottish Dominie) had read widely and well. He was, of course, versed in mediaeval Latin, and probably knew a few of the European vernaculars then taking shape. He certainly knew English. He had, with attention, read Chaucer, who was even then much thought of in these islands, though he had not yet reached that nearly deified position to which the Professors of 'Eng. Lit.' and their followers have since elevated him.

Printed below are two extracts from Henryson. The first is a by-product rather than an example of his classical study and is an Aesopian fable modernised (or, more accurately, mediaevalised) and localised. The second, dealing with Henryson's view of the tale of Cressida, is a development from his Chaucerian reading. These selections have been made not only to display the peculiar power of his restrained, ironically expressive Scottish verse, but to show him in the light of an expounder of Scottish wisdom of a highly characteristic kind.

The Preiching of the Swallow is the mediaevalised Aesopian fable. The rendering of the story is Scottish, the scene is Scottish, the description of the flax-making in his own town is Scottish, the style is Scottish. The moral of providing for the future, need it be pointed out, is Scottish. Many jokes have travelled the world over about the Scotsman's care in economy, many sermons and homilies have been preached in praise of it. Some of the jokes are good, some bad; some of the sermons are of value, some are platitudinously and complacently repetitive. *The Preiching of the Swallow*, which is the first eminent encomium on provi-dence in Scottish literature, is neither a joke nor a sermon. It is a poem in which there is some beauty and much wisdom. Let it be noted that, through the swallow's beak, this mediaeval Scottish schoolmaster praises this quality *not* as a virtue in itself but as an urgent necessity for every vigorous Scot. He lives in a country where, however beautifully the summer's day may linger in the long northern manner, the northern winter shall yet surely strike with crippling force. However peaceful may be the scene (even in the douce town of Dunfermline) war and a powerful enemy may come at any moment.

The Testament of Cresseid is Henryson's master work and indeed is one of the most perfect Scottish poems of a comparable length—a complete work of art, full of compassion and tenderness. More to our immediate purpose, it also contains the first flowering in Scottish mediaeval verse of shrewd, ironical, fact-facing Scottish wisdom. On a superficial reading of this poem, students of 'Eng. Lit.' are inclined to stress too much Henryson's debt to Chaucer. This despite the admirable studies of Henryson made by such eminent English scholars as Professors Geoffrey Tillotson and C. S. Lewis. Even these scholars, we think, have failed to assess Henryson's originality, which is much greater than his debt to Chaucer. In fact, Henryson merely takes Chaucer's famous *Troylus and Crysede* as the starting point for what is almost certainly an original invention of his own—what really happened to Cressida. He develops this theme in a highly characteristic Scottish manner. He does not directly criticise Chaucer's view of Courtly Love, but brings a much more sardonic view to bear upon it. It is his own view and a Scottish one.

The author of Henryson's poem, an elderly man, all passion spent, yet with the pulse of its ardour still faintly beating in the veins of his memory, picks up and reads Chaucer's great work. 'But was this *all* that happened?' he asks. The shrewd Scottish poet is not content merely with the tale of a romantic episode in the life of someone else. He wants to know more and in particular what happens to Cresseid. He finds out or pretends to find out. He finds out that the lovely Cresseid fell a prey to leprosy, that dread mediaeval disease manifest even in Dunfermline. Her father faces this grim fact without evasion but without despair. Cresseid herself faces it with horror but as a fact—a fact which she has brought upon herself. In memorable and beautiful words she warns the ladies of Troy and Greece to take heed of her misery for which she alone is responsible. She faces her own misery as self-wrought. No interpretation of the poem which does not make this central is a sound interpretation. The final moral wisdom of this moving work is quite simply (and as a later Scot was to put it) 'Facts are chiels that winna ding.' Facts are relentless. One fact here is lamentably relentless.

It is impossible to print the whole poem or to cut the narrative successfully. We therefore with much regret include only Henryson's opening where he asks whether Chaucer told the whole story. But we begin with *The Preiching of the Swallow*.

I. THE PREICHING OF THE SWALLOW

The ^ahie prudence, and wirking mervellous,   ^ahigh
The profound wit of God Omnipotent,
Is sa perfite, and sa ingenious,
Excellent far all mannis judgement;
^aForquhy to Him all-thing is ay present,   ^afor why, because
Richt as it is, or ony time sall be,
Before the sicht of His divinity. . . .

For God is in his pouer infinite,
And mannis saul is feeble and ower small,
Of understanding ^awaik and unperfite,   ^aweak
To comprehend Him that conteinis all.
Nane suld presume, ^abe ressoun natural,   ^aby
To seirch the secreitis of the Trinity,
Bot ^atrow fermly, and ^blat all ressoun be.   ^abelieve ^blet

Yit nevertheless we may haiff knawledging
Of God Almichty, ^abe his creaturis,   ^aby
That He is gude, fair, ^awyis, and bening;   ^awise
Exemple tak be ^athir joly flouris,   ^athese
Richt sweit of smell, and pleisant of colouris:
Sum green, sum blue, sum purpour, quhite, and
   reid,
Thus distribute ^abe gift of His Godheid.   ^aby

The firmament paintit with ^asternis cleir,   ^astars
From eist to west rolland in circle round,
And everilk planet in his proper spheir,
In moving makand harmony and sound;
The Fire, the Air, the Watter, and the Ground—
^aTill understand it is ^baneuch, I ^cwiss,   ^ato ^benough ^cknow
That God in all His werkis witty is.

Luik weill the fisch that swimmis in the sea,
Luik weill in ^aeirth all kind of bestial;   ^aearth
The ^afoulis fair, sa forcily thay flee,   ^abirds
Scheddand the air with ^apennis grit and small;   ^awings
Syne luik to man, that He made last of all,
Like to His image and His similitude:
^aBe thir we knaw that God is fair and gude.   ^aby these

All creature He made for the behufe
Of man, and to his supportatioun
^aInto this eirth, baith under and abufe,   ^ain
In number, wecht, and due proportioun;
The difference of time, and ilk sessoun,
Concordand till our opportunity,
As daily by experience we may see.

The Somer with his joly mantill of green,
With flouris fair ^afurrit on everilk ^bfent,   ^afurred ^bopening
Quhilk Flora Goddess, of the Flouris Queen,   (of garment)
Hes to that lord as for his sessoun sent,
And Phebus with his goldin ^abeimis ^bgent   ^abeams ^bfair
Hes ^apurfellit and paintit pleisandly,   ^abordered
With heit and moisture ^astilland from the sky. ^adistilling

Syne Harvest ^ahait, quhen Ceres, that   ^ahot
    Goddess,
Hir barnis ^abeinit hes with abundance;   ^afilled, made comfortable
And Bacchus, God of Wine, renewit hes
The ^atume pipis in Italy and France,   ^aempty pipes (of wine)
With winis ^awicht, and liquour of pleisance; ^astrong
And *Copia temporis* to fill hir horn,
That never wes full of ^aquheit nor other corn. ^awheat

Syne Winter wan, quhen Austern Eolus,
God of the Wind, with blastis boreal,
The green garment of Somer glorious
Hes ^aall to rent and revin in piecis small;   ^acompletely torn
Than flouris fair faidit with frost ^amaun fall, ^amust
And birdis blyith chaingit thair notis sweit
^aIn still murning, neir slain with snaw and   ^ainto
    sleit.

^aThir daillis deip with ^bdubbis drounit is,   ^athese ^bpuddles
Baith hill and ^aholt ^bheillit with frostis ^chair; ^awood ^bcovered ^choar
And ^abewis been ^bleifit bair of bliss,   ^aboughs ^bleft bare
^aBe wickit windis of the winter ^bwair.   ^aby ^b(?) wild
All wild beistis than from the ^abentis bair   ^ahill-grass
Drawis for dreid unto thair dennis deip,
Couchand for cauld in ^acoifis thame to keip. ^ahollows

Syne [a]cummis Ver, quhen Winter is away,	[a]comes
The secretar of Somer with his [a]sell,	[a]seal
Quhen [a]columbie [b]up-keikis throw the clay,	[a]columbine [b]up peeps
Quhilk [a]fleeit wes before with frostis [b]fell.	[a]fled [b]dire
The [a]mavis and the [b]merle beginnis to [c]mell;	[a]thrush [b]blackbird [c]mate
The lark [a]on loft, with other birdis [b]haill,	[a]aloft [b]lit. whole
Than drawis furth fra [a]dern, ower doun and dail.	[a]hiding

That samin sessoun, [a]into ane soft morning,	[a]in
Richt blyith that bitter blastis were [a]ago,	[a]gone
Unto the wuid, to see the flouris spring,	
And heir the mavis sing and birdis mo,	
I passit furth, syne luikit to and fro,	
To see the soil that wes richt sessonable,	
Sappy, and to [a]ressave all [b]seidis able.	[a]receive [b]seeds

Moving [a]thusgate, grit mirth I tuik in mind,	[a]thus
Of lauboraris to see the [a]besiness,	[a]busy-ness
Sum [a]makand dyke, and sum the pleuch [b]can wind,	[a]making [b]did guide
Sum sawand seidis fast from place to place,	
The harrowis hoppand in the [a]saweris trace:	[a]sower's
It wes grit joy, to him that [a]luifit corn,	[a]loved
To see thame laubour, baith at een and morn.	

And as I bade under ane bank full [a]bein,	[a]comfortable
In hart gritlie [a]rejosit of that sicht,	[a]rejoiced
Unto ane hedge, under ane hawthorn green,	
Of small birdis thair come ane [a]ferlie flicht,	[a]wonderful
And doun [a]belyfe [b]can on the [c]leifis [d]licht,	[a]quickly [b]did [c]leaves [d]alight
On everilk side about me quhare I stude,	
Richt mervellous, ane meikle multitude.	

Amang the [a]quhilkis ane Swallow loud [b]couth cry,	[a]which (pl.) [b]did
On that hawthorn [a]hie in the [b]crop sittand:	[a]high [b]crest, top
'O ye birdis on bewis, here me by,	
Ye all weill knaw, and [a]wyisly understand,	[a]wisely
Quhare danger is, or peril appeirand	
It is grit wisdom to provide before,	
It to [a]devoid, for [b]dreid it hurt yow more.'	[a]nullify [b]dread

'Schir Swallow,' ^aquod the Lark ^bagain, and ^aleuch, — ^aquoth ^bin reply / ^alaughed

'What haiff ye seen that causis yow to dreid?'
'See ye yon churl,' quod ^ascho, 'beyond yon pleuch, — ^ashe
Fast sawand hemp, lo, see! and ^alinget seid? — ^alint, flax
Yon ^alint will grow in little time indeed, — ^aflax
And thairof will yon churl his nettis mak,
Under the quhilk he thinkis us to tak.

'Thairfore I ^areid we pass when he is gone, — ^aadvise
At ^aeen, and with our naillis scharp and small — ^aevening
Out of the eirth scraip we yon seid anone,
And eit it up; for, ^agif it growis, we sall — ^aif
Have cause to weip here-efter ane and all:
See we ^aremeid thairfore furthwith instante, — ^aremedy
Nam levius lædit quicquid prævidimus ante.

'For clerkis sayis it is nocht sufficient
To consider that is before thine ^aee; — ^aeye
Bot prudence is ane inwart argument,
That ^agarris ane man provide and foresee — ^ainduces . . . to
What gude, what ill, is likelie for to be,
Of everilk thing behald the final end,
And ^aswa fra peril the better ^bhim defend.' — ^aso ^bhimself

The Lark, ^alauchand, the Swallow thus couth scorn, — ^alaughing
And said, 'Scho fishit lang before the net'—
'The ^abarn is ^beith to ^cbusk that is unborn'— — ^abairn ^beasy ^cdres
'All growis nocht that in the ground is set'—
'The neck to ^astoup, quhen it the ^bstraik sall get, — ^astoop ^bstroke
Is soon ^aaneuch'—'Deith on the ^bfayest fall!' — ^aenough ^bnearest to death
Thus scornit thay the Swallow ane and all.

Despising thus hir healthsome ^adocument, — ^aadmonition
The foulis ^aferly tuik thair flicht anone; — ^asuddenly
Sum with ane ^abirr thay ^bbraidit ower the bent, — ^awhirr ^bstarted
And sum ^aagain are to the green-wuid gone. — ^aback
Upon the land quhare I wes left alone,
I tuik my club, and hamewart ^acouth I cairry, — ^acarried (it)
Swa ^aferlyand, as I had seen ane fairy. — ^amarvelling

Thus passit furth ^aquhill June, that joly tide,   ^atill
And seidis that were sawin of beforn
Were growin hie, that ^ahairis micht thame hide,   ^ahares
And ^aals the quailyie ^bcraikand in the corn;   ^aalso ^bcroaking
I muvit furth, betwix midday and morn,
Unto the hedge under the hawthorn green,
Quhare I before the said birdis had seen.

And as I stude, ^abe aventure and case,   ^aquite by chance
The ^asamin birdis as I haiff said yow ^bere—   ^asame ^bearlier
I ^ahope, because it wes thair hanting-place,   ^aexpect
Mair of succour, or yit mair solitair—
Thay ^alichtit doun: and, when thay lichtit were,   ^aalighted
The Swallow ^aswyth put furth ane pietuous   ^aat once
  ^apyme,   ^acry
Said, 'Wo is him can not be-war in time!

'O, blind birdis, and full of negligence,
Unmindfull of your ^aawin prosperitie,   ^aown
Lift up your sicht, and tak gude advertence!
Luik to the lint that growis on yon lee—
Yon is the thing I ^abad, forsuith, that we,   ^abade
^aQuhill it wes weid, suld rute furth of the ^beird—   ^awhile ^bearth
Now is it lint, now is it hie ^aon breird!   ^ain the shoot

'Go yit, quhill it is tender and small,
And pull it up; let it na mair increiss.
My flesch ^agrowis, my bodie quaikis all,   ^agrues, creeps
Thinkand on it I may not sleip in ^apeice.'   ^apeace
Thay cryit all, and bad the Swallow ^aceise,   ^acease
And said, 'Yon lint here-after will do gude,
For ^alinget is to little birdis fude.   ^aflax

'We think, quhen that yon lint ^abollis are ripe,   ^apods
To mak us feist, and fill us of the seid,
Magre yon churl, and on it sing and pipe.'
'Weill,' quod the Swallow, 'freindis, ^ahardily   ^aby all means be it
  beid;
Do as ye will, bot certain ^asair I dreid,   ^asore I dread
Here-efter ye sall find ^aals sour as sweit,   ^aas
Quhen ye are ^aspeldit on yon ^bcarlis speit.   ^askewered ^bfellow's spit

'The [a]awner of yon lint ane [b]foular is,   [a]owner [b]fowler
Richt cautelus and full of subtlety;
His [a]pray full [b]sendill timis will he miss,   [a]prey [b]seldom
[a]Bot gif we birdis all the [b]warrer be;   [a]unless [b]warier
Full mony of our kin he hes [a]gart die,   [a]made die (pron. dee)
And [a]thocht it bot ane sport to spill thair   [a]thought
   blude:
God keip me fra him, and the Haly Rude!'

Thir small birdis havand bot little thocht
Of peril that micht fall [a]be aventure,   [a]by chance
The counsale of the Swallow set at nocht,
Bot tuik thair flicht, and furth togidder [a]fure;   [a]fared
Sum to the wuid, sum [a]markit to the [b]mure.   [a]went [b]moor
I tuik my staff, quhen this wes said and done,
And walkit hame, for it drew neir the [a]none.   [a]noon

The lint ripit, the carle pullit the [a]line,   [a]stalk (of flax)
[a]Rippillit the bollis, and [b]beitis set,   [a]removed the seeds [b]bundles
It steipit in the [a]burn, and dryit syne,   [a]stream
And with ane [a]bittle knockit it, and [b]bet,   [a]'beetle' [b]beat
Syne [a]swingillit it weill, and [b]heckillit in the   [a]'scutched' [b]dressed (it)
   [a]flet;   [a]inner room (?)
His wife it span, and twinit it into threid,
Of quhilk the Foular nettis made indeed.

The Winter come, the wickit wind can blaw,
The wuidis green were [a]wallowit with the   [a]withered
   [a]weit,   [a]wet
Baith [a]firth and fell with frostis were made   [a]woodland
   [a]faw,   [a]streaked, bright
[a]Slonkis and [b]slaik made sliddery with the sleit;   [a]ditches [b]mud (?)
The foulis fair for [a]falt thay fell of [b]feit;   [a]want [b]feet
On [a]bewis bair it wes na [b]bute to bide,   [a]boughs [b]comfort
Bot hyit unto [a]houssis thame to hide.   [a]houses

Sum in the barn, sum in the stack of corn
Thair ludging tuik, and made thair residence;
The Foular saw, and grit [a]aithis hes sworn,   [a]oaths
Thay suld be [a]tane, truly, for thair expense.   [a]taken
His nettis hes he set with diligence,
And in the snaw he [a]schuillit hes ane plain,   [a]shovelled
And [a]heillit it all ower with [b]caff again.   [a]covered [b]chaff

*a*Thir small birdis, seeand the caff, wes glaid;   *a*these
Trowand it had been corn, thay lichtit doun;
Bot of the nettis na presume thay had,
Nor of the Fowlaris false intentioun;
To scraip, and seik thair meit thay made thame
    *a*boun.   *a*ready
The Swallow on ane little branch neir-by,
Dreidand for gyle, thus loud on thame couth cry:

'Into that caff scraip *a*quhill your naillis bleid,   *a*till
Thair is na corn, ye laubour all in vain;
Trow ye yon churl for pietie will yow *a*feid?   *a*feed
Na, na, he hes it here layit for ane *a*train;   *a*trap
Remuve, I *a*reid, or ellis ye will be slain;   *a*advise
His nettis he hes set full privily,
Ready to draw; in time be-war *a*for-thy!'   *a*for that reason

Grit fule is he that puttis in danger
His life, his honour, for ane thing of nocht;
Grit fule is he, that will not glaidly *a*heir   *a*hear
Counsale in time, *a*quhill it avail him nocht;   *a*till
Grit fule is he, that hes na thing in thocht
Bot thing present, and efter what may fall,
Nor of the end, hes na *a*memorial.   *a*remembrance

Thir small birdis for hunger famischit *a*neir,   *a*nearly
Full *a*besy scraipand for to seik thair fude,   *a*busy
The counsale of the Swallow *a*wald not *b*heir,   *a*would *b*hear
*a*Suppose thair laubour did thame little gude.   *a*even tho'
Quhen scho thair fulisch hartis understude,
Sa indurate, up in ane tree scho flew.
With that this churl ower thame his nettis drew.

Allace! it wes grit *a*hart-sair for to see   *a*heart-sore
That bluidy bowcheour beit thay birdis doun,
And for *a*till heir, when thay wist weill to die,   *a*to hear
Thair *a*cairful sang and lamentatioun: *a*full of care
Sum with ane staff he *a*straik to eirth *b*on swoun: *a*struck *b*in a swoon
Of sum the *a*heid he straik, of sum he brak the   *a*head
    *a*crag,   *a*neck
Sum half on life he *a*stoppit in his bag.   *a*stuffed into

E

And quhen the Swallow saw that thay were
    ^adeid,   ^adead
'Lo,' quod scho, 'thus it happinnis mony ^asyis   ^atimes
On thame that will not tak counsale nor ^areid   ^aadvice
Of prudent men, or clerkis that are wyis;
This grit peril I tauld thame mair than ^athryis;   ^athrice
Now are thay deid, and wo is me thairfore!'
Scho tuik hir flicht, bot I hir saw no more.

II. FROM THE TESTAMENT OF CRESSEID

Henryson asks whether Chaucer knew or told the whole story of Cresseid. At this point he takes over the telling of the tale. Sts. 5–10: 'Quha wait gif all that Chaucer wrait was true?'

Thocht ^alufe be ^bhait, yit in ane man of age   ^alove ^bhot
It kindlis nocht sa soon as in youthheid,
Of quhom the blude is flowing in ane rage,
And in the auld the courage ^adoif and ^bdeid,   ^adispirited ^bdead
Of ^aquhilk the fire outward is best ^bremeid;   ^awhich ^bremedy
To help ^abe physic, ^bquhare that nature   ^aby ^bwhere
    faillit,
I am expert, for baith I have ^aassaillit.   ^atried

I mend the fire and ^abeikit me about,   ^awarmed
Than tuik ane drink my ^aspreitis to comfort,   ^aspirits
And armit me weill fra the cauld thairout:
To cut the winter nicht and mak it schort,
I tuik ane ^aquair, and left all other sport,   ^abook
Writtin be worthy Chaucer glorious,
Of fair Cresseid, and worthy Troilus.

And thair I ^afand, efter that Diomeid   ^afound
^aRessavit had that lady bricht of hue,   ^areceived
How Troilus ^aneir out of wit ^babraid,   ^anearly ^bstarted
And weipit sore with visage pale of hue;
For quhilk ^awanhope his ^bteiris ^ccan renew   ^adespair ^btears ^c(he) did
^aQuhill Esperus rejoicit him again,   ^atill
Thus ^aquhile in joy he ^blevit, quhile in pain.   ^asometimes ^blived

Of hir behest he had greit comforting,
^aTraisting to Troy that scho ^bsuld mak   ^atrusting ^bshould return
   retour,
Quhilk he desirit maist of ^aeirdly thing,   ^aearthly
^aForquhy scho was his only paramour;   ^abecause
Bot quhen he saw passit baith day and hour
Of hir ^againcome, than sorrow ^bcan oppress   ^acoming-back ^bdid
His woful hart in cair and heaviness.

Of his distress ^ame neidis nocht rehearse,   ^aneed not
For worthy Chaucer in the samin buik
In gudely termis and in joly verse
Compilit hes his cairis, quha will luik.
To brek my sleip ane uther quair I tuik,
In quhilk I fand the fatal destiny
Of fair Cresseid, that endit wretchitly.

Quha ^await gif *all* that Chaucer ^bwrait was   ^aknows ^bwrote
   true?
Nor I wait nocht gif this narratioun
Be authoreist, or feignit of the new
^aBe sum poeit, throw his inventioun,   ^aby
Made to report the lamentatioun
And woful end of this lusty Cresseid,
And quhat distress scho ^atholit, and quhat   ^asuffered
   ^adeid. . . .   ^adeath

William Dunbar

Such national wisdom as Dunbar throws out in his multifarious poetry gleams in the iridescence of his style. In sheer virtuosity of language and metre he surpasses all other Scottish poets who have yet written. Those Scots who regard Burns as unquestionably the greatest and most varied of our poets can scarcely have read Dunbar with attention (if indeed they are properly aware of him at all) or they would hardly think that.

Dunbar, who was born about 1465 and died either at Flodden in 1513 or possibly some years later in sorrow and retirement, wrote most of his poetry at the Court of James IV, under whose reign he flourished. James is often described as a Scottish Renaissance Prince; and it is tempting to think of Dunbar as affected by the undoubted Renaissance tide of that time. In fact his technically virtuoso style is really the culmination of something that had been going on for a long time in Scotland and is more akin to developments in Celtic and Gaelic verse than to outside trends. He is, or used to be, best known for his aureate poetry (that is, poetry in an ornate style using a high proportion of Latin words and forms) such as *The Golden Targe* and *The Thrissil and the Rose*. At least equally interesting are the poems he wrote in other modes ranging from ordinary courtier-like verse asking the King for favours, to popular morality and popular scurrility such as *The Twa Marrit Wemen*. This last has a kind of down-to-earth, leave-it-to-the-laughing-or-disgusted-reader kind of wisdom of a patently Scottish quality. We have, however, hesitated to include it in this volume. It might even now be legally interpreted South of Tweed as 'having a tendency to corrupt.'

Dunbar was some kind of cleric. It is unnecessary to discuss here the troubled question of how much he was a cleric or in what kind of orders. But it is odd to think that if the author of *The Twa Marrit Wemen* were living today he would be known as the Reverend William Dunbar, though we would be unlikely to see him in Princes Street, Edinburgh, on the mornings of International Rugby matches (the Thrissil versus the Rose) sporting a dog-collar, a handlebar moustache and a muscularly hearty Christian manner.[1] It is, however, characteristic of the man and his calling that he should have turned a part of his genius to the composition of moralistic verses. It is of a much higher standard than any other moralistic verse of the period, and is, therefore, more than most of his rich output, suitable to our purpose in the presentation of Scottish wisdom.

The first of the six pieces printed below is fairly straightforward.

---

[1] Though he was a courtier poet, it is also unlikely that a man of his temperament would nowadays become Dean of the Thistle—or of the Thrissil as he would have called it. R. L. C. L. [I would never have dared to suggest this. M. Mc.L.]

How sall I govern me? asks its own question and gives its own easily understood answer. Unlike most moralistic poetry it has certain amusingly cynical touches, showing an intimate knowledge of the ways of the world. This is highly characteristic of the richly varied Scottish poet. Scottishly wise, too, is the second stanza which recalls that St. Andreapolitan motto which has gone round the world: 'They have said. And they will say. Let them be saying.' A Scottish interpretation of a classical piece of wisdom if ever there was one. Its origin, by the way, is in the city not the University of St. Andrews. The second poem, *Of Discretioun in Asking*, has the same worldliness and the same moral feeling, besides being very smoothly written.

The third poem, *Of Lufe Erdly and Divine*, speaks to us again of the old Scottish conflict between love and beauty and the desire for discipline. In this poem, however, Dunbar treats the theme in a Christian and specifically Catholic manner. He holds that earthly love turns to ashes; but he does not offer, as an alternative to its fleeting delights, only harsh self-subjugation with no apparent reward. As a Christian he believes that Heavenly love, when striven for with the ardour which its pursuit demands, can provide the lover of God, Our Blessed Lady and the Company of Heaven (this was written before the Reformation) with a satisfaction unknown to the earth-bound, flesh-bound lover. This is not the sort of theme Scottish poets often write about either in the past or in the Glasgow tenements or Edinburgh Rose Street salons of today. It expresses not only Scottish wisdom, but a part of eternal wisdom. It expresses it in the Scottish tongue; and therein lies its poignancy for a Scottish Christian reading it over four hundred years after its making. Poetically, too, its refrain is poignant:

'Now cummis age quhare youth has been,
And true lufe risis fro the spleen.'

Does he intend by 'spleen' the melancholy which precedes redemption, or is he airing a piece of contemporary Scottish medical wisdom? At any rate the effect is most haunting.

The fourth example below (*Dunbar at Oxenfurd*) is a genially conceited poem. The poet of the Northern Renaissance Court felt no sense of inferiority in visiting Oxford. He views the place shrewdly and does not take it at its face value. He does not, as some Scottish visitors and professors do today, take it *at its own* valuation. Indeed, while admiring the learning to be found there he makes the then very Scottish point that learning without true wisdom is not of much worth.

On the other hand he makes his point not in the uncouth and graceless manner in which some modern Scottish oafs would do, but in civilised verse. One pauses to reflect what Dunbar would have made of the later Oxford, of the 'home of lost causes,' of the place of meditative and unutilitarian enchantment it was to become before Lord Nuffield turned it into the *Quartier Latin* of Cowley. Dunbar was a wit as well as a poet; he might, had he lingered on through the centuries, have appreciated the mist-enshrouded and isolated atmosphere of witty indolence which was to accumulate before Latin was on the way out, women on the way in, and internal-combustion already there—that atmosphere which is now dispelled. He might have enjoyed the Oxford of *Zuleika Dobson*. He might have echoed the words of two other scholar-priests: 'Trinity had never been unkind to me.' The author of this note admits that there is no evidence that Dunbar thought it worth while to visit Cambridge.

But all Oxford was probably kind and civil to Dunbar when he stayed there; and indeed he undoubtedly enjoyed himself in England in general when he visited the country on an embassy. Readers may recall his *London, thou art the Flour of Cities all*. Dunbar was the first Scottish writer to say nice things about the English; but he said them from a position of equality. Upon his return to Scotland he may well have been the first person to use the well-known remark, 'Some of my best friends are English.'

It is unlikely, however, that he went to the lengths of an ardently aspiring Anglophil Edinburgh-New-Town advocate's wife of my acquaintance. When asked what college her husband had been at she said (without, I think, any reference to the tradition of non-Europeans or to hoary chestnuts of the Dr.-Livingstone-I-presume kind, but with an even older and Caledonian tradition uneasily troubling her): 'Well, *actually*, he was at Balliol, but *most* of his friends were English.'

The last two extracts printed below are highly moralistic in the Scottish way. Indeed, though coming from a Catholic poet before the Reformation, they have a strong strain of puritanism about them. But it is a puritanism expressed with pith and occasional beauty (see the second stanza of the first poem), rare in any modern puritan writing. Dunbar's puritanism, when he allowed it expression, was concerned with morals not aesthetics. His voluptuous sensuousness in words was quite uninhibited. 'Of the Chaingis of Life' expresses that deeply-implanted Scottish sentiment that when the weather is fair you must expect foul to follow. In other words, don't put your trust in the beauty and comfort of nature. 'Of Content' is a powerful statement of the Scottish belief in the virtues of self-sufficiency and independency. What Dunbar is saying here is what Burns repeated three centuries later in 'Contented wi' little and cantie wi' mair.' A man can be poor yet happy if he keeps his self-respect. This again is a continuing theme of Scottish wisdom though not held of much account in commercial newspaper and television owning circles in Scotland today.

I. HOW SALL I GOVERN ME?

> How suld I rule me or in quhat wise,
> I wald sum wyis man wald devise,
> ^aSen I can ^bleiff in no degree,   ^asince ^blive
> Bot sum my manneris will despise.
> *Lord God, how suld I govern me?*

^aGif I be lusty, galland and blyith,   ^aif
 Than will thay say on me full ^aswyith,   ^asoon
'Yon man out of his mind is he,
Or sum hes done him confort kyith!'¹
Lord God, how suld I govern me?

^aGif I be sorrowful and sad,   ^aif
 Than will thay say that I am mad—
I do bot ^adrowp as I wald die,   ^adroop
So will thay ^adeem baith man and lad.   ^ajudge, condemn
Lord God, how sall I govern me?

Be I liberal, gentill, and kind,
^aThocht I it ^btak of noble ^cstrynd,   ^athough ^binherit ^crace
Yit will thay say, baith he and he,
'Yon man is like out of his mind!'
Lord God, how sall I govern me?

Gif I be lusty in mine array,
Than lufe I paramouris, say thay,
Or in my mind ^ais proud and hie,   ^aam
Or ellis I haiff it sum wrang way.
Lord God, how sall I govern me?

And gif I be not ^aweill-beseen,   ^awell-turned-out
Than twa and twa sayis thame between,
'Ill-gydit is yon man, *pardie*—
Be his clething it may be seen!'
Lord God, how suld I govern me?

Gif I be seen in court ^aowre lang,   ^atoo long
Than will thay quhisper thame amang,
My friendis are not worth ane ^aflie,   ^afly (pron. flee)
That I sa lang ^abut guerdon gang!   ^ago without reward
Lord God, how suld I govern me?

In court rewaird ^athan purchase I,   ^a(if) then
Than have thay malice and envy,
And secreitly on me thay ^alie,   ^a(pron. lee)
And dois me sclander privily.
Lord God, how suld I govern me?

   ¹ Literally: 'Or some have shown him comfort!'

Quhow suld my gyding be devisit?
Gif I spend little, I am despisit;
Be I courtas, noble, and free,
A prodigal man than am I *a*prysit.   *a*priced, esteemed
Lord God, how suld I govern me?

Sen all is judgit, baith gude and ill,
And no mannis tung I may *a*haud still,   *a*hold
To do the best my mind sall be:
*a*Lat every man say quhat he will,   *a*let
*The gracious God *a*mot govern me!*   *a*may

II. OF DISCRETIOUN IN ASKING

Of every asking followis nocht
Rewaird, *a*bot gif sum cause *b*war wrocht;   *a*but if *b*were wrought
And quhare cause is, men weill may see,
And quhare nane is, it will be *a*thocht: *a*thought
In asking suld discretioun be.

Ane fule, *a*thocht he haiff cause or nane,   *a*though
Cryis ay, '*a*Gif me,' into a *b*rane;   *a*give *b*rigmarole
And he that dronis ay as ane bee
Suld haiff ane *a*heirer dull as *b*stane: *a*hearer *b*stone
In asking suld discretioun be.

Sum askis mair than he deservis;
Sum askis far less than he servis;
Sum schamis to ask, as *a*braidis of me,[1]   *a*resembles
And all without rewaird he *a*stervis: *a*starves, dies
In asking suld discretioun be.

To ask *a*but *b*servyis hurtis gude fame;   *a*without *b*service
To ask *for* servyis is not to blame:
To serve *and* *a*leiff in beggarty   *a*live
To man and maister is baith schame:
In asking suld discretioun be.

[1] An astonishing statement, coming from Dunbar!

He that dois all his best servyis
May ^aspill it all with ^bcrackis and cryis,   ^aspoil ^bboasts
^aBe foul inopportunity;   ^aby
Few wordis [thay] may serve the wyis:
In asking suld discretioun be.

Nocht neidful is men suld be dumb—
Na thing is gottin ^abut wordis sum,   ^awithout
Nocht sped but diligence we see,
For nathing ^ait-alane will cum: ^aall by itself
In asking suld discretioun be.

Asking wald haiff convenient place,
Convenient time, ^alaisar, and space,   ^aleisure
^aBut haist, or press of grit ^bmenyie,   ^awithout ^bcompany
But hairt abasit, but tung reckless:
In asking suld discretioun be.

Sum micht haiff 'Yea' with little ^acure,   ^acare
That hes oft 'Nay' with grit labour;
All for that time not bide can he,[1]
He ^atynis baith ^beirand and honour: ^aloses ^berrand
In asking suld discretioun be.

Suppose the servand be lang unquit,
The lord sumtime rewaird will it;
Gif he dois not, quhat remedy?
To fecht with fortune is no wit:
In asking suld discretioun be.

III. OF LUFE ERDLY AND DIVINE

Now ^aculit is Dame Venus' brand;   ^acooled
True lufis fire is ay ^akindland,   ^akindling
And I begin to understand,
In feignit lufe quhat folly been:
Now cummis age ^aquhare youth hes been,   ^awhere
And true lufe risis fro the spleen.

[1] 'All because of the time (for which) he cannot wait. . . .'

^aQuhill Venus fire be ^bdeid and cauld,   ^atill ^bdead
True lufis fire never ^abirnis ^bbauld;   ^aburns ^bbold
So as ^athe tae lufe waxis auld,   ^athe one
The tother dois increise more keen:
Now cummis age quhare youth hes been,
And true lufe risis fro the spleen.

No man hes courage for to write
Quhat pleisance is in lufe perfite,
That hes in feignit lufe delyte,
Thair kindness is so contrair ^aclein:[1]   ^aclean
Now cummis age quhare youth hes been,
And true lufe risis fro the spleen.

Full weill is him that may imprent,
Or onywayis his hairt consent,
To turn to true lufe his intent,
And still the quarrel to sustene:
Now cummis age quhare youth hes been,
And true lufe risis fro the spleen.

I haiff experience by ^amysel;   ^amyself
In lufis court ^aanis did I dwell,   ^aonce
Bot quhare I of a joy ^acouth tell,   ^amight
I culd of trouble tell fifteen:
Now cummis age quhare youth hes been,
And true lufe risis fro the spleen.

Before, quhare that I wes in ^adreid,   ^adread
Now haiff I confort for to speid;
Quhare I had ^amaugre to my ^bmeid,   ^abad grace ^breward
I ^atraist rewaird and thankis between: ^atrust (to have)
Now cummis age quhare youth hes been,
And true lufe risis fro the spleen.

Quhare lufe wes wont me to displeise,
Now find I ^ainto lufe grit eise;   ^ain
Quhare I had danger and dis-eise,
My ^abreist all confort dois contene: ^abreast
Now cummis age quhare youth hes been,
And true lufe risis fro the spleen.

[1] i.e. '. . . they are so completely different in kind.'

Quhare I wes hurt with jealousy,
And wald no luver wer bot I,
Now quhare I lufe, I wald all ^awy   ^amen
Als weill as I luvit,¹ I ween:
Now cummis age quhare youth hes been,
And true lufe risis fro the spleen.

Before, quhare I durst nocht, for schame,
My lufe ^adiscure, nor tell hir name,   ^adiscover, reveal
Now think I ^aworship wer and fame,   ^ahonour
To all the warld that it war seen:
Now cummis age quhare youth hes been,
And true lufe risis fro the spleen.

Before, no ^awicht I did complene,   ^aman
So did hir ^adanger me ^bderene;   ^a(bad) influence ^bdisorder
And now I set nocht by a ^abein   ^abean
Hir beauty nor hir twa fair ^aeen: ^aeyes
Now cummis age quhare youth hes been,
And true lufe risis fro the spleen.

I haiff a luve fairer of face,
Quhom-in no danger may haiff place,
^aQuhilk will me ^bguerdon ^cgiff and grace,   ^awhich, who ^breward ^cgive
And mercy ay quhen I ^ame mene: ^amake my complaint
Now cummis age quhare youth hes been,
And true lufe risis fro the spleen.

Unquit I do no thing nor ^asain,   ^abless
Nor ^awairis a luvis ^bthocht in vain;   ^aware, spend ^bthought
I sall be ^aals weill luvit ^bagain,   ^aas ^bin return
Thair may no ^ajangler me ^bprevene: ^arival ^bforestall
Now cummis age quhare youth hes been,
And true lufe risis fro the spleen.

Ane lufe so fair, so gude, so sweit,
So rich, so ruthful, and discreit,
And for the kind of man so meit,
Nevermore sall be, nor yit hes been:
Now cummis age quhare youth hes been,
And true lufe risis fro the spleen.

    ¹ i.e. 'I would all men loved as well as I. . . .'

Is none sa true a lufe as he
That for true lufe of us did die;
He suld be luvit again, ^athink me,   ^amethinks
That wald sa fain our lufe obtene:
Now cummis age quhare youth hes been,
And true lufe risis fro the spleen.

Is none, ^abut grace of God, I ^bwiss,   ^awithout ^bknow
That can in youth consider this;
This false ^adissavand warldis bliss,   ^adeceiving
So gydis man in flouris green:
Now cummis age quhare youth hes been,
And true lufe risis fro the spleen.

IV. DUNBAR AT OXENFURD

To speik of science, craft, or sapience,
    Of virtue, moral ^acunning, or doctrine,   ^ascience, studies
Of jure, of wisdom, or intelligence;
    Of every study, ^alair, or discipline—   ^alearning
    All is bot ^atynt or ready for to ^btyne,   ^alost ^blose
Nocht using it as it suld usit be,
    The ^acraift exercing, considering not the ^bfine: ^atechnique ^bend
A ^aparalous ^bseikness is vain prosperity.   ^aparlous ^bsicknes

The curious probatioun logical,
    The eloquence of ornate ^arethory,   ^arhetoric
The ^anatural science philosophical,   ^aphysics
    The ^adirk appeirance of astronomy,   ^adark
    The ^atheologis sermoun, the fablis of poetry,   ^atheologian's
Without gude life all in the self dois die,
    As May flouris dois in September dry:
A paralous life is vain prosperity.

Quharefore, ye clarkis and grittest of constance,
    Fullest of science and of knawledging,
To us be mirrouris in your governance,
    And in our darkness be lampis in schining,
    ^aOr than in ^bfrustar is your lang leirning;   ^aor else ^bvain
^aGif to your ^bsawis your deedis contrair be,   ^aif ^bsayings
    Your maist accuser sall be your ^aawin ^bcunning: ^aown ^blearning
A paralous seikness is vain prosperity.

V. OF THE CHAINGIS OF LIFE

I seik about this warld unstable
To find ane sentence convenable,
   Bot I can nocht in all my wit
    Sa ^atrue ane sentence find of it,   ^aso
As say, it is ^adessavable.   ^adeceitful

For yesterday, I did declair
Quhow that the seasoun, soft and fair,
   ^aCome in als fresch as ^bpako-fedder;   ^acame ^bpeacock-feather
    This day it ^astangis like ane ^bedder,   ^astings ^badder
Concluding all in my contrair.

Yisterday fair up-sprang the ^aflouris,   ^aflowers
This day thay are all slain with ^aschouris;   ^ashowers
   And ^afoulis in forest that sang cleir,   ^abirds
    Now ^awaukis with a dreiry cheir,   ^awake
Full ^acauld are baith thair beddis and ^bbouris. ^acold ^bbowers

So nixt to summer winter ^abeen;   ^ai.e. is
Nixt efter confort ^acairis kein;   ^acares keen
   Nixt dirk midnicht the mirthful morrow;
    Nixt efter joy ay cummis sorrow:
So is this warld and ay hes been.

VI. OF CONTENT

Quho thinkis that he hes sufficence
Of gudis hes no indigence,
   ^aThocht he have ^bnowder land nor rent,   ^atho' ^bneither
Grit micht, nor ^ahie magnificence: ^ahigh
   He hes aneuch that is content.

Quho had all riches unto Ind,
And wer not satifiet in mind,
   With poverty I ^ahald him ^bschent;   ^ahold ^bdestroyed
Of covetice sic is the kind:
   He hes aneuch that is content.

Tharefore I pray yow, ^abredir deir,   ^adear brethren
Not to delyte in daintyis ^aseir;   ^amanifold
  Thank God of it is to thee sent,
And of it glaidly mak gude cheir:
  He hes aneuch that is content.

Defy the warld, feignit and false,[1]
With gall in hart and hunny in ^ahalse,   ^athroat
  Quha maist it servis, maist sall repent,
Of ^aquhais surcharge sour is the ^bsalse: ^awhose ^bsauce
  He hes aneuch that is content.

^aGif thow hes micht, be gentill and free;   ^aif
And gif thow standis in poverty,
  Of thine ^aawin will to it consent,   ^aown
And riches sall return to thee:
  He hes aneuch that is content.

And ye and I, my bredir all,
That in this life hes lordschip small,
  ^aLat languour not in us imprent—   ^alet
Gif we not climb we tak no fall:
  He hes aneuch that is content.

For quho in warld most covetous is
In world is ^apuirest man, I wiss,   ^apoorest
  And most neidy of his intent:
For of all gudis no thing is his
  That of no thing can be content.

    [1] Pron. 'fauss, hauss, sauss.'

Gavin Douglas

Gavin Douglas is first and foremost a poet's poet. Save for a few snippets in anthologies he has hitherto not been available to the ordinary reader, nor even to the enthusiastic amateur of Scottish poetry. Indeed the rarity of his texts today has prevented many scholars from commenting on him. We are all the more glad therefore to print here, in an easily procurable book, substantial extracts from his work. Naturally the first reason in choosing them was to illustrate the theme, but it is an added pleasure to be able to introduce (as we hope) new readers to Gavin Douglas by using such material to such a purpose.

We trust we may be excused if for a moment we address scholars who know the poems and explain why we have omitted extracts from two large works full of wisdom. We have put in nothing from *King Hart* and *The Palice of Honour*, both wise expositions; but these long poems are entirely allegorical; and the wisdom is, at one level of the allegory, embodied in the poems as a whole. Selection, even condensing, is impossible. The selections which we have made from other works can stand on their own legs. They do, taken by themselves, have bearing upon the Scottish attitude towards certain human problems. They most certainly have their place here.

Gavin Douglas was born about 1474 and died in 1522. In the latter part of his time he was Bishop of Dunkeld. He pursued, as far as we know, a purely ecclesiastical life. There is not much to be discovered about him save in inferences from his poems. And, even in such deduction, we must do no more than speculate carefully.

His poetry is a characteristic product of the Renaissance in the North and particularly in Scotland. He was learned in many tongues, apart, of course, from his knowledge of Latin and Greek. While the substance of his oratory is Scots he draws upon other languages as it suits his purpose. His vocabulary is prodigious. He can use with ease not only Anglic but Icelandic, Gaelic and Latin words as they suit the purpose of his meaning or (is it fanciful to suppose?) his mood. He does this naturally and without affectation or parade of learning. Eighteenth-century men of letters such as the poet Gray found Gavin Douglas's poetry particularly fascinating because of the richness of its linguistic origin. This does tend to make him, as we have said, a poet's poet. No one, however, should find the selection we print here too indigestibly rich for understanding.

His great achievement is his translation of the *Aeneid* and the original prologues or comments which he devised for each of the books. It is the first translation of Virgil's epic into any vernacular. But its distinction is not merely that it was the first. Douglas's *Eneados* is much more than a straight translation, it is a poem in its own rights, and for this very reason it is a good translation. He remains true to the spirit of Virgil; and while he frequently elaborates a phrase of the Latin making two lines into four or five, he is nevertheless striving to bring out all that is there. Inescapably he adds much that is his own. It is a fine poem and a fine translation.

I. THE PROLOGUE TO THE FOURTH BOOK OF THE ENEADOS

'*Joy or Fulischness?*'

In the fourth Book of the *Aeneid* Virgil tells the story of Dido. Naturally this prompts the Bishop of Dunkeld to give us in his own prologue and with considerable force and passion his considered views on the subject of love. Nowhere else in Scottish literature is this theme so fully and richly elaborated.

This extract is the exordium to this prologue addressed to Cytherea and Venus. It begins in conventional terms, but later on the Bishop is stirred up to write some very intense reflections on the illusory nature of passionate or romantic love. It is quite clear that he knows what he is talking about. This passage, so full of rhetorical oxymoron, concludes with the resounding question in couplet form:

> 'O Lufe quhiddir art thou joy or fulischness
> That makis folk sa glaid of thar distress?'

Here are the Bishop of Dunkeld's reflections on that theme:

With beimis [a]schein thou bricht Cytherea,	[a]shiny
Quhilk only schaddowist amang starris [a]lyte,	[a]little
And thy blindit wingit son Cupid, ye twa	
Fosteraris of [a]birning carnal, [b]hait delyte,	[a]burning [b]hot
Your jolly wo [a]neidlingis must I endite,	[a]needs
Beginning with a feignit faint pleisance,	
Continuit in lust, and endit with penance.	

In fragil flesch your fickle seid is [a]saw,	[a]sown
[a]Rutit in delyte, wealth, and fude delicate,	[a]rooted
Nursit with [a]sleuth and mony unscemly [b]saw;	[a]sloth [b]saying
[a]Quhar schame is lost, thar [b]spreidis your burgeonis hait;	[a]where [b]spread
Oft to revolve ane [a]onleiful consait	[a]unlawful concep
[a]Ripis your perilous fruitis and [b]oncorn:	[a]ripens [b]wild oat
Of wickit grain [a]quhou sall gude [b]schaif be schorn?	[a]how [b]sheaf

Quhat is your force bot feibling of the strenth?
Your curious thochtis quhat bot ᵃmusardry?   ᵃfantasy
Your ᵃfremmit glaidness lestis not ane houris   ᵃstrange
    lenth;
Your sport for schame ye daur not specify;
Your fruit is bot unfructuous fantasy;
Your ᵃsary joys been bot jangling and japis,   ᵃsorry
And your true servandis silly goddis ᵃapis.   ᵃapes

Your sweit mirthis are mixt with bitterness;
Quhat is your dreiry gem? a mirry pain;
Your wark onthrift, your quiet is restless,
Your lust liking in langour to remain,
Freindschip turment, your traist is bot a ᵃtrain.   ᵃsnare
O Lufe, quhiddir art thou joy or fulischness,
That makis folk sa glaid of thar distress?

'Twa Luffis'

The extract from Gavin Douglas's Prologue to Book IV of the *Aeneid*
begins 'Lo, quhou Venus can hir servandis acquite!' This refers to a
preceding passage (omitted here) in which Douglas talks about the
devastating effect of passionate and obsessive love on even the strongest,
best and wisest of men, Solomon, Samson, David, Aristotle, Alexander,
Jacob, Hercules and so on. This is a conventional list which serves only
to lead towards the theme which is the subject of the passage included
below.

That theme is that there are two loves, one perfect, the other profoundly imperfect, the one enrichening, the other self-destructive. This
may seem a familiar and oft-repeated distinction. It should be observed,
however, that Douglas is making no crude division between carnal lust
and more elegant erotically mental love. Though he has some highly
flavoured remarks to make about lust this extract is something more
than a prolonged variation upon:—

> 'The expense of Spirit in a waste of shame
> Is lust in action. . . .'

What Gavin Douglas is saying here is that all obsessive love of earthly
creatures, even if it does not express itself in ugly lust, is death. It is
death in that to love a creature more than the Creator, to love a human
being in the flesh more than God is to love mortality. Carnal love is
death even if that carnal love is not expressed in fleshly action. This
be it noted is a comment upon Virgil's story of Dido.

In one of Gavin Douglas's footnotes he says that he took this theme
from St. Augustine's *De Civitate Dei*. He is also clearly reflecting St.
Paul's warning in the Epistle to the Romans against the danger of loving

F

creatures more than the Creator. This Pauline injunction has had an endless fascination for the Scottish mind. It has sometimes been thought of as a Post-Reformation development in our teaching. Yet here is a Pre-Reformation Bishop expounding St. Augustine and Virgil entirely in terms of this Pauline concept. Here indeed (if on no other account) is an excellent reason for including this extract from Gavin Douglas in an anthology devoted to the wisdom of the Scots.

Finally, though it may not be considered relevant to the actual wisdom which this Scottish Bishop (this cleric who clearly had felt the lash of passion in his youth) is expressing, it is impossible to avoid comment on the way he expresses it. He is expressing but one theme and its variations, yet he piles on words in the service of that theme, words which never repeat themselves or become monotonous. They only accumulate force as they march in battalions through his lines. You should listen to their tread. You should read these words aloud.

Lo, ^aquhou Venus can hir servandis acquite!   ^ahow
Lo, quhou hir passiounis unbridlis all thair wit!
Lo, quhou thai ^atyne thameself for schort delyte!   ^alose
Lo, from all grace quhou to mischeif thay flit,
Fra weill to ^asturt, fra pain to ^bdeid, and yit   ^atribulation ^bdeath
Thar been bot few exemple takis of other,
Bot wilfully fallis in the fire, ^aleif brother.   ^adear

Be never owre-set, mine author teichis sa,
With lust of wine nor warkis venereane;
Thai feible the strength, reveilis secreit baith
   twa,
Strife and debait engendris, and ^afeill hes slain;   ^amany
Honesty, prowess, ^adreid, schame, and luck are   ^areverence
   gane
Quhar thay abound; attemper thame ^afor-thy.   ^atherefore
Childer to engender ^aoiss Venus, and not in   ^ause
   vain;
^aHaunt na surfeit, drink bot quhen thou art dry.   ^aindulge

Quhat! is *this* lufe, nice luffaris, 'at ye ^amein,   ^aintend
Or fause dissait, fair ladyis to beguile?
Thame to defoul, and ^aschent yourself ^bbetween,   ^aruin ^bmeanwhile
Is all your liking, with mony subtil wile.
Is *that* true lufe, gude faith and fame to fyle?
Gif lufe be virtue, than is it ^aleiful thing;   ^alawful
Gif it be vice, it is your undoing.

Lust is na lufe, thocht ^aledis like it weill;   ^aladies
This furious ^aflambe of sensuality   ^aflame
Are nane amouris bot fantasy ye ^afeill;   ^afeel
Carnal pleisance, ^abut sicht of honesty,   ^awithout
Haitis himself for-suth, and luffis nocht thee.
Thair ^abeen ^b*twa* luffis, perfite and imperfite,   ^ai.e. are ^btwo
That ane leiful, the tother foul, delyte.

Lufe is ^akindly passioun, engendrit of ^bheit   ^ai.e. natural ^bheat
Kindlit in the hart, owre-spreading all the ^acorss,   ^abody
And, as thou seeis sum person ^awaik in spreit,   ^aweak
Sum ^ahait-birning as ane unbridlit horse—   ^ahot-burning
Like as the patient hes heit of owre gret force,
And, in young babbis, warmness insufficient,
And, ^ainto agit, faillyis and is ^bout-quent,   ^ain ^bquenched

Richt so in lufe thou may be excessive,
Inordinately lufand ony creature;
This lufe, also, it may be defective,
To lufe thine ^aawin and ^bgeif of otheris na ^ccure.   ^aown ^bgive ^ccare
But ^aquhar that lufe is rulit by mesure,   ^awhere
It may be liknit to ane ^ahaill mannis estait,   ^agrown man's
In temperate warmness, ^anowther too cauld nor   ^aneither
    hait.

Thou auld ^ahasard lichour, fy for schame,   ^ahoary
That ^aslotteris furth evermar in sluggardry!   ^aslouchest
Out on thee, auld ^atrat, agit wife, or dame,   ^ahag
^aAschamis na time in ^broust of sin to ly!   ^a(whom it) ashames ^brust
^aThir Venus' warkis in youthheid are folly,   ^athese
Bot ^ainto ^beild thay turn ^cin fury rage;   ^ain ^bold age ^cinto
And ^aquha schameless doublis thar sin—Ha fy!   ^awho
As doith thir vantouris ^aowther in youth or age.   ^aeither

Quhat ^aneidis ^bavant you of your wickitness,   ^aneeds ^bvaunt
Ye that ^abeen ^bforcy ^calane in villainis deed?   ^aare ^bforceful ^calone
Quhy gloir ye in your ^aawin unthriftiness?   ^aown
Eschame ye not rehearse and blaw ^aon breid   ^aabroad
Your awin defame, havand of God na dreid
Nor yit of Hell, provokand otheris to sin,
Ye that list of your ^apalliardry never ^bblin?   ^aharlotry ^bblind

Wald God ye purchast bot your awin mis-
chance,
And war na *bannereris for to *perich mo! *standard-bearers *destroy
God grant sum-time ye turn you to penance,
Refreining lustic inordinate, and cry ho!
And thar affix your lufe and mindis so,
Quhar ever is very joy without offence,
That all *sik beistly fury ye lat go hence. *such

Of *brokeris and sik bawdry quhou suld I *pimps
write,
Of quham the filth stinkis in Goddis *neise? *nose
With *Venus' hen-wifis quhat wise may I *bawds
*flyte, *vituperate
That *straikis *thir wenschis *heidis thame to *stroke *these *heads
pleise?
'Douchter, for thy lufe this man hes gret dis-
eise,'
Quod the *bismeir with the *sleikit speich, *procuress *cozening
'Rue on him, it is merit his pain to *meiss.' *alleviate
Sik *poid mackerellis for Lucifer bein *leich. *whore-mistresses *leech

Eschame, ying virginis and fair damisellis,
*Furth of wedlock for to *distein your *kellis; *outside *stain *coifs
*Traist nocht all *tailis that wantoun *woweris *trust *tales *wooers
tellis,
Yow to deflour purposing, and nocht ellis;
Abhor sik price *or prayer *wirschip sellis. *before *honour
Quhar schame is lost quite schent is woman-
heid;
Quhat of beauty, quhar honesty lyis *deid? *dead

Rue on yourself, ladyis and maidenis ying,
Grant na sik ruth for ever may cause you rue:
Ye fresch gallandis, in *hait desire birning, *hot
Refrein your courage sik paramouris to
persue;
*Grund your amouris on charity all new; *ground
Found yow on ressoun—quhat neidis mair to
preich?
God grant your grace in lufe, as I you teich.

Lo! with quhat thocht, quhat bitterness and
   pain,
Lufe *unseilly breidis in every wicht!   *wretched
Quhou schort quhile doith his fause pleisance
   remain,
His restless bliss quhou soon takis the flicht!
His kindness alteris *in wraith within a nicht: *into a ghost
Quhat is, *bot turment, all his *langsome fare, *without *tedious affair
Begun with *feir, and endit in despair?   *fear

Quhat *sussie, *cure, and strainge imagining, *souci *care
Quhat ways *unleiful, his purpose to attein, *illicit
Hes this fause lust at his first beginning,
Quhou subtil wylis, and mony quiet *mein, *means
Quhat slicht *dissait quently to *flat and *deceit *flatter
   feign!—
Syne in a *thraw can not him-selvin hide, *throe, moment
Nor at his first estait no quhile abide!

II. THE COMMENT

Gavin Douglas began writing a commentary on his translation which
broke off about half-way through. It is possible that the reason for this
was that he had just received the news of Flodden and had lost heart
for commenting on his own work. Nevertheless what we have of the
Bishop's own footnotes are often wise, entertaining and shrewd. We
include, almost at random, three of these notes as footnotes to these
notes of our own.

  (a) This is a brief but characteristic line. By no means all Scots would
agree with it; some would hardly know what it means. But they constantly
need reminding of it by those who do. Douglas had just finished trans-
lating an epic poem of classical antiquity. 'What relevance has this to
our times?' some might ask. 'What's the use of poetry? What's the use
of Latin?' The Bishop answers them.

  (b) This 'wise-saw' is interesting, not for its obvious reference to the
excellence of old wine but for its remark about high venison. We had
long suspected that the disgusting habit of hanging game-meat until it
all but drops off the hook was an importation into Scotland brought in
by the South British game-laws which extended themselves into a
would-be snobbish custom in the larder. (The author of these notes
was in youth nearly poisoned to death by having to eat a long-hung
capercailzie at an Anglo-Scottish upper-class shooting lodge north of
Inverness.) It is agreeable to find that this fifteenth- and sixteenth-

century Scottish Bishop of Dunkeld, who probably kept as good a table as any at the time, did not like his deer-meat rotten; neither do we.

(c) 'Sum pius Aeneas' is a phrase highly familiar to schoolboys in both England and Scotland—for pious is a 'funny word.' Gavin Douglas here gives a characteristic Scottish and shrewd account of the meaning of the Latin 'pius.' Maybe this comment explains why the Scottish eighteenth century found Roman antiquity so congenial to it. Hume and his friends were brought up on Roman rather than Greek tradition. Gavin Douglas here defines piety as serving our native country and, 'thame been conjoint to us in neir degree,' and links this with two subordinate virtues, namely friendship and liberality.

This, as we have often seen above, is the true hierarchy of virtue according to the Scottish tradition. It is to loyalty to those to whom we belong and who belong to us to which we must constantly return as a cardinal principle of virtue and piety. I pause here to reflect how grossly prostituted is this principle in that racket that seeks to make a market out of modern commercial so-called clan loyalty or in the ye-olde-tartane-game organised by so-called Highland chieftains (and chieftainesses) in conjunction with Scottish 'advertising' and Trans-atlantic 'Klan-klubs.'

The Bishop of Dunkeld knew nothing of such things! America had, in his lifetime, only just been discovered, and modern Scotland was yet to come. But the episcopal poet was not without his own deep distresses and his pains. He was certainly writing these lines about the time of Flodden when Scotland, in the cause of the *pietas* of 'amity,' was sacrificing herself for France. As we have already said, he may well have written them after the news of the sacrifice had reached him.

(a) 'Derk Poetry'

Under derk poetry is hid gret wisdom and learning.[1]

(b) 'Venisoun out of Ply'

Wine the elder the better, sa that it be fresch, and every man knawis venisoun out of ᵃply ᵇtynis the ᵃsessoun.[2]

ᵃcondition ᵇloses
ᵃsavour

(c) Piety

That Eneas here commendis his-self, it is not to be tane that he said this for arrogance, bot for to schaw his style, as a king or prince unknawin in an uncouth land may, ᵃbut repreif, rehearse his estait and dignity to mak him be treitit as ᵃaffeiris. And als, because he ᵇtraistit he spak

ᵃwithout censure
ᵃis fitting ᵇtruste

---

[1] On *Eneados*, Prol. I. 192.   [2] On *Eneados*, I. iv, 98.

with a goddess, that scho suld nocht aschame to remain
and talk with him therefore; and because scho was a
woman, he ^aschew that he was a man of autority, with   ^ashowed
quham thay ^aneidis nocht aschame to speik, for he was   ^aneed
that man quhilk by the common voce was ^acleipit 'Eneas   ^acalled
full of piety.' And ^afor that Virgil cleipis him ^bswa all   ^ainasmuch as ^bso
thro this buik, and I interpret that term ^aquhilis for   ^asometimes
'ruth,' quhilis for 'devotioun' and quhilis for 'piety' and
'compassioun,' tharfore ye sall knaw that piety is a virtue
or gude deed ^abe the ^bquhilk we ^cgeiff our diligent and   ^aby ^bwhich ^cgive
debtful laubour to our native country and unto thame
^abeen conjoint to us in neir degree. And this virtue, piety,   ^a(who) are
is a part of justice and hes under him twa other virtueis:
amity, callit 'frendschip,' and liberality.[1]

[1] On *Eneados*, I. vi, 125.

James Harryson

'SCOTTISHMAN'

AN EXHORTATION TO THE SCOTS, 1547

Few people today, surely, will have read or even heard of this remarkable example of Scottish wisdom in its own fashion. It has most certainly not been included in other anthologies. It presents a point of view which certain Scots have long held and still hold. They seldom speak it quite as openly as in this 'Exhortation' and it is doubtful if many, if any of them, now could speak it so well. James Harryson may or may not have been, as he claimed, of our nation, but his subject was certainly Scotland and he addressed himself to the minds of Scots with skill.

His *Exhortation* is an open appeal to Scots to submerge their nationality with England (to allow themselves to be absorbed), and was launched upon the Scots from London as long ago as 1547, but he puts the case for this point of view better than do most present apologists for it. Before giving extracts from it, or making further comments, may I briefly recall the condition of the country in that year?

In 1547 the realm of Scotland was in a distressful state. James V, the last King to live and die a monarch in Scotland, had been dead for five years. His dying words are said to have been, 'Adieu, farewell, it came with a lass, it will pass with a lass.' They were wrung from him by the news that a girl had been born to his Queen as he lay on his deathbed. He meant that the independent crown of the single Scottish realm had come to the Stewarts through a girl (the marriage of Marjorie Bruce with Walter the Steward), and that with the girl who came into the world as he was leaving it, that purely independent Scottish crown would pass from his family. He was right. The girl born in Linlithgow Palace in 1542 was to be Mary Queen of Scots. Her son was to ascend the throne of the United Kingdom.

With the King dead, with the heir to the Scottish throne a female infant all but imprisoned and the small pawn of forces without as well as within Scotland, with the corrupt state of society which had begun to infect the realm before James's death, and now with little to check its spread the kingdom seemed to lose its cohesion. Sir David Lyndesay's famous play *Ane Satyre of the Thrie Estaits*, a version of which has been on three years so successfully presented at recent Edinburgh Festivals, gives an artist's-eye-view of Scotland at the time—the clergy corrupt, the nobles utterly selfish and self-seeking and with none to control them, the burgesses sunk in money-grubbing. As with most artist's-eye-views the black is very black and the white spotless, but it is a notable and noble piece of dramatic writing.

Modern Protestants and Catholics have both claimed it as propaganda.

The Protestants with considerable justification point to the scarifying exposure of the state of the Church so vividly brought out in stage production. The Catholics, on rather shakier ground, hold that Lyndesay was a reformer from within, that he did not attack the then established Faith but man's misuse of it in Scotland. They argue in support that Lyndesay did not attach himself to the Reform party and died, as far as we know, a practising Roman Catholic, and finally that his castigations were received without dissent by undoubted Roman Catholics. Mary of Guise, of all people, as Queen Regent, actually commanded a performance of this then nine-hour play at Linlithgow. I do not enter into this fruitless dispute, and only mention *The Thrie Estaits* here as a powerful expression of the distress of Scotland at that time—an expression which can still make us feel it.[1]

That distress arose not only from the corruption and weakness castigated by Lyndesay but from the fact that the realm was split from top to toe by treachery. This, then, was the opportunity for greater powers

[1] I take this opportunity of explaining why I have not included any extracts from *The Thrie Estaits*. The original drama lasted nine hours; even the successful adaptation for the Edinburgh Festival made by Robert Kemp and produced so splendidly by Sir Tyrone Guthrie lasted three. Further cuts would be undesirable, mere extracts impossible. The thing is a drama, not a poem or a treatise. To feel its impact properly you must see *and hear it* as a unit. To filch speeches or even scenes from it would convey a wrong impression and do an injustice to Lyndesay and his play.

Since I have allowed myself this footnote I cannot resist one further comment which has not, I think, been made before. Lyndesay castigated three estates of the Realm; of these, two have now been either reformed in behaviour or so reduced in power as to be innocuous. The third (the Burgesses) still remains in the capital of Scotland as potent as ever for good or ill.

High places in the Church, of whatever communion, in Scotland are no longer the sinecures of the illegitimate offsprings of Royalty. Great churchmen, whether leading lights in the General Assembly or leaders of other gatherings, no longer loll about the place in voluptuous ease dispensing Church revenues upon the support of concubines. They are (as one reminds oneself were a number of the clergy of Lyndesay's own time) good and decent men. The nobility are no longer even potentially dangerous. Bowler-hatted and industrious, many of them go about their duties so ordinarily that you could not tell them from ordinary men. Some assume picturesqueness at intervals, some few discover the picturesqueness of decadence in their eccentric behaviour, some, rather self-consciously, assume picturesqueness when they dress up for state occasions: that is all. It is a far cry even from the days of Tom Johnston's swingeing attack on Scottish aristocracy, *Our Noble Families*, published just before World War I.

But the Golden Calf is still enthroned. The orisons of his obsequious yet complacent votaries make, if not the loudest, the most powerful sound in the land. Ah! but they too are mostly good and decent men. They did allow the Edinburgh Festival to happen, they did support the production of *Ane Satyre of the Thrie Estaits*; and someone did have the imagination to ask Tyrone Guthrie to produce it. Who that was present at those first sunlit Festivals will forget them?—Mozart's music, the French Players, David Lyndesay's dreams once more taking on the sound of spoken words and the flesh of living actors. Even the Golden Calf seemed to nod in approval.

outside Scotland to intervene. The English saw a chance of absorbing Scotland into a British-island-Protestant-system; the French took the opportunity of hitting at England from the other side of her by trying to keep the status quo in Scotland. Neither the English nor the French were deeply religiously concerned, neither were missionaries. Both were opportunists; so were the majority of Scots in power. There were, of course, in Scotland genuine Protestant heroes and martyrs; there were also those who suffered for the Catholic Faith and not merely for the established order. But on both sides these were in the minority.

It is a reading of history backwards, an over-simplification to think of the tumult of those times as being primarily caused by the religious convictions of sincere men on either side. The tumult arose because the state of the country had made it the cockpit of two other Powers.

There were, of course, plenty of patriot Scots, though few in high places. These (with due respect to the holders of the modern romantic notion of the 'Auld Alliance') were as much disgusted by the presence on their land of the arrogant French nobility and military as they were angered by the threats of force from England. To these patriots, whatever their religious views, neither England nor France offered a solution to the essentially national problem.

Still these patriots were there, and it was considered worth having a shot at them in propaganda. The French, either owing to the language difficulty or because they disdained anything below court diplomacy, do not seem to have tried much in this line. The English made one notable 'Political Warfare' effort—Harryson's *An Exhortation to the Scots*.

No one knows who Harryson was or whether he was a 'Scottishman,' a real Scots Quisling of the kind that has always existed. His work was probably printed in London and is certainly in English. It may well have been penned by an industrious and clever Cockney in the contemporary equivalent of Whitehall or Bush House as were some of the most potent foreign language broadcasts during the last war.

His style is excellent, his matter apparently weighty and his manner cogent. He foretells the advantages that were to come to Scotland fifty-six years later under the Union of the Crowns and a hundred and ten years later when 'ane auld sang' ended and when in 1707 the Scottish Parliament packed up its bag and baggage, and went south to merge and sink without trace at Westminster. Harryson wanted the song to end earlier than it did. He expresses the views of the ordinary bourgeois Scots Unionist of today, but he expresses them far better than they can and do. It is for this reason that I include his *Exhortation* in this volume of wisdom. Here are two powerful extracts:

A United Kingdom

I perceive that love to my country and nation hath made me unawares to have wandered furder than at the first I purposed: wherefore I will make an end, if first I shall repeat that I have already proved unto you, that these two realms were first a monarchy under Brutus, and so left by his order to his sons, by the superiority which was in his ancestors proved by the homages[1] and other things afore alleged, the claim whereof did yet never cease, as also specially by force of your own late Act of Parliament, whereby he ought of right to marry our Princess, the inheritrice of the Crown of Scotland: by occasion whereof we shall be received, not into servitude, but into the same fellowship with Englishmen, the names of both subjects and realms ceasing, and to be changed into the name of Britain and Britons, as it was first, and yet still ought to be.

And how necessary that same form of the governance of one monarch or king is, you see to be more clear than the sun, and the same to be a ready and easy meane, how both to appease all discord, which otherwise will never stint, and also to establish us in everlasting peace, quiet, and tranquillity: unto which effects there is verily none other mean. And the thing itself (though I should hold my peace) doth sufficiently speak and avouch the same to be a way unto both realms most honourable, because not only the Empire shall by that occasion be the more large and strong in itself, and the King the more puissant and famous: profitable, for that discord shall cease, and concord come in place, and thereby the people and commonweal flourish and prosper: and godly, for that we shall agree all in one, and the same the true and Christian religion.[2]

'GENTILLY OFFERED TO YOU'

So far James 'Scottishman' has argued with moving eloquence, addressing his words to the heart and the head as well as to the self-interests of those whom he claimed to be his compatriots. Now, suddenly, he plays upon other emotions—fear and caution. The Lord Protector Somerset

[1] Thus in 1298 Edward I rather dishonestly informed Pope Boniface that 'Alexander [III], King of Scots, our cousin, did homage to Henry, our father, for the Kingdom of Scotland; and afterwards to us.' But according to the much more detailed account in the Register of Dunfermline, the words that King Alexander actually used in doing homage to Edward I were: 'I become your man for the lands that I hold of you in the Kingdom of England for which I owe you homage; reserving my Kingdom.' The Bishop of Norwich replied: 'And be it reserved to the King of England, if he have right to your homage for the Kingdom.' 'To homage for the Kingdom of Scotland,' King Alexander retorted, 'none has right, save God alone; nor do I hold it, save of God alone.' Wha sups wi' the Deil needs a lang spune; and in view of King Edward's later treatment of Scotland it was very wise of King Alexander to make these reservations. See A. O. Anderson, *Early Sources of Scottish History*, 2 vols., Edinburgh 1922, II. 675, n. 3.
[2] Pp. 234 ff.

is on his way to Scotland. If the Scots don't heed the suasions of their compatriot in London the Lord Protector will come North and, rather painfully, protect them *from themselves*.

How familiar the words are! James Harryson was a skilled anticipator of the technique of British P.W.E. in the last war and also of some of Dr. Goebbels's henchmen. On the whole Harryson was better at his job than William Joyce; at any rate, he is more pleasing to the educated ear. Neither Joyce nor our own side of P.W.E., however, produced the big stick in quite such an obvious manner as did Harryson in his references to the avenging and cleansing campaign of the Lord Protector. This was a mistake, and doubly a mistake. Such threats at the end of such arguments are ineffective when addressed to a proud people. It was also a mistake in that the Lord Protector's campaign when it did occur, in the end, after a painful defeat of the Scottish forces, did fail.[1]

'The said Lord Protector'

It remaineth now to say unto you, that the right high, mighty, and excellent prince, Edward, Duke of Somerset, Earl of Hertford, Viscount Beauchamp, Lord Seymour, Governor of the person of the King's Majesty of England, and Protector of all his Realms, Dominions, and subjects, his Lieutenant-General of all his Armies, both by land and by sea, Treasurer and Earl-Marshal of England, Governor of the Isles of Guernsey and Jersey, and Knight of the Most Noble Order of the Garter: A man for his acts and worthiness well known to the world—and you—of whom you have had late experience to your pains, and his dolour, for that, as the loving mother in beating her child weepeth, so in punishing you, he did it loathly, and to his grief, because he pitied your case.

The said Lord Protector is coming towards you, with a puissant and invincible army, having on his side God, and the just cause, and an intent, to receive to mercy, grace, and favour, so many of you as, for the furthering of this marriage and his other godly purposes, will come in to him. And contrarily, to punish and correct the rest that shall remain in their stubborn and wilful disobedience.

[1] Even when the big stick does strike and with apparent forceful success threats of this kind are ineffective against a people truly independent in mind. Obvious examples are the Irish and the Poles. In 1944 Poland's great Eastern neighbour subjected her to a modern version of the Harrysonian technique including the promise of the big stick. After their infamous betrayal at the Battle of Warsaw the Poles felt in the harshest manner the blows of the Soviet stick or knout, and politically they are still in chains. But the minds of the majority of the Polish population are free; so are their hopes.

The writer of this editorial matter cannot resist this apparently intrusive reflection, for he speaks from experience. He is a Scot whose service lay with the Poles in the last war.

Wherefore (O countrymen) considering that, on our part, we have nothing but the wrong and unjust cause, violation of our promises and oaths given to England with conceived words, after mature and just deliberation, calling God and His angels unto witness thereof, who knoweth our infidelity, and will not leave the injury done to Him and them unrevenged. For the regard of God, for your own sakes, and for the tender respect of our country, cast wisely down that armour and weapons that you have so fondly put on and taken in hand: and submit yourselfs humbly to the mercy and clemency of so noble and benign a prince: who is rather come thither lovingly to embrace and receive you, yea, and as your Protector, to defend and assist you, than to punish you according to your deserts.

But, if you shall despise my counsel and abuse his humanity and good offers, how gentle and clement soever he be of his own nature, think you for sure, that God, who will not suffer infidelity to escape long unchastised, will stir up his courage to do vengeance upon you for your insolency and faith broken: the which I write not without sorrow and tears, praying God for His pity and goodness, to give you His grace and better mind, so as you may forsake the errors that now lead you headlong, and may follow these good and wholesome counsels of your most natural and most tender-loving countryman: whereby you may accord (as, by your promises and duties, ye ought to do) to so godly, so honourable, and so profitable conditions as are now gentilly offered you.[1]

[1] Pp. 235 f.

The Complaint of Scotland, 1549

James Harryson's *Exhortation* may have failed to produce the immediate effect he had hoped for, but it did sting out of Scotland a memorable reply; and for this we must be grateful to the London-writing 'Scottishman.' In 1549 there appeared a work entitled *The Complaint of Scotland.* Most educated Scots have (no, we are bound to admit that they *ought* to have) heard of this impassioned piece of patriotic writing, but few, even of these today, will have read it.

Few indeed! But it is difficult to blame them for this. The sad fact remains that there are NO texts save in libraries available to ordinary readers. Still less are they available for children being taught what passes for Scottish history in our schools today. So long as Scottish children grow up ignorant of the very existence of such deposited inheritances of the wisdom of their country so long will the Scottish adults into which they grow be unaware of the traditions of Scottish wisdom of which *The Complaint of Scotland* is so notable an example. In the meantime we must be content with our children being told the story of Bruce and the Spider (ostentatiously omitted from this book) and little else.[1]

No one knows for certain the name of the author of *The Complaint.* He is thought by the texture of his Scots to have come from Fife or the Lothians. He was obviously a highly learned man; indeed some might call his occasional display of erudite knowledge pedantic. Though the possessor of a notable Scots style he was obviously not a professional writer. Learning and lack of professionalism in writing are, however, overwhelmed by the passion of his feeling for his distressful country which grows within him as he writes, and which he expresses magnificently.

The Complaint was without question a reply to Harryson and to Harryson's ideas which may have been publicised elsewhere; but this is deliberately not made apparent at the beginning. The author starts by

[1] The ignorance of Scottish history, tradition and wisdom even amongst responsible people in Scotland can be breath-taking. In the act of composing this note my eye fell upon the current issue of one of Scotland's leading journals (March 14, 1960). In it the Abbey of Arbroath is prominently referred to as the place where Robert the Bruce signed the Declaration of Arbroath. Those who will have read our section on the Declaration will remember that the whole point of that document was that it was signed by the barons. In it they eulogise King Robert (a passage he could not with decency have signed) and add that if he doesn't keep up to the high standard he has set they will get rid of him (a passage he could not have signed). For a leading Scottish journal to say that the 'Declaration of Arbroath' was signed by Bruce is nearly as absurd as if the London *Times* were to say that the 'Magna Carta' had been drawn up by King John and graciously presented to the English Barons at Runnymede. I feel inclined to withdraw earlier remarks about the fame of the Declaration of Arbroath in Scotland.

saying that writers should use their gifts for the common weal, but admits that he had intended merely to write about some general matters on the condition of Scotland which disturbed him, and to compose therefrom a treatise in honour of the Queen Dowager and Regent, Mary of Guise. In the act of composing this formal treatise, however, he is seized with a vision of Dame Scotia, Mother Scotland (the maternal figure that haunts some Scottish minds) and perceives her in distress. It is to her aid that he now turns his impassioned rather than formal and learned plea. What had happened obviously was that through Harryson's book he has become aware of the danger threatening the independence of his Mother Scotland.

In his vision he sees Dame Scotia with her three sons before her. One is the nobility, the other is the clergy and the third is the commonalty. She bitterly reproaches each of them for failing to support and comfort her in her hour of need against her old enemy. She points to the various failings and weaknesses into which each of these sons has fallen. Finally she exhorts them above all to stop quarrelling amongst each other and to unite in giving their mother their strength in her time of danger.

It will be seen that the theme of *The Complaint* is related to that of Sir David Lyndesay's play *The Thrie Estaits*. There is no evidence, however, that the author knew or worked in collaboration with Lyndesay. He does not quote from this famous play. The truth is, of course, that the corruption of the three estates of the Realm of Scotland was at that time so apparent, and that corruption was so obvious a danger to the country, that any patriotic author was impelled to write about it. Lyndesay the artist made a patriotic drama out of Scotland's danger. The anonymous author of *The Complaint of Scotland* wrote an impassioned reply to the propaganda efforts of the William Joyce of the period.

Here are printed below and fully some extracts from this important treatise published at a crucial period in the millennium of Scotland's story as a nation. Apart from its eminence as an historical document it is packed with characteristic Scottish wisdom. Much of it is relevant to the present day, not only in the dilemma in which Scots still find themselves but in touching upon points in the Scottish character which still lie there beneath the surface.

I. A UNITED KINGDOM

This extract from Chapter X is concerned mostly with English prophecies of a United Kingdom.

The author says that the English have put forward a book declaring Scotland a colony of her southern neighbour and that she shall return to that state. This is a clear reference to Harryson's *Exhortation.*

Secondly, he refers to various pagan prophecies, notably that of Merlin, to which the English have given their credence. The prophecies foretell an establishment of Britain under English rule. The author's comment on this is that the English will be surprised to learn what the future has in store.

Thirdly, through the mouth of Dame Scotia, he now makes his own prophecy about that future. His prophecy was indeed fulfilled and in a short time. He says that England and Scotland will be united under one Scottish monarch. Was he thinking of the infant Mary, niece of Henry VIII of England? Maybe. At any rate it was a remarkably accurate prophecy. Though what the author of *The Complaint* would have thought of the regime of James VI and I of Scotland and England one can only guess.

'Under Ane Prince'[1]

The oratours of Ingland, at ther Protectouris instance, hes set furtht ane [a]beuk, quhairby thay intend to [b]preive that Scotland was ane colony of Ingland quhen it was first inhabit. Ther raisouns that thay allege appeiris to them to be invincible, quhoubeit thay be bot frivol. . . .   [a]book [b]prove

There is ane passage in the said beuk, the quhilk the Inglismen hes ane ardent desire to see it cum till effect. The tenor of the passage sayis, that it war very necessair for the weill-fare of Ingland and Scotland, that baitht the realmis war conjoinit togiddir, and to be under the governing of ane prince, and the twa realmis to be callit the Ile of Bertan, as it was in the beginning, quhen the Trojan Brutus conquesst it fra the Giantis. And also the Inglismen giffis ferm credit to diverse profane prophecies of Merlin, and till other auld, corruppit vaticinaris, to [a]quhair imaginit werkis thay give mair faitht nor to the   [a]i.e. which prophecy of Isay, Ezechiel, Jeremy, or to the Evangel: the [a]quhilkis profane prophetis and vaticinaris hes affermit,   [a]which (pl.) in ther rusty time, that Scotland and Ingland sall be under ane prince. The ardent desire, and the disordinate, avaricious affectioun, that Inglismen hes to be violent dominatours of our country, hes provokit them to make cruel [a]weiris contrar us thir mony yeiris bypast, to that   [a]wars effect that ther diabolic, profane prophecies may be fulfillit, nocht regardand [a]giff the will of God hes permittit,   [a]if [a]be His divine gudeness, that sic prophecies cum till effect: [a]by Nor yit thay consider nocht that all prophecies hes doubtsome and double expositiounis. Yit nochtheless I [a]hope in   [a]expect God that the richt sense of ther profane prophecy sall be

---

[1] All references in this section are to *The Complaynt of Scotland*, ed. J. A. H. Murray, E.E.T.S., 1872. Spellings like 'furtht, throucht, witht, withtout,' etc., should throughout be read as equivalent to 'furth, throuch, with, within, without,' etc.

fulfillit in this generatioun, and that Inglismen sall get ther desire—to ther perpetual confusioun. . . .[1]

I believe that thair prophecy sall cum till effect, bot nocht to thair intent, and that Ingland and Scotland *sall* be ane monarchy, under ane prince, in this generatioun, conformand till ane prophecy that I have read in the Inglis chroniclis, in ane beuk callit *Polichronicon*, the quhilk prophecy sayis, that Ingland sall be first conqueist [a]be the Danis, and syne [b]be the Saxons, and thirdly [a]be the Normandis; and ther last conquessing sall be conquesst be the Scottis, quhom Inglismen hauldis maist vile; and fra that time furtht, Ingland and Scotland sall be bot ane monarchy, and sall live under ane prince; and sa Inglis men sall get thair prophecy fulfillit, to ther awin mischeiff.[2]

[a]by [b]by
[a]by

II. SCOTTISH DISUNITY IS ENGLAND'S OPPORTUNITY

In these extracts from Chapters XI and XII, the main theme of *The Complaint* emerges and is stressed—the danger of Scottish disunity.

After first addressing a brief exhortation to her sons to bestir themselves, the Mother develops the theme of the perils of disunity. The enemy have always been ready for peace with a Scotland in which unity and strength have been manifest. When, however, internal weaknesses arise English promises of peace cannot be trusted. Be forever watchful against such a neighbour and potential enemy. And the first thing to watch is the relationships between yourselves, my sons.

In the second extract (which is amusingly appropriate to more modern times), Dame Scotia speaks of the Scots in England. They are on the whole held of little account in that country save when they can be used against the Scots in Scotland. Finally, however, there is deliberate treason within the borders of Scotland. She is aware of it but does not say much about who perpetrates it.

1. *'The Auld Subtil Doggis'*

'Thir wordis before rehearsit (O, ye my three sonnis) suld provoke you to tak courage; therefore I wald that hope of victory war augmentit, and dreid war banist fra you. Wald ye all perpend your just defence and querrel, [a]than

[a]then

[1] Pp. 82 f.   [2] P. 85.

G

hardiness and courage wald return withtin your hartis. And first ye suld consider the people, and the title of them that persecutis you [a]be unjust [b]weiris. . . .[1]   [a]by [b]wars

'All this, weill-considerit, suld inflamb your hartis witht courage to resist ther cruel wrangous assaultis, and to maintein [a]be vailiantness the just defence of your native   [a]by
country. Ye knaw quhou thay and ther forbears hes been your auld mortal enemies twelf hundreth yeiris by-past, makand cruel weir contrar your predecessours [a]be fyir   [a]by fire and
and swerd, daily destroyand your feildis, villagis and   sword
[a]burrowstounis, witht ane ferm purpose to denude Scotland   [a]burgh's-towns
fra your generatioun; and there was never faitht nor promise keipit be them, bot aye quhen ye beleifit till haiff hed maist sure [a]pace betwix you and them, [b]than thay   [a]peace [b]then
lay at the watch, like the auld subtil doggis, [a]bidand   [a]waiting till
quhill conspiratioun or dissensioun suld rise amang you. [a]Than be ther astuce and subtility thay furnest witht   [a]then by
money baitht the parties adversaris to slay doun [a]otheris,   [a]one another
quhilk was ane ready passage to [a]gar them conqueiss our   [a]cause . . . to
realm without [a]straik or battle, throucht the occasioun of   [a]stroke
the social, civil and intestine weir that [a]rang sa cruelly   [a]ruled
throucht our country. . . .[2]

'O ye my three sonnis, the dissensioun and discord that [a]ringis amang you hes done mair destructioun till our   [a]reigns
realm nor quhen the grit army and power of Ingland invadit you. The experience of this [a]samin is manifest,   [a]same
quhou that the Kingis of Ingland hes been mair [a]solist to   [a]solicitous
haiff [a]pace and favour of Scotland quhen justice and   [a]peace
concord governit the Three Estaitis of Scotland, nor till haiff hed the favour and pace of all the rich realmis that the Empriour possessis. And, in opposite, quhen the Kingis of Ingland persavis discord, dissensioun, civil weiris, injustice, and divisioun withtin Scotland, [a]than   [a]then
thay forgit feignit querrellis contrar our realm, in [a]hope   [a]expectation
that ilk Scottis man sall be mortal enemy [a]till his   [a]to
nichtbour. Quharfore I exhort you, you my three sonnis, that ye be diligent to remeid your abusioun of the timis by-past, quhilk sall never cum till effect bot giff that ye remuve and expel dissensioun, discord, and [a]haitrent that   [a]hatred
[a]ringis amang you; for giff ye be enemies to yourselfis,   [a]reigns

[1] P. 85.   [2] P. 86.

than quhy suld the Kingis of Ingland be accusit quhen
thay intend weiris contrar you, considerant that thay haiff
been ever your auld enemies? I wald ^aspeir quhat castel   ^aask
can be lang keipit, quhen the enemies seigis it cruelly
withtout, and withtin the said castel there ringis mortal
weir amang the ^asoudartis, men of weir, quhilkis suld live   ^asoldiers
in ane mutual faithful accord in defence of the said castel
contrar extern violence? . . .[1]

'Wald ye maturely consider the subtilty of Inglismen
ye sall find them appeirand faithtful and humain in thair
adversity; bot quhen thay ar in prosperity, thai are ingrate
^atirrans and cruel abufe all other natioun. Och! quhou   ^atyrants
dangerous is it ^atill ony sort of people till haiff ane cruel   ^ato
tirran ringand abufe them: and to ^aeschaip sic tirranny   ^aescape
your forbears hes ^adebatit your country this mony yeiris   ^afought for
^abe grit manheid and wisdom, quhoubeit it was in danger   ^aby
to be in final eversioun. The chroniclis will certify you
quhou that your noble predecessours and forbears war
slain, and the commont people brocht to vile servitude ane
lang time ^abe the Saxonis blude. And yit sic calamity and   ^aby
persecutioun indurit bot for ane time. For God Almichty,
that knawis your just defence, hes ever schawin grit
favour towart you, therefore ye suld tak courage in your
just querrel. . . .'[2]

2. 'Renegate Scottis'

'^aThan to quhat effect suld ony Scottis men ^bgiff credence,   ^athen ^bgive
or ^atill adhere till Inglismen? Our chroniclis rehearsis of   ^ato
diverse Scottis men of all staitis that hes passt ^ain Ingland.   ^ainto
Sum hes passt for poverty, and sum hes passt in hope to
live at mair eise and liberty nor thay did in Scotland, and
sum hes been denuncit rebellis ^abe the authority, quhilk   ^aby
was occasioun that thay passt in Ingland for refuge, quhom
the Kingis of Ingland hes ^aressavit familiarly, and hes   ^areceived
treittit them, and hes ^agiffin them gold and silver, the   ^agiven
quhilk he did ^another for pity nor humanity, bot rather   ^aneither
that thay suld help to destroy ther awin native country.
Bot yit he wald never giff them heritage nor credit, for the
experience of the ^asamin is manifest presently. For   ^asame

[1] P. 89.   [2] P. 91.

quhoubeit that there be abufe three thousand Scottis men, and ther wifis and childer, that hes dwellit in Ingland [a]thir *[a]these* fifty yeir by-past, and hes [a]conquesst be ther industry *[a]acquired* baitht heritage and gudis, yit nocht ane of them daur grant that thay are Scottis men, bot rather thay [a]maun deny *[a]must* and refuse ther country, ther surname, and kin and frendis. For the Scottis men that dwellis in the southt part of Ingland, thay [a]sweir and mainteinis that thay war born in *[a]swear* the northt part or in the west part of Ingland; and Scottis men that dwellis in the west or in the northt of Ingland, thay maun sweir and maintein that thay war born in Kint-schire, York-schire, in London, or in sum other part of the southt partis of Ingland.

'[a]Than to quhat effect suld ony Scottis men adhere till *[a]then* Inglis men, to [a]gar themselfis becum sclavis, and to *[a]cause . . . to* remaine in perpetual servitude? Therefore we may very weill beleiff, that quhoubeit that the King of Ingland garris treit Scottis men witht gold and silver as thay war his frendis, yit doubtless he wald be richt glaid sa that every Scottis man hed ane other Scottis man in his belly! And als fra time that God sendis tranquillity amang princis, thay that are maist familiar witht the Protectour sall be [a]haldin maist odious in Ingland, and every Inglis *[a]holden* knaif sall call them, despitefully, "Renegate Scottis"; and [a]giff ony of them passis to the Protectour, to regret and *[a]if* lament the abstractioun of his familiarity that he schew to them in the beginning of the weiris, he will answer to them as Augustus Caesar answerit till ane captain of Thrace callit Rhymirales, qua [a]betraisit his maister *[a]betrayed* Antonius, and past to remaine witht Augustus Caesar: . . .[1] "I will haiff na familiarity witht you, for I [a]low bot the *[a]commend* traisoun that cummis to my effect, and lowis nocht the traitours that committis the traison."

'This foresaid exemple may be weill applyit till all Scottis men that beleivis to get mair liberty and honour in Ingland nor thay did in Scotland; for this exemple hes been [a]prectickit [b]thir fife-hundretht yeiris by-gane *[a]practised [b]th* [a]till all Scottis men that hes adherit till Inglis men contrar *[a]to* ther native country, as the chroniclis makis manifest; for quhoubeit that the King of Ingland [a]lowis the traisoun *[a]commands*

[1] Pp. 103 f.

that Scottis men committis contrar ther prince, yit he
lowis nocht the traitours that committis the traisoun.'[1]

III. SCOTS AND ENGLISH

The next two extracts are from Chapter XIII. In the first of them,
which is one of the most famous in *The Complaint*, Dame Scotia places
much of the trouble that has arisen on the fact that some Scots are
bedazzled into paying too much attention to the English. This familiarity
is unhealthy. In fact, she goes on to say, there are not two nations under
the firmament more unlike one another than the English and the Scots.
She elaborates this, a favourite theme of hers.

In the second of these passages, Dame Scotia concludes by saying
that treason in Scotland can never be prevented so long as familiarity
exists between some of her people and their ancient enemies. This
advice of the good lady's is hardly practicable today. We clearly must
not only live but mix with the English. Our problem is how to preserve
our national character in such circumstances. As Dame Scotia rightly
says earlier, we shall never have the respect of the English unless we are
ourselves. And we cannot be ourselves unless we respect ourselves. The
duty of self-respect in the nation of Scotland is as clamant today as
when *The Complaint of Scotland* was written.

1. *'On Baitht the Bordours'*

'There is no thing that is occasioun (O, ye my three
sonnis!) of your adhering to the opinion of Ingland contrar
your native country, bot the grit familiarity that Inglis
men and Scottis hes hed on baitht the Bordours, [a]ilk ane   [a]each
witht otheris, in marchandise, in selling and buying horse
and [a]nolt and scheip, outfang and infang, ilk ane amang   [a]cattle
otheris, the [a]quhilk familiarity is express contrar the lawis   [a]which
and consuetudis baitht of Ingland and Scotland.

'In the dayis of Moses, the Jewis durst nocht have
familiarity witht the Samaritanis, nor witht the Philistians,
nor the Romans witht the Africans, nor the Greikis witht
the Persans, be raisoun that ilk ane repute otheris to be
of ane barbour nature; for every natioun reputis otheris
natiouns to be barbarians, quhen ther twa naturis and
complexiouns are contrar till otheris; and there is nocht
twa natiouns under the firmament that are mair contrar
and different fra otheris nor is Inglis men and Scottis men,

[1] P. 105.

quhoubeit that thay be withtin ane ile, and nichtbours, and of ane langage. For Inglis men are subtil, and Scottis men are facile. Inglis men are ambitious in prosperity, and Scottis men are humain in prosperity. Inglis men are hummil quhen thay are subjeckit ^{a}be force and violence, and Scottis men are furious quhen thay are violently subjeckit. Inglis men are cruel quhen thay get victory, and Scottis men are merciful quhen thay get victory. And to conclude, it is unpossible that Scottis men and Inglis men can remain in concord under ane monarchy or ane prince, because ther naturis and conditiouns are as indefferent as is the nature of scheip and wolvis. . . . ^{a}by

'I ^{a}trou it is as unpossible to gar Inglis men and Scottis men remain in gude accord under ane prince, as it is unpossible that twa Sunnis and twa Munis can be at one tyme togidder in the ^{a}lift, ^{b}be raisoun of the grit difference that is betwix ther naturis and conditiouns. Quharfore, as I haiff before rehearsit, there suld be na familiarity betwix Inglis men and Scottis men, because of the grit difference that is betwix ther twa naturis. . . .'[1] ^{a}am sure ^{a}sky ^{b}by

2. 'Ane Heirand Damsel'

'It is nocht possible to keip ane realm fra conspiratioun and traisoun, fra time that the people of that realm usis familiarity witht ther enemies. There is ane auld proverb that sayis, that "Ane ^{a}heirand damsel and ane ^{b}speikand castel, sal never end witht honour"; for the damsel that heiris and giffis eiris to the amorous persuasiouns of dissolute young men, sall be eisily persuadit to ^{a}brack hir chaistity. ^{a}Siclike, ane speikand castel, that is to say, quhen the captain or sodiours of ane castel usis familiar speich and communing witht ther enemies, that castel sall be eisily conquesst, ^{a}be raisoun that familiarity and speich betwix enemies ^{a}generis traisoun. . . .'[2] ^{a}hearing ^{b}speaking ^{a}break ^{a}likewise ^{a}by ^{a}engenders

IV. THE YOUNGEST SON'S REPLY

This series of extracts, all from Chapter XV, together forms an important short section of *The Complaint of Scotland.*

For the first time we hear another voice than that of Dame Scotia.

[1] P. 106.   [2] P. 108.

Moreover (and this is significant) the voice is not from one of the great ones but from 'Labour.' It is not John the Commonweal, nor the Burgesses, as in Lyndesay's play, who are speaking, but the oppressed labourer. He voices justifiable but now familiar complaints. In 1549 it was new to hear them, at least in Scotland.

He claims that he is woefully mistreated by his two elder brothers, the nobility and clergy. However hard he works for them he gets no credit or relief. He does not wish to betray his Mother Scotland, but when the English come with promises of better treatment is he to be blamed for listening to them? This point can be compared with the passage in Barbour[1] which says that the ordinary people need have no allegiance to those who will not protect them. Nevertheless he indignantly denies treachery in his heart, and appeals to his Mother to protect him from his elder brothers.

This appeal from the common man can be paralleled in other literatures of the time, but it is the first appearance in Scotland. It would be a mistake to suppose that what is called modern democracy had its origin in Scottish wisdom.

1. *Vox Populi*

'O my dolorous mother, quhilk sum-time aboundit in prosperity, and nou thou art *a*spulyit fra all felicity throucht *a*despoiled grit afflictioun of langorious tribulatioun, *a*ressaiff thy *a*receive *a*repreiff in patience for ane correctioun, and nocht for ane *a*reproof invective despite. I knaw that thy complaint is nocht disraisounable nor withtout cause, yit nochtheless my displeisure is wonder bitter, in sa far as I haiff baitht the *a*domage and the reproach of thy mischeiff, the quhilk I *a*damage deserve nocht till haiff, *a*be raisoun of my innocence. *a*by

'Allace, the adversity of ane innocent is mair *a*nor cruel, *a*than quhen he enduris punitioun for ane crime that ane transgressour committis. I may be comparit to the dull ass in so far as I am compellit to bear ane importable *a*birding, for I *a*burden am *a*dung and *b*broddit to *c*gar me do and to *d*thole the *a*beaten *b*prodded thing that is abufe my power. *c*cause . . . to
*d*suffer

'Allace, I am the merk of the butt, contrar the quhilk every man schutis arrows of tribulatioun.

'Allace, quhou is justice sa evil-treitit quhilk is occasioun that every man usis all extreme extortiouns contrar me as far as ther power can execute.

'Allace, I laubour nicht and day witht my handis to noureis *a*lasche and inutil idle men, and thay recompence *a*lazy

[1] Cp. above, p. 42.

me witht hunger, and witht the [a]sourd. I sustein ther life   [a]sword
witht travail and witht the sweat of my body, and thay
persecute my body witht outrage and [a]herschip, [b]quhill I   [a]ravaging [b]till
am becum ane beggar: Thay live throcht me, and I die
throcht them.

'Allace, O my natural mother, thou repreiffis and accusis
me of the faultis that my twa brether committis daily, my
twa brether Noblis and Clergy, quhilk suld defend me,
thay are mair cruel contrar me nor is my auld enemies of
Ingland! Thay are my natural brether, bot thay are my
mortal enemies of very deed!

'Allace, quhou can I tak patience, considerand that there
can na thing be [a]eikit to my persecutioun bot cruel [b]deid?   [a]added [b]death
I die daily in ane trance throucht the necessity that I haiff
of the gudis that I wan witht my laubours. My cornis
and my cattle are reft fra me. I am exilit fra ma [a]tackis   [a]holdings
and fra my steadingis. The [a]mailis and [b]fermis of the   [a]tenancies [b]ren.
grund that I laubour is [a]hichtit to sic ane price, that it is   [a]raised
force to me wife and bairns to drink watter. The [a]teindis   [a]tithes
of my cornis are nocht [a]alanerly hichtit abufe the fertility   [a]only
that the grund may bear, bot as weill thay are [a]tane furtht   [a]taken
of my handis be my twa [a]tirran brether.   [a]tyrant

'And quhen I laubour [a]be marchandrise or [a]be mechanic   [a]by
craftis, I am compellit to [a]len and to first it to my twa   [a]lend
cruel brether, and quhen I [a]craiff my debtis quhilk suld   [a]crave
sustein my life, I am [a]bostit, hurt, and oft-timis I am slain.   [a]threatened
Therefore laubouraris to [a]burcht and land and [b]be sea-burd,   [a]burgh [b]by
thay endure daily sic violence that it is nocht possible that
esperance of releiff can be imaginit. For there is na thing on
the laubouraris of the grund to burcht and land, bot [a]arrage,   [a]agriculture
[a]carage, taxatiounis, violent spuilyie, and all other sortis   [a]transport
of adversity, quhilk is unmercifully execute daily. The
weir is cryit contrar Ingland, bot the actis of the weir
is executit contrar the laubouraris, and consumis ther
miserable life.

'O, my natural mother, my complaint is heavy to be
tauld, bot it is mair displeisand to sustein my piteous
desolatioun. I am banist fra my house, I am bostit and
manacit [a]be my frendis, and I am assailyit be them that   [a]by
suld defend me. The laubouraris are ane notable member
of ane realm, withtout the quhilk the noblis and clergy

can nocht sustein ther stait nor ther life, yit notheless thay
are baitht becum my mortal enemies—the quhilk will be
the final eversioun of ther awin prosperity! Therefore I
may compair them till ane man in ane frenesy, quhilk bitis
his awin membris witht his teitht, throuch the quhilk his
body becummis consumit. . . .'[1]

2. *'I am thair Eldest Brother'*

'I am *a*haldin *b*be the vulgar people for thair youngest   *a*holden *b*by
brother, bot I am thair eldest brother in vera deed. For
I was . . . born lang before them, and it was I that first
institute ther faculties. For the *a*police that was inventit   *a*polity
*a*be me and my predecessouris efter the creatioun of the   *a*by
warld hes procreate the stait of my brether. The faculties
and the beginning of Noblis and Spirituality hed bot puir
laubouraris to ther predecessouris. Bot nou, *a*sen thay are   *a*since
cum to stait and dignities throucht me, thay are becum
ingrate and *a*lichtlies me. My twa brether professis them   *a*slight
to be gentil men, and reputis me and all laubouraris to be
rustical and incivil, undauntit, ignorant, dullit slavis. Thay
will nocht consider that all ther gentrice hes proceidit and
descendit fra me. . . .'[2]

3. *The Charge of Treason*

'Thou accusis *me* ower rigorously of conspiratioun and
traisoun, thou knawand weill that traisoun is never *a*generit   *a*engendered
nor inventit in the hartis of the *a*puir commontis; and   *a*poor commons
quhoubeit that thair ignorance culd *a*gar them consave ane   *a*compel . . . to
*a*grundit malice contrar ane prince that hes perpetrate   *a*deep-seated
exactiounis on the people, yit notheless thay haiff nothir
prudence nor knawledge till convoy and till execute ony
point of traisoun. . . .[3]

'And quhoubeit that thou wald allege that *we* can nocht
*a*purge us of traisoun in sa far as we haiff *b*tane assurance   *a*clear ourselves
of Inglis men, allace thou suld nocht impute our assurance   *b*taken
for traisoun nor for ane crime, for thou *a*wait weill that   *a*knowest
we that are laubouraris of the grund culd nocht resist the
Inglis men; for we that hed our wivis and bairnis, our

---

[1] Pp. 122 ff.   [2] P. 128.   [3] P. 130.

cattle and corn, and our gudis in the ᵃboundis quhilk the   ᵃdistricts
Inglis men possesst violently, ᵃgart it ᵇbe force till us to   ᵃcaused . . . to
be assurit, or ellis we hed lossit all our gudis, and ourselfis   ᵇby
till haiff been slain. For it is weill knawin that sum of us
wald nocht be assurit, in ᵃhope that my twa brether,   ᵃexpectation
Noblis and Spirituality, wald haiff defendit us, and till
haiff resistit our enemies. Bot ᵃsic vain hope that we hed   ᵃsuch
of my brethers supply hes gart mony of us be ᵃherrit   ᵃharried
furtht of house and ᵃherbery, quhilk is occasioun that   ᵃshelter
mony of us are beggand our meit ᵃathort the country, and   ᵃacross
there is nocht ane of us that are herrit ᵃbe Inglis men that   ᵃby
can get other ᵃtack or steading, or cou or ox, fra our twa   ᵃholding
brether, to help us in this extreme poverty. . . .[1]

'Quharfore I exhort thee (O my desolate mother) that
thou impute nocht the assurance of the puir commontis
to proceid of traisoun, bot rather that thou accuse my twa
sophistic brether, quhilkis suld and culd have releivit and
restorit thee to thy first stait; for God knawis weill that I
am innocent of thy accusatioun, and the remeid of thy
afflictioun lyis nocht in my possibility!'[2]

V. DAME SCOTIA REPLIES

In the next series, all from Chapters XVI–XIX, Dame Scotia replies
to her youngest son, and then goes on to reproach her elder sons for
their neglect of the commonweal. Though necessarily subdivided in the
text below these replies are here dealt with as one.

Mother Scotland here emerges as Caledonia stern and wild, particularly stern. She refuses to listen to the complaints of any Scotsmen
against any others when the realm is in danger. Her sons must be more
manly. Having heard the labourer's complaints she yet notices his own
faults, malice, inconstancy and brutality. Dame Scotia is no modern
sympathiser with the proletarian virtues. The notion that the Scottish
tradition is fundamentally democratic must be received with qualification.
Dame Scotia believes and proclaims that all those parts of Scotland
must work together for their country's good. She says that the Common
People have no political sense and that to hand government over to them
would be to surrender to mob-rule.

In the last two divisions of this series of extracts she turns to rebuke
the other sons. The nobles have no real nobility in them. They mistreat
their other brothers and have no right now in their degenerate state to
bear those tokens of nobility which they so proudly display. While

Dame Scotia has little sympathy with a head-counting, vote-catching democracy she has no use for nobles empty of nobility. This is, of course, characteristically Scottish. Finally she turns to rebuke the clergy. Though she has given the other sons the benefit of her accusations the clergy must not think that this lets them off. They have neglected their duty as shepherds and sunk into selfishness. All three sons are to blame, those who have suffered as well as those who have selfishly inflicted suffering. Caledonia in this extract is stern to all—stern but not without hope or love.

1. *Labourers*

'O thou my youngest son, callit "laubouraris to Burgh and Land," I will nocht giff eirise to thy excusatiouns nor to thy purgatiouns, because, as Cicero writis in ane orison, that na man suld be admittit to be witness in his awin cause. . . .[1]

'Nor yit I will nocht adhere to thy accusatiouns contrar thy twa brether, be raisoun that ane guilty man suld accuse no man of crime. . . .[2]

'Nor yit I will nocht adhere to the accusatiouns that ony ane of you hes contrar others. . . .[3]

'For thou and all thy sect callit Laubouraris to Burgh and Land, deservis no less punitioun nor dois thy twa brether Noblis and Clergy. For ᵃgiff thou and thy sect   ᵃif hed as grit liberty, as hes thy twa brether, doubtless ye wald be mair cruel ᵃnor the wyild beistis of the desertis   ᵃthan of Araby.

'The practic of this samin is ᵃpresently, and ever hes   ᵃnow been in timis by-past, sen the warld began. For as sune as ye that are commont people are unbridlit and furtht of subjectioun, your ignorance, inconstance, and incivility, ᵃpulsis you to perpetrate intolerable exactiouns. For all   ᵃdrive the insurrectiounis that ever occurrit on ony realm contrar the prince and the public weill, hes proceidit of the ignorance and obstinatioun of the commont people. Therefore none of you suld have liberty, bot rather ye suld be daily dauntit and halden in subjectioun, because that your hartis is full of malice, ignorance, variance, and inconstance.

'For the maist part of you all giffis ᵃlowing till vicious   ᵃcommendation men, and ye hauld virtuous men abhominable, and quhen

---

[1] P. 137.   [2] P. 138.   [3] P. 139.

ye are all ^aconvenit togither for the avancing of ane gude   ^aassembled
purpose, ye cry and berkis ^ailk ane contrar others, that   ^aeach
nocht ane of you knawis quhat ane other sayis. And quhen
ye haiff ^aflittin and berkit ^bbut rhyme or raisoun all the   ^avituperated
lang day, ye accord nocht nor condescendis prudently on   ^bwithout
ane substantial, constant purpose, and he that is the maist
^acummersome cryer, and maist obstinate contrar raisoun,   ^aobstructive
ye repute him for the maist prudent man of the realm.
^aThan quhen he gois, all the ^blave rinnis and followis him,   ^athen ^brest
like the brutal scheip that will nocht pass throucht the ^aslop   ^aopening
of ane ^adyke for the manacing of ther hird, ^bquhill ane   ^awall ^btill
of the werst of the flock ^amak fore-gait, ^bthan all the   ^alead the way
lave followis. And all this proceidis of your variance and   ^bthen
inconstance. I ^await nocht quhidder ane calme sea in   ^aknow
winter, or the course of the Mune, or ane misty morning
in simmer, or the commont people, quhilk of them suld
prefer others in variance! . . .[1]

'There is nocht ane mair ignorant, and ane mair blind
thing in this warld, as is till adhere to the judgement of
the commont people, quhilk hes nother consideratioun nor
raisoun. For all ther deliberatiouns proceidis of ther first
apprehensiouns. Therefore, giff the enterprises of the
commont people cummis till ane gude ^afine, Fortune   ^aend
deservis mair ^alowing nor dois ther prudence. . . .[2]   ^acommendatio

'I can nocht compair the commont people that are
unbridlit bot until beistis that are of ane ^awaur nature nor   ^aworse
brutal beistis, as we may see daily. For brutal beistis
keipis ane better ordour in ther beistly nature nor dois
unbridlit commont people that are ^adotit witht raisoun.   ^aendowed
We may see ^abe experience, that horse, ^bnolt, scheip,   ^aby ^bcattle
doggis, wolvis, lyons, and all other brutal beistis, ilk ane
will defend ther awin nature contrar the violence of other
beistis. . . .[3]

'Bot it is nocht ^asiclike amang the people, for every man   ^alikewise
settis his felicity to destroy his nichtbour. And ^aals the   ^aalso
undauntit brutal beistis that hes ther liberty on feildis and
forrestis—none of them eitis, drinkis, nor sleipis, bot
quhen ther natural appetite requiris. Nor the male witht
the femmel committis nocht the werkis of natur, bot in the
saisoun of generatioun. Bot the people that hes liberty

[1] Pp. 139 f.   [2] P. 140.   [3] P. 140.

keipis nocht sa gude regiment. For thay consider nother the virtue of temperance, nor the vice of intemperance, bot rather subjectis themselfis to satiate ony sperk of the foul lust that ther disordinate sensual appetite provokis them till imagine, as to eit, drink, and sleip abuse meisure at all timis, contrar ther natural appetite. And als to commit fornicatioun, adultery, homicide, and diverse other extortiouns and injuries contrar ther nichtbour, therefore thay deserve to be repute mair brutal ^anor beistis that are   ^athan brutal of nature.

'And quhoubeit that sum of them applyis them to virtue, quhen thay are ^ahaldin in subjectioun, throucht the quhilk   ^aholden thay becum industrious in policy and in conquessing of riches, ^abe marchandrise, or ^abe mechanic craftis, or ^abe   ^aby laubouring of the corn-landis, or be service, yit nochtheless, as sune as ony of them, ^abe sic honest industrious   ^aby such occupatiouns, hes conqueist grit riches or heritagis, thay becum mair ambitious and arrogant ^anor ony gentil man,   ^athan spiritual or temporal, that are descendit of the maist noble barouns of the country. . . .'[1]

'O my yongest son, this answer may be sufficient to the severe accusatioun that thou hes pronuncit contrar thy twa brether. In time to cum, thou sall first correct thyself ^aor thou accuse thy nichtbour.'[2]   ^abefore

2. Nobility

'O my eldest son, Noblis, this severe reproach contrar thy youngest brother is no occasioun to ^agar thee ^bgloir, for   ^acause ... to ^bglory giff thou hed grace to ken thyself, thou wald sune ^apersave   ^aperceive that thy vicious life deservis ane mair extreme reproach. For the vice of thy youngest brother suld be supportit be raisoun of his ignorance and of his poverty, bot thou can have na excusatioun to cullour thy mischeivous conversatioun, and the violent extortiouns that thou daily committis contrar thy twa brether, Laubouraris and Clergy. And ^aals thou art the special cause of my ruin, for thou and   ^aalso thy sect that professis you to be noblis and gentil men, there is nocht ane sperk of nobilness nor gentrice amang the maist part of you. And nou, because mony of you

---

[1] Pp. 140 ff.   [2] P. 143.

ascribis sa grit gloir of your pretendit gentrice and nobilness, I will descrive the stait of nobilness and gentilness, to that effect that ye may persave your grit error. . . .[1]

'O my eldest son, Nobilis and Gentil Men, the armis that ye bare in your scheildis and in your ᵃseillis in your ᵃseals signetis, and als is paintit on your wallis, and in your glasin windowis, thay war give to your predecessours be the Prince for ane ᵃtaiken of nobilness, for the noble actis ᵃtoken that thay hed dune for the commont weill of the realm, and ye that are there successours ye bear the samin armis for ane taiken that ye are obleist to follow the futesteppis of your predecessours in virtue, or ellis ye merit to be degradit fra the armis that ye bear, and fra the gentrice that ye profess. . . .[2]

'Bot allace, O ye my eldest son, there is nocht mony of you that meritis to ᵃweir the enseignyie of the ᵇFleice, ᵃwear ᵇFleece of the Cockle, nor of the ᵃGartan, nor yit there is nocht ᵃGarter mony of you that meritis to be born in ane chariot to ᵃressave the triumph of the palm-tree nor of the laur-tree; ᵃreceive for your imbecility, avarice, and contentioun that ᵃringis ᵃreigns amang you rather deservis degrading fra your pretendit gentrice, ᵃnor ye deserve ᵇlowing or commendation for ᵃthan virtue. Therefore ye are in grit error quhen ye profess ᵇcommendin you to be gentil men, and syne committis no actis ᵃeffeirand for your professioun; bot wald ye consider the ᵃbefitting origin of your gentrice, ᵃthan ye wald nocht be sa arrogant ᵃthen as to desire the gloir and the stait of ane dignity that ye deserve nocht. . . .[3]

'O my eldest son, Noblis and Gentil Men, quhy will ye nocht consider ᵃthir wordis before rehearsit? Quhilk ᵃthese wordis suld be occasioun to ᵃgar you mortify your vain ᵃcause . . . to ᵃconsait of your pretendit gentrice. Ye profess you to be ᵃconceit gentil men, bot your werkis testifeeis that ye ar bot incivil villainis. Ye wald be repute and callit virtuous and honest, quhoubeit that ye did never ane honest act; and ye repute other men for villainis that did never ane villain act. It appeiris that quhen your noble predecessours decessit, thay tuik ther virtue and gentrice witht them to ther sepulture, and thay left na thing witht you bot the style of ther gentrice. The wordis of the holy man Job may be

[1] Pp. 143 f. [2] P. 148. [3] Pp. 149 f.

weil applyit to this samin purpose quhen he said, "*Mortui sunt nobiles, et innobiles sunt filii eorum*"—quod he: "all nobil men are decessit, and ther sonnis and successouris are bot villainis." The wordis of Job are ower manifest in our country, for I see no thing amang gentil men bot vice. For honesty is maculate, ignorance is ^aprisit, prudence is scornit, chestity is baneist, the nichtis are ower schort to gentil men to commit ther libidinous lust, and the dayis are ower schort to them to commit extortiouns on the ^apuir people. Ther blasphematioun of the name of God corruptis the air. The ^aprodig pride that ^aringis amang gentil men is detestable, nocht ^balanerly in costly clething abufe ther stait, bot as weill in prodig expensis that thay mak on horse and doggis, abufe ther rent or riches.

[a]esteemed

[a]poor
[a]prodigious
[a]reigns [b]only

'Ane man is nocht repute for ane gentil man in Scotland, ^abot giff he mak mair expensis on his horse and his doggis nor he dois on his wife and bairnis. The poiettis feignis that the Grecian Diomeid hed horse that ^aeit men, and als thay haiff feignit that Actaeon was transformit ^ain ane ^ahart, and there-efter he was stranglit to ^bdeid witht his awin doggis. . . .[1] Allace, ther is ower mony horse in Scotland, like Diomeidis horse, that eitis the puir people, and there is ower mony doggis in Scotland that wirries ther master, as Actaeon was wirriet! . . .[2]

[a]unless

[a]ate
[a]into
[a]stag [b]death

'O ye my eldest son, Noblis and Gentil Men, I exhort you to correct yourselfis of the articlis of this accusatioun, and ^aals that ye adhere till all virtuous besiness, and that ye accord and agree witht your twa brether, Laubouraris and Clergy, to that effect that ye may releiff me of my afflictioun. For doubtless giff that dissensioun and rancour remainis amang you, in schort dayis your auld enemies sall occupie your heritagis and dwelling placis, and the posterity of your generatioun sall be put furtht of rememorance. . . .'[3]

[a]also

3. Spirituality

'O my sicond son, Spirituality, thou hes heard the familiar repreiff that I have pronuncit, be the way of correctioun

[1] Pp. 155 f.   [2] Pp. 156 f.   [3] P. 157.

to thy twa brether, Noblis and Laubouraris; bot my
accusatioun contrar them, is na purgatioun to thee. For
thou deservis nocht ^aalanerly ane mair invective reproach   ^aonly
for thy demeritis, bot as weill thou deservis to be puneist
really, and to be degradit fra thy holy office. The maist
part of the vicis that thy two brether hes committit may be
supportit and excusit, ^abe raisoun of ther ignorance; bot   ^aby
thou can nocht allege ignorance for thy excusatioun,
considerand that God hes giffin thee His Law in thy
moutht to be distribute betwix thee and thy twa brcther,
as is writin in the sicond cheptour of the prophet Malachias,
^aquhilk sayis: "*Labia enim sacerdotis custodiunt scientiam,*   ^awho
*et legem requirent ex ore eius, quia angelus Domini exercituum
est*"—that is to say: "The lippis of the preist sall keip the
science of God, and the people sall desire the Law to be
^aschawin to them, furtht of his moutht, because he is the   ^ashown
messengeir of the Lord."

'O thou my sicond son, this autority that God hes given
to thee, is wonder grit. Therefore, ^asen God hes ^bdotit   ^asince
thy faculty in maist honourable dignity and autority, abufe   ^bendowed
the stait of thy twa brether, nocht ^aalanerly in the knaw-   ^aonly
ledge of divine science, bot als weill in humanity as ^aintill   ^ain
science liberalis, and in moral and natural philosophy, the
^aquhilk gracis and properties are nocht grantit ^bbe God   ^awhich ^bby
for thy particularity, bot rather God hes ordaind thee to
be ane dispensatour of His giftis amang the ignorant
people.

'Therefore I wald thou war ^asolist to distribute the   ^asolicitous
talent that the Lord ^ageff ^btill His servand. And thou can   ^agave ^bto
nocht distribute it better ^anor to purchase unity and   ^athan
concord betwix thee and thy twa brether; for the prudence
and autority that the Lord hes giffin to thee suld ^asuppreme   ^asuppress
ther ignorant error and obstinatioun. Therefore, as lang as
thou are necligent in thy office, sa lang sall ther ay be
dissensioun, discord, and ^ahaterent in the realm, quhilk   ^ahatred
sall be occasioun of thy awin ruin. Therefore I exhort
thee tile animadvert and to perpend maturely ^athir wordis,   ^athese
in dreid that thou repent thy necligence quhen thou hes
na ^alasyar nor opportunity to remeid thy abusioun.'[1]   ^aleisure

[1] Pp. 157 f.

VI. AND SA FARE WEILL

In this farewell from Chapter XX, the afflicted lady makes a final exhortation to her three sons. She blames each of them for abusing his particular faculties in the community. All are at fault for the discord and bickering that goes on amongst them which, she says, is nothing more than a way of hurting themselves. She says that their behaviour is monstrous rather than human. She goes on to tell a painful but amusingly apposite story drawn from classical antiquity. Heraclitus and Democritus went through the world together. The one found nothing to laugh at, the other was laughing all the time. If these two philosophers, she says, were to come to the modern realm of Scotland the one would certainly not laugh (though he might weep), the other would do nothing but laugh. On this sad but sardonic note we can leave that remarkable work *The Complaint of Scotland*.

No, we do not leave it thus. It is impossible to say good-bye to *The Complaint* without one or two further editorial reflections.

The work is by a passionate pedant, a type that one can recognise time and again in Scotland. Our countrymen have prized learning and have often struggled against the adversity of circumstances, remoteness and poverty, to attain it. They do not therefore always wear learning lightly. But they are a passionate people and sometimes they will use their learning to passionate purposes. *The Complaint* is an example. The author is a learned man rather than an author, but his passionate love for his mother country has turned him for the purposes into an author—and a very effective one too.

His learning, his argument and his passion are, in this work, all bent to the one purpose, the salvation of his country; but the result is far more than mere chauvinism. Its literary quality apart, *The Complaint* time and again expresses a Scottish form of wisdom on an eternal theme, love of country. And indeed how much of what he has to say is relevant today!

Who was the author? There have been a few candidates put forward; but the most diligent research of scholars has failed to discover any sure indication as to the identity of this learned, likeable and characteristic Scotsman of four centuries ago. The South of Scotland, and particularly Edinburgh where this anthology of Scottish wisdom is being compiled, is haunted by ghosts. Some of these 'affable familiar ghosts' (some far from affable) are the stock-in-trade of the town guides and hucksters. Their names are bandied about amongst the tourists as easily and as lucratively as are those of the various brands of Scotch sweetmeats, Scotch whiskies and Scotch tartans in 'ye aulde Scotch shoppies.'

There are other ghosts who are nameless and of whose actions when they were in the flesh no guides or tourists have heard; but they are still perceptible. They are perceptible at times even now amid the distressing disfigurement and gross vulgarisation of the modern city. There are times when the haar comes up from the Forth and blots out

H

the scars of the 1960s leaving only the large bulk of the town dimly recognisable, and when even the sounds of traffic seem muted by the mist. It is at such times that one becomes aware of these nameless phantoms—of their memory.

Amongst these ghosts there are few that we would more wish to meet and talk with than the author of *The Complaint of Scotland*.

1. *'Contentioun and Discord'*

'O ye my three sonnis, I haiff accusit every ane of you, particularly in special for the abusioun of your faculties and officis, the quhilk abusioun is the cause of the contentioun and discord that *ᵃ*ringis amang you, the quhilk   *ᵃ*reigns
contentioun and discord hes dune mair *ᵃ*domage in your   *ᵃ*damage
country *ᵃ*nor the grit army of Ingland hes dune. I wald   *ᵃ*than
*ᵃ*speir ane question, quhat medicine can help ane *ᵇ*seik   *ᵃ*ask *ᵇ*sick
man that hurtis himself wilfully, and provokis his awin
seiknese daily? Or quhat city can endure, quhen it is *ᵃ*seigit   *ᵃ*besieged
and assailyit withtout *ᵃ*be enemies, and withtin the city   *ᵃ*by
ringis mortal *ᵃ*weir amang the governours and inhabitantis?   *ᵃ*war

'O ye my three sonnis, quhat can the warld estime of you, quhen ye are sa *ᵃ*solist on the ruin of your prosperity,   *ᵃ*solicitous
and on the demolitioun of your commont weill? Your
conditiouns and coversatiouns is mair like *ᵃ*till barbarian   *ᵃ*to
people *ᵃ*nor it is to Christin people. Ye lament heavily the   *ᵃ*than
cruel weirs, and ye cry and desyris *ᵃ*pace *ᵇ*at God—ye   *ᵃ*peace *ᵇ*from
haiffand rancour in your hartis contrar your nichtbours!
Ye desire mercy at God—ye haiffand ane drawin *ᵃ*sourd   *ᵃ*sword
in your hand to slay ane innocent! Ye wald be *ᵃ*lowit witht   *ᵃ*esteemed
all men—and ye haiff na cherity to na man!

'Quhy suld God deliver you fra your enemies? *ᵃ*Sen   *ᵃ*since
that ye are mortal enemies to yourselfis, your honour
is *ᵃ*tynt; sen that your vailiantness is chaingit *ᵇ*in   *ᵃ*lost *ᵇ*into
*ᵃ*berking on others like cattis and doggis, ye haiff left the   *ᵃ*barking
protectioun of your commont *ᵃ*salute, and ye are becum   *ᵃ*safety
*ᵃ*sodjours and pensionaris to your enemies, and als ye are   *ᵃ*mercenaries
becum enemies to your awin weilfare and prosperity. . . .'[1]

2. *'Matter aneucht. . . .'*

'I wait nocht quhidder that I sall judge you to becum frenetic or brutal, for your conversatiouns in general is ane

[1] Pp. 165 f.

monstrous thing rather nor humain, as your werkis testifeeis. The historiographouris rehearsis that the twa prudent
philosophouris, Heraclites and Democrites, passt throucht
the warld to have ane universal judgement of the conversatioun of mankind. Than, quhan thay war passand throucht
the warld, and pursuand the vice and the vanity, and evil
conversatioun of every country, and als pursuand the grit
*a*solistness of diverse staitis in *b*conquessing riches,   *a*solicitude *b*acquiring
heritagis, dignities, offices, and autorities, sum *a*be avarice,   *a*by
sum *a*be violence and extortiouns, and sum be ane inexor-   *a*by
bitant solistness contrar raisoun, and sum be *a*raif and   *a*rapine
*a*spuilyie, and sum be traisoun, and sum be dissensioun   *a*plundering
and mortal *a*feid, nocht haiffand respect nor rememorance   *a*feud
of the schort peregrinatioun of this miserable life, nor yit
haiffand premeditatioun of the future eternal beatitude
that God hes promist till faithtful men. *a*Than Heraclites   *a*then
began to weip and lament for pity that he hed of the
extreme disraisounable abusioun that *a*rang amang the   *a*reigned
universal people. Bot Democrites *a*leucht and scornit ther   *a*laughed
folliful conversatioun and *a*solist vanity.   *a*solicitous

'Allace! war thay twa philosophours *a*instantly passand   *a*at this moment
throucht the realm of Scotland, Heraclites wald murn and
lament for pity our misery and our afflictioun, the *a*quhilk   *a*which
hes occurrit and daily occurris throuch our awin occasioun.
And siclike Democrites, *a*persavand our folliful mis-   *a*perceiving
governance and our miserable obstinate conversatioun, he
wald *a*laucht and scorn us *b*be grit derisioun.   *a*laugh *d*by, with

'For doubtless thir twa philosophours wald find matter
*a*aneucht to weip for us, and als to laucht us to scorn.'[1]   *a*enough

3. *Neutrality*

'O ye my three sonnis, ony of you that is suspeckit of
traisoun suld do sum vailiant act contrar your enemies . . .
to that effect that the remainant of the people may giff
confidence to you, *a*quhilk will be occasioun that the   *a*which
*a*haill body of the realm will hasyard ther livis and ther   *a*whole
gudis in your company for the just defence of your
commont weill and your native country. Allace! the
suspicioun that the people hes contrar sum of you is

[1] Pp. 168 f.

nocht causeless, for men of small experience may ^apersave ^aperceive
that ther is diverse men of Scotland that are becum neutral;
that is to say, thay will ^another tak ane plain part witht   ^aneither
Ingland nor witht Scotland, for quhen ^athir neutral men   ^athese
^aspeikis witht Inglis men, thay lament heavily the incon-   ^aspeak
stance of the lordis of Scotland that hes brokin ther promit
and ^aband, the ^bquhilk was honestly contrackit, to compleit   ^abond ^bwhich
ane marriage betwix our noble Princess, ^aHeritour of   ^aheir(ess)
Scotland, and Edward the young King of Ingland, the
quhilk contract ^abeand fulfillit wald haiff been the cause   ^abeing
of ane perpetual unity betwix the twa said realmis; and
quhen ^athir said neutral men speikis witht Scottis men,   ^athese
thay regret and lamentis heavily the dissensioun and
divisioun that ringis amang the noblis of Scotland, quhilk
is occasioun that the Inglis men ^abe ther falseheid and   ^aby
subtilty persecutis our realm without any just title. Of
this sort the neutral Scottis men enterteinis baitht the
realmis ^aquhile on to the time that ane of the realmis   ^atill
^aconquess the tother, and ^bthan thay will adhere till his   ^aconquer ^bthe
opinioun that conquessis the victory. . . .¹

'Quharfore I exhort you, O ye my three sonnis, that giff
ony of you be suspeckit that ye haiff bene neutral in timis
by-past, that nou ye purge you witht sum vailiantness
contrar your enemies, to that effect that ye may revenge
the extreme violent ^adomage that ye haiff susteinit ^bbe the   ^adamage ^aby
unjust weiris of Ingland. And quhoubeit that your auld
enemies wald desist fra ther unjust weiris, and that thay
wald treit ^apace witht you, yit nochtheless ye suld nocht   ^apeace
condescend to ^asic pace, ^bbot giff the King of Ingland wald   ^asuch ^bunless
restore and reform the domage and violence that ye have
endurit. . . .'²

4. In Defens

'Every man is ^aoblist to defend the gudis, heritages and   ^aobliged
possessiouns that his antecestours and forbearis hes left to
them; for as Thucydides hes said in his sicond ^abeuk,   ^abook
quod he, it is mair dishonour till ane person to ^atyne the   ^alose
thing that his antecestours and forbearis hes conquesst
^abe grit laubours ^bnor it is dishonour quhen he failyis in   ^aby ^bthan
the conquessing of ane thing that he intendit till have

¹ Pp. 180 f.   ² Pp. 184 f.

conquessit fra his mortal enemy. Be this raisoun, every
noble man suld be very ^asolist to defend his just querrel;   ^asolicitous
for ^asiclike as ane man offendis his conscience quhen he   ^alikewise
dois violence, extortiouns, and ^adomage till his nichtbour,   ^adamage
siclike ane honest man offendis and hurtis his conscience,
quhen he defendis ^ahim nocht in his just querrel contrar   ^ahimself
his enemies, and als revengis him nocht of the violence
and domage that his enemies hes perpetrate contrar him.

'Quharfore I exhort you, my three sonnis, that ye
condescend in ane faithful accord: ^athan doubtless God   ^athen
sall releive you of the grit afflictioun that ye have endurit
^abe the incredule ^bseid of Ingland, and als I believe that   ^aby ^bseed
he sall mak you ane instrument till extinct that false
generatioun furtht of rememorance: and sa fare weill!'[1]

[1] P. 186.

Proverbial Maxims

Scots are fond of making collections of proverbs, maxims and wise-saws easily memorised. Selections are occasionally included here in chronological order of the appearance in which the collections were made. In Part II we shall meet eighteenth- and nineteenth-century proverbs, some of them drawn from an earlier time. Here, however, is a composite and anonymous collection of proverbs made in sixteenth-century Scotland.[1]

The principle which governs these versified sayings has nothing to do with logic, it is purely metrical. As originally printed, the last word of each line is made to rhyme internally with the word in the middle of the next. (We have not followed this laboriously ingenious lay-out below.) In the first making of this collection there was then as much rhyme as reason. Nevertheless, casually embedded in it, there are flashes of knowledge and wisdom. Much of this is common to many nations. All here are expressed Scottishly.

Scottish is the stress placed on legal maxims. Scottish are references to clan and to laws. Amusingly Scottish is the advice about one's behaviour and state of mind at table and at prayer. Characteristic also of our nation is the warning to a man who spends his money on 'ane hure' (whore). Not only will he waste his substance but he will suffer social degradation. It is worth pausing here to take a glance at 'the wisdom of the Scots' today on this subject.

The Scottish wanton has always been amongst the most socially outcast of her kind in Europe—the drabbest of the drabs. Her offence against respectability and the social conventions is considered worse than the frailty of her flesh. There is a good deal of the reckless casting of first stones in Scotland. The episode from St. John's Gospel of the woman taken in adultery and the adjuration to 'he that is without sin' has not been a favourite theme for exposition from the Scots pulpit.

The plot of Walter Scott's great and humane novel *The Heart of Midlothian* is built upon a barbarous Scots law which (in certain circumstances) used to punish the mother of an illegitimate child with death and let the father go 'Scot-free.' This pun is nonetheless shamefully appropriate for having been made here almost accidentally.

In fairness it should be added that this was an unusually savage statute of Scots law of the past. Moreover Scots law today, and for some time, is and has been much more humane on questions of sexual morality than the English one. Nor are Scots lawyers behindhand in denouncing cant on this most cant-ridden subject when it comes to their notice. It was unfortunately true and admittedly representative of a certain element in Scottish opinion that the one dissentient on the committee that made the generally wise findings of the Wolfenden report should have been a Scot.

[1] From the Maitland Folio MS., Ed. W. A. Craigie, S.T.S., 1919.

However, in the ensuing lively and amusing controversy in the press, popular cant received a severe drubbing from the Scots legal fraternity and from members of the learned professions. Scots common sense and wisdom reasserted themselves. There is a strong smack of Scots common sense in these old maxims and jingles reprinted here.

Mony man makis rhyme,
    and luikis to na ressoun;
Ane king seikand tressoun,
    he may find land;
[a]Traist nocht in the [b]band   [a]trust [b]bond
    that is oft broken;
Quhen ane fule hes spoken,
    he hes all done;
The man suld have iron [a]schone   [a]shoes
    suld bide ane other mannis [a]deid;[1] [a]death
Quhen the [a]faut is in the [b]heid,   [a]fault [b]head
    the memberis are [a]seik;   [a]sick
Ane woman, [a]thocht scho seem meik, [a]though
    scho is [a]ill to knaw;   [a]difficult
Mony man [a]glosis the law   [a](mis)interpret
    oft aganis the [a]puir;   [a]poor
He that spendis his gude on ane [a]hure [a]whore
    hes baith [a]skaith and schame;   [a]harm
He that can nocht gang hame,
    he is ane [a]puir man;   [a]poor
Ane man, quhen he began,
    suld think on the end;
He that glaidly wald spend
    suld [a]preiss for to win;   [a]strive
Commounly [a]till sin   [a]to
    makis loud schame;
Better is gude name
    than ill-won [a]geir;   [a]property
Quha usis maist for to [a]sweir   [a]swear
    is nocht best [a]trowit;   [a]believed
Ane tree is [a]eith [b]bowit   [a]easily [b]bent
    quhen that it is young;
He that rulis weill his tung
    may be callit [a]wyis;   [a]wise

[1] i.e., That man should have iron shoes (who) should wait for another man's death.

[a]Geir won at the dice   [a]property
  [a]richis never the [b]air;   [a]enriches [b]heir
Ane woman that is fair
  may happin be gude;
Ane colt of ane gude [a]stude   [a]stud
  oft [a]happinnis best;   [a]turns out
Gudis may nocht [a]lang lest   [a]long last
  that is ill-won;
Ane [a]werk weill begun   [a]work (n.)
  makis the better end;
[a]Preiss never to spend   [a]strive
  meikle on ane fule;
It is eith to cry 'Hail Yule!'
  on [a]ane otheris mannis cost;   [a]another man's
He suld have hunger in frost,
  in [a]heit that will nocht [b]wirk;   [a]heat [b]work (vb.)
Obey weill to Haly Kirk,
  and thou sall fare the better;
[a]Bandis, boyis or fetteris   [a]bonds
  is nocht like marriage;
Ane woman keipit in cage
  is ane ill [a]tressour;   [a]treasure
Eit and drink with [a]messour,   [a]measure
  and defy the [a]leich;   [a]leech, doctor
Ane man of meikle speich
  may sum-time lie;
Think that thou [a]maun die,   [a]must
  thou sall nocht glaidly sin;
Ane man may be of gude kin,
  and be little worth;
Ane fule biddis joy [a]furth,   [a]forth
  and is baith spur and wand;
Better is man [a]but land,   [a]without
  [a]na land but man;   [a]than
He that is cummit of ill clan,
  wyismen suspectis;
Ane scabbit [a]scheip infectis   [a]sheep
  all the [a]haill flock;   [a]whole
Quhairof servis the lock,
  and the theif in the houss?

It makis ane wantoun mouss,
   ane unhardy cat;
Ane swine that is fat
   is cause of his *a*awin *b*deid;   *a*own *b*death
Part never in *a*feid   *a*feud
   fra hame with thy wife;
Flee ay fra strife,
   for ane sweit thing is *a*peice;   *a*peace
All may nocht be *a*lieis   *a*(pron. leeis)
   that mony sayis;
Thou may mend twa 'Nayis'
   with anis-said 'Yea';
He is nane so little fae
   bot he may quhilis noy;[1]
It is *a*either-er to destroy   *a*easier
   *a*be far *b*nor to *c*bigg;   *a*by *b*than *c*build
*a*Quha that usis to thig   *a*who
   is *a*laith to *b*leiff the craft;[2] *a*loath *b*leave
Ane auld man is full daft
   that weddis ane young woman;
*a*He *b*maun *c*trow in sum man, *a*one *b*must *c*believe
   or *a*leiff ane ill life;   *a*live
Be thou jealous of thy wife,
   scho will be the *a*waur;   *a*worse
He that *a*tuichis pick or tar   *a*touches
   may nocht weill be *a*clein;   *a*clean
Ane wound quhen it is *a*green   *a*fresh
   it is best *a*haillit;   *a*healed
Ane *a*byle lang *b*beilit   *a*boil *b*lit. boiled
   *a*maun *b*breik at the last;   *a*must *b*breech, i.e.
Unkindness by-past   come to a head
   may nocht be *a*foryet;   *a*forgotten
Be blyith at the *a*meit   *a*meat
   and sad at the prayeris;
For little mair or less
   thou mak no debate;[3]

---

[1] i.e., prob., 'He is not so little of an enemy that he is not sometimes a nuisance.'

[2] It was formerly a custom that anybody who came 'thigging' had to be given whatever he requested. This proverb means, of course, that anybody who makes a practice of 'thigging' will be reluctant to give it up.

[3] i.e., don't argue about trifles.

Leif never the ^ahie-gait   ^ahighroad
   for the by-road;
Quha that ^adoutis nocht God   ^afears
   sall nocht fare weill;
He that covetis all
   is ^ahable all to tyne;   ^aliable
Put mony to the ^ascule,   ^aschool
   for all will nocht be clerkis;
At all doggis that barkis,
   men suld nocht be muvit;
He that is weill luffit,
   he is nocht ^apuir;   ^apoor
Greit laubour and ^acure   ^acare
   makis ane man auld;
Ane gude tale ill-tauld
   is ^aspilt in the telling;   ^aspoilt
In buying and selling
   is mony ^afause aith;   ^afalse oath
Commounly gude claith
   is ay best ^acheip;   ^acheap
Quha ^apreissis ^bfarrest to leip   ^astrives ^bfarthest
   is able gang aback;
And thus in ane morning of May
   this matter culd I mak—

FINIS

Amen, etc.

Sir Richard Maitland of Lethington

Sir Richard Maitland of Lethington (not to be confused with his tortuous son, William Maitland of Lethington, Queen Mary's Chancellor) is an underrated or neglected Scottish poet. He made his Maitland collection from which the following are taken and which included many of his own poems. His verse and his sometimes rather sad wisdom are marked by an urbane charitable tone not often to be heard in the utterances of our brave, struggling but withal contentious people. Some of Maitland's verses are dull, but others are memorable for their large-mindedness and humanity. They throw a light upon what was passing through the minds of some wise Scotsmen who were not forward protagonists in the great events of the time, yet who lived through the upheaval of the sixteenth century which changed the face of the country and who suffered its impact personally. They represent, therefore, a small but valuable part of the passing wisdom of Scotland.

The first quotation below, *To be put in ony Publict Houss*, might seem, at first sight, to be a trifle sententious. When you examine it, however, you see the good sense in it. If only people had tried to follow these maxims in the frequenting of public houses, how much better a tradition of taverns we would have. Indeed if such a poem could be hung up in our modern public houses, and if people paid attention to it, these would be better places to drink in. Note in the second line the adjuration to 'have faith in Christ ay constantly.' No one today could mention faith in Christ in a modern public house without causing acute embarrassment. Indeed in some places one might be turned out for using 'bad language.' The Name of Christ is usually only mentioned in such circumstances to give added force to an oath. Next time you visit a public house in Scotland raise your glass in silent (yes, it had better be silent) salutation to the gentle shade of the elder Maitland of Lethington and to his forgotten Scottish wisdom.

The Blyithness that hes been is a wise and modest poem, full of a healthy and ordered love of life which overcomes the sadness latent in it. Maitland lived to a great age. He could remember a time when, with all its imperfections, Scotland was composed of an integrated society. He is almost the only Scottish poet who spoke for a unified society and not merely for certain sections or factions of it. In these sane, healthy, modulated lines, Maitland laments the passing of such a Scotland. He knows that when people break up society by embittered faction it will be difficult to build it again. But his lament is not only political. He bewails the loss of so much beauty and of so much spiritual value. Here indeed is a half-forgotten form of Scottish wisdom.

Of Papists and Protestants requires little comment. Neither the modern Scottish Papist nor the modern Scottish Protestant can (historically speaking) find much 'flattering unction' in it. Maitland, an essentially Christian as well as wise old man, looks back with distaste at the corruption of the clergy under the old regimen, and then with a distress equally strong at the arrogance and failings of their Reformed successors (amongst which note their failure to suppress fornication, adultery and oppression of the poor). Long before Milton said it this old Scotsman had discovered for himself that 'new Presbyter is but old Priest writ large.' We who live in times when corruption, arrogance and the mortal bitterness of religious dispute are seemingly passing can but join Maitland in his last lines when he prays for Christian unity.

The Folly of ane Auld Man is full of a shrewd and caustic irony that is highly expressive, and characteristic of Scottish wisdom. It is interesting to observe that the wise charity which animated the author of *The Blyithness that hes been* and *Of Papists and Protestants* does not prevent him from writing a searching comment on the folly of old age. We draw the reader's attention to the pleasingly vigorous imagery which he uses. Having begun the third stanza in fine lyrical style he ends pungently:

> 'Ane auld gray beird on ane quhite mouth to lay
> Into ane bed, it is ane piteous sicht—
> The ane cryis "Help!" the other wantis micht.'

Thence he proceeds through mercantile sea-faring and farming analogies to lament the amorous perplexities of a foolish old man trying to make love to a young woman. His manner is quite inoffensive but distinctly Freudian; and it is also wise. Maitland was one of those sixteenth-century Scottish poets who had lived through so much that they accepted age (with its disadvantages as well as its recompenses) as something inevitable. Maybe poor Sir Richard had suffered some of the distressing humiliations of the 'Auld Man' so graphically described here, maybe not, but he is certainly in a position to philosophise about it.

The Blind Baronis Comfort is again a musing upon the dilemma of age. The old man whose lands have been ravaged would like revenge upon the ravagers but is aware that such thoughts of vengeance are inconsistent with his Christian principles. 'Oh, Lord, make me better—but not just yet,' is an old cry; here it is spoken in Scots.

The last thoughts of the old man are highly colloquially expressed in *Thocht I be Auld*. Here Maitland is in the mood of allowing himself more regret for youth than comfort in old age. 'Of Venus' play past is the heit . . . I am sa auld.' And no wonder too! He lived to be eighty-nine. His view, however, that one of the recompenses for the passing years is that his wife can no longer be jealous of him is pretty thin. More convincing is his relief at not having to play football. But how charmingly and how realistically *and wisely* we hear the old gentleman talking to us across the centuries!

I. TO BE PUT IN ONY
PUBLICT HOUSS

Dreid God and lufe Him faithfully,
Have faith in Christ ay constantly,
And, with thy nichbour, cherity;
For grace on God ay call,
Obey and serve the Quein truly,
Keip Justice, ^apeax and unity,   ^apeace
Fra all sort of seditioun ^aflie,   ^aflee
And do ressoun till all.

Hate pride, invy, and lichory,
All ire, ^asweirness, and gluttony,   ^areluctance
Avarice and idolatry,
All tressoun and debaitis,
Lufe virtue, richt, and honesty;
In cheritable deedis exercit be,
All ^aleifsome promise ^bkeip justly   ^alawful ^bkeep
^aTill all manner of ^bstaitis.   ^ato ^bestates (of society)

Keip you fra prodigality,
Oppressioun, wrang and cruelty,
And fra all vice and vanity,
And grund you upon truth;
^aHant gude and honest company,   ^afrequent
Use wyis counsale and gravity,
Do all your thingis discreitly,
And of the puir have ruth.

II. THE BLYITHNESS THAT HES
BEEN

Quhare is the blyithness that hes been
Baith ^ain burgh and landwart seen?   ^ain town and country
Amang lordis and ladyis ^aschein,   ^abrilliant
Dauncing, singing, game and play:
Bot now I ^await nocht quhat thay ^bmein—   ^aknow ^bmean
All mirriness is worn away.

For now I ^aheir na word of Yule,   ^ahear
In kirk, on ^acausay, nor in ^bscule;   ^acauseway ^bschool
Lordis ^alattis thair kitchingis ^bcule   ^alet ^bcool
And drawis thame to the abbay,
And scant hes ane to keip thair ^amule—   ^amill
All hous-haldaris is worn away.

I saw no ^agysaris all this ^byeir,   ^aguisers[1] ^byear
Bot kirkmen cled like men of ^aweir   ^awar
That never cummis in the ^aqueir,   ^achoir
Like ruffianis is thair array,
To preich and teich that will nocht ^aleir—   ^alearn
The kirk-gudis thay waste away.

Kirkmen afore war gude of life,
Preichit, teichit, and ^astainchit strife,   ^astaunched
Thay feirit ^another swerd nor knife: ^aneither
For lufe of God, the suth to say,
All honourit thame, baith man and wife—
Devotioun was nocht away.

Our faderis wyis was and discreit,
Thay had baith honour, men, and ^ameit,   ^ameat
With lufe thay did thair tenantis ^atreit   ^atreat
And had ^aaneuch in ^bpoise to lay,   ^aenough ^bstore
Thay wantit nother malt nor ^aquheit—   ^awheat
And mirriness was nocht away.

And we ^ahald nother Yule nor ^bPace,   ^acelebrate ^bEaster
Bot ^aseikis our meit from place to place   ^aseek
And we have nother luck nor grace;
We ^agar our landis double pay,   ^acompel . . . to
Our tenantis cryis 'Allace, allace!'—
That ruth and pity is away.

Now we have mair, it is weill ^akend,   ^aknown
Nor our forebearis had, to spend,
Bot far less at the ^ayeiris end,   ^ayear's
And never hes ane mirry day—
God will na richess to us send,
Sa lang as honour is away.

---

[1] Children dressed up for a festival, especially Hallowe'en.

We waste far mair now like vain fulis,
We and our page, to ^aturse our ^bmulis,   ^acarry ^bslippers
Nor thay did ^athan that held grit Yulis,   ^athen
Of ^ameit and drink said never 'Nay'—   ^ameat
Thay had lang formis ^aquhare we have stulis,   ^awhere
And mirriness was nocht away.

Of our ^awanthrift sum ^bwytis playis,   ^aunthrift ^bblame
And sum thair wantoun vain arrayis,
Sum the wyte on thair wifis layis
That in the Court wald gang so gay
And ^acairis nocht ^bquha the merchant payis—   ^acare ^bwho
^aQuhill ^bpairt of land be put away.   ^atill ^bpart

The kirkmen keipis na professioun,
The temporal men committis oppressioun,
Puttand the puir from thair possessioun.
Na kind of ^afeir of God have thay—
Thay ^acummer baith the kirk and sessioun,   ^aencumber
And chassis cherity away.

Quhen ane of thame susteinis wrang,
We cry, 'For justice, ^aheid and hang!'   ^abehead
Bot quhen our nichbour we ^aowre-gang,   ^aover-go
We laubour justice to delay—
Affectioun blindis us sa ^alang,   ^along
All equity is put away.

To mak actis we have sum ^afeill: ^a'feel,' skill
God wait gif yat we keip thame weill—
We cum to bar with ^ajack of ^bsteill,   ^ajacket ^bsteel
As we wald ^abost the judge, and ^bfray: ^athreaten ^bintimidate
Of ^asic justice I have na ^bskeill—   ^asuch ^bskill
Quhair rule and ordour is away!

Our lawis are ^alichtlit for abusioun,   ^adisregarded
Sumtime ^ais cloakit with collusioun,   ^aare
Quhilk causis of blude the greit effusioun,
For na man ^aspairis now to slay—   ^aforbears
Quhat bringis countryis to confusioun,
Bot ^aquhare that justice is away?   ^awhere

Quhare is the ^awyte, ^bquha can schaw us?   ^ablame ^bwho
Quha bot our noblis that suld knaw us
And till honourable deedis draw us?
^aLat never commoun-weill decay—   ^alet
Or ^aellis sum mischeif will ^bfaw us   ^aelse ^bbefall
And nobleness we put away!

Put our ^aawin lawis to executioun,   ^aown
Upon trespassouris mak punitioun,
To cruel folk ^aseik na remissioun: ^aseek
For ^apeax and justice lat us pray—   ^apeace
In dreid sum strange new institutioun
Cum, and our custom put away.

Amend your livis ane and all,
And be-war of ane sudden fall,
And pray to God that made us all
To send us joy that ^alestis ay   ^alasts
And lat us nocht to sin be thrall—
Bot put all vice and wrang away!

III. PAPISTIS AND PROTESTANTIS

O gracious God, almichty and eterne,
For Jesus' sake, Thy son, we ask at Thee
Us to defend, conserve us and guberne,
And tak fra us, Lord, for thy greit mercy
Thir ^aplaigis that appeiris presently—   ^aplagues
Pest, poverty, and maist unkindly ^aweir,   ^awar
Hunger, and dearth that now is like to be,
Throw ^adeid of beistis and scant of corn this yeir.   ^adeath

Bot, Lord, this cummis of Thy just judgement
For punischment of our iniquity,
That never of our sinnis will repent,
Bot persevere in impiety:
We are sa soppit in sensualitie
Baith spiritual and temporal estait,
The people all misguidit ^ahaillalie   ^awholly
Not regnis now bot trouble and debate.

Sum-time the preistis thocht thay did weill
Quhen that thay made thair ^abairdis and   ^abeards
   ^aschuif thair croun,   ^ashaved
Usit round cappis and gounis to thair ^aheill,   ^aheel
And ^aMess and Matinis said of thair fassoun,   ^aMass
Thocht that all vicis ^arang in thair persoun,   ^areigned
Leichary, gluttony, vain-gloir and avarice,
With sword and fire, for zeill of religioun,
Of Christian people oft made sacrifice.

For ^aquhilk God hes thame puneist richt   ^awhich
   schairply,
Bot had thay left thair auld abusioun
And turnit thame fra vice to God truly,
And ^asyne ^bforthocht thair wrang intrusioun   ^athen ^brepented
Into the kirk be false elusioun,
The Word of God syne preichit faithfully—
Thay had not cummit to sic confusioun,
Nor ^atholit had, as yit, sic misery.   ^asuffered

Now is Protestantis risen us amang,
Sayand thay will mak reformatioun—
Bot yit as now ma vicis never rang,
As pride, invy, false dissimulatioun,
^aDissait, adultery, and fornicatioun,   ^adeceit
Thift, reif, slauchter, oppressioun of the
   puir,
Of policy plain alteratioun—
Of ^awrangous geir now na man   ^awrongly acquired property
   ^atakis cure.   ^aconcerns himself

Thay think it weill, ^aand thay the Pape do   ^aif
   call
'The Antichrist,' and Mess 'idolatry,'
And syne eit flesch upon the Fridayis all,
That thay serve God richt then accordingly,
^aThocht in all thing thay ^bbleiff maist wickedly: ^athough ^blive
Bot God commandit us His Law to keip—
First honour Him, and syne have cherity
With our nichtbour, and for our sinnis
   weip.

Think weill, that God, that puneist the Papistis,
Is yit *a*on life, and you to puneisch able,   *a*alive
As He did thame, that in your sinnis insistis,
As Goddis Word wer *a*hauldin bot ane fable: *a*holden
Bot *a*gif your *b*hairt on God be firm and stable,   *a*if *b*heart
*a*Thocht that His Word *b*into your mouth ye   *a*tho' *b*in
     have,
Except your life be thairto conformable,
In word and work ye bot yourself *a*dissave.   *a*deceive

I *a*mein not here of faithful Christianis,   *a*am thinking
Nor ministeris of Goddis Word truly,
That at the *a*samin steidfastly remainis,   *a*same (time)
In word and work, without hypocrisy:
Bot I do mein of thame *a*allanerlie   *a*alone
That callit are the 'fleschly Gospellaris,'
Quha in thair wordis appeiris richt godly,
Bot yit thair workis the plain contrar declaris.

Bot thocht of Papistis and Protestantis sum
Hes baith gane wrang and Goddis Law trans-
     gressit,
Keip us, gude Lord, that never mair we cum
To sic errour, bot grace to do the best,
That with all men Thy true faith be confesst,
That Christian folk may *a*leiff in unity,   *a*live
Virtue set up and all vicis suppresst,
That all the world, gude Lord, may honour
     Thee!

IV. THE FOLLY OF ANE AULD MAN

Amang follyis, ane grit folly I find—
Quhen that ane man past fifty yeiris of age
That in his vain *a*consait growis sa blind   *a*conceit
As for to join himself in mairriage
With ane young lass: *a*quhare blude is in ane   *a*where
     rage
Thinkand that he may serve hir appetite—
*a*Quhilk gif he faill, *b*than scho will him despite.   *a*which *b*then

Aigit men suld joice in moral ^atailis,   ^atales
And nocht in ^atailis: for folly is to mairry   ^a(skirt-) tails
Fra time that baith ^athair strenth and nature   ^aone's
  faillis
To tak ane wife, and bring ^athameself   ^aoneself
  ^ain tairy: ^ainto difficulty
For fresch Maii and cauld Ianuary
Agreeis nocht upon ane sang in June—
The treble ^awantis that suld be sung ^babune.   ^ais lacking ^babove

Men suld tak voyage at the larkis sang
And nocht at ^aeen, quhen passit is the day;   ^aevening
Efter mid-age, the luvar lyis full lang;
Quhen that his hair is turnit ^alyart gray,   ^ahoary
Ane auld gray beird on ane ^aquhite mouth   ^awhite
  to lay
^aInto ane bed, it is ane piteous sicht—   ^ain
The ane cryis 'Help!' the other wantis micht.

Till have been merchand, ^abygane mony   ^abygone
  ^ayeir,   ^ayears
In ^aHandwarp, ^bBurges, and the toun of   ^aAntwerp ^bBruges
  Berry,
Syne in to ^aDeip for to ^btyne all his ^cgeir,   ^aDieppe ^blose ^cstock
With vain consait to ^apuir himself and   ^aimpoverish
  ^aherry—   ^aharry
Grit peril is for to pass ^aowre the ferry   ^aover
Into ane ^aleikand boat, nocht nailit fast,   ^aleaking
To ^abeir the sail nocht havand ane ^bsteiff   ^abear ^bstiff
  mast.

To tak ane ^amailing that grit laubour requiris,   ^aholding (of land)
Syne ^awantis ^bgraith for to manure the land—   ^ais lacking ^bgear
Quhen ^aseid wantis, ^bthan men of ^cteilling   ^aseed ^bthen ^ctilling
  tiris—
Than ^acumis ane ^bfindis it waste lyand,   ^acomes ^b(that) finds
Yokis his ^apleuch, teillis at his ^bawin hand: ^aplough ^bown
Better had been the first had never ^akend it   ^aknown
^aNor thole that schame—and sa my tail is   ^athan suffer
  endit.

V. THE BLIND BARONIS COMFORT

Blind man, be blyith, ^athocht that thou be wrangit,   ^atho'
Thocht Blyith[1] be herryit, tak na melancholy
Thou sall be blyith when that thay sall be hangit
That Blyith hes ^aspuilyit so maliciously.   ^adespoiled
Be blyith and glaid that nane ^apersave in thee   ^aperceive
That thy blyithness consistis into richess,
Bot thou art blyith that thou eternally
Sall ^aring with God in eternal blyithness.   ^areign

Thocht thay have spuilyit Blyith of gude and geir,
Yit have thay left lyand still the land,
Whilk to transport wes not in thair power—
Nor yit will be, ^athocht no man thame gainstand: ^atho'
Therefore be blyith, the time may be at hand
When Blyith sall be yit, with Goddis grace,
Als weill ^apleneist as ever thay it ^bfand—   ^aplenished ^bfoun·
When sum sall rue the ^arinning of that race!   ^arunning

Ay to be blyith outwartly appeir
That ^abe na man it may persavit be   ^aby
That thou ^apansis for ^btinsale of thy geir,   ^aart pensive ^blos·
That thy unfreindis that are proud and hie
Be blyith and glaid of thy adversity:
Thairfore be stout and lat thame understand
For loss of geir thou takis na ^asussie—   ^asouci
For yit behind thou hes ^aaneuch of land.   ^aenough

Be blyith and glaid ay in thy intent
For ^aleisome blyithness is ane happy thing.   ^alawful
Be you not blyith, what ^availlis land or rent?   ^aavails
^aAnd thou be blyith, is cause of lang ^bleving;   ^aif ^bliving
Be thou not blyith, thocht thow were ane king,
Thy life is not bot cair without blyithness:
Thairfore be blyith, and pray God us to bring
Till His blyithness and joy that is endless.

[1] Blythe, in Lauderdale, one of Sir Richard's estates. Rollent Foster, Captain of Wark, who harried it, is said to have 'spuilyit . . . furth of the said barony, fowr thousand scheip . . . , two hundreth nowlt [cattle], thretty horss and meiris [mares]. . . .' The raid occurred when Sir Richard was 'three score and xiiii yeiris of age and growin blind, in time of peice [peace], when nane of that cuntra lippint for [counted on] sic thing.'

VI. [a]THOCHT I BE AULD   [a]though

[a]Thocht that this warld be very strainge,   [a]though
And [a]theiffis hes done my rowmis rainge   [a]thieves have ravaged my lands
  And [a]teind my [b]fauld   [a]emptied [b]folds
Yit I wald [a]leiff and [b]bide ane chainge,   [a]live [b]await
  Thocht I be auld.

Now me to [a]spoilyie sum men not [b]spairis   [a]despoil [b]forbear
To tak my [a]geir na Capitain[1] [b]cairis   [a]stock [b]scruples
  Thay ar sa bauld:
Yit time may cum may mend my [a]sairis,   [a]hurts
  Thocht I be auld.

Sum now [a]be force of men of [b]weir   [a]by [b]war
My houss, my landis, and my geir
  Fra me thay hauld:
Yit, as I may, [a]sall mak gud cheir,   [a]shall (I)
  Thocht I be auld.

Sa weill is [a]kend my innocence   [a]known
That I will not for none offence
  [a]Flyte like ane [b]scauld,   [a]vituperate [b]scold
Bot thank God and tak patience
  [a]For I am auld.   [a]that

For eild and my infirmity,
Warm claithis are better for me
  To keip fra cauld,
Nor in Dame Venus' [a]chalmer be,   [a]chamber
  For I am auld.

Of Venus' play past is the [a]heit   [a]heat
For I may not the [a]misteris [b]beit   [a]needs [b]satisfy
  Of Meg nor [a]Mald,   [a]Maud
For ane young lass I am not [a]meit,   [a]fit
  I am sa auld.

---

[1] Foster, the Englishman who harried Blythe, was Captain of Wark.

The fairest wench in all this toun,
Thocht I hir had in hir best goun
      Richt bravely ^abrauld,   ^abedecked
With hir I micht not play the ^aloun,   ^ayouth
      I am sa auld.

My wife sum-time wald ^ataillis ^btrow   ^atales ^bbelieve
And mony ^aleisingis weill allow   ^alies
      ^aWer of me tauld—   ^a(that) were
Scho will not ^aeindle on me now,   ^abe jealous of me
      I am sa auld.

My horss, my ^aharness, and my ^bspeir,   ^abody-armour ^bspear
And all other my ^ahosting geir   ^afield-kit
      Now may be ^asauld   ^asold
I am not able for the ^aweir,   ^awar
      I am sa auld.

Quhen young men cummis fra the green,
Playand at the futeball ^ahad been,   ^a(that) had
      With broken ^aspauld,   ^ashoulder-blade
I thank my God I want my een,
      I am sa auld.

Thocht I be ^asweir to ride or ^bgang,   ^areluctant ^bgo
Thair is sumthing I wantit lang
      Fain have I wald—
And thame punisch that did me wrang,
      Thocht I be auld!

Alexander Montgomerie

The first of the two parts of this anthology ends with substantial extracts from Alexander Montgomerie's long poem *The Cherry and the Slae*. We hesitated about including this poem and about how much of it we should put in. In hesitating, and therefore examining it again with care, we found much profit. We ended by deciding to include it, and much of it. We were convinced not only (as we had always been) of its merits— its occasional beauty, its charm, its wit, its observation, its swing and style, its civilised form, but also of its suitability to this anthology of wisdom. We reached our decision with pleasure and with the conviction (not strange to us) that we were right.

We had hesitated because many critics, professors, editors of earlier Scottish verse, lecturers and the like have dismissed the bulk of this ingenious, fertile and often inspiring allegorical poem (precisely that part of it that is to our purpose) as a piece of arid argument in verse masquerading as poetry. It is true that they praise the much anthologised opening of the poem with its evocative description of a Scottish rustic scene in the luxuriance of summer; but this praise is only used as a stick with which to beat the author of the contents of the remaining 107 stanzas. As one editorial critic has put it: 'The old fauna and flora of the Rose-garden' (a reference to mediaeval French romantic poetry) 'are given a new life and conviction.' The editor-critic then dismisses the rest of the poem as a 'digressive, rambling disputation on general questions of behaviour with rather commonplace counsels of cautious and commercial morality' (if this is true why bother to edit a poem of 114 stanzas of which you only approve of the first seven?).

We do not agree with this harsh, uneconomical, indeed, to us, superficial judgment. This is not to say that we are insensitive to the purely decorative poetry at the beginning, but we look beyond. We are as fond of the odour of roses as is any professor on his rostrum sniffing with homesick longing, and through the smell of chalk and the hot-water pipes of the lecture-room, the scents from his faded youth. We are indeed fond of roses, we revel in them, thorns and all. But we also delight in wisdom, particularly if we find it felicitously and sometimes movingly expressed. We believe that much of *The Cherry and the Slae* contains this wisdom and of a characteristic Scottish kind. We have, therefore, included much of it.

Alexander Montgomerie, of a well-connected Scottish family and linked by blood remotely with Royalty, was born about 1545 and disappeared probably to his death about 1611. He is therefore a near contemporary of Shakespeare's, and, like Shakespeare, he lived through a period of great change in his country; but the change was profounder and, from the point of view of the country's fortunes, was deeper in Scotland than in England.

It was during this period that the Reformation was established in both countries. England began to feel her way towards maritime power and towards the founding of the English Empire. One of the most important steps in this Imperial movement was the acquisition of Scotland (though it may not have been thought of in such terms by the generality of England at the time).

In 1603 James VI of Scotland went to England to ascend the throne of the United Kingdom—placed firmly in London; he was to remain there, for all practical purposes, for the rest of his life. This may have been a fairly important fact for England, but it was a matter of life and death for Scotland. A dynasty of Scottish descent might thereafter sit in London, but the establishment of a United Kingdom on a now officially Protestant island meant the inevitable progress towards a greater union. A union of Parliaments really became inescapable from 1603 onwards.

Montgomerie's contemporary Shakespeare, then, lived to see the enlargement of his native country and its gain in power, Montgomerie to see the loss of Scotland's power and the beginning of its decline. He saw what the unknown author of the *Complaint of Scotland* almost certainly never lived to see, the definite acceptance by Scotland of an inferior status in this island and her practical disappearance from the councils of Europe not only as a separate kingdom but as a nation.

Montgomerie was a Catholic and was involved in some Scottish Catholic conspiracies of his time. As to how far he was an ardent Scottish patriot we cannot be sure. We certainly have no evidence of explicit patriotic writing from him of the kind in *The Complaint*. But as a fervent Catholic in the Scotland of the late sixteenth century he would certainly have looked upon Protestantism as having been introduced into Scotland and fomented in Scotland by England. His religion then drove him into the traditional Scottish tongue which he would have regarded as the proper vehicle for Scottish literature uncontaminated by Englishry or Protestantism.

At the same time, though he lived for fifty-one years after the establishment of the Reformation in Scotland, he was the last true pre-Reformation poet and scholar to be influenced by European culture while expressing himself in Scots. Of course Urquhart and Hume, to name but two of many after him, drew much of their inspiration from France and Europe rather than from England, but Montgomerie was the last in the Catholic-Scots-European tradition. As a survivor, a late survivor from the period when Scotland was both an independent kingdom and a part of Europe, he is a fitting writer to choose to end the first part of this anthology.

In an unexpected way he does in his style offer a link with the future. The complicated and individual manner of the stanza he adopted in *The Cherry and the Slae* was used by many other Scottish post-Reformation poets, most of them inferior to him and most of them pedantic. One was not inferior, and was certainly not pedantic. Robert Burns used this difficult stanza form on more than one occasion and most notably and brilliantly in the *recitativi* of *The Jolly Beggars*.

Montgomerie also anticipated rather than influenced a form of Scottish

writing very different from *The Jolly Beggars*. As will later be shown in
the last two stanzas of this curious allegorical poem he rises to the
heights of an eloquence which in form, style and content reminds one of
the metrical versions of the Psalms of David. Thus did this scholarly,
Catholic, pre- (and just post-) Reformation, European, Scottish poet act
as a link between his times and those of the seventeenth- and eighteenth-
century highly Protestant Scottish psalm singers. Thus also he acts as
a link between his times and ours.

His poem elaborates, decorates, argues about, amuses itself with,
cavorts around and touches with wit, sometimes beauty the theme sung
by a later Scottish poet and man of action—Montrose:

> He either fears his fate too much,
> Or his deserts are small,
> That puts it not unto the touch,
> To win or lose it all.

These well-known lines are included in this place not only because
they are apt but to remind the reader that they are by a a Scots
Presbyterian and a signatory of the Solemn League and Covenant at
that. It is not only Scots Catholics who will risk all to win or lose all—
far from it! A noble example of the Presbyterian power to put it to the
touch to 'win or lose it all' was the 'Disruption' of 1843—a fact still
remembered in the Kirk as if it had happened yesterday. At the
Disruption a large body of beneficed clergy 'walked out.' They walked
out of the General Assembly, out of their manses, out of any prospect
of livelihood and all on a matter of conscience. They did not lose the
day.

The habit of labelling nations and peoples as if they were the contents
of bottles in a chemist's shop is tiresome and misleading. The French
are 'excitable and unreliable,' the English are 'phlegmatic and under-
sexed,' the Scots are 'cautious and canny'; there's the label, and there
you are. If what comes out of the bottle (a Foch for the French, a
Nelson for the English, a Montrose for the Scots) disagrees with the
label there must be something wrong with the bottle, never with the
label.

The label of 'cautious' on the Scotch bottle, the legend that the Scot
can never be induced to put it to the touch to 'win or lose it all,' that he
abhors the notion of 'all or nothing' has been so often and so patently
refuted in history, legend and literature that there is no point in citing
examples here. There is, however, one illustration to the purpose.

The well-known and international saying about throwing away the
scabbard after drawing the sword in a perilous venture is much approved
of in Scotland. 'Gentlemen, I have thrown away the scabbard,' is such
a favourite remark with us that you would think we had invented it.
Indeed, so much is this exhortation to 'all or nothing' a delight in
Scottish ears that it has been adapted to convivial use. Even in these
degenerate days you may in Scotland sit down to an evening's social
pleasure with us, and, before the business of the night begins, you may

see your host slowly draw the stopper from a large flagon, slowly look at it and then hurl it into the fire saying: 'Gentlemen, I have thrown away the cork.'

Montgomerie would have been all for throwing away the cork. But, being the learned, amusing, fanciful as well as poetic and passionate fellow he was he would have lingered over and decorated his gesture with a hundred different sleights of hand and verbal tricks.

With a long, strong, slow, loving pull culminating and exploding in a popularly applauded pop he would have drawn it from the flagon-neck. He would then have gazed at it in mock surprise, tossed it into the air, caught it behind his back, flicked it with his finger and thumb up his sleeve, transferred it with a thrust of his elbow and a wriggle of his shoulder-blades, while it was still underneath his coat, to the other sleeve, have shaken it out again and have pretended, while producing many reasons for doing so, to put it back into the flagon before a drop had been drunk. Then, and only then, and with a gesture combining beauty, abandon and nobility would he have hurled it to sizzle in the flames.

At least that, from a reading of *The Cherry and the Slae*, is what one believes he would have done. To complete the parallel one might point out that the applause that would greet the delicious drawing of the cork from the flagon-neck and the pleasing pop therefrom corresponds to the praise that has been lavished on the opening poetical seven stanzas of the work (see reference above). Moreover, amongst the assembled company at the flagon-opening exploit there would inevitably be a number of earnest, thirsty and pedantic drinkers. These would be as bored by the skilful prestidigitation and patter of the performance as are the usual run of critics by the verbal complications of Montgomerie's delightful prolongation of his argument. They would be so bored that they would fail to applaud the final gesture of the throwing of the cork into the flames.

Just so, the critics have failed to praise the nobility of our poet's concluding stanzas in which, with full-throated Scots vigour, he thanks God for having rewarded the belief in 'all or nothing' or in 'Gentlemen, I have thrown away the scabbard,' or 'the cork' or what you will. But we must get on. The mere reading of *The Cherry and the Slae* has provoked a digression less felicitous than his.

The allegory on the theme of 'all or nothing' in *The Cherry and the Slae* is contained in this story.

A youth finds himself by a river bank obviously somewhere in Scotland. Here he encounters Cupid at his sport of flying about in the air and shooting arrows, wantonly. Cupid persuades the youth to 'take a lane,' as we would say in modern Scots parlance, of his gear and 'try a shot' at flying about and shooting arrows. Alas! as others before him who have taken a lane of the gods, the youth suffers a bad toss. Heedless of the example of Icarus he flies too high and falls—having already clumsily wounded himself with one of the little god's arrows. Upon the youth's fall and wounding Cupid flies away and deserts him.

Fainting, the youth now approaches the river bank where he sees high up on a crag over the torrent a cherry-tree laden with fruit. More humbly by its base there is situate a bush of slaes, or bitter sloe-berries. The stricken youth, convinced that only the tasting of pure fruit will relieve his sickness and pain, tries to climb to the cherries, but fails owing to the terrifying steepness of the crag. Is he to put up, then, with very inferior bitter but available slaes or shall he summon up courage to attain the excellence of the high-hung cherries?

To him there now appear various counsellors who conduct a debate on the great question. At first they debate directly with him. Dread, Danger and Despair (note the Scottish love of alliteration) implore him not to be so foolish as to aspire to what they believe to be the dangerously remote cherry. After all, will not the slae, lying close at hand, 'satisfie to slocken'? But such satisfaction is not to the poetic young man's liking. Courage and Hope, of course, are all for his trying for the cherry and are so eloquent that the opponents retire shrugging their shoulders at his folly.

But senior advocates (Queen's Counsel as it were) in the form of Wisdom and Experience and Reason now enter and make it clear that the youth must not allow himself to be swayed by either side until he has really examined the position fairly in the light of what his advisers have to say. The slae-supporters then return and the debate continues. After a bit it continues amongst the counsel themselves and now about the youth himself. The question is how to make a man of him. This too will be referred to in the annotation of the poem. It is an important point.

We are now about two-thirds of the way through the work. The debate now until near the end swings to and fro illustrating Mont-gomerie's lively acquaintance with Scottish committee manners. At length it is agreed that the cherries are ultimately desirable and must be pursued. But how best to pursue them? Here again the curse of committee-rule raises its head in the most amusing manner. The problem is at last resolved by the decision to choose a leader of the expedition. That leader is Wisdom; under his guidance they all lead and escort their young friend and client to his cherry-laden goal.

And now an unexpected thing happens. The high and hitherto inaccessible tree, as if in reward for this display of well-planned courage (note well-planned) bursts into miraculous ripeness and drops its fruit into the young man's mouth who, at once, finds himself relieved of his fever and pain. The poem ends in a Psalm-like paean of praise to God.

The Cherry and the Slae is in our opinion a straightforward allegorical poem on the theme of courage supported by reason. The introduction of the Cupid episode at the beginning has led some commentators into the belief that it is an allegory on love based on Montgomerie's own experience. Should he, with his poet's eye fixed above him, and with the excuse of good blood in his veins, aspire to the refined delights that might be enjoyed in the love and possession of a high-born but difficult lady—the cherry? Or should he 'satisfie' himself 'to slocken' with the slae, and content himself like many other humbler and less accomplished voluptuaries before him with the rough-and-tumble pleasures of a douce and docile country wench in the hay ?

We do not agree with this reading. Nor do we agree with Mrs. H. M. Shire's clever (rather too clever) notion that Montgomerie began the work as a love allegory and then converted it into a poetical political pamphlet aimed at James VI. The idea being that the slae is the Crown of Scotland, and that the United Crowns of England and Scotland is the difficult cherry towards which His Majesty should courageously aspire.

No, the poem is surely neither amorous nor political in purpose. It is a piece of abstract Scottish wisdom cast into the form of Renaissance Scots verse, and as such it is presented here.

We present it divided into three parts and introduced and annotated.

THE CHERRY AND THE SLAE

The Debate in Progress

The Cherry and the Slae consists of 114 stanzas. We begin about a third of the way through and proceed with various minor omissions and larger divisions to allow of annotation. This, perhaps, is the place to say something about Montgomerie's stanza.

It may or may not have been Montgomerie's own invention, but he was certainly the first to use it well; and, as we have said, it was often imitated by Scots poets after him, but only once successfully and by Burns. It contains fourteen lines of varying length and complicated metre involving two turns in each stanza and internal rhymes in the last short lines. Some people have found this too light and artificial a form for a long poem containing debate. There can, indeed, be no doubt that occasionally the artificiality of the poet's inverted form weighs upon the invention of his spirit, but only occasionally.

One way to free him from this weight is to read him aloud. I am aware that I have made this recommendation before and with other Scottish poets, but I do not apologise for repeating it; indeed I shall repeat it in my notes once more before *The Cherry and the Slae* is ended. If you read some of the stanzas aloud you will *hear* how delightfully the poet rings the changes. And, when they come off, you will hear how effective for emphasis are the internal rhymes that tie the stanzas up. You will perceive also how the bob-lines at the end of the arguments give a lively and realistic swing to the arguments themselves.

Reading aloud too will, I hope, draw your attention to the pleasing effect of the alliteration. Alliteration is a long-founded and still continuing tradition in our verse by which (in Gaelic as well as in Scots, by the way) we achieve what is to us a musical appeal. Like rhyme it can, in unskilful hands, become laboured and affected. Like rhyme, properly and easily used, it can add life to the verse.

If you read Montgomerie's alliterations aloud to yourself you will find that nearly always they are natural and unforced and help to make the metrical pattern of the poem.

Another quality in Montgomerie's poem often missed by the critics which may be discovered by the reader who reads aloud is the excellent characterisation of the various disputants. The conversational springy rhythm of the stanzas brings this out. Note, by the way, how these characters amusingly (to us but not to themselves) rely on proverbs, wise-saws and the like to enforce their arguments. Sancho Panza and Polonius were both adept at this sort of thing. No one has suggested that these two characters are dull; neither are the counsellors in *The Cherry and the Slae*. We begin with the stanza in which Danger is ending an argument and is answered by Hope.

'Bot yet to mind the proverb call,
"Quha usis perillis perisch sall,"
   Schort quhile thair life them lastis.'
'And *I* haiff hard,' quod HOPE, 'that he
Sall never schape to sail the sea
   That for all perillis *a*castis.   *a*casts
Hu mony throucht despair are *a*deid,   *a*dead
   That never perillis *a*preiffit!   *a*tried
Hu mony also, *a*gif thou reid,   *a*if
   Of lifis we have releiffit—
     *a*Quha being e'en *b*deing,   *a*who *b*dying
       *a*But danger and despair   *a*without
     Ane hunder, I wonder—
       Bot thou hes *a*hard declair.   *a*heard

'*a*Gif we twa *b*hald not up thy *c*hairt,   *a*if *b*hold *c*heart
 *a*Quhilk is the cheif and noblest pairt, *a*which
   Thy wark wald not gang weill:
Considering thae companions can
Persuade ane silly semple man,
   To haizart for his *a*heill: *a*health
Suppose thay haiff *a*dissaiffit sum,   *a*taken in
 *a*Or thay and we micht *b*meit,   *a*before *b*meet
Thay get na credit quhair we cum,
   In ony man of *a*spreit: *a*spirit
     *a*Be reasoun, thair treasoun,   *a*by
       *a*Be us is first espyit,   *a*by
     Reveiling thair *a*deilling,   *a*dealing
       *a*Quhilk dow not be denyit. . . .   *a*which cannot

'Quhat ^agif Melancholie cum in,	^aif

'Quhat *a*gif Melancholie cum in,   *a*if
And get ane grip *a*or thou begin,   *a*before
   *a*Than is thy laubour lost: *a*then
For he will *a*hald thee hard and fast,   *a*hold
Till time and place and fruit be past,
   Till thou give up the ghost:
Than sall be graven on the stane
   That on thy *a*graiff is laid: *a*grave
"Sum-time thair *a*levit *b*sic a ane"—   *a*lived *b*such
   Bot here sall it be said:
   "Here lyis nou but price nou,
      *a*Into dishonourit bed: *a*in
   Ane cowart, as thou art,
      That from his fortune fled."

'Imagine, man, *a*gif thou were laid   *a*if
In graiff and syne micht *a*heir this said,   *a*hear
   Wald thou nocht *a*sweit for schame?   *a*sweat
Yes, faith, I doubt not bot thou wald:
Thairfore, gif thou hes *a*eyis, behald,   *a*eyes
   Quhou thay wald *a*smore thy fame: *a*smother
Go to, and mak na mair excuse,
   Nou life or honour loss:
And *a*outher them or us refuse,   *a*either
   Thair is na uther *a*choce: *a*choice
   Consider togider
      That we can never dwell:
   At lenth ay, at strength ay,
      Thae pultronis we expell!'

The Debate continues

The debate continues with Danger and the pro-slae counsellors going off in a shoulder-shrugging huff. Enter the seniors in the form of Experience, Reason and Wit and still also called Wisdom; the word is significant and appropriate to our purpose. These seniors say that for a true decision all counsellors must be recalled. After some bickering (some of it omitted here) the debate takes a new departure.

The counsellors now all talk amongst themselves *about* the young man. The question is not so much the desirability of the cherry, the suitability of the second-rate slae and so on, but quite simply what is the best way to make a true full man of the youth who faces his dilemma. The consideration of this debate is important in our contention that the poem is more than a merely personal love allegory. It is an expression of a point of view of wisdom; the same point of view (already referred to) expressed in the recent stage presentation of Lyndesay's *The Thrie Estaits*.

It might just be possible for supporters of Mrs. Shire's ingenious theory that the poem was eventually addressed to James VI to say that this passage supports their theory. They might say that in urging James VI to aspire to the cherry of the throne of the United Kingdom Montgomerie was urging him to the making of his manhood. But we think this far-fetched.

We cannot, however, resist this comment. If Montgomerie's purpose was to make a man of James by sending him down to London it singularly failed when the King did eventually go there. If the London gossip of what went on at the Court of James I of England be even approximately true the last thing that happened to James was that he was made a man of there; rather the reverse. His dallyings with 'Steenie' Buckingham and other favourites were hardly the sort of thing that Mother Scotia of *The Complaint* would have approved of in any of her brood, least of all in a prince; indeed it may be doubted whether the good lady had ever heard of such 'carryings-on.' None of her sons had been to a 'good public school.'

James's unfortunate temperament may have been native to him in harsh and hilly Edinburgh, but it flowered in him in the city of the plain by the banks of the Thames. Whatever else it did, the cherry of London did not act as a masculating influence upon him 'when Royal James obtained the crown' of the United Kingdom.

Quod DANGER, '*a*Sen I understand   *a*since
That counsel can be na command,
    I haiff na mair to say:
Except *a*gif that thou think it gude,   *a*if
Take counsel yit *a*or ye conclude,   *a*before
    Of wyser men nor thay:
They are bot rackless, young, and rasch,
    Suppose ye think us *a*fleid: *a*frightened
*a*Gif of our fallowschip you *b*fasch,   *a*if *b*trouble
    Gang with thame, hardly *a*beid: *a*be it[1]
    God speid you, thay *a*leid you   *a*lead
    That hes not meikle wit:
    Expell us, and tell us
    Heirefter comes not yit.'

[1] i.e., 'and good luck to you!'

Quhile DANGER and DESPAIR reteirit,
EXPERIENCE came in and ^aspeirit, ^aasked
 Quhat all the matter ^ameinit: ^ameant
With him came RESSOUN, WIT, and
 SKILL,
And thay began to speir at WILL,
 'Quhair mak ye to, my freind?'
'To pluck yon lusty CHERRY, lo!'
 Quod he, 'and nocht the SLAE!'
Quod thay, 'Is thair na mair ado,
 Or ye win up the brae?
  Bot to it, and do it,
   Perforce the fruit to pluck?
  Weill, brother, some uther
   Wer ^ameiter to conduck.' ^afitter

'I grant ye *may* be gude aneuch,
Bot yit the hazard of yon ^aheuch ^acliff
 Requiris ane graver guide:
Als wyis as ye are *may* gang wrang;
Thairfore tak counsel ^aor ye gang, ^abefore
 Of sum that standis beside.
Bot quhilk wer yon three ye forbade
 Your company richt nou?'
Quod WILL, 'Three preichouris, to
 persuade
  The poisonit SLAE to ^apou: ^apull
   They ^atrattlit and rattlit ^atattled
   A lang half-hour and mair:
  Foul ^afall thame! they call thame ^abefall
   DREID, DANGER and DESPAIR.

'Thay are mair ^afaschious nor of ^bfeck, ^atroublesome ^bvalu
Yon ^afaizardis durst not for thair neck ^adastards
 Climb up the craig with us.
Fra we determinit to die,
Or else to climb yon CHERRIE tree,
 Thay ^abade about the ^bbuss ^alingered ^bbush

Thay are conditionate like the cat—
  They wald not ^aweit their feit: ^awet
Bot yit, gif of the fruit we gat,
  Thay wald be fain to ^aeit!   ^aeat
    Thocht thay, nou, I say, nou,
      To hazard hes na hairt:
      Yit luck we, and pluck we
        The fruit, *they* wald have pairt!

'Bot fra we get our voyage wun,
  Thay sall nocht ^athan the CHERRY ^bcun, ^athen ^btaste
  That wald not enterprise.'
'Weill,' quod EXPERIENCE, 'ye boast;
Bot he that countis without his ^aost,   ^ahost
  Oft-times he countis twice.
Ye sell the bear-skin on his back,
  Bot ^abide ^bquhill ye it get: ^await ^btill
Quhen ye haiff done it is time to ^acrack; ^atalk, brag
  Ye fisch before the net.
    Quhat haste, ^aschir, ye taste, ^aschir, ^asir
      The CHERRY or ye ^apow it   ^apull
      Be-war yit, ye are yit
        Mair talkative ^anor ^btrowit!' ^athan ^bbelieved

'Call DANGER back again,' quod SKILL,
'To see quhat he can say to WILL,
  We see him schod sa strait!'
'We may nocht trow quhat ^ailk ane tellis,' ^aeach
Quod COURAGE. 'We concludit ^aellis,   ^aelse
  He servis not for our mate!
For I can tell you all ^aperqueir,   ^a*par cœur*
  His counsel ^aand ye will.'   ^aif
Quod WILL,'Quhairto suld he cum here?
  He can not hald him still.
    He speikis ay, and seikis ay
      Delay of time ^abe driftis: ^aby tricks
    He greivis us and ^adeivis us   ^adeafens
      With sophistry and schiftis.'

K

Quod RESSOUN, 'Quhy was he debard?
The tale is ill ^amay not be ^bhard,   ^a(that) may ^bheard
  Yit let us ^aheir him ^banis.'   ^ahear ^bonce
Than DANGER to declair began
Quhou HOPE and COURAGE tuik the
  man,
  And led him ^aall thair lanis: ^aall on their own
For they wald haiff him up the hill,
  ^aBot ^bouther stop or stay: ^awithout ^beither
And quha was welcomer ^anor WILL?   ^athan
  He wald be foremaist ay.
    He culd do, and suld do,
      Quha-ever wald, nor nocht:
    Sic speiding, proceiding,
      Unlikely was, I thocht. . . .

Quod SKILL, 'Quhat, wald we langer
  strive?
Far better late than never thrive:
  Cum, lat us help him yit.
^aTint time we may not get again,   ^alost
We waste bot present time in vain.'
  'Be-war with that,' quod WIT.
'Speik on, EXPERIENCE, lat see!
  We think *you* hold you dumb,'
'Of bygones I haiff hard,' quod he,
  'I knaw not thingis to cum.'
    Quod RESSOUN, 'The sessoun,
      With ^asleuthing, slides away: ^adelay
    First tak him, and mak him
      A man, if that you may!'

Quod WILL, '^aGif he be not a man,   ^aif
I pray you, schirs, quhat is he, than?
  He luikis like ane, at leist!'
Quod RESSOUN, 'Gif he follow thee,
And mind not to remain with me,
  Nocht but a brutal beist!

A man in shape dois nocht consist,
  For all your taunting ^ataillis.   ^atales
Thairfore, Schir WILL, I wald ye ^awist,   ^aknewest
  Your metaphysic faillis.
    Go leir, yet, a yeir, yet,
      Your logic at the sculis:
    Some day, than, ye may, than,
      Pass ^aMaister with the mulis.'   ^ai.e. *of Arts*

Quod WILL, 'I mervel quhat ye mein,
Suld I nocht trow mine awin twa een,
  For all your logic sculis?
Gif I did not, I wer not wyis!'
Quod RESSOUN, 'I haiff tauld you thrice
  Nane ^aferlyis mair ^bnor fulis.   ^awonders ^bthan
Thair are mair sensis nor the sicht,
  Quhilk ye owerhail for haste.
To wit, if ye remember richt,
  Smell, heiring, touch, and taste.
    All quick things have sic things,
      I mein baith man and beist,
    ^aBe kind ay we find ay   ^aby
      Few lackis thame, at the leist.

So, by that consequence of thine,
Or syllogism said like a swine,
  A cow may leirn thee ^alear.   ^alearning
Thou usis only but the ^aeyis: ^aeyes
Scho touchis, tastis, smellis, heiris, and
    seeis,
  Which matchis thee, and mair.
But sen na triumph ye intend,
  As presently appeiris,
Schir, for your clergy to be ^akend,   ^aknown
  Tak ye twa assis eiris;
    No mitre ^aperfyter   ^amore perfect
      Gat Midas for his ^ameid: ^aportion
    That hude, schir, is gude, schir,
      To ^ahap your brain-seik ^bheid.   ^awrap ^bhead

'Ye haiff na ^afeill for to define,   ^aunderstanding
Thoucht ye haiff cunning to decline,
   A man to be a mule:
With little wirk, yet ye may ^avou 'd   ^aavow it
To grow a gallant horse and gude,
   To ride thairon at Yule;
Bot to our ground when we began,
   For all your gustless jestis,
I maun be maister of the man,
   But thou to brutal beistis:
     So we twa maun be twa,
       To cause baith kindis be knawin:
     Keep mine, ^athan, fra thine, ^athan,   ^athen
     And ilk ane use thair ^aawin.'   ^aown

Than WILL as angry as an ape,
Ran rampand, ^asweirand, rude and   ^aswearing
   ^arape,   ^aquickly
   Saw he nane uther schift.
He wald nocht want ane inch his will,
E'en quhither it did him gude or ill,
   For ^athretty of his thrift.   ^athirty
He wald be foremaist in the feild,
   And maister, if he micht:
Yea, he suld rather die than yeild,
   ^aThoucht RESSOUN had the richt.   ^athough
     'Sall he, nou, mak me, nou,
       His subjeck or his sclaiff?
     No, rather, my father
     Sall quick go to the graiff!

'I ^aheicht him, ^bquhill mine hairt is   ^apromised ^btill
   ^ahaill,   ^awhole
To perisch first, ^aor he prevail,   ^abefore
   Cum efter quhat so may.'
Quod RESSOUN, 'Doubt ye not, indeed,
Ye hit the nail upon the heid,
   It sall be as ye say.

> Suppose ye spur for to aspire,
>   Your bridle wants a bit;
> That ^amear may leive you in the mire,   ^amare
>   As ^asiccar as ye sit.   ^asure
>   Your sentence, repentance,
>   Sall leir you, I belieff,
>   And anger you langer,
>   Quhan ye that practic ^aprieff.   ^atry
>
> 'As ye haiff ^adytit your ^bdecreit,   ^acomposed ^bdecree
> Your prophecy to be complete,
> Perhaps, and to your painis,
> It hes been said, and may be so,
> A wilful man wants never wo,
>   ^aThoucht he gettis little gainis.   ^athough
> Bot ^asen ye think it an easy thing,   ^asince
>   To mount abuve the Mune,
> Of your awin fiddle tak a ^aspring,   ^atune
>   And dance when ye have done.
>   If than, schir, the man, schir,
>   Like of your mirth, he may:
>   And ^aspeir first, and ^bheir first,   ^aask ^bhear
>   Quhat he himself will say.'

The Debate is ended

We now come to the last and longest extract from the poem printed
here. It leads, after a few omissions, to the end of the whole allegory.

In the part omitted before this final extract the counsellors all turn
to the youth and urge him to accept their ordered findings under the
chairmanship of Reason. The young man gratefully agrees.

As will be seen below, Reason assumes the chair and the debate
continues. Even now when some form of order has been agreed upon
it is amusing to see how many red herrings the ingenious members of
committee can draw across the path of the deliberations. How well
Montgomerie understood the insufferable committee-mindedness of
certain Scots. Whisky has by some been thought to be the Curse of
Scotland. Others have believed that it is the Nine of Diamonds. It is
more likely to be committees. Montgomerie might have agreed.

Passing over various other points that arise we now come to an
important climax in the allegory. It is eventually agreed that only the
cherry can cure the young man's deep sickness. This sickness came
about by his fall, and it was only as a result of this fall that he was

granted the vision of the cherry. Is not this vision of perfection a heritage from an earlier Scottish tradition, an earlier and anonymous Scottish poet? Is it not the vision, in another form, that which Thomas the Rhymer beheld?

But how is he to attain to it? There must be a leader of the expedition who shall conduct this youth on his dangerous quest. It is significant, it is apt for our purpose that they choose WISDOM. Once again we pause to reflect that the committee-minded Scots are not usually so happy in their decisions. They don't like choosing leaders, and if they do they often (just because they are unaccustomed to choosing) choose the wrong one. Scotsmen always respond to a great leader. How seldom do they find one!

And so, under the leadership of WISDOM, the expedition proceeds to its happy and successful ending. As has been already said the youth's well-supported courage leads to the cherry-tree bending to discharge its ripe, curative and glorious fruit into his very mouth. This is where the poem rises to great heights in the praise of God. That praise begins in the modulation of the rhythm at the sixth line of the second last stanza: 'God bless'd our interprise.' Thereafter it proceeds in the afore-mentioned Psalm-like manner to the end.

This is the last time that I shall adjure any reader to read aloud, but it is irresistible. All Scots and surely many English are familiar with the solemn yet inspiring measure of our metrical version of the Psalms of David when sung or spoken aloud with force and meaning. That metrical version, so beloved of, so deep a source of inspiration to the Covenanters, was yet to come.

Here, and in an allegorical poem by Alexander Montgomerie (certainly no Covenanter), is that unmistakable measure sounding out from nearly four hundred years ago.

EXPERIENCE then ᵃsmirkling smilit,	ᵃsmirking
'We are na bairnis to be beguilit,'	
Quod he, and schuik his ᵃheid:	ᵃhead
'For authouris quha allegis us,	
They may not ga about the buss,	
For all thair ᵃdeidly feid:	ᵃdeadly feud
For we are equal for you all,	
Na persounis we respeck.	
We haiff been sa, are yit, and sall	
Be ᵃfand sa in effeck.	ᵃfound
If we wer as ye wer,	
We had come unrequirit:	
But we, nou, ye see, nou,	
Do nathing undesirit.	

'There is a sentence said by sum,
"Let nane uncallit to counsel cum,
   That welcome *a*weinis to be."   *a*thinks
Yea, I haiff hard ane uther yit,
"Quha cum uncallit, unservit suld
   sit"—
   Perhaps, schir, sa may ye.'
'Gudeman, *grande merci* for your
   *a*geck!'   *a*taunt
Quod HOPE, and lawly *a*loutis;   *a*bows
'*a*Gif ye wer sent for, we suspeck,   *a*whether
   Because the doctours doubtis.
      Your yeiris, nou, appeiris, nou,
         With wisdom to be vext.
      Rejoicing in glosing
         Till you have *a*tint your text.   *a*lost

'Quhair ye wer sent for, lat us see
Quha wald be welcomer nor we.
   Pruve that, and we are payit.'
'Weill,' quod EXPERIENCE, 'be-war,
You knaw nocht in quhat case ye are,
   Your tongue has you betrayit.
The man may *a*aiblins *b*tyne a *c*stot,   *a*perhaps *b*lose *c*ox
   That can not count his *a*kinch;   *a*kine
In your *a*awin bow ye are *b*owreschot,   *a*own *b*overshot
   *a*Be mair *b*nor half an inch.   *a*by *b*than
      Quha wat, schir, gif that, schir,
         Is sour quhilk seemis sweit?
      I *a*feir, nou, ye *b*heir, nou,   *a*fear *b*hear
         A dangerous *a*decreit. . . .   *a*decree

'Confront him further face for face,
Gif yit he rues his rackless race,
   Perhaps and ye shall *a*heir.   *a*hear
For ay since Adam and since Eiff,
*a*Quhilks first thy *b*leisingis did beleiff,   *a*who (pl.) *b*lyings
   I *a*sauld thy doctrine deir.   *a*sold

Quhat has been done, e'en to this day,
   I keip in mind almaist;
Ye promise further than ye pay,
   Schir HOPE, for all your haste.
     Promitting unwitting,
       Your *a*hechtis ye never *b*huikit,   *a*promises *b*regarded
     I schaw you I knaw you,
       Your bygones I haiff *a*buikit.   *a*booked

'I wald, in case ane count were *a*craiffit,   *a*craved
*a*Schaw thousand thousands thou *b*dissaiffit,   *a*show *b*deceived
   Quhair thou was true to ane;
And, by the contrair, I may vant—
*a*Quhilk thou *b*maun (thocht it greive thee)   *a*which *b*must
   grant—
   I *a*trumpit never a man.   *a*deceived
Bot truly tauld the nakit truth,
   To men that *a*mellit with me,   *a*meddled
For *a*nouther rigour, nor for ruth,   *a*neither
   But only *a*laith to *b*lie.   *a*loath *b*pron. lee
     To sum yit to cum yit
       Thy succour shall be slicht:
     Quhilk I, than, maun try, than,
       And register it richt.'

'Ha, ha!' quod HOPE, and loudly *a*leuch,   *a*laughed
'Ye're bot a prentice at the *a*pleuch,   *a*plough
   EXPERIENCE ye *a*preiff,   *a*test, try
Suppose all bygones as ye spak,
Ye are na prophet worth a *a*plack—   *a*$\frac{1}{3}$d.
   Nor I bound to beleiff:
Ye suld nocht say, schir, *a*quhill ye see—   *a*till
   Bot, quhen ye see it, say.'
'Yit,' quod EXPERIENCE, 'at thee
   Mak many *a*mintis I may,   *a*threatening gestures
     *a*Be singis, nou, and thingis, nou,   *a*by signs
      *a*Quhilk ay before me *b*beiris,   *a*(I) who *b*bear
     Expressing, by guessing,
       The peril that appeiris.

Than HOPE replyit, and that with pith,
And wyisly ^aweyit his wordis thairwith,   ^aweighed
  Sententiously and schort;
Quod he, 'I am the anchor-grip,
That ^asaiffis the sailoris and thair schip,   ^asaves
  From peril, to thair port.'
Quod he,[1] 'Oft-times that anchor ^adrivis,   ^adrags
  As we haiff ^afand before,   ^afound
And losses mony thousand livis,
  ^aBe schipwrack on the schore.   ^aby
    Your grippis, oft, bot slippis, oft,
    Quhen men haiff maist to do,
    ^aSyne ^bleivis thame, and ^creivis thame,   ^athen ^bleave ^cdeprive
    Of thy companions too.

'Thou leivis thame nocht thysel ^aalane,   ^aalone, only
Bot to their greiff, quhen thou art gane,
  ^aGars COURAGE quit them ^bals.'   ^adost cause . . . to ^balso
Quod HOPE, 'I wald ye understude,
I grip fast gif the ground be gude,
  And ^afleitis quhair it is false;   ^a(I) shift
Thair suld na ^afalt with me be found,   ^afault (pron. faut)
  Nor I accusit at all;
^aWyte ^bsic as suld have ^csoun't the ground,   ^ablame ^bsuch ^csounded
  Before the anchor fall:
    Thair ^aleid ay at ^bneid ay   ^alead ^bneed
    Micht warn thame, gif they wald,
    Gif thay ^athair wald stay ^athair   ^athere
    Or have gude anchor ^ahald.   ^ahold

^aGif ye ^breid richt, it was nocht I,   ^aif ^bread
Bot only Ignorance, quhairby
  Thair ^acarvellis all were cloven;   ^asmall vessels
I am not for a ^atrumpour ^btane.'   ^adeceiver ^btaken
'All,' quod EXPERIENCE, 'is ane;
  'I haiff my process proven—

---

[1] EXPERIENCE

To wit, that we wer callit ^ailk ane   ^aeach
  To cum, before we came:
That nou objectioun ye haiff nane,
  Yoursel may say the same.
    Ye are, nou, too far, nou,
      Come fordwart for to flee:
    ^aPersaiff, than, ye haiff, than,   ^aperceive
      The werst end of the tree.'

Quhen HOPE was gallit ^ainto the quick,   ^ain
Quod COURAGE, kickand at the prick,
  'We ^alat you will to wit: ^alet
Mak he you welcomer ^anor we,   ^athan
Than "Bygones, bygones," fare weill he,
  Except he seik us yit.
He understandis his ^aawin estait,   ^aown
  Lat him his cheiftainis chuse,
Bot yit his battle will be ^ablate,   ^ahalf-hearted
  Gif he our force refuse.
    Refuse us, or chuse us,
      Our counsel is, he clim':
    But stay he, or stray he,
      We have na help for him!

'Except the CHERRY be his ^achose,   ^achoice
Be ye his freinds, we are his foes,
  His doingis we despite.
Gif we ^apersaiff him ^bsattlit sa   ^aperceive ^bsettled
To satisfie him with the SLAE,
  His company we quite.'
Than DREID and DANGER grew so glaid,
  And ^aweinit that thay had wun,   ^aassumed
Thay ^athoct all ^bseillit that thay had said   ^athought ^bsealed
^aSen they had first begun.   ^asince
    Thay thocht, than, thay ^amocht, then,   ^amight
      Without a pairty ^apleid: ^aplead
    Bot yit, thair, with WIT, thair,
      Thay wer ^adung doun indeed.   ^aknocked

'Schirs, DREID and DANGER,' ^athan quod WIT,[1]   ^athen
Ye did yoursellis to me submit—
   EXPERIENCE can pruve.'
'That,' quod EXPERIENCE, 'I passt:
Thair awin confessioun made thame fast,
   Thay may na mair remuve.
For gif I richt remember me,
   This maxim ^athan thay made—   ^athen
To wit, the man with WIT suld ^awey   ^aweigh
   Quhat philosophis haiff said.
     Quhill sentence repentance
      Forbade him deir to buy:
     Thay knew, than, hou true, than,
      And pressit nocht to reply.'

^aThocht he ^bdang DREID and DANGER dumb[2]   ^athough ^bknocked
Yet COURAGE could not he owercum,
   HOPE ^ahecht him sic ane hire: ^apromised
He ^athocht himsel, ^bhou sune he saw   ^athought ^bas soon as
His enemyis wer laid sa law,
   It was na time to tire.
He hit the iron quhile it wes ^ahait,   ^ahot
   In case it suld grow cauld;
For he esteimit his foes defait,
   Quhen ^aanis he ^bfand thame ^cfauld.   ^aonce ^bfound ^cyield
     'Thocht we, nou,' quod he, nou,
      'Have been sa free and frank,
     Unsocht, yit, ye ^amocht, yit,   ^amight
      For kindness ^acund us thank. . . .   ^ahave felt grateful
                                           to us

'Quhen ye have done sum douchty deedis,
^aSyne ye suld see hou all succeidis,   ^athen
   To write thame as they wer.'
'Freind, ^ahuly! haste nocht half sa fast,   ^agently
Leist,' quod EXPERIENCE, 'at last
   Ye buy my doctrine deir!

---

[1] WIT seems, in what follows, to be the same as WISDOM: but this is not absolutely certain.
[2] The text reads 'down': 'dumb' is only a guess, but at least it makes sense, and rhymes, too.

HOPE puttis that haste into your [a]heid,   [a]head
  Quhilk [a]bylis your barmy brain;   [a]boils
Hou-be-it [a]fulis haste cummis huly speid,   [a]fools'
  Fair [a]hechtis makis fulis be fain.   [a]promises
    [a]Sic smiling, beguiling,   [a]such
      Biddis [a]feir nocht for na [b]freitis: [a]fear [b]omens
    Yit I, nou, deny, nou,
      That all is gold that [a]gleitis. . . .   [a]glitters

'Yit,' quod EXPERIENCE, 'quhat [a]than?   [a]then
Quha may be meitest for the man,
  Lat us *his* answer haiff.'
Quhen thay submittit thame to me,
To RESSOUN I was fain to flee,
  His counsel for to craiff.
Quod he, '[a]Sen you yoursellis submit   [a]since
  To do as I [a]decreit,   [a]decree
I sall advise with SKILL and WIT,
  Quhat thay think may be meit.
    Thay cried, than, we bide, than,
      'At RESSOUN for refuge:
    Allow him, and [a]trow him,   [a]believe, trust
      As governour and judge!' . . .

Than RESSOUN [a]rase with gesture grave   [a]rose
[a]Belyve convening all the [b]lave   [a]promptly [b]rest
  To see quhat thay wald say;
With silver sceptre in his hand,
As cheiftain chosen to command,
  And thay bent to obey.
He pausit lang before he spak,
  And in a study stude:
[a]Syne he began and silence brak—   [a]then
  'Come on,' quod he, 'conclude,
    Quhat way, nou, we may, nou,
      Yon CHERRY cum to catch:
    Speik out, schirs, about, schirs—
      Haiff done—lat us dispatch!

Quod COURAGE, 'Scourge him first that
   ^ascarris   ^ascares
Much musing memory bot marris:
   I tell you mine intent.'
Quod WIT, 'Quha will not pairtly ^apance,   ^athink
In perillis perischis perchance;
   ^aOwre-rackless may repent.'   ^aover, too
Than quod EXPERIENCE and spak,
   'Schir, I have seen thame baith,
In ^abairnliness and lye-aback,   ^ainfantility
   ^aEschaip and cum to ^bskaith.   ^aescape ^bharm
       Bot quhat, nou, of that, nou?
      ^aSturt followis all extreimis: ^atrouble
     Retain, than, the ^amein, than,   ^amean
       The surest way *it* seemis.

'Quhair sum hes furtherit, sum hes failit;
Quhair pairt hes perischit, pairt prevailit:
   Alike all can not luck.
Than either venture with the ane,
Or with the tither lat alane,
   The CHERRIE for to pluck.'
Quod HOPE, 'For ^afeir folk must not   ^afear
   ^afasch.'   ^aworry
   Quod DANGER, 'Lat not licht.'
Quod WIT, 'Be ^anouther rude nor rasch,   ^aneither
   Quod RESSOUN, 'Ye have richt.'
       The rest, than, ^athocht best, than,   ^athought
        Quhen RESSOUN said it sa,
      That roundly and soundly
       They suld togidder ga,

To get the CHERRY in all haste,
As for my safety servand maist,
   ^aThocht DREID and DANGER feirit   ^athough
The peril of that irksome way,
Leist that thairby I suld dechay,
   That than sa ^awaik appeirit;   ^aweak

Yit HOPE and COURAGE hard beside,
  ^aQuhilks with thame wald contend,   ^awho (pl.)
Did tak in hand us for to guide,
  Unto our journeyis end;
    Impledging, and waging,
      Baith twa their livis for mine:
    Providing the guiding
      To thame wer grantit syne.

Than DREID and DANGER did appeill,
Alleging it could nocht be weill,
  Nor yit wald thay agree,
But said thay suld sound thair retreit,
Because thay thocht thame na wise ^ameit   ^asuitable
  Conductoris unto me,
Nor to na man in mine estait,
  With ^aseikness sair oppresst,   ^asickness
For thay tuik ay the neirest ^agate,   ^aroad
  Omitting oft the best:
    'Thair neirest ^aperqueirest   ^adearest in heart
      Is alwayis to thame baith:
    Quhair thay, schir, may say, schir,
      "Quhat recks thame of your skaith?"

'Bot as for us twa, nou we sweir,
^aBe him before quhom we appeir,   ^aby
  Our full intent is nou
To have you ^ahaill, and alwayis was,   ^awhole, cured
That purpose for to bring to pass;
  So is nocht thairis, I trow.'
Than HOPE and COURAGE did ^aattest   ^acall to witness
  The goddis of baith ^athir pairtis   ^athese (?) parties
Gif thay wrocht nocht all for the best
  Of me, with upricht hairtis.
    Our cheiftain, than, liftan'
      His sceptre, did enjoin:
    'Na mair, thair, uprair, thair!'
      And sa thair strife was done.

Rebuikand DREID and DANGER ^asair   ^asore
^aSuppose they meinit weill evermair   ^aeven though
  To me, as thay had sworn:
Because thair nichbouris thay abusit,
In so far as thay had accusit
  Thame, as ye hard beforn.
'Did ye nocht ^aellis,' quod he, 'consent   ^aelse
  The CHERRY for to ^apou?'   ^apull
Quod DANGER, 'We are weill content:
  But yit—the manner hou?
    We sall nou, e'en all, nou,
      Get this man with us thair;
    It ^arestis, and best is,   ^aremains
      Your counsel shall declair.'

'Weill said!' quod HOPE and COURAGE,
    nou,
'We thereto will accord with you,
  And sall abide by thame.
Like as before we did submit,
Sa we repeit the ^asamin yit,   ^asame
  We ^amind not to ^breclaim.   ^ahave no intention
Quham thay sall chuse to guide the   ^bgo back on it
    way,
  We sall him follow straicht,
And ^afurther this man quhat we may,   ^ahelp on
  Because we have sa ^ahecht.   ^apromised
    Promitting, ^abut flitting,   ^awithout shifting
      To do the thing we can;
    To pleise, baith, and eise, baith,
      This silly ^aseikly man.'   ^asickly

Quhen RESSOUN hard this, than, quod he,
'I see your cheifest stay to be,
  That we haiff namit na guide.'
The worthy counsel hes, thairfore,
^aThocht gude that WIT suld ga before,   ^athought
  For perillis to provide.

Quod WIT, 'Thair is but ane of three,
  ^aQuhilk I shall to you schaw,   ^awhich
Quhairof the first twa may nocht be,
    For ony thing I knaw.
        The way, here, so ^astay, here,   ^asteep
            Is that we can nocht clim'
        E'en owre, nou, we fowr, nou:
            That will be hard for him.

'The nixt, gif we ga doun about,
  ^aQuhill that this bend of craigis run out: ^atill
      The streim is thair sa ^astark,   ^astrong
And also passis wading-deip,
And braider far nor we ^adow leip—   ^acan possibly leap
      It suld be idle wark!
It growis ay braider neir the sea,
  ^aSen over the ^blinn it came;   ^asince ^bwaterfall
The running-^adeid dois signifie   ^adead
      The deipness of the same.
        I ^aleive, nou, to ^bdeive, nou,   ^acease ^bdeafen,
            Quhow that it swiftly slidis,   i.e. bore (you)
        As sleiping, and creiping—
            Bot Nature sa providis.

'*Our* way, than, lyis about the linn
Quhairby, I warrand, we sall win,
      It is sa straicht and plain;
The water also is so ^aschald,   ^ashallow
We sall it pass, e'en as we wald,
      With pleisure and ^abut pain.   ^awithout
For, as we see the mischeiff grow,
      Oft, of a ^afeckless thing,   ^atrivial
Sa likewise dois this river flow
      Furth of a pretty spring,
        Quhais throat, schir, I ^awat, schir,   ^aknow
            You may stop with your ^aneiff—   ^afist
        As you, schir, I trow, schir,
            EXPERIENCE, can ^apreiff.'   ^atest

'That,' quod EXPERIENCE, 'I can—
All that ye said sen ye began
   I knaw to be of truth.'
Quod SKILL, 'The ^asamin I appruve.'   ^asame
Quod RESSOUN, 'Than lat us remuve,
   And sleip na mair in ^asleuth!   ^asloth
WIT and EXPERIENCE,' quod he,
  'Sall cum before, apace;
The man sall cum with SKILL and me,
   ^aInto the second place.   ^ain
     ^aAtowre, nou, you fowr nou,   ^aout over
      Sall cum ^ainto ^bane band,   ^ain ^bone
      Proceiding, and leiding
       Ilk uther ^abe the hand.'   ^aby

As RESSOUN ordainit, all obeyit,
Nane was ower-rasch, nor nane
    affrayit,
   Our counsel was sa wise:
As of our journey WIT did note,
We fand it true in every jote,
   God blissit our interprise.
For e'en as we come to the tree,
   Quhilk, as ye hard me tell,
Could not be clum'—thair suddenly
   The fruit for ripeness fell:
     Quhilk hasting and tasting,
      I fand mysel releivit
     Of cairis all, and sairis all,
      Quhilk mind and body greivit!

Praise be to God, my Lord, thairfore,
Who did mine health to me restore,
   Being so long time pined:
Yea, blessed be His Holy Name,
Who did from death to life reclaim
   Me, who was so unkind!

L

All nations also magnifie
This everliving Lord;
Let me with you, and you with me,
To laud Him ay accord,
Whose luve, ay, we pruve, ay,
To us abuve all thingis,
And kiss Him, and bless Him,
Whose Glore eternal ªringis!   ªreigns

With these Covenanting-like lines from the pen of Alexander
Montgomerie at the end of the sixteenth century we conclude
Part I of The Wisdom of the Scots.

PART TWO

Introduction

The preface to this anthology included the remark that in the first part would be found 'the purer matter of the book, the more purely Scottish, more purely wise.' There was the implication too that the second part which would cover the centuries of Scotland's slow loss of nationality would be shorter, containing less purely national wisdom: this was a mistake.

It would, I suppose, be a tidier thing for me to do to go back and moderate these implications, but I have thought it better to let them stand. I took the reader into my confidence on how and why I undertook this book at the beginning. Work of such kind grows beneath one's hand as one writes, researches and writes again. I venture to suggest that, while keeping the form of the book, it is more interesting to show how it grew than to present the whole thing as an object achieved in one's own mind from the beginning: it was no such thing.

In talking about moderating any earlier implications I do not withdraw anything said about Scotland's decline in national status in the last three and a half centuries. It is surely impossible for any unbiased or unsentimental person to deny this. What I would moderate is the impression I may have left that Scottish wisdom of the kind to our purpose here declined obviously. In fact the Scottish character not only survived but often hardened as Scotland lost her independence. But it survived and hardened in individuals—often lonely individuals regarded in their time as unrepresentative, but now seen by us as highly national.

It is from these Scottish individuals, standing out so clearly against the background of their deteriorating country, that the rich material for this second part comes. At least it seems rich to us; and we have had rich pleasure in collecting it and writing about it. It is only necessary to mention their names to feel the force of their individual Scottishness. Urquhart, Montrose, Lord Belhaven, Hume, Boswell, Burns, Walter Scott, and (leaving aside a number of other names from the past and middle-past to come down to the present with a bang—yes, a bang, not a whimper) C. M. Grieve, here's richness. And it is a richness that many another country, such as Sweden or Switzerland, which has remained independent, or others which have become free, might envy.

The wisdom of the Scots in the last three and a half centuries has been the wisdom of individuals. From these individuals we have chosen certain obvious mountain peaks; Hume, Burns, Scott are examples. We have also allowed ourselves a few highly Scottish eccentrics, oddities or unusual people—Urquhart, some of the judges and lawyers, perhaps Smollett and certainly the anonymous coiners of the Scottish proverbs.

These have been our own choice; inevitably then we have left out others who would be other people's choice. Once again there is no need to apologise for this. We do not necessarily have any aversion from our omissions, nor do we necessarily think them unimportant. They just didn't fit into the shape of the book, and there was no reason to force them in.

To save any critic the trouble of detecting what we have left out of Scottish wisdom from the year of 1611 down to the present here are some of the more glaring examples. We put in no sermons, no theological writing or speaking on any of the many sides of the religious divisions in Scotland of the period; our reason for this is the same as that given in Part I. We have omitted the patriotic Fletcher of Saltoun because of his illiberal opinions. We have also excluded the splendid rhetoric of pro- and anti-Jacobite argument or speech from the pulpit or sometimes the scaffold. We have given nothing from Hogg's *Memoirs of a Justified Sinner* which is narrative rather than wisdom. After the Union we have included no single utterance by a Scottish politician or even a statesman (such as Gladstone) of pure Scottish descent. We have chosen Scottish individuals speaking for the most part for themselves; but in so doing for Scotland; even so we have left out some individuals (no names here) whom we should like to have put in, but for whom we could not find space.

This second half of the book has been more crowded than we had anticipated—crowded with character. That has been one of the most pleasurable and hopeful elements in compiling it. The Scottish character lives on. Anyone who gets far enough will observe that the end is a note of hope.

M. McL.

Sir Thomas Urquhart, Knight of Cromartie

This delightful seventeenth-century north-eastern Scottish character compounded out of scholarship, fanciful wisdom, a passionate love of ideas, swashbuckling humour, anti-Presbyterianism, Scottish patriotism, deep seriousness and apparent frivolity, combining to present a habit of mind and expression in the Scot which at once repels and attracts, delights and infuriates, the foreigner, especially if he be an Englishman, a Teuton, or a North American, employing a style of writing in which terse and trenchant epithets besprinkle enormous sesquipedalian and periphrastic sentences, claimed to be able to trace his descent directly from Adam, and, as a Scottish laird of lineage, was well placed to make a genealogy beginning to prove that beginning. Indeed he published a proof of his descent covering over a hundred generations.

Born in 1611 (the year of Alexander Montgomerie's disappearance from human ken and exactly a century before the birth of David Hume), Urquhart died in 1660, the year of the Restoration of Charles II, the news of which event produced in him a burst of such purely happy laughter that it killed him. He may have died laughing for, with, on account of and not at a Royal Occasion, but spent a considerable part of his lifetime not only fighting against but laughing at the King's enemies. His method of attack on Presbyterianism was pure ridicule.

When imprisoned by Cromwell after fighting with the Royalist forces at Worcester, he employed his time by composing a fantastical work ΕΚΣΚΥΒΑΛΑΥΡΟΝ or 'the discovery of a most exquisite Jewel.' The ostensible reason for this work was a plea for his freedom and the restitution of his estates. This Jewel contains amongst other things Urquhart's invention of a universal language which he claimed would be of such benefit to mankind as to merit its author's immediate release upon the world. Some regard these plans for a universal language as an example of pedantic absurdity, others look upon it as an overblown joke. We agree with neither point of view. It is a huge piece of real Renaissance learning and wisdom conceived in the Scottish manner and animated by the full flood of that type of Scottish humour which (much to the pleasure of true Scots) never knows when to stop. In our eyes the longer it goes on the funnier it becomes—and the wiser.

A Scottish friend of ours at Balliol College, Oxford, remembers being tackled about the 'Jewel' by a fellow-collegian neither (for once) Scots nor even English, but Jewish. Cohen (for such was this excellent Balliol man's name) was much exercised by the problem of a universal language and had been writing an article on the subject for publication in *Mind*, but he did not feel happy about it. 'What on earth,' said he, 'is the point of having a language with eleven genders?'

'Does it not occur to you,' our friend replied to him, 'that Urquhart was being funny as well as learned?'

'But it isn't funny.'

'Why not?'

'Because it goes on for so long.'

'That's the whole point of the joke.'

But a deadlock had been reached; and, for once, a Jew and a Scot (even though both sons of Balliol) did not understand each other.

Urquhart is best known for his translation of Rabelais, a labour which must certainly have been one of love to his learned, fantastical and scatological mind. His other works, from which we have made our selection of his wisdom, are today extremely rare. The Maitland Club made a collection of his writings in 1834; but, as far as can be ascertained, this can only be consulted by the student if he lives in Edinburgh, Glasgow, London or Oxford. (Our thanks are due to the Keepers of the Reference Room of the Edinburgh Public Library who made available to us for copying the single volume they possess.) Once again we take pleasure in introducing a Scottish rarity to the general reader.

It would be an easy and superficial judgment to dismiss Sir Thomas Urquhart as a learned, pedantic and amusing eccentric—unrepresentative of the true tradition of Scottish wisdom. This is to overlook the fact that the Scottish eccentric is or (let us sadly admit it) was the Scottish norm. A strong and ridicule-using opponent of Presbyterianism, Urquhart yet shared with his Presbyterian compatriots that passion for ideas which is one of their most admirable characteristics; and he was certainly not the ordinary type of cavalier as represented in romantic historical fiction. He loved ideas for their value and only if they were ideas which produced good—but more of this later. A European Scot and detester of the Presbyterian system, he yet had no use for the Church of Rome. He praised with equal pride and gusto the achievements of the Scottish professional soldiers on either side of the Thirty Years War, claiming that, as there was always a Scot on the winning side in each battle, Scotland was never defeated. A north-easterner from that part of Scotland most chary of words, he must surely have been responsible for the most enormous sentences penned in the languages of these islands. Full of a capacity for humorous exaggeration, his feet never left the ground from which he had started arguing. Utterly unlike most of his contemporaries and compatriots he is yet a prototype of so many Scots before and after him.

Such was Sir Thomas Urquhart, Knight of Cromartie. We print four extracts from his prose below. All are taken from the Maitland Club edition of his works already referred to.

THE WISDOM OF THE SCOTS MILITARY TRADITION AND A MOST NOTABLE EXAMPLE OF HUMANE WISDOM

This comes from the beginning of 'The Discovery of a most exquisite Jewel' (hereinafter called, for brevity, 'the Jewel') composed in the Cromwellian prison.[1] Urquhart's ostensible reason for this composition

[1] Maitland Club, pp. 218–20.

was his release. He realised that there were, apart from his politics, a number of facts which the English would hold against him. The first was his Scottish nationality.

He begins then by speaking of those Scottish qualities which, it seemed to him, must surely command general admiration. Amongst these is the Scottish military tradition. Though Urquhart does not mention this in this context, this tradition derives directly from Bruce and the Wars of Independence. If Scotland was to keep her freedom and identity she must preserve her soldierly heritage. This was indeed as true in the seventeenth as in the fourteenth century. Urquhart, however, confines his remarks to a catalogue of Scottish military prowess in Europe at a time when the professional skill of the Scottish military commander as well as the bravery of the Scottish professional soldier was much in demand. This military skill was indeed a great quality of ours. No doubt we had, by reason of our perilous circumstances, to put it at the forefront of our achievements. In doing so, alas! we forfeited some of the gentler and more amenable qualities of culture which are so conspicuously lacking in a modern Scotland where soldiering is already becoming out of date.

It is conceivable that such a thought may have crossed Urquhart's mind, for he drags into this list of Scottish soldiers the names of two heroes of his who could hardly have been described as great military commanders—the Admirable Crichton and Napier of Merchiston. Crichton it is true was almost as nimble and adept in the use of his sword in personal combat as in the use of his mind, but there is no evidence that he ever led troops in the field. Napier of Merchiston had no military experience, but the device by which Urquhart introduces him into this context is particularly ingenious and delightful, and, for us at this time, particularly à propos.

He recounts how it is commonly reported (and be it noted that when concerned with a matter of so grave import Urquhart, though of fictive and inventive mind, is careful to mention a report as a report), commonly reported that Napier had invented a destructive machine which could have revolutionised warfare in his time. By this engine, which from other reports that have come to us would seem to have been composed of an ingenious system of burning glasses, Napier claimed to have been able to clear a field of four miles circumference of 'all living creatures above a foot in height.' Indeed he demonstrated this invention in a country place in Scotland (other reports again say upon a flock of sheep upon the Pentland Hills) and convinced observers that by this machine he could 'kill thirty thousand Turks, without the hazard of one Christian.'

When Napier fell sick of the disease which was to kill him a friend besought him to describe this invention so that it might be used by posterity and not be buried with him. Napier's wise and humane refusal to bequeath such a legacy of destruction to mankind is reported with touching approval by Urquhart. It is indeed deplorable that the scientists who made the events of Hiroshima and Nagasaki possible and the politicians who made that possibility a fact had not possessed the

Scottish wisdom of Napier of Merchiston. Urquhart's approval of
Napier in this decision is an example of what we meant when we said
earlier that, though he had a passion for ideas, they had to be ideas that
produced good. Good ideas, in fact! How that essential phrase has been
weakened and degraded!

Now, as steel is best resisted and overcome by steel, and that the
Scots, like Ishmael, whose hand was against every man, and every
man's hand against him, have been of late so ingaged in all the wars
of Christendome, espousing, in a manner, the interest of all the princes
thereof; that, what battel soever, at any time these forty yeers past
hath been struck within the continent of Europe, all the Scots that
fought in that field, were never overthrown and totally routed; for if
some of them were captives and taken prisoners, others of that nation
were victorious, and givers of quarter; valour and mercy on the one
side, with misfortune and subjection upon the other side, meeting one
another in the persons of compatriots on both sides; so the gold and
treasure of the Indias not being able to purchase all the affections of
Scotland to the furtherance of Castilian designes, there have been of
late several Scotish colonels under the command of the Prince of
Orange, in opposition of the Spagniard; viz. Colonel Edmond, who
took the valiant Count de Buccoy twice prisoner in the field; Sir
Henry Balfour, Sir David Balfour, Colonel Brog, who took a Spanish
general in the field upon the head of his army; Sir Francis Henderson,
Colonel Scot, Earl of Bucliugh, Colonel Sir James Livistoun, now Earl
of Calander, and lately in these our tourmoyles at home lieutenant-
general of both horse and foot, besides a great many other worthy
colonels, amongst which I will only commemorate one, named Colonel
Dowglas, who to the States of Holland was often times serviceable, in
discharging the office and duty of general engineer; whereof they are
now so sensible, that, to have him alive againe, and of that vigour and
freshness in body and spirit, wherewith he was endowed in the day
he was killed on, they would give thrice his weight in gold; and well
they might; for some few weeks before the fight wherein he was
slaine, he presented to them twelve articles and heads of such wonderful
feats for the use of the wars both by sea and land, to be performed by
him, flowing from the remotest springs of mathematical secrets, and
those of natural philosophy, that none of this age saw, nor any of our
fore-fathers ever heard the like, save what out of Cicero, Livy,
Plutarch, and other old Greek and Latin writers we have couched,
of the admirable inventions made use of by Archimedes in defence of
the city of Syracusa, against the continual assaults of the Romane

forces both by sea and land, under the conduct of Marcellus. To speak really, I think there hath not been any in this age of the Scotish nation, save Neper and Crichtoun, who, for abilities of the minde in matter of practical inventions useful for men of industry, merit to be compared with him; and yet of these two notwithstanding their excellency in learning, I would be altogether silent, because I made account to mention no other Scotish men here, but such as have been famous for souldiery, and brought up at the schoole of Mars, were it not that, besides their profoundness in literature, they were inriched with military qualifications beyond expression. As for Neper, otherwayes designed Lord Marchiston, he is for his logarithmical device so compleatly praised in that preface of the author's, which ushers a trigonometrical book of his, intituled *The Trissotetras*, that to add any more thereunto, would but obscure with an empty sound, the clearness of what is already said; therefore I will allow him no share in this discourse, but in so far as concerneth an almost incomprehensible device, which being in the mouths of the most of Scotland, and yet unknown to any that ever was in the world but himself, deserveth very well to be taken notice of in this place; and it is this: he had the skill, as is commonly reported, to frame an engine, for invention not much unlike that of Architas Dove, which, by vertue of some secret springs, inward resorts, with other implements and materials fit for the purpose, inclosed within the bowels thereof, had the power, if proportionable in bulk to the action required of it, for he could have made it of all sizes, to clear a field of four miles circumference, of all the living creatures exceeding a foot of hight, that should be found thereon, how neer soever they might be to one another; by which means he made it appear that he was able, with the help of this machine alone, to kill thirty thousand Turkes, without the hazard of one Christian. Of this it is said, that, upon a wager, he gave proof upon a large plaine in Scotland, to the destruction of a great many herds of cattel, and flocks of sheep, whereof some were distant from other half a mile on all sides, and some a whole mile. To continue the thred of the story, as I have it, I must not forget, that, when he was most earnestly desired by an old acquaintance and professed friend of his, even about the time of his contracting that disease whereof he dyed, he would be pleased, for the honour of his family, and his own everlasting memory to posterity, to reveal unto him the manner of the contrivance of so ingenious a mystery; subjoining thereto, for the better perswading of him, that it were a thousand pities that so excellent an invention should be buryed with him in the grave, and that after his decease nothing should be known thereof; his answer was, That for the ruine and overthrow of man, there were too many devices already framed, which, if he could make to be fewer, he would with all his might endeavour to do; and that therefore seeing the malice and rancor rooted in the heart of mankind will not suffer them to diminish, by any new conceit of his, the number of them should never be increased. Divinely spoken, truly.

THE UNIVERSAL LANGUAGE

Given here are some extracted paragraphs from the heart of 'the Jewel,'[1] Urquhart's adumbration of his language plans. We have already hinted at what we feel about this mixture of high spirits and of learning, and avoid the temptation, by quoting in advance, to draw the reader's attention to any of the higher flights of fancy quoted below. Let Sir Thomas Urquhart's words *and* tone of voice in the printed page speak for themselves.

This, however, we would point out: though funny this is no more purely a joke than is *Alice in Wonderland*. Indeed it is (though just as extravagant in expression) more based on fact—the fact of an idea; and ideas were what Urquhart passionately believed in. Never for one moment does Urquhart imply that the idea of a universal language was funny. No doubt the pedestrianly pedantic attempts of some of his friends at Aberdeen University at that time to form such a language may have seemed to him ridiculous. But he, he the much more poetic, philosophical and generally learned knight, set out to think of a language which could express all *his* ideas from poetry, through philosophy, mathematics and science to ejaculations of Divine Praise. In setting out to do this he set out despite himself to do a funny thing. Then (then not despite but because of himself) he perceives the humour of the situation and proceeds to decorate his previous, cherished and firmly believed-in idea with the high, involuted and convoluted jinks of pure fancy.

Urquhart loved ideas first and words second, and liked playing with both. We will leave him to his wise and learned sport without further comment save this. One of Sir Thomas's descendants whom we know has, in conversation, drawn attention to a common but fantastical modern word which would have delighted Urquhart—'Macadamised.'[2] Mac is Gaelic, Adam is Hebrew, ise comes from the Greek and ed is a Saxon ending. Was there ever such a combination? It is a pity Urquhart did not live to learn of it.

70. Now to the end the reader may be more enamored of the

[1] Maitland Club, pp. 315–20.
[2] In drawing attention to this word another one has come to us. What about demacadamised? That introduces a fifth and Latin root.

language, wherein I am to publish a grammer and lexicon, I will here set down some few qualities and advantages peculiar to it self, and which no language else, although all other concurred with it, is able to reach unto.

71. First, There is not a word utterable by the mouth of man, which, in this language, hath not a peculiar signification by it self, so that the allegation of Bliteri by the Summulists will be of small validity.

72. Secondly, Such as will harken to my instructions, if some strange word be proposed to them, whereof there are many thousands of millions, deviseable by the wit of man, which never hitherto by any breathing have been uttered, shall be able, although he know not the ultimate signification thereof, to declare what part of speech it is; or if a noune, into what predicament or class it is to be reduced, whether it be the signe of a real or notional thing, or somewhat concerning mechanick trades in their tooles or tearmes; or if real, whether natural or artificial, complete or incomplete; for words here do suppone for the things which they signifie, as when we see my Lord General's picture, we say, there is my Lord General.

73. Thirdly, This world of words hath but two hundred and fifty prime radices, upon which all the rest are branched; for better understanding whereof, with all its dependant boughs, sprigs, and ramelets, I have before my lexicon set down the division thereof, making use of another allegory, into so many cities, which are subdivided into streets, they againe into lanes, those into houses, these into stories, whereof each room standeth for a word; and all these so methodically, that who observeth my precepts thereanent, shall, at the first hearing of a word, know to what city it belongeth, and consequently not be ignorant of some general signification thereof, till, after a most exact prying into all its letters, finding the street, lane, house, story, and room thereby denotated, he punctually hit upon the very proper thing it represents in its most specifical signification.

74. Fourthly, By vertue of adjectitious syllabicals annexible to nouns and verbs, there will arise of several words, what compound, what derivative, belonging in this language to one noune or to one verb alone, a greater number than doth pertaine to all the parts of speech in the most copious language in the world besides.

75. Fifthly, So great energy to every meanest constitutive part of a word in this language is appropriated, that one word thereof, though but of seven syllables at most, shall comprehend that which no language else in the world is able to express in fewer then fourscore and fifteen several words; and that not only a word here and there for masteries

sake, but several millions of such, which, to any initiated in the rudiments of my grammar, shall be easie to frame.

76. Sixthly, In the cases of all the declinable parts of speech, it surpasseth all other languages whatsoever, for whilst others have but five or six at most, it hath ten, besides the nominative.

77. Seventhly, There is none of the learned languages but hath store of nouns defective of some case or other; but in this language there is no heteroclite in any declinable word, nor redundancie or deficiency of cases.

78. Eighthly, Every word capable of number, is better provided therewith in this language than by any other; for in stead of two or three numbers, which others have, this affordeth you four; to wit, the singular, dual, plural, and redual.

79. Ninthly, It is not in this as other languages, wherein some words lack one number, and some another, for here each casitive or personal part of speech is endued with all the numbers.

80. Tenthly, In this tongue there are eleven genders; wherein likewise it exceedeth all other languages.

81. Eleventhly, Verbs, mongrels, participles, and hybrids, have all of them ten tenses besides the present; which number no language else is able to attaine to.

82. Twelfthly, Though there be many conjugable words in other languages defective of tenses, yet doth this tongue allow of no such anomaly, but granteth all to each.

83. Thirteenthly, In lieu of six moods which other languages have at most, this one enjoyeth seven in its conjugable words.

84. Fourteenthly, Verbs here, or other conjugable parts of speech, admit of no want of moodes, as doe other languages.

85. Fifteenthly, In this language the verbs and participles have four voices, although it was never heard that ever any other language had above three.

86. Sixteenthly, No other tongue hath above eight or nine parts of speech, but this hath twelve.

87. Seventeenthly, For variety of diction in each part of speech, it surmounteth all the languages in the world.

88. Eighteenthly, Each noun thereof, or verb, may begin or end with a vowel or consonant, as to the peruser shall seem most expedient.

89. Nineteenthly, Every word of this language, declinable or indeclinable, hath at least ten several synonymas.

90. Twentiethly, Each of these synonymas, in some circumstance of the signification, differeth from the rest. . . .

93. Three and twentiethly, Every word in this language signifieth as well backward as forward, and how ever you invert the letter, still shall you fall upon significant words, whereby a wonderful facility is obtained in making of anagrams. . . .

98. Eight and twentiethly, By this language, and the letters thereof, we may do such admirable feats in numbers, that no cyfering can reach its compendiousness; for whereas the ordinary way of numbring by thousands of thousands of thousands of thousands, doth but confuse the hearer's understanding, to remedy which I devised, even by cyfering it self, a far more exact maner of numeration, as in the treatise of arithmetick which I have ready for the press is evidently apparent. This language affordeth so concise words for numbering, that the number for setting down, whereof would require in vulgar arithmetick more figures in a row then there might be grains of sand containable from the center of the earth to the highest heavens, is in it expressed by two letters.

99. Nine and twentiethly, What rational logarithms do by writing, this language doth by heart, and by adding of letters, shall multiply numbers, which is a most exquisite secret.

100. Thirtiethly, The digits are expressed by vowels, and the consonants stand for all the results of the Cephalisme, from ten to eighty-one inclusively, whereby many pretty arithmetical tricks are performed.

101. One and thirtiethly, In the denomination of the fixed stars, it affordeth the most significant way imaginary; for by the single word alone which represents the star, you shall know the magnitude, together with the longitude and latitude, both in degrees and minutes, of the star that is expressed by it. . . .

103. Three and thirtiethly, As for the yeer of God, the moneth of that yeer, week of the moneth, day of that week, partition of the day, hour of that partition, quarter and half quarter of the hour, a word of one syllable in this language will express it all to the full.

104. Four and thirtiethly, In this language also, words expressive of herbs represent unto us with what degree of cold, moisture, heat, or driness they are qualified, together with some other property distinguishing them from other herbs.

105. Five and thirtiethly, In matter of colours, we shall learn by words in this language the proportion of light, shadow, or darkness, commixed in them. . . .

107. Seven and thirtiethly, For attaining to that dexterity which

Mithridates, king of Pontus, was said to have, in calling all his souldiers, of an army of threescore thousand men, by their names and surnames, this language will be so convenient, that if a general, according to the rules thereof, will give new names to his soldiers, whether horse, foot, or dragoons, as the French use to do to their infantry by their *noms de guerre*, he shall be able, at the first hearing of the word that represents the name of a souldier, to know of what brigade, regiment, troop, company, squadron, or division he is, and whether he be of the cavalry or of the foot, a single souldier or an officer, or belonging to the artillery or baggage. Which device, in my opinion, is not unuseful for those great captains that would endear themselves in the favour of the souldiery. . . .

112. Two and fourtiethly, No language but this hath in its words the whole number of letters, that is, ten vowels, and five and twenty consonants, by which means there is no word escapes the latitude thereof.

113. Three and fourtiethly, As its interjections are more numerous, so are they more emphatical in their respective expression of passions, then that part of speech is in any other language whatsoever.

114. Four and fourtiethly, The more syllables there be in any one word of this language, the manyer several significations it hath; with which propriety no other language is endowed. . . .

119. Nine and fourtiethly, For writing of missives, letters of state, and all other manner of epistles, whether serious or otherways, it affordeth the compactest stile of any language in the world; and therefore, of all other, the most requisite to be learned by statesmen and merchants.

120. Fiftiethly, No language in matter of prayer and ejaculations to Almighty God is able, for conciseness of expression, to compare with it; and therefore, of all other, the most fit for the use of church-men, and spirits inclined to devotion. . . .

123. Three and fiftiethly, In many thousands of words belonging to this language, there is not a letter which hath not a peculiar signification by it self. . . .

125. Five and fiftiethly, All the languages in the world will be beholding to this, and this to none. . . .

127. Seven and fiftiethly, The greatest wonder of all is, that of all the languages in the world, it is the easiest to learn; a boy of ten yeers old, being able to attaine to the knowledge thereof, in three moneths space; because there are in it many facilitations for the memory, which no other language hath but it self. . . .

LOGOPANDECTEISION

When Urquhart was released from the Cromwellian prison he extended
and published further plans for his Universal Language. To this he added
an introduction under the above heading.[1] We extract from it the
following story. It amusingly and, we think, charmingly illustrates
Urquhart's idea of ideas properly used being more potent than mere
action for its own sake. That reads like a truism, but as Urquhart
expresses it here it gains freshness in the telling. It is a characteristic
piece of Urquhartian Scottish wisdom, drawn from a sporting analogy.

49. Of these examples there are many, which to summe up in one
of a more disproportioned mistake then any of the rest, I will tell
you, that there happening a gentleman of very good worth to stay
awhile at my house, who, one day amongst many other, was pleased,
in the deadst time of all the winter, with a gun upon his shoulder, to
search for a shot of some wild fowl; and after he had waded through
many waters, taken excessive pains in quest of his game, and by means
thereof had killed some five or six moor fowls and partridges, which
he brought along with him to my house, he was by some other gentlemen, who chanced to alight at my gate, as he entred in, very much
commended for his love to sport; and, as the fashion of most of our
countrymen is, not to praise one without dispraising another, I was
highly blamed for not giving my self in that kind to the same exercise,
having before my eys so commendable a pattern to imitate; I answered,
though the gentleman deserved praise for the evident proof he had
given that day of his inclination to thrift and laboriousness, that
nevertheless I was not to blame, seeing whilst he was busied about
that sport, I was imployed in a diversion of another nature, such as
optical secrets, mysteries of natural philosophie, reasons for the
variety of colours, the finding out of the longitude, the squaring of
a circle, and wayes to accomplish all trigonometrical calculations
by sines, without tangents, with the same compendiousness of
computation, which, in the estimation of learned men, would be
accounted worth six hundred thousand partridges, and as many
moor-fowles.

50. But notwithstanding this relation, either for that the gentlemen
understood it not, or that they deemed the exercise of the body to be
of greater concernment then that of the minde, they continued firme
in their former opinion, whereof I laboured not to convince them,

[1] Maitland Club, p. 331.

M

because I intended, according to their capacities, to bear them company.

51. In the mean while that worthy gentleman, who was nothing of their mind, for being wet and weary after travel, was not able to eat of what he had so much toyled for, whilst my braine recreations so sharpened my appetite, that I supped to very good purpose. That night past, the next morning I gave six pence to a footman of mine, to try his fortune with the gun, during the time I should disport my selfe in the breaking of a young horse; and it so fell out, that by I had given my selfe a good heat by riding, the boy returned with a dozen of wild fouls, half moor foule, half partridge, whereat being exceeding well pleased, I alighted, gave him my horse to care for, and forthwith entred in to see my gentlemen, the most especiall whereof was unable to rise out of his bed, by reason of the Gout and Sciatick, wherewith he was seized for his former day's toyle.

52. Thus seeing matters of the greatest worth may be undervalued by such as are destitute of understanding, who would reap any benefit by what is good, till it be appreciated, should be charie of its prestitution; let this therefore suffice, why to this preface or introduction, I have not as yet subjoyned the Grammar and Lexicon.

A PARAGRAPH ON PUNISHMENT

Urquhart composed a humorously pedantic plea against the punishment of witches.[1] It was not very effective, as it was based on the grounds that, as we teach schoolboys ancient mythology, it is not logical to punish old women for practising race-memories of it. The plea, however, does contain one paragraph on the punishment of murder and the punishment of fornication. This seventeenth-century, considerably pre-Wolfenden-report is, we think, of interest. At any rate, here it is as a tail-piece to the Knight of Cromartie's wisdom.

22. To punish a fornicator for murther, or a theef for fornication, is an act of injustice, because the first begetteth rather then kills, and the other rather takes then gives; and to chastise one for an offence which he hath not committed, is a meer oppressing of the innocent, for that whatever secret sin he have that may deserve it from above, it is without any cause knowne to him that inflicts the correction.

[1] Maitland Club, p. 355.

James Graham, Marquis of Montrose

'Montrose,' as Mark Napier, the nineteenth-century Scottish historian, has well said, 'was a hero, not a poet. He might have been a poet, had he not been a hero. He was a man of poetic genius unquestionably; and there are some things written by him that can never die.'

True; but it might be added that among his undying poems there is one that is almost never printed without being cut to its detriment, misquoted according to earliest sources and misunderstood.

His famous *To His Mistress* containing the well-known lines:

> 'He either fears his Fate too much
> Or his Deserts are small,'

has eighteen stanzas instead of the usual four now commonly allowed to it and is 'addressed to no flesh and blood' woman, as is too often supposed, but to an ideal for which he was to suffer death. Were it not that the epithet has become so fouled one might venture to call it a 'political' poem. John Buchan, in his *Life of Montrose*, says this of it:

'This is the song of a man who has at last found assurance, the confession of a soul which has the vision of a noble purpose and holds no risk too high in its ultimate attainment. . . . Almost every metaphor is drawn from the language of contemporary politics, but the language is warmed and coloured by a passion of loyalty—to an ideal rather than to a person, for with Montrose, in Plato's words, the quest of truth did not lack the warmth of desire.'[1]

There is no need of further comment or explanation of why we include such a wedding of wisdom and poetry in noble verse among the 'wisdom of the Scots' save this. We would remind readers of what we recalled in Part I. Montrose was a Scot who presented, as his countrymen often do, an incarnation of things usually taken to be in opposition. He was a Cavalier and the best soldier the Royal Charles Stuarts ever had yet he was a Presbyterian and a signatory of the Solemn League and Covenant. Here is his poem in full and according to the earliest reliable sources. For these we are indebted to Mr. J. L. Weir's definitive book *Poems of Montrose*, John Murray, 1938, pp. 19–24.

MONTROSE TO HIS MISTRESS

An Excellent New Ballad, to the Tune of
'I'll never love thee more'

My dear and only Love, I pray
This noble World of thee,
Be govern'd by no other Sway
But purest Monarchie.

[1] *Montrose*, by John Buchan, 1928, p. 152.

For if Confusion have a Part,
　　Which vertuous Souls abhore,
And hold a Synod in thy Heart,
　　I'll never love thee more.

Like *Alexander* I will reign,
　　And I will reign alone,
My Thoughts shall evermore disdain
　　A Rival on my Throne.
He either fears his Fate too much,
　　Or his Deserts are small,
That puts it not unto the Touch,
　　To win or lose it all.

But I must rule, and govern still,
　　And always give the Law,
And have each Subject at my Will,
　　And all to stand in awe.
But 'gainst my Battery if I find
　　Thou shun'st the Prize so sore,
As that thou set'st me up a Blind,
　　I'll never love thee more.

Or in the Empire of thy Heart,
　　Where I should solely be,
Another do pretend a Part,
　　And dares to Vie with me,
Or if Committees thou erect,
　　And goes on such a Score,
I'll sing and laugh at thy Neglect,
　　And never love thee more.

But if thou wilt be constant then,
　　And faithful of thy Word,
I'll make thee glorious by my Pen,
　　And famous by my Sword.
I'll serve thee in such noble Ways
　　Was never heard before:
I'll crown and deck thee all with Bays,
　　And love thee evermore.

My dear and only Love, take heed,
  Lest thou thy self expose,
And let all longing Lovers feed
  Upon such Looks as those.
A Marble Wall then build about,
  Beset without a Door;
But thou let thy Heart fly out,
  I'll never love thee more.

Let not their Oaths, like Vollies shot,
  Make any Breach at all;
Nor Smoothness of their Language plot
  Which way to scale the Wall;
Nor Balls of Wild-fire Love consume
  The Shrine which I adore:
For if such Smoak about thee fume,
  I'll never love thee more.

I think thy Virtues be too strong
  To suffer by Surprise:
Which Victual'd by my Love so long,
  Their Siege at length must rise,
And leave thee ruled in that Health
  And State thou was before:
But if thou turn a Common-Wealth,
  I'll never love thee more.

But if by Fraud, or by Consent,
  Thy Heart to Ruine come,
I'll sound no Trumpet as I wont,
  Nor march by Tuck of Drum:
But hold my Arms, like Ensigns, up,
  Thy Falshood to deplore,
And bitterly will sigh and weep,
  And never love thee more.

I'll do with thee as *Nero* did
  When *Rome* was set on fire;
Not only all Relief forbid,
  But to a Hill retire;

And scorn to shed a Tear to see
  Thy Spirit grown so poor:
But smiling, sing until I die,
  I'll never love thee more.

Yet for the Love I bare thee once,
  Lest that thy Name should die,
A Monument of Marble-stone
  The Truth shall testifie;
That every Pilgrim passing by,
  May pity and deplore
My Case, and read the Reason why
  I can love thee no more.

The golden Laws of Love shall be
  Upon this Pillar hung;
A simple Heart, a single Eye,
  A true and constant Tongue.
Let no Man for more Love pretend
  Than he has Hearts in store:
True Love begun shall never end;
  Love one and love no more.

Then shall thy Heart be set by mine,
  But in far different Case:
For mine was true, so was not thine,
  But lookt like *Janus* Face.
For as the Waves with every Wind,
  So sails thou every Shore,
And leaves my constant Heart behind,
  How can I love thee more?

My Heart shall with the Sun be fix'd
  For Constancy most strange,
And thine shall with the Moon be mix'd,
  Delighting ay in Change.
Thy Beauty shin'd at first most bright,
  And wo is me therefore,
That ever I found thy Love so light,
  I could love thee no more.

The misty Mountains, smoaking Lakes,
    The Rocks resounding Echo;
The whistling Wind that Murmur makes,
    Shall with me sing Hey ho.
The tossing Seas, the tumbling Boats,
    Tears droping from each Shore,
Shall tune with me their Turtle Notes,
    I'll never love thee more.

As doth the Turtle chaste and true
    Her Fellow's Death regrete,
And daily mourns for his Adieu,
    And ne'er renews her Mate;
So though thy Faith was never fast,
    Which grieves me wond'rous sore,
Yet I shall live in Love so chast,
    That I shall love no more.

And when all Gallants rides about
    These Monuments to view,
Whereon is written in and out,
    Thou traiterous and untrue;
Then in a Passion they shall pause,
    And thus say, sighing sore,
Alas! he had too just a Cause
    Never to love thee more.

And when that tracing Goddess *Fame*
    From East to West shall flee,
She shall Record it to thy Shame,
    How thou hast loved me;
And how in Odds our Love was such,
    As few has been before;
Thou loved too many, and I too much,
    That I can love no more.

Scots Law

It is with surprise that some foreigners learn that there is in Scotland a legal system separate from that in England, a system which in company with the Established Presbyterian Church of Scotland survived the Treaty of Union of 1707. It still, after a fashion, and in the face of many difficulties, continues to survive the deep erosions into and serious infringements of that Treaty which have come about from the mere size of the dominant partner in the Union, the weight of London, the power of the Westminster Parliament and the supineness of the Scots themselves. How long it will continue to survive in a healthy condition and without the power of legislation in Edinburgh is a matter debated by eminent Scots lawyers themselves. Many of us have (in silence, of course, from lack of expert knowledge on the subject) heard them at it.

However, at the time of writing it does survive. And, just as a member of the Archbishop of Canterbury's vast and variegated flock is surprised to find himself, in the sense of not belonging to the Established Church, a Nonconformist three miles north of Berwick[1] (the Pope also, in the unlikely event of his visiting either England or Scotland, would be a Nonconformist) so does the English visitor to Scotland still surprisingly find himself subject to certain different laws and a number of different legal regulations. The facts that civil marriage used to be more easily contracted in Scotland than in England, and that the age for marriage without parental consent still is lower, have been popularised in Gretna Green fiction and are still the basis of many a lurid and inaccurate press story. There is also a fairly general knowledge that the verdict of Not Proven exists in Scotland, but even learned and sympathetic English lawyers are often unaware of the many other differences.

I lack the knowledge to speak even generally about these differences. At random, however, and from my own observation I mention the

[1] The Monarch, by one of those extraordinary compromises which only the English (and in this instance one must admit the British) can invent, is capable of belonging to two fundamentally different forms of Protestantism at the same time. In England the Queen is head of the Church of England. When at Braemar she becomes if not exactly a rigid member of the Church of Scotland a suppliant in its fold while worshipping at Crathie Kirk. Queen Victoria, indeed, while remaining head of the Church that contained Dr. Pusey and later the first Anglo-Catholics pushed her preference for the Presbyterian system so far as to make her communion for the last forty years of her life only according to the Church of Scotland rites. What did Mr. Gladstone think? Similarly what do the modern Anglo-Catholics who claim the Princess Margaret as one of their devotees think of her attendance at Crathie? And what do the logically and historically correct, strongly Episcopal-opposed members of the Church of Scotland think of a system which allows their Monarch to appoint Bishops on one side of a river and on the other worship in a national and Established Church whose foundations rest upon its repudiation of Bishops? These are questions to which we have never received satisfactory answers.

following. There is no Coroner's Court in Scotland, and a death whether it turns out to be murder or suicide is *primarily* investigated *in private* by the Procurator Fiscal. There are some English arguments against this private investigation, and they have (certainly in the past they had) weight. But today the amount of human misery saved by keeping the reporters out of the publicity ballyhoo of a suicide case does make our system in this respect more civilised. Moreover, when a man is charged with murder in Scotland there is no public preliminary examination before a Magistrate. The first the public, and consequently the jury, hear of the details of the case are at the trial. In these days of mass publicity in a sordid case this is surely an advantage. There are other differences which sometimes surprise visitors. A jury consists of fifteen not twelve members who, in cases of crime, may, apart from having three verdicts to choose from, come to a majority decision.

These are fairly obvious differences with which lawyers on both sides of the Border are familiar. The deeper difference between the Scottish and the Anglo-American systems can, by painful compression, be summed up thus. Scots law owes far more to Roman, Continental, and in particular French and Dutch origins than does the other. This also should be added. The continual struggle with England until the Union of the Crowns was, to put it mildly, unpropitious to the early growth and establishment of Scots law. In the seventeenth century and in an era of comparative peace, yet before the Union of Parliaments and therefore while legislation still lived in Edinburgh, it was possible to codify our system. It was fortunate for us that that great legal genius Lord Stair was at hand to do this. His *Institutions of the Law of Scotland* published in 1681 are the foundation of Scots law as it exists today.

Clearly I had to take selections from Stair's great work, and in this I was helped by a learned lawyer to whom I express due gratitude. Once I had digested the proper portions of Stair I was in some difficulty as to how to illustrate the theme of Scots wisdom from the innumerable Scottish judgments, the speeches in the Scottish courts and the writings about Scots law. I am not expert in law, nor even if I were should the fascinating subject of law bulk too largely in this anthology primarily devoted to literature and character.

Character was perhaps the operative word that guided me. Again on advice from those who know far more about Scots law than I do, I did not pursue a Scottish legal theme but made selections that appealed to me as illustrating the Scottish character in thought and speech. In one instance (the famous speech for the defence at Madeleine Smith's trial) I was impelled to give an extract almost solely on grounds of its eloquence—and highly Scottish eloquence at that. This brief portion of this anthology, then, does not, of course, pretend even to be a hurried conspectus of Scots law. It is a personal choice that has had the tolerant approval of some legal friends.

One extract in strict chronological order should have come into Part I of this anthology, one is in the eighteenth century, and others are more modern, coming down to the year in which these words are written. I have placed this 'Scots Law' section in the seventeenth century, however, simply because of Stair, with whom any study of our law must inevitably begin and who lived in that century.

VISCOUNT STAIR

Sir James Dalrymple, first Viscount Stair (1619–95), was an eminent figure in Scottish politics as well as a Judge at the time of the Revolution. We are concerned here only with his legal achievements. It would be an impertinence to attempt to evaluate his *Institutions*. This is what the great Lord Cooper said:

'Then came Stair. The publication of his *Institutions* in 1681 marked the creation of Scots Law as we have since known it—an original amalgam of Roman Law, Feudal Law and native customary law systematised by resort to the law of nature and the Bible, and illuminated by many flashes of ideal metaphysics. To this work and its author every Scots lawyer has since paid a tribute of almost superstitious reverence, and the resort still occasionally made to Stair in the House of Lords and the Privy Council suggests that it is not only in the estimation of his fellow-countrymen that he falls to be ranked amongst the great jurists of all time.'

The extracts herein made from the *Institutions of the Law of Scotland* are taken from the 1832 edition by John S. More. These extracts are divided into two sections. The first is from the dedication to the King (Charles II) setting forth the intention of the work, the second is from the body of the work itself. I have subdivided each section under (a), (b), (c), etc.

Under guidance I have followed no set theme in this selection and hope to do no more than to give examples of Stair's method and thought and incidentally of his agreeable and lucid style.

The extracts are, for the most part, self-explanatory. But the following points may be made in particular about I(c), where Stair says 'For we are happy in having so few and so clear statutes,' about I(d) and II(c). First, the general tradition of Scots statute law was that the Act of the Estates was short and virtually laid down a principle which had to be worked out by practice and judicial decision. If a statute was not observed or acted upon for a long time it was impliedly repealed by falling into desuetude—something not recognised in England and applying only to Scots Acts before 1707.

The doctrine of *stare decisis* or the slavish following of precedent was not in accord with Scots method, though it has now crept in from England. One decision even of a superior court was not, in our practice, binding: but once a *course* of decisions had laid down the same rule then that rule did become binding on later judges. This is particularly relevant to II(c).

The reader's attention is drawn also to II(f). In England until 1923 the law was that a single act of adultery by a wife entitled the husband to divorce. But a wife could not obtain a divorce unless his adultery was accompanied by cruelty or desertion for over two years. It is perhaps also worth noting that until just over a hundred years ago divorce in England required a private Act of Parliament and was a very costly affair. Whatever one's view of divorce may be, Scotland has at least long had the credit of (*a*) not discriminating between the sexes, and (*b*) not making divorce the luxurious prerogative of the rich.

Here are our extracts from Stair's *Institutions of the Law of Scotland.*

I. From the Dedication to the King

MAY IT PLEASE YOUR MAJESTY,

(*a*) I do humbly present to your Majesty, a Summary of the Laws and Customs of your ancient Kingdom of Scotland, which can be no where so fitly placed, as under the rays of your royal protection. I am confident it will tend to the honour and renown of your Majesty, and your princely progenitors, that you have governed this nation so long and so happily, by such just and convenient laws, which are here offered to the view of the world, in a plain, rational, and natural method: In which, material justice (the common law of the world) is, in the first place, orderly deduced from self-evident principles, through all the several private rights thence arising, and, in the next place, the expedients of the most polite nations, for ascertaining and expeding the rights and interests of mankind, are applied in their proper places, especially those which have been invented or followed by this nation. So that a great part of what is here offered is common to most civil nations, and is not like to be displeasing to the judicious and sober any where, who doat not so much upon their own customs as to think that none else are worthy of their notice. . . .

(*b*) A quaint and gliding style, much less the flourishes of eloquence, (the ordinary condiment and varnish, which qualify the pains of reading,) could not justly be expected in a treatise of law, which, of all subjects, doth require the most plain and accurate expression. To balance which, the nauseating burden of citations are, as much as can be, left out.

(*c*) We do not pretend to be amongst the great and rich kingdoms of the earth; yet we know not who can claim preference in antiquity and integrity, being of one blood and lineage, without mixture of any other people, and have so continued above two thousand years; during all which, no foreign power was ever able to settle the dominion of a strange Lord over us, or to make us forsake our allegiance to your Majesty's royal ancestors, our native and kindly kings; whereas most of the other kingdoms are compounds of divers nations, and have been subjugated to princes of different and opposite families, and ofttimes foreigners. The great monarchies, which did design universality, are all broken in pieces, and there is no family that can claim a just title to redintegrate any of them. There is no Emperor or King except yourself, but knows to what other family their predecessors did succeed, and when, and by what means. It is evident, what a mixture hath been in Greece and Italy, in France and Spain, in England and elsewhere. This nation hath not been obscure and unknown to the world; but the most famous nations have made use of our arms, and have still, in grateful remembrance, retained trophies and monuments of our courage and constancy. There be few wars in Christendom, wherein we have not had considerable bodies of soldiers regimented and commanded by themselves, and ofttimes general officers commanding them and whole armies of strangers, with great reputation and gallantry, which did advance them above the natives of those countries where they served. Neither have we wanted the fame of learning, at home and abroad, in the most eminent professions, divine or human. And as every where the most pregnant and active spirits apply themselves to the study and practice of law, so those that applied themselves to that profession amongst us, have given great evidence of sharp and piercing spirits, with much readiness of conception and dexterity of expression; which are necessary qualifications both of the bench and bar, whereby the law of this kingdom hath attained to so great perfection, that it may, without arrogance, be compared with the laws of any of our neighbouring nations. For we are happy in having so few and so clear statutes.[1] Our law is most part consuetudinary, whereby what is found inconvenient is obliterated and forgot. Our forms are plain and prompt, whereby the generality of the judicious have, with little pains, much insight in our law, and do, with the more security, enjoy their rights and possessions.

(d) We are not involved in the labyrinth of many and large statutes,[2] whereof the posterior do ordinarily so abrogate or derogate from the prior, that it requires a great part of a life to be prompt in all those windings, without which no man, with sincerity and confidence, can consult or plead, much less can the subjects, by their own industry, know where to rest, but must give more implicit faith to their judges and lawyers than they need, or ought, to give to their divines. And we do always prefer the sense, to the subtilty, of law, and do seldom trip by niceties or formalities.

[1] See annotation above to this section.   [2] *Ibid.*

II. From the Text

(*a*) Law is the dictate of reason, determining every rational being to that which is congruous and convenient for the nature and condition thereof.   (Book I, title 1, 1.)

(*b*) Before we come to the customs of Scotland, there lies this block in the way of all human laws, that seeing, as hath been said, equity and the law of nature and reason is perfect and perpetual, then all laws of men's constitution seem not only to be dangerous, in that they may impinge upon the perfect law of God, but also to be useless and unprofitable, seeing that men may live better and more safely by the devices of men; so that it may be thought that those, who, instead thereof, embrace the laws of men, may meet with the reproof of the Israelites, who were said *to reject God from reigning over them.* This reason is so pressing, that if the law of nature, and of reason, were equally known to all men, or that the dispensers thereof could be found so knowing, and so just, as men would and ought to have full confidence and quietness in their sentences, it would not only be a folly, but a fault, to admit of any other law. But the prime interest of men being to enjoy their rights, not only in safety and security, but in confidence and quietness of mind, that they may clearly know what is their right, and may securely enjoy the same; therefore human laws are added, not to take away the law of nature and reason, but some of the effects thereof, which are in our power. And therefore, as by the law of nature man is a free creature, yet so he may engage himself, and being engaged by the same law of nature, he must perform; so men's laws are nothing else but the public sponsions of princes and peoples; which therefore, even by the law of nature, they ought and must perform.   (I, 1, 15.)

(*c*) Surely they are most happy, whose laws are nearest to equity, and most declaratory of it, and least altering of the effects thereof, except in cases eminently profitable, like unto those now pointed to.[1] Yea, and the nations are more happy, whose laws have entered by long custom, wrung out from their debates upon particular cases, until it came to the consistence of a fixed and known custom. For thereby the conveniences and inconveniences thereof, through a tract of time, are experimentally seen; so that which is found in some cases convenient, if in other cases afterwards it be found inconvenient, it proves abortive in the womb of time, before it attain the maturity of a law.

[1] See annotation above to this section.

But, in statutes, the lawgiver must at once balance the conveniences and inconveniences, wherein he may, and often doth, fall short; and there do arise *casus incogitati*, wherein the statute is out, and then recourse must be had to equity. But those statutes are best, which are approbatory, or correctory, of experienced customs. And in customary law, though the people run some hazard at first of their judges' arbitrament; yet when that law is come to a full consistence, they have by much the advantage in this, that what custom hath changed is thrown away and obliterated, without memory or mention of it; but in statutory written law, the vestiges of all the alterations remain, and ordinarily increase to such a mass, that they cease to be evidences and securities to the people, and become labyrinths, wherein they are fair to lose their rights, if not themselves; at least, they must have an implicit faith in those, who cannot comprehend them, without making it the work of their whole life.   (I, 1, 15.)

(*d*) Liberty . . . is the most native and delightful right of man, without which he is capable of no other right; for bondage exeemeth man from the account of persons, and brings him in rather among things *quae sunt in patrimonio nostro*. And the encroachments upon, and injuries against, the right of liberty, of all others are the most bitter and atrocious.   (I, 2, 2.)

(*e*) Though liberty be the most precious right, yet it is not absolute, but limited: 1st, By the will of God and our obediential obligations to him, and to men, by his ordinance. And though man hath power of his own person, yet hath he no power of his own life, or his members, to dispose of them at his pleasure, either by taking away his life, or amputation, or disabling, of any member, either by himself, or by giving power to any other so to do, unless it be necessary for preserving the whole; but he is naturally obliged to God to maintain his life. So likewise men may be restrained or constrained by others, without encroachment upon the law of liberty, in the pursuance of other obediential obligations. . . . But in matters of utility and profit, where the natural liberty is not hemmed in with an obligation, there, unless by his own delinquency or consent, man cannot justly be restrained, much less constrained, upon pretence of his utility or profit; for liberty is far preferable to profit; and, in the matter of utility, every man is left to his own choice, and cannot, without injury to God and man, be hindered to do what he pleaseth, or be compelled to do what he pleaseth not, in things wherein he is free.   (I, 2, 5.)

(*f*) The affection of the property and chastity of women, and the animosity and jealousy, that ariseth in men naturally upon the breach thereof, do evince, that by the law of nature every man ought to content himself with his own wife, and women not to be common.[1] For as no man can endure the communication of his own, so it must necessarily follow, that he should not encroach upon another's property. (I, 4, 3.)

(*g*) For unfolding this right [sc. dominion, or property], and the progress thereof, both according to the order of time and nature, advert, *first*, That when God created man, he gave him dominion or lordship over all the creatures of the earth, in the air, and in the sea, *Gen*. i, verses 28 and 29, with power to man to dispose of the creatures, even to the consumption thereof; and it is like, that during man's innocency, there was upon the part of the creatures a great subjection and subserviency to man, till afterwards, when he revolted from God, the creatures revolted also from him. Yet God's dominion over man, and man's dominion over the creatures, remaineth still in right; so that he hath a legal power and warrant to dispose of them, though not so much possession, or natural power, being less able to master them than before. This dominion of the creatures was given by God, when there was yet no man but Adam and Eve only; whence some do infer, that Adam was not only governor of this whole inferior world, but that he was proprietor of it, and that all rights of government or property behoved to be derived from his disposal, or by succession to him, and that his monarchy did descend by primogeniture of his male race; so that if the person could be known, that doth, by progress, represent Adam, he would be the only righteous monarch of the world.

(II, 1, 1.)

It is a false and groundless opinion which some hold, that man, by his fall, hath lost his right to the creatures, until by grace he be restored, and that the sole dominion of them belongs to the saints, who may take them by force from all others. For, by the whole strain of the law of God, he still alloweth dominion and property of the creatures in man, without distinction, and prohibiteth all force or fraud in the contrary, which sufficiently cleareth that subtilty of man's forfeiture.

(II, 1, 1.)

(*h*) The first [sc. real right] is that of commonty, which all men have of things, which cannot be appropriated. (1) As, *first*, The air is common to all men, because it can have no limits or bounds, and because all men every where must necessarily breathe it. *Secondly*,

[1] See annotation above to this section.

Running waters are common to all men, because they can have no bounds; but water standing, and capable of bounds, is appropriated. *Thirdly,* The vast ocean is common to all mankind as to navigation and fishing, which are the only uses thereof, because it is not capable of bounds; but where the sea is inclosed, in bays, creeks, or otherwise is capable of any bounds or meiths, as within the points of such lands, or within the view of such shores, there it may become proper, but with the reservation of passage for commerce, as in the land. So fishing without these bounds is common to all, and within them also, except as to certain kinds of fishes, such as herrings, &c. *Fourthly,* All the wild and free creatures, which are in the property of none, are in some sort common to all, as fishes, fowls, bees, &c. But in respect that property hath taken hold of all that is appropriable, these are rather said to belong to none, as being by common consent declared void by all, that property thereof may be inferred by occupation and possession, without respect to the person's necessity or use, as was in the ancient community, but that simply whoever possesseth that which belongeth to none, doth thereby acquire the property thereof; which yet is restricted as to some kinds, as hawks and swans in some countries, and whales, extraordinary great fishes, salmon and herring fishings, &c, which are *inter regalia,* or are excluded from the property of the commons.   (II, 1, 5.)

THE KING VERSUS THE COURT OF SESSION

Before coming down to more modern times we return to a time nearly a century before Stair. In 1599 the Court of Session stood up to the monarch James VI who was then still in Edinburgh before the Union of the Crowns. The late Lord Birkenhead said of this incident: 'A nobler and more courageous expression of judicial independence was never made.' Given below is Lord Normand's account of it taken from his speech when he was elected President of the International Law Association at its forty-sixth meeting in 1954.[1] It requires no comment.

In 1599 a litigation took place here in Edinburgh in which a minister of the Presbyterian Church, Mr. Robert Bruce, claimed a stipend or emolument attaching to his clerical office as a parish minister. The stipend was also claimed by Lord Hamilton as lay donatory under a Crown grant of the revenues out of which the stipend was payable. The then King James VI, a monarch who fully deserved the description

[1] Report of the Forty-sixth Conference of the International Law Association, 1954, pp. 9 and 10.

'the wisest fool in Christendom' and a convinced upholder of the divine right of Kings, had his own reasons for disliking Mr. Robert Bruce. He appeared in person in the Court of Session to demand that it should dismiss the claim of Bruce and find in favour of Hamilton. The President of the Court, Alexander Seton, thereupon stood up and said to the King that he was President and had first place to speak, and therefore he said to the King that he was their King and they his subjects bound to obey him in all humility, which they all would do in all things for their lives, lands and gear, but that in matter of law and conscience, being sworn to justice, they would do as their consciences led them unless he commanded them to the contrary, in which case he said he would not vote at all nor no honest man there. The Lord of Newbattle, another judge, then also stood up and said to the King that it was said in the town, to his slander and theirs, that they durst not do justice but as the King commanded them; which he said should be seen to the contrary. He would vote against him in the right in his own presence. The Lords of Session all but one voted for Mr. Robert Bruce, 'whereat the King raged marvellously and is in great anger with the Lords of Session.' This account of the case we owe to the letter of an eye-witness, George Nicolson, addressed to Sir Robert Cecil, then a minister of Queen Elizabeth in London. Nicolson added, 'The King swears he will have Mr. Robert Bruce's cause reversed, which the President understanding says he will pen in Latin, French and Greek to be sent to all the judges in the world to be approved, and that by his vote it shall never be reversed, and so say the whole Session.' Surely never was the supremacy of the law over the state more fearlessly and resoundingly proclaimed.

INSANITY IN DEFENCE

Many people including Scots readers may learn with astonishment that the first Scots judge to deal with insanity as defence in a humane fashion was Lord Braxfield. Braxfield, indeed, anticipated most English judges in this.

Braxfield has a black reputation as a hanging Judge, an inveterate anti-reformer and the possessor of a 'coarse' old Scots tongue. This reputation arises from Cockburn's bitter references to him in his 'Memorials' and also from the fact that Stevenson took him as a subject in his classic portrait of the Scottish Judge in that great unfinished novel *Weir of Hermiston*. He needs no defence here, but those who are curious to learn the truth about this remarkable Scottish 'original' are referred to the late William Roughead's writings on him.

N

In 1788 there came before him Sir Archibald Gordon Kinloch who had killed his brother in a fit of madness. Here below is Braxfield's address to the jury.[1] It anticipates in a remarkable way our modern attitude.

Gentlemen of the Jury,—That Sir Francis Kinloch was killed by the hand of the pannel is proved beyond a doubt; you have therefore to consider the defence on his part set up. Now it will occur to any man of sound sense and judgment that there are different degrees of insanity.

If a man is totally and permanently mad, that man cannot be guilty of a crime; he is not amenable to the laws of his country. There is no room for placing the pannel in that predicament; for as a person totally and absolutely mad is not an object of punishment, so neither is he of trial.

The next insanity that is mentioned in our law books is one that is total but temporary. When such a man commits a crime he is liable to trial, but when he pleads insanity, it will be incumbent on him to prove that the deed was committed at a time when he was actually insane.

There is still another sort of distemper of the mind, a partial insanity, which only related to particular subjects or notions; such a person will talk and act like a madman upon those matters; but still if he has as much reason as enables him to distinguish between right and wrong, he must suffer that punishment which the law inflicts on the crime he has committed. You have therefore to consider the situation of the pannel, whether his insanity is of this last kind or whether he was, at the time he committed the crime, totally bereaved of reason. For if it is your opinion from the evidence that he was capable of knowing that murder was a crime, in that case you have to find him guilty.

Gentlemen, this is a question of some nicety. You have the testimony of certain witnesses that he was correct and coherent in his answers; and you have on the other hand evidence that he was totally deranged by a fever in the West Indies. In regard to a later period the conduct of the family with respect to him is also to be considered. It has been observed for the prosecutor that no steps were taken to secure him till just before the accident happened; whence it is attempted to be inforced that the family thought his disorder only a sort of melancholy and not a derangement of such degree as required confinement. I must

[1] *The Riddle of the Ruthvens*, by William Roughead, 'With Braxfield on the Bench,' pp. 453 *et seq.*

say that if this event had taken place eight days sooner than it did, this circumstance would have come with very great force against the pannel; but in the actual circumstances of the case it comes with more force in his favour, and is a consideration of weight upon his side. For it is proved that a nurse had actually been provided to take care of him, and a strait-waistcoat prepared to put on him; and pity it is that this plan was not timeously put in execution.

Gentlemen, I shall not take up more of your time. You will consider the evidence well, and decide according to your consciences. If you are convinced that he knew right from wrong, you will return a verdict of guilty. On the other hand, if it shall appear to you that he was not able to distinguish between moral good and evil, you are bound to acquit him. But, gentlemen, I think that in all events a verdict of not guilty is not the proper verdict for you to return. I think you ought to return a special verdict, finding that the pannel was guilty of taking the life of his brother, but finding also that he was insane at the time.

THE DEFENCE OF MADELEINE SMITH

The trial of Madeleine Smith on the charge of murder which took place in Edinburgh in 1857 remains one of the most famous of its kind in the annals of English and Scottish Justice. It is so well known that all we need to say here is that Madeleine, a young girl of good family in mid-Victorian Glasgow, was accused of poisoning her seedy French lover. The verdict was Not Proven. She was an enigmatic figure who lived to be over ninety, and died within the memory of some now living, in 1928 in New York.

The question of her guilt or innocence has been ceaselessly debated for over a hundred years. One thing is certain. She owed her escape from the verdict of Guilty largely to the skill and superb eloquence of her counsel, John Inglis. It is on account of its eloquence alone that I give two extracts from his long and celebrated speech for the defence. Its opening is classic. Who, reading this, even on the cold printed page, can deny the quality of Scottish legal eloquence?

Having posed that question I would ask the reader to exercise his imagination on the question of how the speech was delivered. No counsel either in Scotland or England addresses the jury in this fashion now. It would be considered unpardonably theatrical. Yet John Inglis, the responsible Dean of Faculty (that is head of the Scottish bar), was no histrionic appealer to the gallery. He was a skilful, assiduous, conscientious and tireless lawyer who eventually became one of our greatest Lord Presidents of the Court of Session.

The two extracts printed below come from the opening and end of his long address.[1] Between them he marshalled his facts in the most lucid, telling and weighty manner, yet the conventions of the time allowed, even called for the use of eloquence in its proper place. He rose to the occasion superbly. His words which read here with the measured balance of fine prose were, of course, spoken without notes and in the recognisably Scottish tones of a Scotsman born and bred. They may have been, to English ears, rugged tones, without the polish of a Southron accent, yet they came from his heart and from his sense of duty. To have heard the Dean of Faculty deliver this speech in 1857 must have been to have heard native Scottish eloquence of the time at its best.

The Beginning of the Speech

Gentlemen of the jury, the charge against the prisoner is murder, and the punishment of murder is death; and that simple statement is sufficient to suggest to us the awful solemnity of the occasion which brings you and me face to face. But, gentlemen, there are peculiarities in the present case of so singular a kind—there is such an air of romance and mystery investing it from beginning to end—there is something so touching and exciting in the age, and the sex, and the social position of the accused—ay, and I must add, the public attention is so directed to the trial, that they watch our proceedings and hang on our very accents with such an anxiety and eagerness of expectation, that I feel almost bowed down and overwhelmed by the magnitude of the task that is imposed on me. You are invited and encouraged by the prosecutor to snap the thread of that young life, and to consign to an ignominious death on the scaffold one who, within a few short months, was known only as a gentle and confiding and affectionate girl, the ornament and pride of her happy home. Gentlemen, the tone in which my learned friend, the Lord Advocate, addressed you yesterday could not fail to strike you as most remarkable. It was characterised by great moderation—by such moderation as I think must have convinced you that he could hardly expect a verdict at your hands—and in the course of that address, for which I give him the highest credit, he could not resist the expression of his own deep feeling of commiseration for the position in which the prisoner is placed, which was but an involuntary homage paid by the official prosecutor to the kind and generous nature of the man. But, gentlemen, I am going to ask you for something very different from commiseration; I am going to ask you for that which I will not condescend to beg, but which I will loudly and importunately demand—that to which every prisoner is

[1] *The Trial of Madeleine Smith*, edited by Tennyson Jesse, pp. 233 and 273–4.

entitled, whether she be the lowest and vilest of her sex or the maiden whose purity is as the unsunned snow. I ask you for justice; and if you will kindly lend me your attention for the requisite period, and if heaven grant me patience and strength for the task, I shall tear to tatters that web of sophistry in which the prosecutor has striven to involve this poor girl and her sad, strange story.

The Ending of the Speech

I have thus laid before you, as clearly as I could, what I conceive to be all the important branches of this inquiry separately, and as calmly and deliberately as I could; and I now ask you to bring your judgment— to bring the whole powers with which God has endowed you—to the performance of your most solemn duty. I have heard it said that juries have nothing to do with the consequences of their verdicts, and that all questions of evidence must be weighed in the same scale, whether the crime be a capital one or merely penal in a lower degree. I cannot agree to that proposition. I cannot too indignantly repudiate such a doctrine. It may suit well enough the cramped mind of a legal pedant, or the leaden rules of a heartless philosophy; but he who maintains such a doctrine is entirely ignorant of what materials a jury is, and ought to be, composed. Gentlemen, you are brought here for the performance of this great duty, not because you have any particular skill in the sifting or weighing of evidence—not because your intellects have been highly cultivated for that or similar purposes—not because you are a class or caste set apart for the work; but you are here because, as the law expresses it, you are indifferent men—because you are like, not because you are unlike, other men; not merely because you have clear heads, but because you have warm and tender hearts—because you have bosoms filled with the same feelings and emotions, and because you entertain the same sympathies and sentiments as those whose lives, characters, and fortunes are placed in your hands. To rely, therefore, upon your reason only, is nothing less than impiously to refuse to call to your aid, in the performance of a momentous duty, the noblest gifts that God has implanted in your breasts. Bring with you then to this service, I beseech you, not only your clear heads, but your warm hearts—your fine moral instincts, and your guiding and regulating consciences—for thus, and thus only, will you satisfy the oath which you have taken. To determine guilt or innocence by the light of intellect alone is the exclusive prerogative of infallibility; and when man's presumptuous arrogance tempts him to usurp the attribute of Omniscience, he only exposes the weakness and frailty of his own nature. Then, indeed,

> 'Man, proud man,
> Dressed in a little brief authority,
> Most ignorant of what he's most assured,
> Plays such fantastic tricks before high Heaven,
> As make the angels weep.'

Raise not, then, your rash and impotent hands to rend aside the veil in which Providence has been pleased to shroud the circumstances of this mysterious story. Such an attempt is not within your province, nor the province of any human being. The time may come—it certainly will come—perhaps not before the Great Day in which the secrets of all hearts shall be revealed—and yet it may be that in this world, and during our own lifetime, the secret of this extraordinary story may be brought to light. It may even be that the true perpetrator of this murder, if there was a murder, may be brought before the bar of this very Court. I ask you to reflect for a moment what the feelings of any of us would then be. It may be our lot to sit in judgment on the guilty man. It may be the lot of any one of you to be empanelled to try the charge against him. Would not your souls recoil with horror from the demand for more blood? Would not you be driven to refuse to discharge your duty in condemning the guilty, because you had already doomed the innocent to die? I say, therefore, ponder well before you permit anything short of the clearest evidence to induce or mislead you into giving such an awful verdict as is demanded of you. Dare any man hearing me—dare any man here or elsewhere say that he has formed a clear opinion against the prisoner—will any man venture for one moment to make that assertion? And yet, if on anything short of clear opinion you convict the prisoner, reflect—I beseech you, reflect—what the consequences may be. Never did I feel so unwilling to part with a jury—never did I feel as if I had said so little as I feel now after this long address. I cannot explain it to myself, except by a strong and overwhelming conviction of what your verdict ought to be. I am deeply conscious of a personal interest in your verdict, for if there should be any failure of justice I could attribute it to no other cause than my own inability to conduct the defence; and I feel persuaded that, if it were so, the recollection of this day and this prisoner would haunt me as a dismal and blighting spectre to the end of life. May the Spirit of all Truth guide you to an honest, a just, and a true verdict! But no verdict will be either honest, or just, or true,

unless it at once satisfies the reasonable scruples of the severest judgment, and yet leaves undisturbed and unvexed the tenderest conscience
among you.

LORD SANDS ON INDECENCY

In 1930 Lord Sands gave judgment on appeal in a comparatively
obscure and not very important case concerning the sale of indecent
or obscene prints in a small shop in the back streets of Glasgow. In
view of the recent disputes on obscene and indecent publications it
cannot be said that he anticipated modern views or came to any unusual
decisions even for thirty years ago. It should be remembered that Scots
law on obscene publication differed and still differs from English law,
particularly in the matter of intention; this is too complicated to enter
into here. Lord Sands' judgment is, however, lucid, easy to follow and
interesting. Extracts are given below.

They are included here less for these admirable qualities than for
the patent Scottishness of style. His Lordship clearly loved playing with
ideas in an almost Urquhartianly humorous manner. Yet he put forward
these ideas without a smile and with that gravity of demeanour which
only heightened the humour. Once more the reader is asked to imagine
the following speech delivered in undoubtedly Scottish tones. We would
also draw his attention to this delightful illustration: 'A picture of Mrs.
Brown, to which only the very straitlaced might take exception if displayed as a work of art in a remote city, might become grossly indecent
if displayed in Brown's drawing-room in Edinburgh.' There is another
passage worthy of note. It is the one beginning 'I have no doubt but
that there are a few pictures of the nude in the fine collection of the
Glasgow Gallery.' Here speaks the voice of a Scots lawyer who might
have come out of the pages of Walter Scott.

Lord Sands, 1930[1]

This case concerns the keeping for sale of indecent or obscene prints.
I do not think that the two words 'indecent' and 'obscene' are
synonymous. The one may shade into the other, but there is a difference of meaning. It is easier to illustrate than define, and I illustrate
thus. For a male bather to enter the water nude in the presence of
ladies would be indecent, but it would not necessarily be obscene.
But if he directed the attention of a lady to a certain member of his
body his conduct would certainly be obscene. The matter might
perhaps be roughly expressed thus in the ascending scale—Positive—
Immodest; Comparative—Indecent; Superlative—Obscene. These,
however, are not rigid categories. The same conduct, which in certain

[1] MacGowan v. Langmuir, Justiciary Cases, pp. 13–17.

circumstances may merit only the milder description, may in other circumstances deserve a harder one. 'Indecent' is a milder term than 'obscene,' and as it satisfies the purposes of this case if the prints in question are indecent, I shall apply that test.

In using the expression indecency in relation to this case, I am, of course, referring to decency and indecency in relation to sex, and to nudity, and to physiological functions; for the words 'decent' or 'indecent' are often used in relation to matters of conduct which have no such significance. 'Indecent,' in the sense which I am considering, I take to mean contrary to decency in relation to exposure, gesture, or language, in accordance with the standards which prevail in the country at the time. These standards have varied in different ages, and they vary today in different countries. If I recollect aright, this observation is as old as Herodotus. There is nothing indecent in the human frame. Such a suggestion would be a libel upon nature. But the most venerable record in history recognises that, while nakedness is innocent, shame comes with the consciousness of nakedness—'They were both naked, the man and his wife, and were not ashamed . . . and the eyes of them both were opened, and they knew that they were naked; and they sewed fig leaves together and made themselves aprons.' Except among some of the lowest savages the public exposure of certain parts of the human body to the gaze of members of the opposite sex has been regarded as indecent so far back as historical records extend. Even the wave-tossed and half-drowned Ulysses—

> 'With his strong hand broke from a goodly tree
> A leafy bough that he might hide his shame'

before he ventured to approach fair Nausicaa and her maidens. The story of the sons of Noah shows that in certain circumstances this veto was not limited to exposure as between members of the opposite sex.

It can hardly, I think, be regarded, speaking generally, as not indecent to depict or portray for promiscuous public exhibition what it would be indecent to display. No doubt the absence of reciprocal consciousness in the former case is a circumstance which in certain cases may make a difference, but this qualification is a limited one. To put it quite plainly; on the assumption that it would be indecent for a woman to stand nude in a shop window as an advertisement, it would, in my view, be indecent to display in that shop window a life-size photograph of the woman in a state of frank nudity. One may perhaps concede that there might be a difference in degree for the reason I have indicated. Under a convention, however, which extends

far back in the history of civilisation, an exception has been recognised
to the general rule that, what it is deemed indecent publicly to expose,
it is indecent to depict for public exhibition. That convention concerns
works of art. There have been differences of opinion as to how far
that convention should extend, but into that one need not enter. The
concession, if such it be regarded, to art is hedged in certain ways.
The nude must be impersonal. A picture of the nude, which a house-
holder might display in his drawing-room as a work of art, would,
however perfect in that regard, be regarded as grossly indecent if the
person depicted was his wife or daughter. This, as it appears to me,
illustrates the relativity of indecency, and how impossible it may
often be to pronounce upon it apart from circumstances. A picture of
Mrs. Brown, to which only the very straitlaced might take exception
if displayed as a work of art in a remote city, might be grossly indecent
if displayed in Brown's drawing-room in Edinburgh.[1] There is another
very well recognised limitation. Even as regards the accurate depicting
of the female frame, there is one limitation which has from classical
times been observed, in disregard of fidelity, except in debased forms
of art.

We must, I think, recognise and accept the convention which shields
works of art, but we must confine it within the limits to which it
properly extends. A representation of nudity in what is not a work of
art is not to be regarded as protected because similar realism in a work
of art would not be regarded as indecent. Further, I am not prepared
to affirm that the question whether a picture is decent or indecent
falls to be determined simply upon a consideration of the picture as
being or not being a work of art, irrespective of the circumstances
under which it is exhibited. Few, I think, would contest the proposition that a picture of the nude, which might quite legitimately be
exhibited in a public gallery, might be a most inappropriate adorn-
ment of the sixth form room in a public school. I am not prepared to
take it that, because this may be a work of art which might be exhibited
without offence in a public gallery, it is a matter of mere expediency,
and not of decency, whether it should be exhibited in the classroom.
I refuse to divorce the picture from the circumstances by which it is
surrounded, and I affirm that the picture as so exhibited is an indecent
picture. Rightly or wrongly, a high protection is accorded to works
of art, but in order to claim that protection, in my view, it is necessary
to show that they are exhibited simply as works of art, without any
erotic appeal beyond what may be inevitable.

[1] See annotation above.

There is not, in my view, any absolute standard of indecency. There is always an element of relativity. There is no indecency in the illustrations in medical works of human anatomy, which it would be highly indecent to display in a shop window. Charts and realistic coloured illustrations, which might be exhibited in a medical class-room, might be grossly indecent as adornments of a place of public worship, or even of a private sitting-room. Again, many great libraries contain collections of prints and books carefully guarded from public scrutiny. These are kept, and quite properly kept, as records of human ideas and manners for historical and scientific purposes, and there is no indecency in such preservation. But it might be grossly indecent to put them in general circulation, or even to exhibit them indiscriminately to the curious.

To turn, however, from these general considerations to the more squalid consideration of what has been established in the present case. The charge against the appellant is that he did keep for sale in his shop indecent or obscene prints or representations, contrary to the Glasgow Corporation Order Confirmation Act, 1914, section 21. The charge being one of keeping indecent prints for sale, the magistrate was, in my view, entitled to take into account the whole circumstances, the number of the prints, their mode of display, and their get up, as suggestive on the one hand of sale as works of art to those interested therein, or on the other hand of popular sale in virtue of some other allurement. The magistrate was, in my view, entitled to take all these things into account, not merely for the purpose of determining whether all these prints were being kept for sale, but also, as explained in what I have said as to the relative element, for the purpose of determining the question whether, in the circumstances, the prints were indecent. The magistrate has found the appellant guilty of the charge; in other words he has found that the prints were indecent or obscene. The magistrate is the judge of that matter, and he is final unless he has erred in law, or unless there were no facts upon which a magistrate could reasonably reach the conclusion at which he arrived. . . .

I have no doubt but that there are a few pictures of the nude in the fine collection of the Glasgow Gallery. But, unless it is unlike other similar galleries, one might wander there for an hour without encountering one of the class who congregate round the appellant's shop window. It would be mere affectation, it would be contrary to common sense, to suggest that the appeal in this latter case is to artistic taste. Beyond all doubt or question it is to prurient curiosity. The magistrate having found that these prints, kept for sale in the manner in which they are sold, are indecent, it appears to me that it would be out of the question that we should hold that this was an unreasonable conclusion, merely because of an expression of opinion by the magistrate that works of art with similar nudity might be exhibited in an art gallery. It was quite open to the appellant to have urged upon the magistrate that these prints were kept for exposure for sale on account of their appeal to artistic taste, and not with the intention of exciting the appeal to erotic emotions, which latter intention, according to authorities so eminent as Lord Justice-Clerk Macdonald and Chief Justice Cockburn, is one of the touchstones of indecency. I do not know whether this consideration was urged upon the magistrate, but, if it was, I am not surprised that he declined to entertain such a ridiculous suggestion.

In my view, we are not called upon to disturb the conviction. I am under no apprehension that the view I take need cause any embarrass-ment to merchants who have albums or collections of artistic prints for exhibition and sale to connoisseurs or those who are interested in art.

The Act of Union

The Union between the Parliaments of England and Scotland occurred in 1707 and 'ane auld sang' ended. Little comment is called for. All that need be done is sadly to record some reporting and editorial remarks and one famous reported speech by a Scottish peer taken from Daniel Defoe's *History of the Union*, which he wrote as a spectator of the proceedings in Edinburgh. We have used the first edition of this work, to which all references are made.

Defoe was an amiable and industrious journalist who was also touched with genius.[1] He sincerely liked the Scots and sincerely believed that the Union was as much to their advantage as to that of the English. During his period as an agent sent up from England to propagate the idea of a Union he made many Scottish friends, and not only amongst those of his own political views. He was no underhand James Harryson 'Scottishman.' Englishmen of his honest and forthright kind, especially if they write and speak as well as he did, are still well liked in Scotland. Even the strongest opponents of the Union today bear the memory of Defoe no ill-will.

Defoe's mellifluously composed dedication to the Queen (for which we have, unfortunately, no space) in its own manner and of its kind puts the 1707 case for the Union as well as it could be put—better indeed than did many of the pro-Union Scottish speakers.

Lord Belhaven's still remembered speech is the most forceful, and certainly the most eloquent one against the Union. We would draw attention to only two points in it. It will be observed that, in the flood of his patriotic expression, Belhaven evokes the familiar female image of Caledonia. It was the image seen by the anonymous author of the *Complaint of Scotland*. It is a sister to the image (as we shall see) that appeared to Burns in his poem *The Vision*. It is the image with which in quotation from Thomas of Ercildoun this anthology opened. The other point which it would be a pity to miss is the pathos of the reporter's interpolated statement '*No Answer*' after Belhaven's appeal for a truce to internal Scottish dissension.

The final editorial reporting from Defoe's pen which is printed here requires only one comment. It will be noticed that the Earl of Marchmont's sour little reply to Belhaven evoked appreciative laughter. Laughter of this kind is still heard in Scotland today.

[1] He wrote his *Robinson Crusoe* at the age of fifty-eight. *Crusoe* is one of the greatest novels in English, but it is worth noting that the greatest novel in any language was also begun at the same age. Cervantes composed the first part of *Don Quixote* in his fifty-ninth year. This irrelevant piece of information is thrown out in order to cheer up any professional writer in the last gasp of his fifties—'the youth of old age.' And for further encouragement it may be added that Cervantes wrote the splendid second part (that rarely successful thing a sequel) of *Quixote* when he was sixty-nine.

But there was another sound than laughter that rang out high over the High Street of Edinburgh on the day when the Act of Union was passed in the Scottish Parliament. According to tradition some unknown individual managed to get into the belfry of the High Kirk of St. Giles and played upon the bells there the then well-known tune 'Why Should I be Sad upon my Wedding-Day?'

In those days this tune was played in slow time as a lament. Later the melody was turned into the brisker dance tune of 'I was at a Wedding at Inveraray, but all they gave me was shell-fish.' Inveraray is, of course, the seat of the Duke of Argyll, head of the Campbell clan. It is understandable then that later still, in the nineteenth century, the tune took its present form of 'The Campbells are Coming.' There are some Macdonalds who, even today, would regard this as a more sombre piece of music than 'Why Should I be Sad upon my Wedding-Day?'

The melody began, however, as a lament; and as such it was played on the bells of St. Giles on the passing of the Act of Union in 1707. It was, in truth, the end of an old song.

I. FROM LORD BELHAVEN'S SPEECH[1]

Next spoke the Lord *Beilhaven*, but without answering what had been said by M. *Seton*, he made a long premeditate Speech, the Nature of which will be best understood by Reading it at length, which being so much talk'd of in the World, I have also inserted here, tho' I shall not trouble the Reader with many more Speeches in this whole History.

My Lord Chancellor,

'When I consider this Affair of an UNION betwixt the Two Nations, as it is express'd in the several *Articles* thereof, and now the Subject of our Deliberation at this time; I find my Mind crowded with variety of very Melancholy Thoughts, and I think it my Duty to disburden my self of some of them, by laying them before, and exposing them to the serious Consideration of this Honourable House.

'I think I see *a Free and Independent Kingdom* delivering up That, which all the World hath been fighting for, since the days of *Nimrod*; yea, that for which most of all the Empires, Kingdoms, States, Principalities and Dukedoms of *Europe*, are at this very time engaged in the most Bloody and Cruel Wars that ever were, *to wit*, A Power to Manage their own Affairs by themselves, without the Assistance and Counsel of any other.

[1] From Defoe's *History of the Union*, pp. 32–41.

'I think I see *a National Church*, founded upon a Rock, secured by a *Claim of Right*, hedged and fenced about by the strictest and pointedest Legal Sanction that Sovereignty could contrive, voluntarily descending into a Plain, upon an equal level with *Jews*, *Papists*, *Socinians*, *Arminians*, *Anabaptists*, and other Sectaries, &c.

'I think I see *the Noble and Honourable Peerage of Scotland*, whose Valiant Predecessors led Armies against their Enemies upon their own proper Charges and Expenses, now divested of their Followers and Vassalages, and put upon such an Equal Foot with their Vassals, that I think I see a petty *English* Excise-man receive more Homage and Respect, than what was paid formerly to their *quondam Maccallanmores*.

'I think I see *the present Peers of* Scotland, whose Noble Ancestors conquered Provinces, over-run Countries, reduc'd and subjected Towns and fortify'd Places, exacted Tribute through the greatest part of *England*, now walking in the Court of Requests like so many *English* Attornies, laying aside their Walking Swords when in Company with the *English* Peers, lest their Self-defence should be found Murder.

'I think I see *the Honourable Estate of Barons*, the bold Asserters of the Nation's Rights and Liberties in the worst of Times, now setting a Watch upon their Lips and a Guard upon their Tongues, lest they be found guilty of *Scandalum Magnatum*.

'I think I see *the Royal State of Burrows* walking their desolate Streets, hanging down their Heads under Disappointments; wormed out of all the Branches of their old Trade, uncertain what hand to turn to, necessitate to become Prentices to their unkind Neighbours; and yet after all finding their Trade so fortified by Companies, and secured by Prescriptions, that they despair of any success therein.

'I think I see *our Learned Judges* laying aside their Practiques and Decisions, studying the Common Law of *England*, gravelled with Certioraries, *Nisi prius's*, Writs of Error, Verdicts indovar, *Ejectione firmæ*, Injunctions, Demurrs, &c. and frighted with Appeals and Avocations, because of the new Regulations and Rectifications they may meet with.

'I think I see *the Valiant and Gallant Soldiery* either sent to learn the Plantation Trade Abroad; or at Home Petitioning, for a small Subsistance as the Reward of their honourable Exploits, while their old Cores are broken, the common Soldiers left to Beg, and the youngest *English* Corps kept standing.

'I think I see *the Honest Industrious Tradesman* loaded with new

Taxes, and Impositions, disappointed of the Equivalents, drinking Water in place of Ale, eating his fat-less Pottage, Petitioning for Encouragement to his Manufacturies, and Answered by counter Petitions.

'In short, I think I see *the Laborious Plew-man*, with his Corns spoiling upon his Hands, for want of Sale, Cursing the day of his Birth, dreading the Expense of his Burial, and uncertain whether to Marry or do worse.

'I think I see the Incureable Difficulties of the *Landedmen*, fettered under the Golden Chain of Equivalents, their pretty Daughters Petitioning for want of Husbands, and their Sons for want of Imployments.

'I think I see *our Mariners*, delivering up their Ships to their *Dutch* Partners; and what through Presses and Necessity, earning their Bread as Underlings in the Royal *English* Navy.

'But above all, *My Lord*, I think I see *our Ancient Mother* CALEDONIA, like *Cæsar* sitting in the midst of our Senate, Rufully looking round about her, Covering her self with her Royal Garment, attending the Fatal Blow, and breathing out her last with a *Et tu quoque mi fili.*

'Are not these, *My Lord*, very afflicting Thoughts? And yet they are but the least part Suggested to me by these Dishonourable Articles; should not the Consideration of these things vivifie these *dry Bones* of ours? Should not the Memory of our Noble Predecessors *Valour and Constancie*, rouse up our drouping Spirits? Are our Noble Predecessors Souls got so far into the *English Cabbage-Stock and Colliflowers*, that we should shew the least Inclination that way? Are our Eyes so Blinded? Are our Ears so Deafned? Are our Hearts so Hardned? Are our Tongues so Faltered? Are our Hands so Fettered, that in this our day, I say, *My Lord, That in this our day, that we should not mind the things, that concern the very Being and Well-being of our Ancient Kingdom, before the day be hid from our Eyes.*

'No, *My Lord*, GOD *forbid, Man's Extremity is* GOD's *Opportunity: He is a present Help in time of need; and a Deliverer, and that right early.* Some unforeseen Providence will fall out, that may cast the Ballance; some *Joseph* or other will say, *Why do ye strive together, since you are Brethren?* None can Destroy *Scotland*, save *Scotland*'s self; hold your Hands from the Pen, you are Secure. Some *Judah* or other will say, *Let not our hands be upon the Lad, he is our Brother.* There will be a JEHOVAH-JIREH and *some Ram will be caught in the Thicket*, when the bloody Knife is at our Mothers Throat; Let us up then, *My Lord*,

208   THE WISDOM OF THE SCOTS

and let our Noble Patriots behave themselves like Men, and we know
not how soon a Blessing may come. . . .

'For the Love of GOD then, *My Lord*, for the Safety and Wellfare
of our Ancient Kingdom, whose sad Circumstances I hope we shall
yet Convert unto Prosperity and Happiness! We want no Means, if
we Unite, GOD blesseth the Peace-makers, we want neither Men nor
Sufficiency of all manner of things necessary, to make a Nation happy:
all depends upon Management, *Concordia res parvæ crescunt*. I fear
not these Articles, tho they were ten times worse than they are, if we
once Cordially forgive one another, and that according to our Proverb,
bygones be bygones and fair play to come. For my part in the sight of
GOD and in the presence of this Honourable House I heartily forgive
every Man, and beggs that they may do the same to me, and I do
most humbly propose, that his Grace *My Lord Commissioner* may
appoint an *Agape*, may order a Love-Feast for this Honourable House,
that we may lay aside all self designs, and after our Fasts and
Humiliations may have a day of Rejoicing and Thankfulness, may eat
our Meat with Gladness, and our Bread with a Merry Heart, then
shall we *sit each Man under his own Fig-tree*, and *the Voice of the Turtle
shall be heard in our Land*, a Bird famous for Constancy and Fidelity.

'*My Lord*, I shall make a Pause here and stop going on further in
my Discourse till I see further, if his Grace my Lord Commissioner
receive any Humble Proposals for removing Misunderstandings
among us, and putting an end to our Fatal Divisions, upon Honour
I have no other design, and I am Content to begg the favour upon
my bended knees.'

No Answer

'*My Lord Chancellor*, I am sorry, that I must pursue the Threed of
my Sad and Melancholy Story: what remains, I am afraid, prove as
afflicting as what I have said; I shall therefore Consider the Motives,
which have ingaged the two Nations to enter upon a Treaty of Union
at this time: in general, *My Lord*, I think both of them had in their
View to better themselves by the Treaty; but before I enter upon the
Particular Motives of each Nation, I must inform this Honourable
House, that since I can Remember, the two Nations have altered their
Sentiments upon that Affair, even almost to Downright Contradiction,
they have changed Headbands, as we say, for *England* till of late never
thought it worth their pains of Treating with us; the good Bargain
they made at the Beginning, they resolve to keep, and that which we
call an Incorporating Union was not so much as in their thoughts.

The first Notice they seem'd to take of us, was in our Affair of
Caledonia, when they had most effectually broke off that design in a
manner very well known to the World, and unnecessary to be repeated
here, they kept themselves quiet during the time of our Complaints
upon that Head. In which time our Sovereign, to satisfie the Nation
and allay their Heats, did condescend to give us some good Laws,
and amongst others that of Personal Liberties and of Peace and War;
but *England* having declared their Succession and extended their
Intail without ever taking Notice of us; our Gracious Sovereign
QUEEN ANNE was Graciously pleased to give the Royal Assent to
our *Act of Security*, and to give us a hedge to all our Sacred and Civil
Interests, by Declaring it High Treason to endeavour the Alteration
of them, as they were then Established. Thereupon did follow the
Threatning and Minatory Laws against us by the Parliament of
England and the unjust and unequal Character of what Her Majesty
had so Graciously Condescended to in our Favours: Now *My Lord*
whether the desire they had to have us ingaged in the same Succession
with them; Or whether that they found us like a free and independent
People breathing after more Liberty than what formerly was lookt
after: Or whether they were afraid of our *Act of Security* in case of
Her Majesties Decease: which of all these Motives has induced them
to a Treaty I leave it to themselves, this I must say only, they have
made a good Bargain this time also.

'For the particular Motives that induced us, I think, they are
Obvious to be known; we found by sad Experience, that every Man
hath advanced in Power and Riches, as they have done in Trade, and
at the same time considering that no where through the World, Slaves
are found to be Rich, though they should be adorned with Chains of
Gold, we thereupon changed our Notion of an Incorporating Union
to that of a Federal one; and being resolved to take this Opportunity
to make Demands upon them, before we enter into the Succession, we
were content to Impower Her Majesty to Authorise and Appoint
Commissioners to Treat with the Commissioners of *England*, with as
ample Powers as the Lords Commissioners from *England* had from their
Constituents, that we might not appear to have less Confidence in
Her Majesty, nor more narrow hearted in our Act than our Neighbours
of *England*: and thereupon last Parliament, after Her Majesty's
Gracious Letter was Read, Desiring us to declare the Succession in the
first place, and afterwards to appoint Commissioners to Treat; we
found it necessary to renew our former *Resolve*, which I shall Read
to this Honourable House.'

o

II. DEFOE'S REPORT OF THE END OF THAT
DAY'S PROCEEDINGS[1]

'The time had been taken up with their length, and the House, as well as the Nation, was, at this time, in an Unusual Ferment, so not many Replies were made. Mr. *Seton*, who made the first Speech, stood up to Answer the Lord *Beilhaven*, but, as he had already spoken, the Orders of the House, *viz. That the same Member could not speak twice in the same Cause*, were urged against his speaking, and the Earl of Ma——mont then standing up the Lord Chancellor gave him place. The Earl of *Ma——monts* Speech was short and occasioned some laughter. It was to this Purpose, *viz. He had heard a long Speech and a very terrible one, but he was of Opinion, it required a short Answer*, which he gave in these Words, *Behold he Dream'd, but, lo! when he awoke, he found it was a Dream*; This Answer, some said, was as Satisfactory to the Members, who understood the Design of that Speech, as if it had been Answered Vision by Vision.

'After these two Speeches, several Members spoke *Pro* and *Con*; But the Debate, in Close of the Day, turned so Warm, That, at the Desire of the House, it was Adjourned to the next *Sederunt*.'

[1] Defoe's *History of the Union*, p. 44.

David Hume

Hume proclaimed himself, in the triumphant peroration of a passage quoted below, 'a citizen of the world.' He was indeed; and it may seem an impertinence here to state the obvious: that is that his was one of the greatest philosophical minds which Europe and the Western world has produced since Aristotle. That impertinence may be slightly reduced by the consideration that there are those who would deny this fact. It is, however, so.

Having stated that fact, it may seem an added impertinence to claim the wisdom of so large a figure as a part of the wisdom of the Scots. Does he not (whether you receive or repel the conclusions of his philosophy) pass beyond nationality? Maybe, but his roots were in his nation, deep in his nation. His cast of thought can be shown to be Scottish; his way of expressing himself was certainly Scottish.[1] Among our major writers no man, not even Burns or Scott, has been more consciously, more passionately Scottish, more devoted to the fact of Scotland. Citizen of the world though he was, no man than himself would have been more offended by the notion that his international status denied, precluded or overshadowed his Scottish nationality.

David Hume was the younger son of the Laird of Ninewells in Berwickshire, and it is worth noting by our modern levellers that he was conscious and proud of his gentle birth. A younger son, however, of a Laird in the thin time of the earlier half of the eighteenth century in Scotland had a particularly thin time. This temporal leanness, with David Hume, only excited his powers and led his ambitions in the direction of the Scottish intellectual life of the period, and of which he was to become so luminously characteristic an example.

He did not inherit the paternal estate and at no time had prospects of it. He had no competence beyond a sum of about £40 a year; he was educated with his elder brother and had, in his eyes, to justify himself before Esau. No mess of pottage, however, or even porridge changed plates. He became precocious and energetic in mind, and turned his powers and hopes towards literary fame for which, even from early life, he evidently longed. Judged by the standards which he set himself in this respect he achieved much of his ambition and attained happiness. Happiness, sunniness of temperament were, indeed, marks of his personality, but, in common with the rest of mankind who get what they want, he was touched by that melancholy which is the birthright of all thinking mortals and is the occupational complaint of being a success. But he had his own remedy for this.

This is not the place in which to discourse on Hume's philosophy; but there are one or two characteristics which should be mentioned.

[1] The much-mentioned debating point that Hume occasionally 'purged' his style of 'Scoticisms' will be dealt with and Scotched later on.

The first is its singular comprehensiveness. Most people have not fully appreciated this, owing to the essentially Oxonian habit which has moulded the academic tradition of Hume. This concentrates almost entirely to the exclusion of everything else on Hume's epistemology, on his doctrine of cause and effect which is contained in Book I of the *Treatise of Human Nature* and ignores practically everything else.

Hume's philosophy of Human Nature is meant to be a complete account of the fundamental principles of Human Nature, of man as an individual, his passions, his understanding, that is his knowledge, science and reasoning powers and those aspects of his nature which are relevant in a study of man as a social animal. In this Hume anticipated all modern sociological and anthropological study of man, and he gave a philosophical framework within which all modern studies can be accommodated—and economics. He taught Adam Smith.

Many, perhaps most, people would say that he did not adequately appreciate man's spiritual side. But apart from this, which is, of course, a matter of controversy (and even more, of course, a controversy which cannot be discussed here), there is no doubt that he gave a thorough and searching account of Human Nature which largely stands today.

The first and greatest of his works was the *Treatise of Human Nature*. After this he went on to write a number of essays in which he tried to make the fundamental principles of the treatise intelligible and palatable not only to leisured readers of the male but also of the female sex. In other words, he recognised that if he wished to put his ideas across they would have to be in a good literary form. David Hume was an excellent example of the social and sociable animal whom he was studying.

In his maturer years he produced his *Histories*. These are largely neglected now because Hume did not have access to the documents available to historians today. But this neglect is unjust. His history was, after all, one of the products of one of the greatest intellects of modern times. Hume's history is not just an attempt to establish what happened in the past and why. Rather it is an endeavour to find illustration in the concrete facts of history of the ultimate principles of Human Nature as already discussed in his philosophy. This gives his history a lasting and universal character which it shares with the historical writings of Thucydides and Livy and other great ancient writers. This citizen of Edinburgh was indeed a citizen of the world, and an heir of the ages as well.

Hume's last great work was his *Dialogues concerning Natural Religion*. It is profoundly sceptical (need it be added that the word is used in its dictionary, not popular, sense), but, famous though the work is, its origins are usually unknown or neglected. Its beginnings lie in a notebook which Hume kept about 1729 when he was no more than eighteen. Even at that age he was seeking to free himself from the rigid constraints of the Presbyterian system as defined in the Westminster Confession. His method of doing so was, it seems, to try to assemble reasonable arguments, independent of the Westminster Confession, for the existence

of God. The effect upon the youth was disturbing. Indeed, in an effort
to seek support for the common belief about God, it may be said that
he experienced a profound upheaval of thought.

In the 1750s he returned to the subject which he had been pursuing
in the notebooks and wrote the first draft of the work which was later
the *Dialogues*. He tried to persuade his friend Gilbert Elliott to formulate
and write in defence of the common opinion. Elliott, not being a
philosopher, funked this task and wriggled out of it.

In the last year or two of his life Hume re-wrote the *Dialogues* for
himself. It was now that they became so outspokenly sceptical. He
bequeathed them to his nephew Baron Hume, the great writer of Scots
criminal law, to be published posthumously. Baron Hume had a deep
affection and admiration for his uncle. His dicta are responsible for the
modern doctrine in Scottish judge-made law of Diminished Responsibility—that doctrine of which the English Courts of Criminal Appeal have
recently been making such heavy weather. It is clear that Baron Hume
received inspiration for his dicta from his uncle David.

Printed below are eight extracts from Hume's published works and
letters. They can do no more than give a hint as to the quality of his
extraordinary mind and the highly agreeable nature of his eighteenth-
century Scottish personality. Near the end there is an abbreviated
account of Boswell's celebrated last meeting with him on Hume's death-
bed, also a codicil to Hume's will which is characteristic and *à propos*.
Each extract is headed with an editorial note. As there is a good deal of
Hume here this is better than a general conspectus.

I. A TREATISE OF HUMAN NATURE[1]

1. *Conclusion of This Book*[2]

It is the habit of the Oxonian philosophers already mentioned to dismiss
and pooh-pooh this splendid 'conclusion' of Hume's First Book in his
Treatise as 'just a piece of literature': and so it is. It is a triumphant
piece of literature, one of the most excellent examples of lucid thought
expressed in literature in the eighteenth century; it is yet moving literature. It is one of the most sustained, lofty yet impassioned pieces of
confessional writing known to us in any language composed in that
century. Not Rousseau, not any of the other harbingers of the Romantic
Movement surpass this classically composed aria of self-revelation.

It is the keynote of Hume's philosophy that, when confronted with
any awkward question, he could never, never for any reason of convenience, still less of comfort, evade it. He had to go on worrying at it
until he achieved, if not a complete answer, the end of the question.
It was this honest and pertinacious pursuit of argument for and against

---

[1] All references in this section are to David Hume, *A Treatise of Human
Nature*, Ed. L. A. Selby-Bigge, Oxford, 1946.
[2] *Treatise*, I. IV, vii; *ed. cit.*, pp. 263 ff.

coming to rest, eventually and only, upon a probability (and not necessarily a desirable probability) that led to his fundamental scepticism.

Yet he was a man, very much a man with human feelings, as well as a philosopher. He gained no sense of priggish superiority from the scepticism to which his form of reasoning led him. Quite the contrary; indeed he who loved his friends and often admired their intellects, who enjoyed the companionability of that most companionable of cities, eighteenth-century Edinburgh, endured a sense of loss amounting to personal desolation when he realised the end to which his system of thought was leading him.

This is the place to say that it is not only the honest sceptic who has to endure such distress. Many a man who has made an act of faith at the end of a process of reasoning which has led him to that act by almost unwilling steps and ineluctable experiences has reached a conclusion that is far from comfortable, which demands an unceasing discipline, especially among his fellows, which is far from easy, which, like Hume, isolates him from those he loves and for whom he has affection and admiration. Newman's distress was as poignant as Hume's. There are pages in the *Apologia Pro Vita Sua*, and in the conclusion to the first book of *The Treatise*, in which, across the gulf of Faith and Scepticism, the nineteenth-century English cardinal-to-be and the Scottish David Hume speak to one another.

But Hume also speaks to *us* most intimately. The burden of his self-revelation, the resolution which informs it is summed up in Hume's own maxim: 'Be a philosopher, but, amidst all your philosophy, be a man.' How vivid and effective is Hume's metaphor of the sea of life upon which the leaky boat of his thought sets out! It was a metaphor which Byron was later to use with such poetic effect in *Childe Harold* and *Don Juan*. There was a touch of philosophy in the Aberdonian poet's conception of the sea, and of poetry in that of the Edinburgh philosopher. The cold grey sea is particularly harsh upon the coasts of Lothian and Aberdeenshire.

But before I launch out into those immense depths of philosophy, which lie before me, I find myself inclin'd to stop a moment in my present station, and to ponder that voyage, which I have undertaken, and which undoubtedly requires the utmost art and industry to be brought to a happy conclusion. Methinks I am like a man, who having struck on many shoals, and having narrowly escap'd shipwreck in passing a small frith, has yet the temerity to put out to sea in the same leaky weather-beaten vessel, and even carries his ambition so far as to think of compassing the globe under these disadvantageous circum-stances. My memory of past errors and perplexities, makes me diffident for the future. The wretched conditions, weakness, and disorder of the faculties, I must employ in my enquiries, encrease my apprehension. And the impossibility of amending or correcting these faculties, reduces me almost to despair, and makes me resolve to perish on the barren rock, on which I am at present, rather than venture myself upon that boundless ocean, which runs out into immensity. This sudden view of my danger strikes me with melancholy; and as 'tis usual for that passion, above all others, to indulge itself, I cannot forbear feeding my despair, with all those desponding reflections, which the present subject furnishes me with in such abundance.

I am first affrighted and confounded with that forelorn solitude, in which I am plac'd in my philosophy, and fancy myself some strange uncouth monster, who not being able to mingle and unite in society, has been expell'd all human commerce, and left utterly abandon'd and disconsolate. Fain wou'd I run into the crowd for shelter and warmth; but cannot prevail with myself to mix with such deformity. I call upon others to join me, in order to make a company apart; but no one will hearken to me. Every one keeps at a distance, and dreads that storm, which beats upon me from every side. I have expos'd myself to the enmity of all metaphysicians, logicians, mathematicians, and even theologians; and can I wonder at the insults I must suffer? I have declar'd my dis-approbation of their systems; and can I be surpriz'd, if they shou'd express a hatred of mine and of my person? When I look abroad, I foresee on every side, dispute, contradiction, anger, calumny and detraction. When I turn my eye inward, I find nothing but doubt and ignorance. All the world conspires to oppose and contradict me; tho' such is my weakness, that I feel all my opinions loosen and fall of themselves, when unsupported by the approbation of others. Every step I take is with hesitation, and every new reflection makes me dread an error and absurdity in my reasoning.

For with what confidence can I venture upon such bold enterprizes, when beside those numberless infirmities peculiar to myself, I find so many which are common to human nature? Can I be sure, that in leaving all establish'd opinions I am following truth; and by what criterion shall I distinguish her, even if fortune shou'd at last guide me on her foot-steps? After the most accurate and exact of my reasonings, I can give no reason why I shou'd assent to it; and feel nothing but a *strong* propensity to consider objects *strongly* in that view, under which they appear to me. Experience is a principle, which instructs me in the several conjunctions of objects for the past. Habit is another principle, which determines me to expect the same for the future; and both of them conspiring to operate upon the imagination, make me form certain ideas in a more intense and lively manner, than others, which are not attended with the same advantages. Without this quality, by which the mind enlivens some ideas beyond others (which seemingly is so trivial, and so little founded on reason) we cou'd never assent to any argument, nor carry our view beyond those few objects, which are present to our senses. Nay, even to these objects we cou'd never attribute any existence, but what was dependent on the senses; and must comprehend them entirely in that succession of perceptions, which constitutes our self or person. Nay farther, even with relation to that succession, we cou'd only admit of those perceptions, which are immediately present to our consciousness, nor cou'd those lively images, with which the memory presents us, be ever receiv'd as true pictures of past perceptions. The memory, senses, and understanding are, therefore, all of them founded on the imagination, or the vivacity of our ideas.

No wonder a principle so inconstant and fallacious shou'd lead us into errors, when implicitely follow'd (as it must be) in all its variations. 'Tis this principle, which makes us reason from causes and effects; and 'tis the same principle, which convinces us of the continu'd existence of external objects, when absent from the senses. But tho' these two operations be equally natural and necessary in the human mind, yet in some circumstances they are directly contrary, nor is it possible for us to reason justly and regularly from causes and effects, and at the same time believe the continu'd existence of matter. How then shall we adjust those principles together? Which of them shall we prefer? Or in case we prefer neither of them, but successively assent to both, as is usual among philosophers, with what confidence can we afterwards usurp that glorious title, when we thus knowingly embrace a manifest contradiction? . . .

But what have I here said, that reflections very refin'd and metaphysical have little or no influence upon us? This opinion I can scarce forbear retracting, and condemning from my present feeling and experience. The *intense* view of these manifold contradictions and imperfections in human reason has so wrought upon me, and heated my brain, that I am ready to reject all belief and reasoning, and can look upon no opinion even as more probable or likely than another. Where am I, or what? From what causes do I derive my existence, and to what condition shall I return? Whose favour shall I court, and whose anger must I dread? What beings surround me? and on whom have I any influence, or who have any influence on me? I am confounded with all these questions, and begin to fancy myself in the most deplorable condition imaginable, inviron'd with the deepest darkness, and utterly depriv'd of the use of every member and faculty.

Most fortunately it happens, that since reason is incapable of dispelling these clouds, nature herself suffices to that purpose, and cures me of this philosophical melancholy and delirium, either by relaxing this bend of mind, or by some avocation, and lively impression of my senses, which obliterate all these chimeras. I dine, I play a game of back-gammon, I converse, and am merry with my friends; and when after three or four hours' amusement, I wou'd return to these speculations, they appear so cold, and strain'd, and ridiculous, that I cannot find in my heart to enter into them any farther.

Here then I find myself absolutely and necessarily determin'd to live, and talk, and act like other people in the common affairs of life. But notwithstanding that my natural propensity, and the course of my animal spirits and passions reduce me to this indolent belief in the general maxims of the world, I still feel such remains of my former disposition, that I am ready to throw all my books and papers into the fire, and resolve never more to renounce the pleasures of life for the sake of reasoning and philosophy. For those are my sentiments in that splenetic humour, which governs me at present. I may, nay I must yield to the current of nature, in submitting to my senses and understanding; and in this blind submission I shew most perfectly my sceptical disposition and principles. But does it follow, that I must strive against the current of nature, which leads me to indolence and pleasure; that I must seclude myself, in some measure, from the commerce and society of men, which is so agreeable; and that I must torture my brain with subtilities and sophistries, at the very time that I cannot satisfy myself concerning the reasonableness of so painful an application, nor have any tolerable prospect of arriving by its means at truth and certainty. Under what obligation do I lie of making such an abuse of time? And to what end can it serve either for the service of mankind, or for my own private interest? No: If I must be a fool, as all those who reason or believe any thing *certainly* are, my follies shall at least be natural and agreeable. Where I strive against my inclination, I shall have a good reason for my resistance; and will no more be led a wandering into such dreary solitudes, and rough passages, as I have hitherto met with.

These are the sentiments of my spleen and indolence; and indeed I must confess, that philosophy has nothing to oppose to them, and expects a victory more from the returns of a serious good-humour'd disposition, than from the force of reason and conviction. In all the incidents of life we ought still to preserve our scepticism. If we believe, that fire warms, or water refreshes, 'tis only because it costs us too much pains to think otherwise. Nay if we are philosophers, it ought only to be upon sceptical principles, and from an inclination, which we feel to the employing ourselves after that manner. Where reason is lively, and mixes itself with some propensity, it ought to be assented to. Where it does not, it never can have any title to operate upon us.

At the time, therefore, that I am tir'd with amusement and company, and have indulg'd a *reverie* in my chamber, or in a solitary walk by a river-side, I feel my mind all collected within itself, and am naturally *inclin'd* to carry my view into all those subjects, about which I have met with so many disputes in the course of my reading and conversation. I cannot forbear having a curiosity to be acquainted with the principles of moral good and evil, the nature and foundation of government, and the cause of those several passions and inclinations, which actuate and govern me. I am uneasy to think I approve of one object, and disapprove of another; call one thing beautiful, and another deform'd; decide concerning truth and falshood, reason and folly, without knowing upon what principles I proceed. I am concern'd for the condition of the learned world, which lies under such a deplorable ignorance in all these particulars. I feel an ambition to arise in me of contributing to the instruction of mankind, and of acquiring a name by my inventions and discoveries. These sentiments spring up naturally in my present disposition; and shou'd I endeavour to banish them, by attaching myself to any other business or diversion, I *feel* I shou'd be a loser in point of pleasure; and this is the origin of my philosophy.

But even suppose this curiosity and ambition shou'd not transport me into speculations without the sphere of common life, it wou'd necessarily happen, that from my very weakness I must be led into such enquiries. 'Tis certain, that superstition is much more bold in its systems and hypotheses than philosophy; and while the latter contents itself with assigning new causes and principles to the phænomena, which appear in the visible world, the former opens a world of its own, and presents us with scenes, and beings, and objects, which are altogether new. Since therefore 'tis almost impossible for the mind of man to rest, like those of beasts, in that narrow circle of objects, which are the subject of daily conversation and action, we ought only to deliberate concerning the choice of our guide, and ought to prefer that which is safest and most agreeable. And in this respect I make bold to recommend philosophy, and shall not scruple to give it the preference to superstition of every kind or denomination. For as superstition arises naturally and easily from the popular opinions of mankind, it seizes more strongly on the mind, and is often able to disturb us in the conduct of our lives and actions. Philosophy on the contrary, if just, can present us only with mild and moderate sentiments; and if false and extravagant, its opinions are merely the objects of a cold and general speculation, and seldom go so far as to interrupt the course of our natural propensities. The CYNICS are an extraordinary instance of philosophers, who from reasonings purely philosophical ran into as great extravagancies of conduct as any *Monk* or *Dervise* that ever was in the world. Generally speaking, the errors in religion are dangerous; those in philosophy only ridiculous.

I am sensible, that these two cases of the strength and weakness of the mind will not comprehend all mankind, and that there are in *England*, in particular, many honest gentlemen, who being always employ'd in their domestic affairs, or amusing themselves in common recreations, have carried their thoughts very little beyond those objects, which are every day expos'd to their senses. And indeed, of such as these I pretend not to make philosophers, nor do I expect them either to be associates in these researches or auditors of these discoveries. They do well to keep themselves in their present situation; and instead of refining them into philosophers, I wish we cou'd communicate to our founders of systems, a share of this gross earthy mixture, as an ingredient, which they commonly stand much in need of, and which wou'd serve to temper those fiery particles, of which they are compos'd. While a warm imagination is allow'd to enter into philosophy, and hypotheses embrac'd merely for being specious and agreeable, we can never have any steady principles, nor any sentiments, which will suit with common practice and experience. But were these hypotheses once remov'd, we might hope to establish a system or set of opinions, which if not true (for that, perhaps, is too much to be hop'd for) might at least be satisfactory to the human mind, and might stand the test of the most critical examination. Nor shou'd we despair of attaining this end, because of the many chimerical systems, which have successively arisen and decay'd away among men, wou'd we consider the shortness of that period, wherein these questions have been the subjects of enquiry and reasoning. Two thousand years with such long interruptions, and under such mighty discouragements, are a small space of time to give any tolerable perfection to the sciences; and perhaps we are still in too early an age of the world to discover any principles, which will bear the examination of the latest posterity. For my part, my only hope is, that I may contribute a little to the advancement of knowledge, by giving in some particulars a different turn to the speculations of philosophers, and pointing out to them more distinctly those subjects, where alone they can expect assurance and conviction. Human Nature is the only science of man; and yet has been hitherto the most neglected. 'Twill be sufficient for me, if I can bring it a little more into fashion; and the hope of this serves to compose my temper from that spleen, and invigorate it from that indolence, which sometimes prevail upon me. If the reader finds himself in the same easy disposition, let him follow me in my future speculations. If not, let him follow his inclination, and wait the returns of application and good humour. The conduct of a man, who studies philosophy in this careless manner, is more truly sceptical than that of one, who feeling in himself an inclination to it, is yet so over-whelm'd with doubts and scruples, as totally to reject it. A true sceptic will be diffident of his philosophical doubts, as well as of his philosophical conviction; and will never refuse any innocent satisfaction, which offers itself, upon account of either of them.

Nor is it only proper we shou'd in general indulge our inclination in the most elaborate philosophical researches, notwithstanding our sceptical principles, but also that we shou'd yield to that propensity, which inclines us to be positive and certain in *particular points*, according to the light, in which we survey them in any *particular instant*. 'Tis easier to forbear all examination and enquiry, than to check ourselves in so natural a propensity, and guard against that assurance, which always arises from an exact and full survey of an object. On such an occasion we are apt not only to forget our scepticism, but even our modesty too; and make use of such terms as these, *'tis evident, 'tis certain, 'tis undeniable*; which a due deference to the public ought, perhaps, to prevent. I may have fallen into this fault after the example of others; but I here enter a *caveat* against any objections, which may be offer'd on that head; and declare that such expressions were extorted from me by the present view of the object, and imply no dogmatical spirit, nor conceited idea of my own judgment, which are sentiments that I am sensible can become no body, and a sceptic still less than any other.

2. *Reason and Passion*[1]

Hume here is speaking in an impassioned way. The operative word is 'ought'—'Reason is and *ought* only to be . . .' In other words 'If only you Wesminster Confession moralistic tyrants would just stop trying

From *Treatise*, I. III, iii; *ed. cit.*, p. 415.

to make humanity something it cannot possibly be, how much happier we would be!' It is possible that this is one of the sources whence his nephew Baron Hume (referred to earlier) got the first germ of the idea from which later judges in Scotland derived the concept of 'Diminished Responsibility,' one of Scotland's great practical contributions to human wisdom.

We speak not strictly and philosophically when we talk of the combat of passion and of reason. Reason is, and ought only to be the slave of the passions, and can never pretend to any other office than to serve and obey them.

3. *Hunting and Philosophy*[1]

This extract is an odd echo of the Urquhart shooting-philosophical story we printed earlier. Hume (with recollection perhaps of his elder brother's sporting tastes on his estate) draws an analogy from the chase. The philosopher does not endure the arduous exercise of prolonged mental investigation merely for the miserable half-truths he brings back, but for the zest of hunting for them.

To illustrate all this by a similar instance, I shall observe, that there cannot be two passions more nearly resembling each other, than those of hunting and philosophy, whatever disproportion may at first sight appear betwixt them. 'Tis evident, that the pleasure of hunting consists in the action of the mind and body; the motion, the attention, the difficulty, and the uncertainty. 'Tis evident likewise, that these actions must be attended with an idea of utility, in order to their having any effect upon us. A man of the greatest fortune, and the farthest remov'd from avarice, tho' he takes a pleasure in hunting after partridges and pheasants, feels no satisfaction in shooting crows and magpies; and that because he considers the first as fit for the table, and the other as entirely useless. Here 'tis certain, that the utility or importance of itself causes no real passion, but is only requisite to support the imagination; and the same person, who over-looks a ten times greater profit in any other subject, is pleas'd to bring home half a dozen woodcocks or plovers, after having employ'd several hours in hunting after them. To make the parallel betwixt hunting and philosophy more compleat, we may observe, that tho' in both cases the end of our action may in itself be despis'd, yet in the heat of the action we acquire such an attention to this end, that we are very uneasy under any disappointments, and are sorry when we either miss our game, or fall into any error in our reasoning.

[1] *Treatise*, II. III, x; *ed. cit.*, pp. 451 ff.

4. *Allegiance*[1]

Here again is an echo, doubtless unconscious, of an earlier piece of Scottish wisdom. The reader may recall Barbour's view of allegiance, i.e. that the ordinary man owes allegiance to his sovereign only in so far as that sovereign is able to protect and govern him well. If that sovereign becomes impotent to do so the duty of allegiance lapses. Hume agrees. He is a Scottish Tory, but an empirical Tory without any of the mystique of primogeniture mixed up in his political philosophy. He was a Tory who could say 'of course the subject has the right of rebellion, but,' he added to the horror of the eighteenth-century Whigs, '*but*, if he's got any sense, he'll never use it because of the appalling consequences that flow from it.'

The general opinion of mankind has some authority in all cases; but in this of morals 'tis perfectly infallible. Nor is it less infallible, because men cannot distinctly explain the principles, on which it is founded. Few persons can carry on this train of reasoning: 'Government is a mere human invention for the interest of society. Where the tyranny of the governor removes this interest, it also removes the natural obligation to obedience. The moral obligation is founded on the natural, and therefore must cease where *that* ceases; especially where the subject is such as makes us foresee very many occasions wherein the natural obligation may cease, and causes us to form a kind of general rule for the regulation of our conduct in such occurrences.' But tho' this train of reasoning be too subtile for the vulgar, 'tis certain, that all men have an implicit notion of it, and are sensible, that they owe obedience to government merely on account of the public interest; and at the same time, that human nature is so subject to frailties and passions, as may easily pervert this institution, and change their governors into tyrants and public enemies. If the sense of common interest were not our original motive to obedience, I wou'd fain ask, what other principle is there in human nature capable of subduing the natural ambition of men, and forcing them to such a submission. Imitation and custom are not sufficient. For the question still recurs, what motive first produces those instances of submission, which we imitate, and that train of actions, which produces the custom? There evidently is no other principle than common interest; and if interest first produces obedience to government, the obligation to obedience must cease, whenever the interest ceases, in any great degree, and in a considerable number of instances. . . .

[1] From *Treatise*, III. II, ix–x; *ed. cit.*, pp. 552 ff.

But tho', on some occasions, it may be justifiable, both in sound politics and morality, to resist supreme power, 'tis certain, that in the ordinary course of human affairs nothing can be more pernicious and criminal; and that besides the convulsions, which always attend revolutions, such a practice tends directly to the subversion of all government, and the causing an universal anarchy and confusion among mankind. As numerous and civiliz'd societies cannot subsist without government, so government is entirely useless without an exact obedience. We ought always to weigh the advantages, which we reap from authority, against the disadvantages; and by this means we shall become more scrupulous of putting in practice the doctrine of resistance. The common rule requires submission; and 'tis only in cases of grievous tyranny and oppression, that the exception can take place. . . .

Whoever considers the history of the several nations of the world; their revolutions, conquests, increase, and diminutions; the manner in which their particular governments are establish'd, and the successive right transmitted from one person to another, will soon learn to treat very lightly all disputes concerning the rights of princes, and will be convinc'd, that a strict adherence to any general rules, and the rigid loyalty to particular persons and families, on which some people set so high a value, are virtues that hold less of reason, than of bigotry and superstition. In this particular, the study of history confirms the reasonings of true philosophy; which, shewing us the original qualities of human nature, teaches us to regard the controversies in politics as incapable of any decision in most cases, and as entirely subordinate to the interests of peace and liberty. Where the public good does not evidently demand a change; 'tis certain, that the concurrence of all those titles, *original contract, long possession, present possession, succession,* and *positive laws,* forms the strongest title to sovereignty, and is justly regarded as sacred and inviolable. But when these titles are mingled and oppos'd in different degrees, they often occasion perplexity; and are less capable of solution from the arguments of lawyers and philosophers, than from the swords of the soldiery. Who shall tell me, for instance, whether *Germanicus,* or *Drusus,* ought to have succeeded *Tiberius,* had he died while they were both alive, without naming any of them for his successor? Ought the right of adoption to be receiv'd as equivalent to that of blood in a nation, where it had the same effect in private families, and had already, in two instances, taken place in the public? Ought *Germanicus* to be esteem'd the eldest son, because he was born before *Drusus*; or the younger, because he was adopted after the birth of his brother? Ought the right of the elder to be regarded in a nation where the eldest brother had no advantage in the succession to private families? Ought the *Roman* empire at that time to be esteem'd hereditary, because of two examples; or ought it, even so early, to be regarded as belonging to the stronger, or the present possessor, as being founded on so recent an usurpation? Upon whatever principles we may pretend to answer these and such like questions, I am afraid we shall never be able to satisfy an impartial enquirer, who adopts no party in political controversies, and will be satisfied with nothing but sound reason and philosophy.

5. *Chastity and Modesty*[1]

There may be blunt downright John Bulls who would hold that the meaning of these melodiously expressed (and rather humorous) paragraphs of Hume's was better and more tersely put by a celebrated English contemporary of his. When asked whether adultery was worse in a married man or woman the Englishman replied that of course it was worse in the woman. 'If the master of the house lie with a maid servant no worse harm may come of it than a clap; but if his lady lie with the groom of the chambers the whole succession is in peril.' This passage from the *Treatise*, however, shows how well Hume knew and accepted the standards and customs of his time, even though he probably did not allow himself the same latitude as did most of his contemporaries. He always thought it was silly to try to change things. If they are going to change, they'll change anyhow; if not, it's a waste of time trying to alter them. Moral cranks please note.

There are some philosophers, who attack the female virtues with great vehemence, and fancy they have gone very far in detecting popular errors, when they can show, that there is no foundation in nature for all that exterior modesty, which we require in the expressions, and dress, and behaviour of the fair sex. I believe I may spare myself the trouble of insisting on so obvious a subject, and may proceed, without farther preparation, to examine after what manner such notions arise from education, from the voluntary conventions of men, and from the interest of society.

Whoever considers the length and feebleness of human infancy, with the concern which both sexes naturally have for their offspring, will easily perceive, that there must be an union of male and female for the education of the young, and that this union must be of

[1] From *Treatise*, III. II, xii; *ed. cit.*, pp. 570 ff.

considerable duration. But in order to induce the men to impose on themselves this restraint, and undergo chearfully all the fatigues and expences, to which it subjects them, they must believe, that the children are their own, and that their natural instinct is not directed to a wrong object, when they give a loose to love and tenderness. Now if we examine the structure of the human body, we shall find, that this security is very difficult to be attain'd on our part; and that since, in the copulation of the sexes, the principle of generation goes from the man to the woman, an error may easily take place on the side of the former, tho' it be utterly impossible with regard to the latter. From this trivial and anatomical observation is deriv'd that vast difference betwixt the education and duties of the two sexes.

Were a philosopher to examine the matter *a priori*, he wou'd reason after the following manner. Men are induc'd to labour for the maintenance and education of their children, by the persuasion that they are really their own; and therefore 'tis reasonable, and even necessary, to give them some security in this particular. This security cannot consist entirely in the imposing of severe punishments on any transgressions of conjugal fidelity on the part of the wife; since these public punishments cannot be inflicted without legal proof, which 'tis difficult to meet with in this subject. What restraint, therefore, shall we impose on women, in order to counter-balance so strong a temptation as they have to infidelity? There seems to be no restraint possible, but in the punishment of bad fame or reputation; a punishment, which has a mighty influence on the human mind, and at the same time is inflicted by the world upon surmizes, and conjectures, and proofs, that wou'd never be receiv'd in any court of judicature. In order, therefore, to impose a due restraint on the female sex, we must attach a peculiar degree of shame to their infidelity, above what arises merely from its injustice, and must bestow proportionable praises on their chastity.

But tho' this be a very strong motive to fidelity, our philosopher wou'd quickly discover, that it wou'd not alone be sufficient to that purpose. All human creatures, especially of the female sex, are apt to over-look remote motives in favour of any present temptation: The temptation is here the strongest imaginable: Its approaches are insensible and seducing: And a woman easily finds, or flatters herself she shall find, certain means of securing her reputation, and preventing all the pernicious consequences of her pleasures. 'Tis necessary, therefore, that, beside the infamy attending such licences, there shou'd be some preceding backwardness or dread, which may prevent their first approaches, and may give the female sex a repugnance to all expressions,

P

and postures, and liberties, that have an immediate relation to that enjoyment.

Such wou'd be the reasonings of our speculative philosopher: But I am persuaded, that if he had not a perfect knowledge of human nature, he wou'd be apt to regard them as mere chimerical speculations, and wou'd consider the infamy attending infidelity, and backwardness to all its approaches, as principles that were rather to be wish'd than hop'd for in the world. For what means, wou'd he say, of persuading mankind, that the transgressions of conjugal duty are more infamous than any other kind of injustice, when 'tis evident they are more excusable, upon account of the greatness of the temptation? And what possibility of giving a backwardness to the approaches of a pleasure, to which nature has inspir'd so strong a propensity; and a propensity that 'tis absolutely necessary in the end to comply with, for the support of the species?

But speculative reasonings, which cost so much pains to philosophers, are often form'd by the world naturally, and without reflection: As difficulties, which seem unsurmountable in theory, are easily got over in practice. Those, who have an interest in the fidelity of women, naturally disapprove of their infidelity, and all the approaches to it. Those, who have no interest, are carried along with the stream. Education takes possession of the ductile minds of the fair sex in their infancy. And when a general rule of this kind is once establish'd, men are apt to extend it beyond those principles, from which it first arose. Thus batchelors, however debauch'd, cannot chuse but be shock'd with any instance of lewdness or impudence in women. And tho' all these maxims have a plain reference to generation, yet women past child-bearing have no more privilege in this respect, than those who are in the flower of their youth and beauty. Men have undoubtedly an implicit notion, that all those ideas of modesty and decency have a regard to generation; since they impose not the same laws, *with the same force*, on the male sex, where that reason takes not place. The exception is there obvious and extensive, and founded on a remarkable difference, which produces a clear separation and disjunction of ideas. But as the case is not the same with regard to the different ages of women, for this reason, tho' men know, that these notions are founded on the public interest, yet the general rule carries us beyond the original principle, and makes us extend the notions of modesty over the whole sex, from their earliest infancy to their extremest old-age and infirmity.

Courage, which is the point of honour among men, derives its merit, in a great measure, from artifice, as well as the chastity of women; tho' it has also some foundation in nature, as we shall see afterwards.

As to the obligations which the male sex lie under, with regard to chastity, we may observe, that according to the general notions of the world, they bear nearly the same proportion to the obligations of women, as the obligations of the law of nations do to those of the law of nature. 'Tis contrary to the interest of civil society, that men shou'd have an *entire* liberty of indulging their appetites in venereal enjoyment: But as this interest is weaker than in the case of the female sex, the moral obligation, arising from it, must be proportionately weaker. And to prove this we need only appeal to the practice and sentiments of all nations and ages.

II. AN ENQUIRY CONCERNING HUMAN UNDERSTANDING

Sophistry and Illusion[1]

This ending of the enquiry concerning Human Understanding comes from Hume's revised version of the *Treatise*, Book I. In it he reaffirms that there are only two kinds of reasoning: probable reasoning concerning matter of fact and existence; and demonstrative reasoning concerning number and quantity, that is, mathematical reasoning which yields certainty; but this can, so Hume states, never be applied to matter of fact. Thus we may state with certainty that two and two make four, but if we see two apples and then add another two to them we cannot be certain that we shall have four. We are ignoring the possibility that there may be a minute apple concealed behind one of the large and original ones, or that we are drunk and seeing double or intemperately abstinent and only seeing half or suffering from similar delusions.

This passage from Hume ends with the famous adjuration to commit to the flames any volumes of divinity or school metaphysics which do not answer to his conditions of demonstrative reasoning. It was a courageous adjuration when written and reads resonantly yet. We confess that by attuning ourselves, patriotically and for the purposes of these annotations, to the philosophy of doubt, we have reached a position where we are uncertain even that two and two do make four. Maybe this is no more than an evocation of an early prejudice. In our youth and at school in Edinburgh it was the mathematical treatises that were forced upon us which we were most inclined to commit to the flames.

The existence, therefore, of any being can only be proved by arguments from its cause or its effect; and these arguments are founded

---

[1] From *An Enquiry concerning Human Understanding*, XII, iii; in *Enquiries*, Ed. Selby-Bigge, Oxford, 1946, pp. 164 ff.

entirely on experience. If we reason *a priori,* anything may appear able to produce anything. The falling of a pebble may, for aught we know, extinguish the sun; or the wish of man control the planets in their orbits. It is only experience, which teaches us the nature and bounds of cause and effect, and enables us to infer the existence of one object from that of another. Such is the foundation of moral reasoning, which forms the greater part of human knowledge, and is the source of all human action and behaviour.

Moral reasonings are either concerning particular or general facts. All deliberations in life regard the former; as also all disquisitions in history, chronology, geography, and astronomy.

The sciences, which treat of general facts, are politics, natural philosophy, physic, chemistry, &c. where the qualities, causes and effects of a whole species of objects are enquired into.

Divinity or Theology, as it proves the existence of a Deity, and the immortality of souls, is composed partly of reasonings concerning particular, partly concerning general facts. It has a foundation in *reason,* so far as it is supported by experience. But its best and most solid foundation is *faith* and divine revelation.

Morals and criticism are not so properly objects of the understanding as of taste and sentiment. Beauty, whether moral or natural, is felt, more properly than perceived. Or if we reason concerning it, and endeavour to fix its standard, we regard a new fact, to wit, the general tastes of mankind, or some such fact, which may be the object of reasoning and enquiry.

When we run over libraries, persuaded of these principles, what havoc must we make? If we take in our hand any volume; of divinity or school metaphysics, for instance; let us ask, *Does it contain any abstract reasoning concerning quantity or number?* No. *Does it contain any experimental reasoning concerning matter of fact and existence?* No. Commit it then to the flames: for it can contain nothing but sophistry and illusion.

III. A CITIZEN OF THE WORLD

In 1763 to 1765 Hume accompanied Lord Hertford to France and was for some months *Chargé d'Affaires* for the United Kingdom at the Embassy in Paris. While there he was, in the stiffly cautious yet sly language of the *D.N.B.,* 'intimate with the Comtesse de Boufflers.' In fact the relationship between this extraordinary Scotsman and this remarkable Frenchwoman (both, however, highly characteristic of their countries) was a poignant affair of the heart and the intellect. It is possible, just possible, that today there are still middle-aged people who are capable of enjoying and enduring the feelings that arise from such a relationship, at once complex and simple—but not many, we think.

But in 1765 these feelings were sufficiently powerful in the breast of the fifty-four-year-old Edinburgh philosopher to make him consider remaining in France and spending the rest of his life as the *ami* of Madame de Boufflers. His old friend Gilbert Elliott heard a rumour to this effect, and this information appalled that respectable Lowland Scottish, or rather North British, gentleman. In the extract from his letter to Hume printed below one can almost hear the outraged flat Lothian tones growing even flatter in indignation. The word precipiece (with the last syllable then pronounced as it was then spelled) must have been satisfactory to say and agreeably sharp to write. One seems to hear, on reading it, not only the flatness of the voice but the scratch of the pen. The attempt to get under his friend David Hume's guard by using a French couplet of verse at the end of his argument would have been pathetic were it not ridiculous. This, we regret to say, is another example of Scottish wisdom. Hume had a respect as well as liking for Elliott, but his friend must have been a stupid or a highly unobservant man to have adjured David to 'continue still an Englishman.' Maybe he was only taunting him. If so, he got what he deserved.

Hume's reply, which was wrung from him in exacerbation, should leave no one in any doubt as to his feelings about being considered an Englishman. Overriding his irritation at such an accusation is his triumphant assertion near the end: 'I am a citizen of the World.' Edinburgh in those days was a remote city, but intellectually it was not a provincial one; London was. Hume had had enough of London-English provincialism.

There is a sad prickly little phrase, 'our just pretensions to govern them,' which deserves comment from today. This is just the sort of remark which if made now by a Scot produces, and rightly, from the good-natured English a smile of contemptuous indifference. This indeed is all that our pathetic yet nevertheless insufferable boasting of the 'Here's-tae-us-wha's-like-us' kind deserves. It was different then. Angry though he was, Hume meant what he said, and with justification.

In the eighty years after the Union, and during the intellectual torpor of the southern English, stuck fast in the suet and 'pudding-time' of the first three Georges, Scots did feel, in matters of the mind, the superiors of the English. Smarting under the political humiliations of that same Union they did feel capable of taking it out of them by governing them. For all our flatulent *fanfaronnade* at St. Andrew's nights dinners and the like, do we really feel that now?

If so, we have precious little to show for our boast in two hundred years. We have provided a certain number of men of learning and of literature. We have contributed to the sciences and occasionally to the arts. We have made excellent soldiers. We have poured out our blood sometimes because our bodies have been evicted, sometimes to make money, and sometimes just because we found living at home intolerable, sometimes for adventure to help the English (and help them most notably) in the founding of their Empire, but what of our pretensions to govern them? In general it comes down to the claim uttered with self-satisfaction, that wherever you go in the English-speaking world you will find a Scotsman at the head of a department. The Head of a Department!

Now and again the British system of politics regurgitates a Prime Minister who is, or who claims to be, a Scot. With the exception of the great-hearted Gladstone (and he for all his almost unmixed Scottish blood was a Liverpool Etonian who spent nearly all his life in England), what mark have any left on the Government of the United Kingdom? If Hume were able to speak now he would hardly call our pretensions to govern the English just. But it was a different matter then.

We commend this letter and other personal writings of Hume for the attention of those who have accepted Lytton Strachey's view of him as a detached insentient and purely ironic sceptic withdrawn from human feelings. This Cambridge and Bloomsbury provincial view of the Edinburgh 'philosopher' is even more unjust than the Oxonian one. It is difficult to believe that a man of Strachey's intelligence could have bothered to read much of Hume's writings before himself wrote about him as he did.

In the letter from Brussels, Elliott says:[1]

Before I conclude, allow me in friendship also, to tell you, I think I see you at present upon the very brink of a precipiece. One cannot too much clear their mind of all little prejudices, but partiality to ones country is not a prejudice. Love the French as much as you will, many of the Individuals are surely the proper objects of affection, but above all continue still an Englishman. You know better than any body, that the active powers of our mind are much too limited, to be usefully employed in any pursuit more general than the service of that portion of mankind which we call our country. General benevolence, & private friendship will attend a generous mind, & a feeling heart, into every country. But political attachment confines itself to one.

> Mon fils sur les humains, que ton âme attendrie,
> Habite l'univers, mais aime sa Patrie.

This provoked the following outburst from Hume:[2]

I cannot image what you mean by saying that I am on a Precipice. I shall foretell to you the Result of my present Situation almost with as great Certainty as it is possible to employ with regard to any future

---

[1] *Letters of David Hume*, Ed. J. Y. T. Greig, Oxford, 1932, I. 469, n. 3.
[2] *Loc. cit.*

Event. As soon as Lord Hertford's Embassy ends, which probably may not continue long, some Zealot, whom I never saw, & never coud offend, finding me without Protection, will instantly fly, with Alacrity, to strike off that Pension which the King & the Ministry, before I woud consent to accept of my present Situation, promisd should be for Life. I shall be oblig'd to leave Paris, which I confess I shall turn my Back to with Regret. I shall go to Thoulouse, or Montauban, or some Provincial Town in the South of France, where I shall spend, contented, the rest of my Life, with more Money, under a finer Sky, & in better Company than I was born to enjoy.

From what human Motive or Consideration can I prefer living in England to that in foreign Countries? I believe, taking the Continent of Europe, from Peterburg to Lisbon, & from Bergen to Naples, there is not one that ever heard my Name, who has not heard of it with Advantage, both in point of Morals & Genius. I do not believe there is one Englishman in fifty, who, if he heard that I had broke my Neck to night, would not be rejoic'd with it. Some hate me because I am not a Tory, some because I am not a Whig, some because I am not a Christian, and all because I am a Scotsman. Can you seriously talk of my continuing an Englishman? Am I, or are you, an Englishman? Will they allow us to be so? Do they not treat with Derision our Pretensions to that Name, and with Hatred our just Pretensions to surpass & to govern them? I am a Citizen of the World; but if I were to adopt any Country, it woud be that in which I live at present, and from which I am determin'd never to depart, unless a War drive me into Swisserland or Italy.

IV. MY OWN LIFE

In 1776, the last year of his life, Hume prepared a manifesto preparatory to staging the death of David Hume, or, as he would have preferred to put it, of 'David Hume, Esquire, Philosopher.' This took the form of the relict among his papers 'My Own Life.' It is his autobiography composed on seven pages. To have attempted such a feat in such a space was, of course, a vain and ironic *tour de force*.

Vain. Hume never pretended to ignore the fact that his intelligence and reasoning powers were greater than those of nearly all his contemporaries. He may therefore be called vain. Of course he was vain, and had every right to be. For all his friendliness, his good humour, his sociability and his charm, mock-modesty would have sat ill upon him.

There is also irony in a man of such intellectual stature, leaving behind him a seven-page autobiography. It was an irony which may have been lost on his contemporaries, particularly those of his contemporaries who opposed him, but it is not lost on us. Every sentence of 'My Own Life' is, for those who have soaked themselves in Hume, packed with meaning, and full of devotion. Comment is superfluous. We print the last paragraph.[1]

To conclude historically with my own Character—I am, or rather was (for that is the Style, I must now use in speaking of myself; which emboldens me the more to speak my Sentiments) I was, I say, a man of mild Dispositions, of Command of Temper, of an open, social, and cheerful Humour, capable of Attachment, but little susceptible of Enmity, and of great Moderation in all my Passions. Even my Love of literary Fame, my ruling Passion, never soured my humour, notwithstanding my frequent Disappointments. My Company was not unacceptable to the young and careless, as well as to the Studious and literary: And as I took a particular Pleasure in the Company of modest women, I had no Reason to be displeased with the Reception I met with from them. In a word, though most men any wise eminent, have found reason to complain of Calumny, I never was touched, or even attacked by her baleful Tooth: And though I wantonly exposed myself to the Rage of both civil and religious Factions, they seemed to be disarmed in my behalf of their wonted Fury: My Friends never had occasion to vindicate any one Circumstance of my Character and Conduct: Not but that the Zealots, we may well suppose, wou'd have been glad to invent and propagate any Story to my Disadvantage, but they coud never find any which, they thought, woud wear the Face of Probability. I cannot say, there is no Vanity in making this funeral Oration of myself; but I hope it is not a misplac'd one; and this is a Matter of Fact which is easily cleard and ascertained.

V. THE DYING HUME TALKS TO BOSWELL

There is an episode in Scott's *The Heart of Midlothian* which might be described as the most deliberately funny and sardonic death-bed scene in fiction. The extract from Boswell's Journal printed here is not fiction but fact, and fact as few but Boswell could report it; and he certainly did not intend to make this death-bed scene funny, though we may indeed extract humour from Boswell's own absurdities. All the same he did, willingly or unwillingly, give us what must be one of the most good-humoured near death-bed scenes ever recorded.

Boswell's account of the dying Hume has been called 'one of the

[1] *Letters of David Hume*, ed. Greig, I. 7.

greatest scoops in journalism.' It requires little comment save what is to the purpose in presenting the character of Hume. His gaiety and good humour when wasting away from an enervating and mentally depressing liver complaint would be incredible were they reported by anyone but Boswell and in such patently veracious words. The whole interview rings as true as the finest glass.

No doubt Hume could have thought of more cogent arguments for annihilation and against personal immortality at another time and place and faced with another opponent of whom he was less fond. As it was, he was content, with idle and surely smiling good temper, to marshal the more obvious reasons, to keep his flag flying and, incidentally, to lead his younger and desperately serious friend into absurdities such as the statement that disembodied spirits do not take up space. As if Hume hadn't thought of that one! We draw attention to his kind remarks about the Stuarts; not the sort of thing the ordinary reader associates with Hume.

This scene then is reprinted here less to show Hume's capacity in argument on the most important question that faces man than for another purpose. It is an example of his death-defying courage, his luminous good humour and his greatness of mind in triumphing over the matter of his body at its approaching dissolution. It is also reprinted here (if his shade, or his memory or the memory of his memory will forgive us), to the greatness of his soul.

An Account of My Last Interview with David Hume, Esq.

Partly recorded in my Journal, partly enlarged from my memory,
3 March 1777[1]

On Sunday forenoon the 7 of July 1776, being too late for Church, I went to see Mr. David Hume, who was returned from London and Bath, just a dying. I found him alone, in a reclining posture in his drawing-room. He was lean, ghastly, and quite of an earthy appearance. He was drest in a suit of grey cloth with white metal buttons, and a kind of scratch wig. He was quite different from the plump figure which he used to present. He had before him Dr. Campbell's *Philosophy of Rhetorick*. He seemed to be placid and even cheerful. He said he was just approaching to his end. I think these were his words. I know not how I contrived to get the subject of Immortality introduced. He said he never had entertained any belief in Religion since he began to read Locke and Clarke. I asked him if he was not religious when he was young. He said he was, and he used to read the *Whole Duty of Man*; that he made an abstract from the Catalogue of vices at the

---

[1] Hume's *Dialogues*, edited by Norman Kemp Smith, pp. 76–9.

end of it, and examined himself by this, leaving out Murder and
Theft and such vices as he had no chance of committing, having no
inclination to commit them. This, he said, was strange Work; for
instance, to try if, notwithstanding his excelling his school-fellows, he
had no pride or vanity. He smiled in ridicule of this as absurd and
contrary to fixed principles and necessary consequences, not adverting
that Religious discipline does not mean to extinguish, but to moderate,
the passions; and certainly an excess of pride or vanity is dangerous
and generally hurtful. He then said flatly that the Morality of every
Religion was bad, and, I really thought, was not jocular when he said
'that when he heard a man was religious, he concluded he was a rascal,
though he had known some instances of very good men being religious.'
This was just an extravagant reverse of the common remark as to
Infidels. I had a strong curiosity to be satisfied if he persisted in dis-
believing a future state even when he had death before his eyes. I was
persuaded from what he now said, and from his manner of saying it,
that he did persist. I asked him if it was not possible that there might
be a future state. He answered It was possible that a piece of coal put
upon the fire would not burn; and he added that it was a most unreasonable fancy that he should exist for ever. That immortality, if it were at
all, must be general; that a great proportion of the human race has
hardly any intellectual qualities; that a great proportion dies in infancy
before being possessed of reason; yet all these must be immortal; that
a Porter who gets drunk by ten o'clock with gin must be immortal;
that the trash of every age must be preserved, and that new Universes
must be created to contain such infinite numbers. This appeared to
me an unphilosophical objection, and I said, 'Mr. Hume, you know
Spirit does not take up space'. . . .

I asked him if the thought of Annihilation never gave him any
uneasiness. He said not the least; no more than the thought that he
had not been, as Lucretius observes. 'Well,' said I, 'Mr. Hume, I
hope to triumph over you when I meet you in a future state; and
remember you are not to pretend that you was joking with all this
Infidelity.' 'No, No,' said he, 'But I shall have been so long there
before you come that it will be nothing new.' In this style of good-
humour and levity did I conduct the conversation. Perhaps it was
wrong on so aweful a subject. But as nobody was present, I thought
it could have no bad effect. I however felt a degree of horrour, mixed
with a sort of wild, strange, hurrying recollection of My excellent
Mother's pious instructions, of Dr. Johnson's noble lessons, and of
my religious sentiments and affections during the course of my life.

I was like a man in sudden danger eagerly seeking his defensive arms; and I could not but be assailed by momentary doubts while I had actually before me a man of such strong abilities and extensive inquiry dying in the persuasion of being annihilated. But I maintained my Faith. I told him that I beleived the Christian Religion as I beleived History. Said he: 'You do not beleive it as you beleive the Revolution.' 'Yes,' said I, 'but the difference is that I am not so much interested in the truth of the Revolution; otherwise I should have anxious doubts concerning it. A man who is in love has doubts of the affection of his Mistress, without cause.' I mentioned Soame Jennyns's little book in defence of Christianity, which was just published but which I had not yet read. Mr. Hume said, 'I am told there is nothing of his usual spirit in it.' He had once said to me on a forenoon, while the sun was shining bright, that he did not wish to be immortal. This was a most wonderful thought. The reason he gave was that he was very well in this state of being, and that the chances were very much against his being so well in another state; and he would rather not be more than be worse. I answered that it was reasonable to hope he would be better; that there would be a progressive improvement. I tried him at this Interview with that topick, saying that a future state was surely a pleasing idea. He said No, for that it was allways seen through a gloomy medium; there was allways a Phlegethon or a Hell. 'But,' said I, 'would it not be agreeable to have hopes of seeing our friends again?' and I mentioned three Men lately deceased, for whom I knew he had a high value: Ambassadour Keith, Lord Alemoor, and Baron Muir. He owned it would be agreeable, but added that none of them entertained such a notion. I believe he said, such a foolish, or such an absurd, notion; for he was indecently and impolitely positive in incredulity. 'Yes,' said I, 'Lord Alemoor was a beleiver.' David acknowledged that *he* had *some* belief. I some how or other brought Dr. Johnson's name into our conversation. I had often heard him speak of that great Man in a very illiberal manner. He said upon this occasion, 'Johnson should be pleased with my *History*.' Nettled by Hume's frequent attacks upon my revered friend in former conversations, I told him now that Dr. Johnson did not allow him much credit; for he said, 'Sir, the fellow is a Tory by chance.' I am sorry that I mentioned this at such a time. I was off my guard; for the truth is that Mr. Hume's pleasantry was such that there was no solemnity in the scene; and Death for the time did not seem dismal. It surprised me to find him talking of different matters with a tranquillity of mind and a clearness of head which few men possess at any time. Two particulars I remember: Smith's *Wealth of Nations*, which he recommended much, and Monboddo's *Origin of Language*, which he treated contemptuously. I said, 'If I were you, I should regret Annihilation. Had I written such an admirable History, I should be sorry to leave it.' He said, 'I shall leave that history, of which you are pleased to speak so favourably, as perfect as I can.' He said, too, that all the great abilities with which Men had ever been endowed were Relative to this World. He said he became a greater friend to the Stuart Family as he advanced in studying for his History; and he hoped he had vindicated the two first of them so effectually that they would never again be attacked. Mr. Lauder, his Surgeon, came in for a little, and Mr. Mure, the Baron's son, for another small interval. He was, as far as I could judge, quite easy with both. He said he had no pain, but was wasting away. I left him with impressions which disturbed me for some time.

VI. A CODICIL TO HUME'S WILL

Here as one last brief extract is a posthumous example of David Hume's smiling good nature. One of Hume's strongest friendships was with John Home, the playwright and author of *Douglas: A Tragedy*. Though John Home had as a Minister of the Church of Scotland got into considerable hot water for writing a successful play he was never officially unfrocked. He remained in orders and a professing Christian. This never interfered with the warm sentiments of friendship between the Philosopher and the Minister. The only two differences on temporal matters (see below) between the two men were on a taste in wine and on the spelling of their commonly pronounced name. David Hume, though distantly related to the family of the Earls of Home, considered the noble spelling of that Scottish name to be an affectation. He smilingly, affectionately and posthumously drew attention to this belief in the following codicil written in his own hand and dated eighteen days before his death:[1]

[1] David Hume's views on the spelling of his patronymic would have been strengthened by the reading of a newspaper paragraph which has just come to hand while these notes are being written. The present and 14th Earl of Home has just been created Her Majesty's Secretary of State for Foreign Affairs. For some days before the appointment was officially made known his Lordship had suffered embarrassment from public dispute as to whether it was proper in these democratic days for so important a Minister to sit in the House of Lords and not in the Commons. Speaking before his peers in London on July 29, 1960, Lord Home said that "some of the criticisms had tended to get him down." He added, amidst loud laughter, that the pride of his Scottish blood had come to his rescue when he had reflected that "after all the publicity is free." We now know what it is that thrills the blood of our ancient Scottish Peerage—'publicity free.' David Hume's comments on his remote kinsman would have been interesting.

The Codicil[1]

I leave to my friend Mr. John Home of Kilduff ten dozen of my old claret, at his choice; and one single bottle of that other liquor called port. I also leave him six dozen of port provided that he attests under his hand signed John *Hume* that he has himself alone finished that bottle at two sittings. By this concession he will at once terminate the only two differences that ever arose between us on temporal matters.

CONCLUDING REMARKS ON HUME'S MANNER OF THOUGHT AND STYLE

These notes are not intended to be a philosophical treatise. It is impossible, however, to finish talking about Hume's essentially Scottish style of expression without touching upon his equally essentially Scottish manner of thought. Apart from his greatness, combined with the accident of his nationality, these two national things in him, his manner of thought and his manner of expression, are the reasons for his inclusion in this Scottish anthology.

Hume's ability to worry away at purely intellectual questions until, not necessarily an answer, but an end had been reached was extraordinary in his time, and remains, in its own kind, an unsurpassed feat. It would be the greatest mistake to confuse this exhaustive Scottish mental energy and pertinacity with Teutonic 'thoroughness.' No true German would be satisfied with Hume's enigmatic and ironic conclusions. These conclusions have been more in tune with certain elements in French thought, and this is only natural, for their origins are Scottish. Hume's voice spoke to the ear and mind of the intellectual France of his time across the body of the then intellectually lethargic England, and indeed his style, as was recognised in eighteenth-century England, sometimes with irritation, was more a Scottish-French style in English rather than an English style.

His irony (again another pleasing quality to the French) is to be discovered in the manner of his conclusions. He thought to the end of what was the tether of mind in his time; the classical example of which is his argument on cause and effect which, even now, every young philosopher reads and which goes on for well over a hundred pages. Hume's process of thought (if we may be forgiven for stating the obvious) goes relentlessly on until it arrives at a position of considered scepticism, but it is his ironic attitude towards this scepticism and his expression of it which is to our purpose.

He balances probability against probability, arriving at no more than a probability, and if it is an uncomfortable probability he ironically comforts one with the thought that it is not necessary to believe this

[1] *The Works of John Home*, Vol. I, p. 162.

probability after all. And behind this there lies the ironically even more uncomfortable fact that you can't be sure about it in any event. You cannot be sure of it or of anything else short of an impulsive act of faith. And an act of faith is, according to Hume, in itself not intellectually satisfying.

Hume (to use his own sporting analogy drawn from the chase his brother was so fond of) goes out over vast fields and muirlands of thought with the fowling-piece of his intellect and returns with only a few woodcock or plover of probability. But it is not these which have provided him with the satisfaction of the chase. The conclusions of probability that he draws are not the important ones. The deeper truth that he has discovered and brought to light in the ardour of his pursuit is latent in the whole balance of his argument. You cannot state it. He has discovered for himself and for many of his readers, yet with the greatest good humour, that life is an enigma. Does that seem to you an obvious conclusion? If so, reflect that no one before Hume had come to it. Here indeed is irony.

The irony of this enigma is discovered in the magnificent architecture of Hume's prose style. It is built upon antithesis. The antitheses are lucidly expressed, yet so attenuated or separated by the rhythm of punctuation within paragraph against paragraph that the mind is exhilarated by the exercise (exercise rather than effort) of following them.

This was an eighteenth-century Scottish way of writing which Hume developed to its finest. Much play has been made by some English critics who have noted that David was sometimes at pains to prune his style of 'Scoticisms.' These Scoticisms were no more than the occasional use of words or phrases uncommon in English South of the Border. Hume did not wish to obscure his meaning to the English by the use of expressions unfamiliar to them, but he made no compromise in his style. It is a style of the English language written by a Scotsman, and by one of the greatest minds Scotland has produced—thinking and writing in a Scottish cultural tradition.

No one in Scotland today, or anywhere else for that matter, writes as Hume did, but his way of thought and argument and perhaps even talk is not entirely gone from us. Scottish lawyers and the better type of 'men of affairs' are still to be found among us who marshal their thoughts and arguments after a fashion in his fashion. Anyone who has tried to state the apparent certainty of an impregnable case to the older kind of Scottish lawyers (even a lawyer on his own side of the case) will know what we mean. He will recognise that the sceptical temperament, ironic and searching, but not necessarily mean-minded, is not dead amongst us. But he will be lucky if that ironic scepticism speak to him with anything like the friendliness that Hume used.

Friendliness, that is the word on which to take leave of Hume. In the enigmatic world of faint probabilities contesting with even fainter ones, of half-truths dissolving, at a touch (so it appeared to his majestic mind), into quarter-truths, there was one thing to which he clung, which was to him sacred—friendship. Despite all that celebrated dourness which afflicts some of our race, despite those inhibitions in temperament which are the legacy of so many harsh and unlovely things in our history, the Scots can be the most friendly and companionable people you will meet anywhere. None of us out of the great men of our past had a greater gift for friendship than David Hume.

It is one of the failings of a Scottish writer to be unable to leave well alone when he is writing about what he likes; the giants among us, notably Walter Scott, as well as the lesser breeds, have succumbed to it. The writer of these notes, too, and without apology, succumbs: he must say yet one more thing, a personal thing, about Hume. He who has had the congenial task of giving form to these notes on Hume, as well as to all the other extracts in this book, would like to pay this tribute to him.

He has his favourites amongst those about whom he has had to write. He has a warm and protective affection for Boswell, a respectful admiration for Henryson, a rather less respectful but nonetheless lively admiration for Dunbar, a poignant curiosity about the anonymous author of *The Complaint of Scotland*, a delight in Burns and a joyful veneration for Scott, but for none does he (a Roman Catholic Scot) feel quite that friendliness that he enjoys for the eighteenth-century sceptic, David Hume—*Le Bon David*.

Tobias Smollett or the Disputatious Scot

The Scots' power of disputatiousness, which is itself a prickly form of wisdom, has often been noted. Sometimes it has been ridiculed, sometimes mentioned with something akin to affection. It has seldom been better observed and described than in the character of Lieutenant Lismahagow from Smollett's *Humphry Clinker*. Smollett wrote this good-humoured masterpiece of a novel as his last book when he was all but dying, an exile from Britain (both his native N.B. and his adopted S.B.) in the sunshine of Italy. The novel is a series of letters supposed to be written by English and Welsh people who, in the progress of the book, happen to visit Scotland. Smollett makes them meet Lismahagow whom the author describes with good-natured mockery, but also with an exile's affection for a 'type'—his own national 'type' whom he was never to see again.[1] Your Scottish addict of disputation will never allow anyone else to praise Scotland. That privilege he reserves for himself. The privilege of running down his native country he also jealously guards as his own. Smollett brings this out well. He must as a member of the small impoverished unpopular group of Scottish literary men who lived in London after the Union have known this 'type' and heard it disputing often. The 'type' still exists.[2] Grotesque though it may seem there is a form of perverse wisdom in its utterances.

When I observed that he must have read a vast number of books to be able to discourse on such a variety of subjects, he declared he had read little or nothing, and asked how he should find books among the woods of America, where he had spent the greatest part of his life. My nephew remarking, that the Scots in general were famous for their learning, he denied the imputation, and defied him to prove it from their works.—'The Scots,' said he, 'have a slight tincture of letters, with which they make a parade among people who are more illiterate than themselves; but they may be said to float on the surface of science, and they have made very small advances in the useful arts.' 'At least,' cried Tabby, 'all the world allows that the Scots behaved gloriously in fighting and conquering the savages of America.' 'I can assure you, madam, you have been misinformed,' replied the lieutenant; 'in that continent the Scots did nothing more than their duty, nor was there one corps in his majesty's service that distinguished itself

---

[1] *Humphry Clinker, Letter from Matt Bramble to Dr. Lewis from Berwick*, The Edinburgh Edition of Smollett, pp. 226–30.

[2] Some readers may even perceive its influence in these editorial annotations.

more than another.—Those who affected to extol the Scots for superior merit, were no friends to that nation.'

Though he himself made free with his countrymen, he would not suffer any other person to glance a sarcasm at them with impunity. One of the company chancing to mention Lord B——'s inglorious peace, the lieutenant immediately took up the cudgels in his lordship's favour, and argued very strenuously to prove that it was the most honourable and advantageous peace that England had ever made since the foundation of the monarchy. Nay, between friends, he offered such reasons on this subject, that I was really confounded, if not convinced.—He would not allow that the Scots abounded above their proportion in the army and navy of Great Britain, or that the English had any reason to say his countrymen had met with extraordinary encouragement in the service. 'When a South and North Briton,' said he, 'are competitors for a place or commission, which is in the disposal of an English minister, or an English general, it would be absurd to suppose that the preference will not be given to the native of England, who has so many advantages over his rival.—First and foremost, he has in his favour that laudable partiality, which, Mr. Addison says, never fails to cleave to the heart of an Englishman; secondly, he has more powerful connections, and a greater share of parliamentary interest, by which those contents are generally decided; and, lastly, he has a greater command of money to smooth the way to his success. For my own part,' said he, 'I know no Scots officer who has risen in the army above the rank of a subaltern, without purchasing every degree of preferment either with money or recruits; but I know many gentlemen of that country, who, for want of money and interest, have grown grey in the rank of lieutenants; whereas very few instances of this ill fortune are to be found among the natives of South Britain. Not that I would insinuate that my countrymen have the least reason to complain. Preferment in the service, like success in any other branch of traffic, will naturally favour those who have the greatest stock of cash and credit, merit and capacity being supposed equal on all sides.'

But the most hardy of all this original's positions were these:—That commerce would, sooner or later, prove the ruin of every nation, where it flourishes to any extent—that the parliament was the rotten part of the British constitution—that the liberty of the press was a national evil—and that the boasted institution of juries, as managed in England, was productive of shameful perjury and flagrant injustice. He observed, that traffic was an enemy to all the liberal passions of the soul, founded

Q

on the thirst of lucre, a sordid disposition to take advantage of the necessities of our fellow-creatures. He affirmed, the nature of commerce was such, that it could not be fixed or perpetuated, but, having flowed to a certain height, would immediately begin to ebb, and so continue till the channels should be left almost dry; but there was no instance of the tide's rising a second time to any considerable influx in the same nation. Meanwhile, the sudden affluence occasioned by trade, forced open all the sluices of luxury, and overflowed the land with every species of profligacy and corruption; a total depravity of manners would ensue, and this must be attended with bankruptcy and ruin. He observed of the parliament, that the practice of buying boroughs, and canvassing for votes, was an avowed system of venality, already established on the ruins of principle, integrity, faith, and good order; in consequence of which, the elected, and the elector, and, in short, the whole body of the people, were equally and universally contaminated and corrupted. He affirmed, that, of a parliament thus constituted, the crown would always have influence enough to secure a great majority in its dependence, from the great number of posts, places, and pensions, it had to bestow; that such a parliament would, as it had already done, lengthen the term of its sitting and authority, whenever the prince should think it for his interest to continue the representatives; for, without doubt, they had the same right to protract their authority *ad infinitum*, as they had to extend it from three to seven years.—With a parliament, therefore, dependent upon the crown, devoted to the prince, and supported by a standing army, garbled and modelled for the purpose, any king of England may, and probably some ambitious sovereign will, totally overthrow all the bulwarks of the constitution; for it is not to be supposed that a prince of a high spirit will tamely submit to be thwarted in all his measures, abused and insulated by a populace of unbridled ferocity, when he has it in his power to crush all opposition under his feet with the concurrence of the legislature. He said, he should always consider the liberty of the press as a national evil, while it enabled the vilest reptile to soil the lustre of the most shining merit, and furnished the most infamous incendiary with the means of disturbing the peace, and destroying the good order of the community. He owned, however, that, under due restrictions, it would be a valuable privilege; but affirmed, that, at present, there was no law in England sufficient to restrain it within proper bounds.

With respect to juries, he expressed himself to this effect.—Juries are generally composed of illiterate plebians, apt to be mistaken, easily misled, and open to sinister influence; for if either of the parties to be tried can gain over one of the twelve jurors, he has secured the verdict in his favour; the juryman thus brought over, will, in despight of all evidence and conviction, generally hold out till his fellows are fatigued, and harassed, and starved into concurrence; in which case the verdict is unjust, and the jurors are all perjured;—but cases will often occur, when the jurors are really divided in opinion, and each side is convinced in opposition to the other; but no verdict will be received, unless they are unanimous, and they are all bound, not only in conscience, but by oath, to judge and declare according to their conviction. What then will be the consequence? They must either starve in company, or one side must sacrifice their conscience to their convenience, and join in a verdict which they believe to be false.—This absurdity is avoided in Sweden, where a bare majority is sufficient; and in Scotland, where two-thirds of the jury are required to concur in the verdict.

You must not imagine that all these deductions were made on his part, without contradiction on mine.—No—the truth is, I found myself piqued in point of honour, at his pretending to be so much wiser than his neighbours.—I questioned all his assertions, started innumerable objections, argued and wrangled with uncommon perseverance, and grew very warm, and even violent in the debate. Sometimes he was puzzled, and once or twice, I think, fairly refuted; but from those falls he rose again, like Antæus, with redoubled vigour, till at length I was tired, exhausted, and really did not know how to proceed, when luckily he dropped a hint, by which he discovered he had been bred to the law; a confession which enabled me to retire from the dispute with a good grace, as it could not be supposed that a man like me, who had been bred to nothing, should be able to cope with a veteran in his own profession. I believe, however, that I shall for some time continue to chew the cud of reflection upon many observations which this original discharged.

I cannot say farewell to Smollett even in this brief extract without mentioning his highly national power and taste in scatological writing. England was pretty good at this sort of thing in the eighteenth century, but it was left to the Irishman Swift and the Scotsman Smollett to beat all comers. In Scotland the taste for scatology lasted until into Queen Victoria's reign. We would have liked to have included a specimen of Smollett's gifts in this kind, but decided regretfully that even we could scarcely call it 'wisdom.'

James Boswell

With a few honourable exceptions people who write about Boswell either damn him with faint apology or damn him outright. Not being Almighty God we do not damn him at all. Nor do we feel called upon to apologise for the weaknesses and oddities of this perhaps excessively human (how often humane) human being and Scotch genius.[1]

Scotch genius maybe, but it is something of a task getting him into a book on the wisdom of the Scots. Nevertheless, in he must be got. To pass over the eighteenth century in our country without mentioning him or quoting from him would be unthinkable. Mentioning him is easy; the difficulty is to stop. Quoting from him is a different matter.

The iridescent quality of Boswell's talent, let alone genius, is such that anyone can plunge into his major work at random and emerge immediately with something quotable—a sentence, a scene, a description. Indeed he must be one of the most easily quotable writers in the language. It is arguable that it is a form of wisdom in Boswell which enabled him to provide such richness not only for our delight but for the good of our minds and souls; but the wisdom is implicit and is seldom quotable *as* wisdom. The dear good man did not go in much for wise homilies or maxims, and when he did try to do so they aren't often worth much.

His wisdom as it reaches us is usually the wisdom of brilliant selective reflection of the wisdom of others; but this form of, however wisely and artistically reflected, wisdom does not lend itself to the kind of quotation that is apt for this anthology. The vulgarest jibe about Boswell is that he was an inspired fool. It would be doing him, and the reader, poor service merely to select some of those examples of brilliant reporting where his 'inspired folly' is generally admitted to have been most remarkable.

Apart from the wisdom which enabled Boswell to select from and reflect the luminous world around him with an excellence which no one before him or since has equalled, the man had other qualities that arose from a kind of wisdom in him and which appear (or ought to appear to anyone with a spark of charity in him) all the more clearly against the background of his naïvety, his outbursts of folly and his weaknesses.

He was wise in his deliberately practised power of hope—not a chuckle-headed braying optimism, but a sustained, and, as it turned out, justified meliorism, a meliorism that his temperament and circumstances must have severely tried. This divine gift, assiduously cultivated, cannot, of course, be claimed as Scottish wisdom, but there is something Scottish in the pathetically dogged way in which Boswell clung to it.

---

[1] One seems to hear from a hundred and eighty-five years ago the venerable growl: 'The Irish are a FAIR PEOPLE,—they never speak well of one another.'

He was wise in that he tended always to look for what could interest him and what he could like in other people. His naïvety in companionship led him over this into some absurd mistakes, and, of course, he had his unconquerable antipathies; but to the end he went half-way to meet people instead of retreating into his shell as they approached. For those of us who have to spend half a century or more amongst our fellow-men on this earth this is a wise thing to do. It is wise and brave to go on doing it in the face of rebuffs.

Looking round on modern Scotland, so full of mean-minded denigration and terror of self-display, it would seem pitiable to claim this as a piece of Scottish wisdom. It is not only the spirit of paradox, however, that prompts this claim. We still, even now, have our Boswells (our lesser Boswells) amongst us; and when a Scotsman does decide to be generous with himself there are few who can do it more wholeheartedly. Also Boswell did not live in modern Scotland but in one of the sunniest periods of her capital's intellectual existence.

Surrounded as he was by so many and such delightful men so persuasively and skilfully vocal in infidelity, he was wise in his continued belief in God and His Revelation. In an age of cynical inhumanity towards the poor he was wonderfully humane (or tried his best to be) in his relations with his poorer clients in the law. Indeed, he imperilled his prospects at the Scottish bar by what seemed, and sometimes still seems, foolish Quixotry. Rather it was, even when unsuccessful, wise humanity. He was wise in his extraordinary capacity for work (just because he believed in himself) even when he had half ruined his constitution by drinking and wenching. He was, for the most part, wise in his friendship; and, if the old aphorism about style being the man has any validity, he showed his wisdom in the way he wrote.

People have perhaps understandably been so impressed by Boswell's dramatic powers as a reporter that they have neglected his style as a writer. It is remarkable. Lucid, muscular, economical, forceful, it yet has, when he wishes to lend it that quality, plenty of colour. Apparently effortlessly produced, it is yet as full of art as is an eighteenth-century melody by one of the Italian or Austrian masters. It is unlikely that he strove long in the act of composition to conceal his natural art; he was almost certainly a born writer, yet a born writer whose gift was enforced by the classical education of a gentleman of the period, by inquisitively voracious reading and by a familiarity with at least three European languages. How many of his most condescending critics today have half the learning in the humanities he had?

This gave him a style of writing which is not only a delight, but which is all his own. Amidst the surge and thunder and reverberation of eighteenth-century English and Scottish, and Scottish-French prose, Boswell's voice sounds clearly, unaffectedly and distinctly—distinctly his own. A man who was able to express himself as Boswell did, must, to some extent, have been wise.

He was also, of course, as we would now say it, a 'bloody fool.' He drank far too much and was always getting stupidly tight at the most inappropriate times and places. His failure as a Lothario, in which role he foolishly fancied himself, drove him to uncontrolled recourse with easy women—a habit amongst all classes of men that is often more common than is generally known, or, outside the Latin races, admitted—and he frequently clapped himself to the permanent detriment of his health. He was often foolish in company (though not to the extent that many people make out) and had a number of minor absurdities.

All this is known, and, owing to recent discoveries, has, of late, been much blown upon and gloated over. But the biggest folly that he is charged with in the eyes of the world is of being an insufferable loose-mouth, a gabster, a man who gave himself away. I shall return to this later, for I propose to allow myself plenty of elbow, or rather cudgel, room when we come to Boswell's detractors.[1]

In the thirty or so years of his writing life Boswell put over three million words on to paper. It is difficult to decide how many of these, those that form the journals and the correspondence with Temple, he wrote with a view to publication or as a basis for publication; but all have now been published, are in the process of publication, or can be consulted in private publications. Interesting and sometimes well written as the journals and the letters are they do not provide much suitable material for this anthology; they are too 'bitty.' But one excerpt is printed to show his wise humanity.

Even though one were to confine oneself for the rest to his three major works published in his lifetime, the *Life of Johnson*, the *Tour to the Hebrides* and *An Account of Corsica*, there would still be difficulty in choosing. There is the difficulty of an embarrassment of riches. More-over, one hesitates to pull out pieces from such well-known works as the first two just to illustrate our theme—especially as such wisdom as Boswell discovers in them are, as we have implied, difficult in their varied manner to pin down. It is extremely difficult to do even part justice to Boswell by quoting him in snatches.

We have chosen, then, only three selections of Boswell's prose to illustrate his way of thought and his style. And of those three, two are from his lesser-known work. There is nothing from the great *Tour to the Hebrides*, and only one excerpt from the *Life of Johnson*. This is not because we hold the *Tour to the Hebrides* to be inferior —in some ways it is a more remarkable work than the *Life*—but because the *Life* offers more apt quotable material. *Corsica* we have used to show Boswell's wisdom on liberty, and because, even now, it is a much neglected book. There will be short annotations before each selection.

But there is still something left to be said *about* Boswell, in particular about his detractors; this is still relevant to our theme. The distaste which Boswell has aroused since his death illustrates a quality in the Scottish mind as it has developed in the last hundred and fifty years and a thing which often passes for wisdom in modern Scotland. That

---

[1] I am reminded of a writing colleague who, complaining of the smallness of his study, said: 'There isn't room here to swing a critic.'

thing is best expressed in the horrible aphorism which might be used by certain Scots—'Hate thy neighbour as thyself.'[1]

Disapproval of James Boswell has never been better or more strongly expressed than by the Clapham-reared Scot Macaulay in his famous review of Croker's edition of the *Life of Johnson*. The stench of Macaulay's malevolence was so strong that it still lingers in the nostrils of men who are unaware of where the smell originally came from, who maybe have never read a line which Macaulay wrote but who derive at second, third, fourth or twentieth hand their opinion of Boswell as a worthless fool from his unforgettable attack.

It is unforgettable not only on account of Macaulay's splendid style but because of its manner. As one reads it one recalls a boxer hitting not merely to score points, not merely to knock out, but to pound his senseless opponent into bloody meat. One hears between the thud of the blows the shrill ululations of the prize-fighter's sadistic pleasure and sees the fleck of foam upon his lips. As a display of pathological ferocity on the part of this strange individual it is unforgettable.

To say that Macaulay's trumpet-voiced Clapham–Scottish wisdom spoke for the establishment of the middle classes in Britain is a truism. What is to our purpose is that the period of his eloquence and power in the United Kingdom coincided with the adoption by his grandfather's country of Scotland of the middle-class qualities as a way of life. This was, with us, a later submission than in England. David Hume, Principal Robertson and later Walter Scott, as well as other literati of Edinburgh's 'Golden Age,' were of good birth though of narrow economical circumstances. They would certainly not have called themselves middle-class, and there was a sunny security in the way their minds worked which was purely aristocratic. Robert Burns may have aspired to something approaching a middle-class status as a farmer and have died in the harness of a civil servant, and a very efficient civil servant too, but he was a peasant. It was not until Scott was dead and the noble Georgian New Town of Edinburgh was barely completed that the capital of Scotland became the profoundly bourgeois city that she is today.

The Scottish, and particularly the Edinburgh, bourgeoisie, once they became conscious of being bourgeois, have, with characteristic and national intemperance, pushed the virtues and failings of the middle-class way of life to the limit. Its virtues need not concern us here, some of its failings do. Amongst these are a deep fear of giving oneself away and a hatred of anyone else who does. The hatred of your self-giving-away neighbour arises from the knowledge, or maybe only the fear that in giving himself away he is *giving away a part of you*. In hating such thou art indeed hating thy neighbour as thyself. It was this feeling that Macaulay so trenchantly expressed for the Scotland that came after the Scotland of Boswell's time.

[1] I yield to the temptation to complete this aphorism. Scotch Puritanism in its most violent extreme, at one time, may be said to have been a corruption of the New Commandment running thus: 'Thou shalt be afraid of the Lord thy God with all thy heart, with all thy soul and with all thy might; and thou shalt hate thy neighbour as thyself.'

He did it better, because more ferociously and openly than anyone else has done. All subsequent detraction of Boswell down to that of the aciduously learned Mr. C. E. Vulliamy is but Macaulay and water. Its theme is the same. The overt objection to him is that he was a sot,[1] a wencher, a toady, and a fool, but it does not take long to discover that his real crime was that he admitted it. It is an old saying that there are really eleven commandments and that the eleventh is: 'Thou shalt not be found out.' In certain sections of Scottish opinion there are twelve commandments, and the twelfth and gravest of all is, 'Thou shalt not give thyself away!' Granted this, James Boswell was indeed the Prince of Sinners.

In fairness to Boswell's own countrymen in the nineteenth century it should be said that Macaulay's diatribe had the effect of making them, almost despite themselves, stand up for him. An understandably clannish pride was offended. As the century proceeded, and as more and more people all over the world kept on saying that Boswell's *Life of Johnson* was not only the best biography in English, but one of the best in any language, and as the generation disappeared that had actually seen Boswell making such a self-admitted fool of himself in Edinburgh and elsewhere, people here began to be more proud of Boswell than ashamed of him. He had joined our small temple of world-wide fame.

Moreover Edinburgh is an odd city; it is a very old city as well as an odd one. Centuries of humanity have flowed along its narrow streets and its wide and gracious streets. In those centuries a lot of Scotsmen other than Boswell have made fools of themselves in something of the same way that he did. 'After all, hadn't poor old so-and-so been almost as ridiculous as Boswell? And after all wasn't Boswell a genius? All over the world people seem to be saying he was.' Certain sections in Edinburgh, with the rest of Scotland following in the rear, almost began to persuade themselves that, since they owned Boswell outright, they owned and understood what the rest of the world called his peculiarities as well as his genius. 'After all, wasn't he one of us?' They weren't far wrong.

Maybe the anglicised Macaulay spoke partly for the thou-shalt-not-give-thyself-away creed of his grandparents' country, but he also spoke for, and in advance of, many, many English critics who find the 'paradox of Boswell' incomprehensible. It is not incomprehensible to us. They (the English critics) cannot understand how a man could be so full of all the extreme qualities of extrovert behaviour, both foolish and wise, and yet be a Scot and a genius. It is the old trouble of the label not agreeing with what is in the bottle. This kind of label is not usually found on a bottle of Scotch—Scotch humanity, that is. The problem does not trouble us. After all, we are inside the bottle and know that the contents are pretty mixed. We only read the label when we get outside.

---

[1] The use of this word recalls an earlier and trenchant piece of Scottish wisdom. The early mediaeval scholar, John the Scot, was carousing at the hospitable board of King Charles the Bold when he had the Royal riddle put to him: 'What is it that separates a Scot from a sot?'
'Only the table,' replied John immediately.

Macaulay, then, on the whole, spoke as much for England as for Scotland when he eructated against Boswell.

While musing on this subject in the National Library of Scotland (just over the Cowgate where Boswell conducted some of the most reprehensible, ridiculous and pitiable of his nocturnal and vertically practised amours) my eye fell by the merest chance upon the volume of Sir Thomas Urquhart's works already referred to containing this rhymed epigram:[1]

Of Lust And Anger

'Lust taking pleasure in its owne delite,
Communicates it selfe to two togither;
But far more base is anger, whose despite
Rejoyceth at the sorrow of another
  For th'one is kindly, th'other sows debate,
  Lust hath a smack of love, but wrath of hate.'

Certainly this is not poetry, and is no more than jingling verse. Yet the coincidence, however, of stumbling across this possibly post-prandial piece of Scottish wisdom by the Knight of Cromartie—wisdom for what it is worth—at that moment was more than I could resist. It is an innocuous way of getting the taste of Clapham out of one's mouth by way of the Cowgate and Cromartie.

And now for James Boswell himself.

CORSICA

We begin with a passage from his *An Account of Corsica: The Journal of a Tour to that Island*, published in 1768. The text is from the first edition, which is the purest. It is important to realise that, long before Boswell was famous as 'Johnson Boswell,' he was comparatively well known as 'Corsica Boswell.' His youthful book, in its time, was a novelty in style and treatment. Moreover, as a large part of Europe was then watching with admiring interest the Corsican struggle for Freedom under the heroic General Paoli, the subject was topical. His *Corsica* was a considerable success at home, and was well received in translation abroad.

It is a long time since the island of Corsica was 'news'; and Boswell's manner in writing about it has long since ceased to be a novelty in travel literature. Indeed his eager personal style has been imitated over and over again by people who may not even know that Boswell ever wrote about Corsica. Nevertheless Boswell's first book remains a remarkable achievement. It is so fresh, so informative, so interesting, and is still so original. Many may have consciously and unconsciously imitated Boswell's first book, but few have equalled him in it, none excelled. It is extraordinary that this little near-masterpiece is as neglected as it is by

[1] Maitland Club, *Works of Sir Thomas Urquhart*, p. 15.

a public that professes to be so interested in Boswell's less happy pro-
ductions. The word happy is used here literally and with no undertones.

It contains much that could have been written by him alone, and as
such shows gleams of what we would claim as Boswellian wisdom.
Corsica is very much to our purpose in beginning our brief selection
from him; so is the subject of liberty.

This passage from *Corsica* on liberty has an odd history. It comes
from the introduction to the body of the work itself and appeared in
the eighteenth-century editions published in Boswell's lifetime. The few
nineteenth and twentieth century more 'modern' editions leave it out.
Maybe later editors found it an example of what they would have called
Boswell's sententiousness. It is not; it is a piece of Scottish wisdom,
deriving directly from Barbour's 'Ah! freedom is a noble thing.' When
Boswell wrote this as a young man Barbour's famous poem, let alone
line, was hardly known; this makes his eighteenth-century version of
the theme all the more remarkable. The tradition must have carried on.
It is possible that a sentence here and there may have in it a note of
Rousseau (whom Boswell had but recently left), but the bulk is Scottish
and in the Scottish tradition, yet applied to the mountain Island of
Corsica instead of to the mountainous land of Scotland. On the title-page
of his first edition Boswell quoted the great words *Non enim propter
gloriam* . . . from the Declaration of Arbroath.

Why did not Boswell echo these sentiments when he visited the
Highlands and Islands of his own country and with Dr. Johnson?
Well, he did, in a way, but very remotely. The real answer is that in
1767 there was real hope for Corsica. By 1773 there was no hope, as
far as human eyes could see, for Gaelic Scotland. It is a part of the
poignant beauty of Boswell's Highland and Hebridean book that in it
we bid farewell to a ghost (the old Highland way of life) in that moment
of suspended mortality just before a ghost becomes a ghost by leaving
the flesh.

Liberty is so natural, and so dear to mankind, whether as individuals,
or as members of society, that it is indispensibly necessary to our
happiness. Every thing worthy ariseth from it. Liberty gives health to
the mind, and enables us to enjoy the full exercise of our faculties.
He who is in chains cannot move either easily or gracefully; nothing
elegant or noble can be expected from those, whose spirits are subdued
by tyranny, and whose powers are cramped by restraint.

There are those who from the darkest prejudice, or most corrupt
venality, would endeavour to reason mankind out of their original and
genuine feelings, and persuade them to substitute artificial sentiment
in place of that which is implanted by GOD and Nature. They would
maintain, that slavery will from habit become easy, and, that mankind
are truly better, when under confinement and subjection to the arbitrary
will of a few.

Such doctrine as this, could never have gained any ground, had it been addressed to calm reason alone. Its partisans therefore have found it necessary to address themselves to the imagination and passions; to call in the aid of enthusiasm and superstition; in some countries to instill a strange love and attachment to their sovereigns; and in others to propagate certain mystical notions, which the mind of man is wonderfully ready to receive, of a divine right to rule; as if their sovereigns had descended from heaven. This last idea has been cherished for ages, from the 'Cara Deum suboles, The beloved offspring of the Gods,' among the Romans, to those various elevated and endearing epithets, which modern nations have thought proper to bestow upon their sovereigns.

But whatever sophisms may be devised in favour of slavery, patience under it, can never be any thing but 'the effect of a sickly constitution, which creates a laziness and despondency, that puts men beyond hopes and fears; mortifying ambition, and other active qualities, which freedom begets; and instead of them, affording only a dull kind of pleasure, of being careless and insensible.'

There is no doubt, but by entering into society, mankind voluntarily give up a part of their natural rights, and bind themselves to the obedience of laws, calculated for the general good. But, we must distinguish between authority, and oppression; between laws, and capricious dictates; and keeping the original intention of government ever in view, we should take care that no more restraint be laid upon natural liberty, than what the necessities of society require.

Perhaps the limits between the power of government, and the liberty of the people, should not be too strictly marked out. Men of taste reckon that picture hard, where the outlines are so strong, as to be clearly seen. They admire a piece of painting, where the colours are delicately blended, and the tints, which point out every particular object, are softened into each other, by an insensible gradation. So in a virtuous state, there should be such a mutual confidence between the government and the people, that the rights of each should not be expressly defined.

But flagrant injustice, on one side or other, is not to be concealed; and, without question, it is the priviledge of the side that is injured, to vindicate itself.

I have been led into these reflections from a consideration of the arguments by which ingenious men in the refinement of politics have endeavoured to amuse mankind, and turn away their attention from the plain and simple notions of liberty.

Liberty is indeed the parent of felicity, of every noble virtue, and even of every art and science. Whatever vain attempts have been made to raise the generous plants under an oppressive climate, have only shewn more evidently the value of freedom.

It is therefore no wonder that the world has at all times been roused at the mention of liberty; and that we read with admiration and a virtuous enthusiasm, the gallant achievements of those who have distinguished themselves in the glorious cause; and the history of states who were animated with the principle of freedom, and made it the basis of their constitution.

Should any one transmit to posterity the annals of an enslaved nation, we should sleep over whole ages of the humbling detail. Every thing would be so poor, so tame, and so abject, that one might as well peruse the records of a prison-house.

But we have a manly satisfaction in reading the history of the ancient Romans; even abstracting from their connections and their broils with other states. Their internal progress alone affords ample matter of speculation to a judicious and spirited observer of human nature. We love to trace the various springs of their conduct, and of their advancement in greatness. We contemplate with pleasure the ferments between the patricians and plebeians, the strong exertions of rude genius, the vigorous exercises and hardy virtues of men uncontrouled by timid subjection.

They who entertain an extravagant veneration for antiquity, would make us believe, that the divine fire of liberty has been long ago exhausted, and that any appearances of it which are to be found in modern times are but feeble and dim. They would make us believe that the world is grown old, that the strength of human nature is decayed, and that we are no more to expect those noble powers which dignified men in former ages.

But the truth is, that human nature is the same at all times, and appears in different lights merely from a difference of circumstances. In the language of the schoolmen, the substance is fixed, the accidents only vary. Rome has yet the seven hills on which the conquerors of the world dwelt, and these are inhabited by Romans. Athens still occupies the space from whence philosophy and genius diffused a radiance to all the nations around, and is possessed by Athenians. But neither of these people now retain any resemblance of their illustrious ancestors; this is entirely owing to the course of political events, which has produced a total change in their manners.

That the spirit of liberty has flourished in modern times, we may appeal to the histories of the Swiss, and of the Dutch; and the boldest proofs of it are to be found in the annals of our own country.

But a most distinguished example of it actually exists in the island of Corsica. There, a brave and resolute nation, has now for upwards of six and thirty years, maintained a constant struggle against the oppression of the republic of Genoa. These valiant islanders were for a long time looked upon as an inconsiderable band of malecontents, as a disorderly troop of rebels, who would speedily be compelled to resume those chains which they had frowardly shaken off. They have however continued steady to their purpose. Providence has favoured them; and Europe now turns her eyes upon them, and with astonishment sees them on the eve of emancipating themselves for ever from a foreign yoke, and becoming a free and independent people.

> Libertas quae sera tamen respexit—
> Respexit tamen et longo post tempore venit.
> VIRG. Eclog. I.
> When a long age of vent'rous toil was past,
> Celestial freedom blest their isle at last.

The smallness of the Corsican state does not render it less an object of admiration. On the contrary, we ought to admire it the more. The ingenius Mr. Hume hath shewn us, that Rhodes, Thebes, and many of the famous ancient states were not so numerous as the people of Corsica now are. If the ten thousand Greeks have gained immortal honour because they were opposed to the armies of the Persian monarch, shall not the Corsicans be found deserving of glory, who have set themselves against a republic, which has been aided at different times by the power of France, and by that of the empire of Germany?

The Corsicans have been obliged to shew particular force of spirit. The Swiss and the Dutch were both assisted by powerful nations in the recovery of their liberties: but during the long and bloody war which Corsica has carried on, the Powers of Europe, who might be supposed friendly to her, have stood aloof, and she has single and unsupported, weathered the storm, and arrived at the degree of consequence which she now holds.

To give an account of this island, is what I am now to attempt. The attempt is surely laudable; and I am persuaded that my readers will grant me every indulgence, when they consider how favourable is the subject. They will consider that I am the first Briton who has had the curiosity to visit Corsica, and to receive such information as to enable him to form a just idea of it; and they will readily make allowance for the enthusiasm of one who has been among the brave islanders, when their patriotic virtue is at its height, and who has felt as it were a communication of their spirit.

BOSWELL FOR THE DEFENCE[1]

Boswell, to put it conservatively, was an odd bundle of contradictions. He was distinctly rocky on the question of negro slavery when it came up in the Scottish courts and even tried to resist Johnson's cogent and noble arguments for freedom. He also had an unpleasing love of attending public executions. At the same time he was a most humane man. He would go to great lengths to save anyone from being hanged, even when the man was, in the popular and official view, worthless. In practice, if not in explicit argument, he might be said to have been an opponent of capital punishment.

His defence of John Reid, the sheep-stealer, in 1774 is a well-known example. The details are too complicated to give here. It is enough to say that Boswell damaged his prospects at the bar in his persistent defence of this pitiable character. I give only one extract from the mass of papers about this case. It is a letter which Boswell sent to the London press in a last-minute bid and unavailing attempt to save his humble client's life. The letter shows Boswell, for all his assiduity in attending executions, in advance of his time on the matter of Capital Punishment.

To The Printer of The London Chronicle

Edinburgh, 13 September 1774

Sir,—The rigour of our present penal laws has been long the subject of complaint. It is to be hoped that the legislature will at least see fit to relax it. In the mean time, the utmost care shall be taken that there should at least be full evidence against an unhappy man before he is dragged to a violent death for theft or any of those lesser crimes which are at present capital by law in England and by practice in Scotland. We have at present in this city a remarkable man lying under sentence of death, being convicted of the theft of a few sheep. His name is John Reid. He is remarkable because he was formerly tried and acquitted by a very worthy jury, notwithstanding which some persons in high office publicly represented him as guilty. In particular one great man of the law exclaimed against him in his speech in the great Douglas Cause. This is a striking specimen of what goes on in this narrow country. A strong prejudice was raised against him, and now

[1] *The Private Papers of James Boswell*, published by the Yale University Press, Vol. VII, pp. 315 and 316.

he was condemned upon circumstantial evidence which several impartial gentlemen of very good skill were of opinion was inconclusive. He has uniformly affirmed that, although the sheep were found in his possession, he had obtained them by a fair and honest bargain from another man. His case is very much similar to that of Madan, who was lately in the cart at Tyburn just going to be turned off, as guilty of a robbery upon circumstantial evidence, when Merritt appeared and confessed that he was the man who had committed the crime. But the man from whom Reid got the sheep has not as yet been so conscientious as Merritt. He has maintained an obstinate denial; but having been transported for housebreaking, he will probably confess in America.

A respite for fourteen days was sent to Reid from the office of Lord Rochford, from whence Madan's respite also was sent. But, according to my information, an opinion from Scotland was desired upon the case: an opinion from that very man who exclaimed in the Civil Court against a man acquitted by a jury in the Criminal Court, when his life was staked upon the issue.

The determination of the Sovereign is expected here with anxiety. I wish to avoid strong expressions. I would turn my mind only towards mercy. This will reach you on Saturday. It is entreated that you may insert it directly, as it may perhaps have influence in some manner that we cannot exactly foresee, and an express with a pardon, or with another respite till there can be time to hear from America, will prevent what I am afraid would have a wretched appearance in the annals of this country. I am, Sir, your constant reader,

A ROYALIST.

THE LIFE OF JOHNSON

Boswell's masterpiece is the large quarry in which those who wish to find examples of his social folly just lying about, or deliberately and naïvely exposed, are most richly rewarded. He is frequently made to look a fool in speech or in conduct and in the rebukes which he called down upon himself from his revered friend. His general comments, which appear incidentally, are sometimes dead wrong, e.g. on the negro question referred to above, and are often sententious. The *Life* is not the place people usually go to in search of Boswellian wisdom.

Was this role of near buffoon consciously or unconsciously assumed for artistic effect—in order to show up by contrast the dignity and wisdom of his subject? If it was conscious it must have been so heroic and so superbly sustained as to have been a wise achievement. Even if it was unconscious it was remarkable. A subconscious self that can sustain for artistic effect a self-portrait of this kind for so long, in so large a book, in such a limited style, and through so many months of weary conscious effort, is unusual. But to sum it up simply, to have written the best biography in the language in so new a manner and at such length was an achievement of wisdom.

Nevertheless, there are passages where all except his most implacable denigrators would admit that he shows himself not only as an affectionate and affection-arousing individual, but as a wise one, at any rate a wise observer of character and the world. From these, after much hesitation, we decided to choose only one example. To apologise to other lovers of the *Life* for our choice would be in vain. But we believe that the example we do give shows Boswell's wisdom at its best. It is his celebrated discourse on 'The English Malady.'[1]

Under this name eighteenth-century physicians referred to that inexplicable and painful melancholy which can seize the constitutions of some of the sanest, best and wisest of us. It was an insular complaint at that time, being more found in Britain than anywhere else, but it was not confined to England. Boswell, for instance, suffered from it just as much as did Johnson. Indeed, lacking Johnson's heroic powers of self-control, he suffered from its effects more grievously. The bottle and the brothel were for him often no more than anodynes for his distress from this malady.

The important thing to note, the consoling thing to reflect on, for those who know how crippling, degrading and eventually destructive this complaint can be, is how much these two men in their two ways triumphed over it, how much they achieved despite it—and this before the days of psychotherapy, psychiatry and all the rest of it. In this passage here quoted, Boswell is speaking from the heart and the head—and for the soul.

The 'morbid melancholy,' which was lurking in his constitution, and to which we may ascribe those particularities, and that aversion to regular life, which, at a very early period, marked his character, gathered such strength in his twentieth year, as to afflict him in a dreadful manner. While he was at Lichfield, in the college vacation of the year 1729, he felt himself overwhelmed with an horrible hypochondria, with perpetual irritation, fretfulness, and impatience; and with a dejection, gloom, and despair, which made existence misery. From this dismal malady he never afterwards was perfectly relieved; and all his labours, and all his enjoyments, were but temporary interruptions of its baleful influence. How wonderful, how unsearchable are the ways of God! Johnson, who was blest with all the powers of genius and understanding in a degree far above the ordinary state of human nature, was at the same time visited with a disorder so afflictive, that they who know it by dire experience, will not envy his exalted

[1] *Life of Johnson*, Dent, Everyman's Edition, Vol. I, pp. 30–2.

endowments. That it was, in some degree, occasioned by a defect in his nervous system, that inexplicable part of our frame, appears highly probable. He told Mr. Paradise that he was sometimes so languid and inefficient, that he could not distinguish the hour upon the town-clock.

Johnson, upon the first violent attack of this disorder, strove to overcome it by forcible exertions. He frequently walked to Birmingham and back again, and tried many other expedients, but all in vain. His expression concerning it to me was 'I did not then know how to manage it.' His distress became so intolerable, that he applied to Dr. Swinfen, physician in Lichfield, his god-father, and put into his hands a state of his case, written in Latin. Dr. Swinfen was so much struck with the extraordinary acuteness, research, and eloquence of this paper, that in his zeal for his god-son he shewed it to several people. His daughter, Mrs. Desmoulins, who was many years humanely supported in Dr. Johnson's house in London, told me, that upon his discovering that Dr. Swinfen had communicated his case, he was so much offended, that he was never afterwards fully reconciled to him. He indeed had good reason to be offended; for though Dr. Swinfen's motive was good, he inconsiderately betrayed a matter deeply interesting and of great delicacy, which had been entrusted to him in confidence: and exposed a complaint of his young friend and patient, which, in the superficial opinion of the generality of mankind, is attended with contempt and disgrace.

But let not little men triumph upon knowing that Johnson was an HYPOCHONDRIACK, was subject to what the learned, philosophical, and pious Dr. Cheyne has so well treated under the title of 'The English Malady.' Though he suffered severely from it, he was not therefore degraded. The powers of his great mind might be troubled, and their full exercise suspended at times; but the mind itself was ever entire. As a proof of this, it is only necessary to consider, that, when he was at the very worst, he composed that state of his own case, which shewed an uncommon vigour, not only of fancy and taste, but of judgement. I am aware that he himself was too ready to call such a complaint by the name of *madness*; in conformity with which notion, he has traced its gradations, with exquisite nicety, in one of the chapters of his RASSELAS. But there is surely a clear distinction between a disorder which affects only the imagination and spirits, while the judgement is sound, and a disorder by which the judgement itself is impaired. The distinction was made to me by the late Professor Gaubius of Leyden, physician to the Prince of Orange, in a conversation which

R

I had with him several years ago, and he explained it thus: 'If (said he) a man tells me that he is grievously disturbed, for that he *imagines* he sees a ruffian coming against him with a drawn sword, though at the same time he is *conscious* it is a delusion, I pronounce him to have a disordered imagination; but if a man tells me that he *sees* this, and in consternation calls to me to look at it, I pronounce him to be *mad*.'

It is a common effect of low spirits or melancholy, to make those who are afflicted with it imagine that they are actually suffering those evils which happen to be most strongly presented to their minds. Some have fancied themselves to be deprived of the use of their limbs, some to labour under acute diseases, others to be in extreme poverty; when, in truth, there was not the least reality in any of the suppositions; so that when the vapours were dispelled, they were convinced of the delusion. To Johnson, whose supreme enjoyment was the exercise of his reason, the disturbance or obscuration of that faculty was the evil most to be dreaded. Insanity, therefore, was the object of his most dismal apprehension; and he fancied himself seized by it, or approaching to it, at the very time when he was giving proofs of a more than ordinary soundness and vigour of judgement. That his own diseased imagination should have so far deceived him, is strange; but it is stranger still that some of his friends should have given credit to his groundless opinion, when they had such undoubted proofs that it was totally fallacious; though it is by no means surprising that those who wish to depreciate him, should, since his death, have laid hold of this circumstance, and insisted upon it with very unfair aggravation.

Amidst the oppression and distraction of a disease which very few have felt in its full extent, but many have experienced in a slighter degree, Johnson, in his writings, and in his conversation, never failed to display all the varieties of intellectual excellence. In his march through this world to a better, his mind still appeared grand and brilliant, and impressed all around him with the truth of Virgil's noble sentiment—

> '*Igneus est ollis vigor et coelestis origo*.'

Robert Burns

It is no derogation of the lambent and imperishable genius of Burns to say that most Scottish anthologies (indeed, until this one we might say all) contain far too much of him. Anthologists rely on Robert Burns because they fear that readers are not interested in other Scottish poets. Whether this be true of the average modern reader of Scottish letters (if indeed such a creature exists), we cannot say, but to suppose such a thing of him is an insult to his intelligence and is certainly unjust to the literature of Scotland and to Burns himself.

Were this a purely poetic or literary compilation we should therefore still be cautious in our selection from Burns. It pretends, however, to be a collection of wisdom; and, again with no derogation of him intended, Burns's singing and narrative output (from which most selections are made) is not conspicuous for wisdom.

Then there is another reason for restraint. Burns is a greater popular poet than any in the world. Because he always spoke for the common people he is more commonly and widely known than Shakespeare. He is known to the Japanese, to the Faroese, to the Chinese, the Indians, the Russians (to the Germans and North Americans, of course), and even to the superbly insular French. Only the English are largely ignorant of him; they regard him, for the most part, as an irritatingly uncouth North British dialect poet whom the Scots are always ramming down their throats. The Scots, too, have heard too much of too little of him to know much about him. Deafened by the flatulent and inevitably repetitive quotations thrown up per annum on each 25th of January, the poet's birthday, indeed it would sometimes seem delivered perennially, they have but little ear-space left for anything else he sang or said. All the same, even in these islands he has been over-anthologised and is in no need of more space of this kind.

It has till recently been a literary dogma (*a*) that Burns wrote in two languages, (*b*) that all his best poems are written in Scots, (*c*) that everything he wrote in English is bad. This may be nationalism, or provincialism or parochialism, or even that 'last refuge of the scoundrel' patriotism, but it is not literary criticism. In fact Burns used all languages available to him; and the powerful effect of his poetry is often due to his subtle change when he modulates between one linguistic key and another. An obvious example for the general reader is to be found in the hackneyed but ever beautiful *Ae fond kiss*.

Except for a celebrated light tail-piece of four lines which we have thrown in to illustrate one gleaming glancing facet of the poet's mind rather than heart, we have chosen but one poem to represent the wisdom of Burns. In this he modulates from the couthiest of vernacular Scots to the most literary post-Augustan Scots-English. No listener need be a trained student of music to appreciate the delights of the bold modulations in the adagio of Beethoven's Ninth Symphony; no reader surely who is sympathetic to the quality of the languages spoken in these islands should fail to receive something of the same effect in the linguistic modulations Burns practises in *The Vision* which we print below.

It was irresistible to mention this linguistic modulation of Burns so triumphantly used in *The Vision*. It is almost equally irresistible to dwell upon the other technical achievements here displayed, the strange poetic perceptions of what was yet to come in poetry. Nobody can fully do justice to this poem without thinking himself back to the time before Wordsworth.[1] It is also irresistible, just because it may seem trivial, to point to the phrase 'A wildly-witty rustic grace' and in pointing to it to think almost exactly a hundred years later to 'She was wild and sweet and witty; let's not say dull things about her.'

But let's not say dull things about Robert Burns's poetic powers. Let his poem speak for itself with only this comment which is germane to our theme of wisdom.

In this poem he expressed the deepest wisdom he knew. In this poem in which the vision of his Muse consoles him for the mundane reflections of how much earthly gain he had lost by following her he gives a comprehensive statement of his own vision of an integrated Scotland. It is a Scottish nation in which each is for all, and all for each, and all are kindly Scots, even the traditional Ayrshire lairds who are here not oppressing their folk but working for the common Scottish weal. All are kindly Scots. And it is a Scotland in which learned and rustic bards have each an essential and honoured place.

Inevitably the mind returns to the vision of an earlier Scottish poet—that of Thomas the Rhymer. It is possible that Burns may have been inspired by the thought of this more ethereal, though nevertheless equally poignant vision. Burns's vision came to him not on the hillside and in the wild free air, but by his own fireside.

The only Scottish poet save Burns who tried to express this same integrated view of Scotland was Sir Richard Maitland of Lethington whom we have quoted in Part I. Charming though Maitland's verse was it bears no comparison with Burns's *The Vision*. Moreover, in Maitland's time the idea of an integrated Scotland was an ideal that could conceivably have been realised. He could remember the ghost of something faintly like it from his own youth. In Robert Burns's time, at the end of the eighteenth century, with the Industrial Revolution dawning, with the old Scotland dying, with innumerable MacJudases computing the sale of their Motherland for less than half of thirty pieces of silver, the poet was granted a vision of a phantom of a ghost of a thing whom none could recall.

Who dare laugh at him for that? All honour to him that he had the courage to believe in it. All gratitude to him that he made a poem of it (and such a poem) which he left to posterity or Scotland to laugh at or to fail to appreciate.

[1] Cp. T. Crawford, *Burns: A Study of the Poems and Songs*, Edinburgh, 1960, pp. 182 ff. Mr. Crawford gives a long and admirable discussion of the poem, which may be commended to the enquiring reader.

I. THE VISION[1]

DUAN FIRST

The sun had closed the winter day,
The curlers ^aquat their roarin' play,   ^aquit
An' hunger'd ^amaukin taen her way   ^ahave
       To kail-yards green,
While faithless ^asnaws ^bilk step betray   ^asnows ^beach
       Where she has been.

The thresher's weary ^aflingin'-tree   ^aflail
The lee-lang day had tirèd me;
And when the day had clos'd his e'e,
       Far i' the west,
^aBen i' the ^bspence, right pensivelie,   ^ainside ^bparlour
       I gaed to rest.

There lanely by the ingle-cheek
I sat and eyed the spewing ^areek,   ^asmoke
That fill'd, wi' ^ahoast-provoking ^bsmeek,   ^athroat- ^bfumes
       The auld clay ^abiggin';   ^abuilding
An' heard the restless ^arattons squeak   ^arats
       About the ^ariggin'.   ^aroof

All in this ^amottie misty clime,   ^amote-filled
I backward mused on wasted time,
How I had spent my youthfu' prime,
       An' done nae-thing,
But stringin' ^ablethers up in rhyme   ^aidle talk
       For fools to sing.

Had I to guid advice but harkit,
I might, by this, hae led a market,
Or strutted in a bank, and clarkit
       My cash-account:
While here, half-mad, half-fed, ^ahalf-sarkit,   ^ahalf-shirted
       Is a' th' amount.

[1] *The Poetry of Robert Burns*, ed. W. E. Henley and T. F. Henderson, 4 vols., Edinburgh and London, 1896, I. 74 (350).

I started, mutt'ring 'blockhead! coof!'
And heaved on high my *waukit loof,   *hard palm
To swear by a' yon starry roof,
   Or some rash *aith,   *oath
That I, henceforth, would be rhyme-proof
   Till my last breath—

When click! the string the *snick did draw;   *latch
An' jee! the door gaed to the wa';
And by my *ingle-lowe I saw,   *firelight
   Now bleezin' bright,
A tight outlandish *hizzie, braw,   *girl
   Come full in sight.

Ye need na doubt I *held my whisht;   *kept silent
The infant aith, half-form'd, was crusht;
I glowr'd as eerie 's I'd been *dusht   *pushed by an ox
   In some wild glen;
When sweet, like modest worth, she blusht,
   An' steppèd *ben.[1]   *into (the inner room)

Green, slender, leaf-clad holly-boughs
Were twisted, gracefu', round her brows;
I took her for some Scottish Muse
   By that same token;
And come to stop these reckless vows,
   *Would soon *been broken.   *(that) would . . .
           *(have) been . . .

A 'hare-brain'd, sentimental trace,'
Was strongly markèd in her face;
A wildly-witty rustic grace
   Shone full upon her;
Her eye, ev'n turn'd on empty space,
   Beam'd keen with Honour.

Down flow'd her robe, a tartan sheen,
Till half a leg was *scrimply seen;   *scarcely
An' such a leg! my bonnie Jean
   Could only peer it;
Sae *straught, sae taper, tight, and clean,   *straight
   *Nane else came near it.   *none

---

[1] Here Burns begins, as Mr. T. Crawford would put it, to modulate from
vernacular Scots into Scots-English. Even so, 'boughs,' 'brows' and 'vows,'
in the next stanza, still rhyme with 'Muse.'

Her mantle large, of greenish hue,
My gazing wonder chiefly drew;
Deep lights and shades, bold-mingling, threw
      A lustre grand;
And seem'd to my astonish'd view
      A well-known land.[1]

Here rivers in the sea were lost;
There mountains to the skies were tost:
Here tumbling billows mark'd the coast
      With surging foam;
There, distant shone Art's lofty boast,
      The lordly dome.

Here Doon pour'd down his far-fetch'd floods;
There well-fed Irvine stately thuds;
Auld hermit Ayr [a]staw thro' his woods,   [a]stole
      On to the shore;
And many a lesser torrent scuds,
      With seeming roar.

Low in a sandy valley spread,
An ancient borough rear'd her head;
Still, as in Scottish story read,
      She boasts a race,
To ev'ry nobler virtue bred,
      And polish'd grace.

By stately tower or palace fair,
Or ruins pendent in the air,
Bold stems of heroes, here and there,
      I could discern;
Some seem'd to muse, some seem'd to dare,
      With feature stern.

My heart did glowing transport feel,
To see a race[2] heroic wheel,
And brandish round, the deep-dyed steel
      In sturdy blows;
While back-recoiling seem'd to reel
      Their Suthron foes.

[1] Not Scotland, but Ayrshire, and especially the part called Kyle.
[2] The Wallaces.—R. B.

His COUNTRY'S SAVIOUR,[1] mark him well!
Bold Richardton's heroic swell;[2]
The Chief on Sark who glorious fell[3],
        In high command;
And he whom ruthless fates expel
        His native land.

There, where a sceptred Pictish shade[4]
Stalk'd round his ashes lowly laid,
I mark'd a martial race, pourtray'd
        In colours strong;
Bold, soldier-featur'd, undismay'd,
        They strode along. . . .

DUAN SECOND

With musing-deep astonish'd stare,
I view'd the heavenly-seeming Fair;
A whisp'ring throb did witness bear
        Of kindred sweet,
When with an elder Sister's air
        She did me greet.

'All hail! my own inspirèd bard!
In me thy native Muse regard!
Nor longer mourn thy fate is hard,
        Thus poorly low;
I come to give thee such reward
        As we bestow.

'Know the great Genius of this land
Has many a light aerial band,
Who, all beneath his high command,
        Harmoniously,
As arts or arms they understand,
        Their labours ply.

[1] William Wallace.—R. B.
[2] Adam Wallace, of Richardton, cousin to the immortal preserver of Scottish independence.—R. B.
[3] Wallace, Laird of Craigie. . . .—R. B.
[4] Coilus, King of the Picts, from whom the district of Kyle is said to take its name. . . .—R. B.

'They Scotia's race among them share:
Some fire the soldier on to dare;
Some rouse the patriot up to bare
                    Corruption's heart:
Some teach the bard, a darling care,
                    The tuneful art. . . .

'And when the bard, or hoary sage,
Charm or instruct the future age,
They bind the wild poetic rage
                    In energy,
Or point the inconclusive page
                    Full on the eye. . . .

'To lower orders[1] are assign'd
The humbler ranks of human-kind,
The rustic bard, the lab'ring hind,
                    The artisan;
All choose, as various they're inclin'd,
                    The various man.

'When yellow waves the heavy grain,
The threat'ning storm some strongly rein;
Some teach to meliorate the plain
                    With tillage-skill;
And some instruct the shepherd-train,
                    Blythe o'er the hill.

'Some hint the lover's harmless wile;
Some grace the maiden's artless smile;
Some soothe the lab'rer's weary toil
                    For humble gains,
And make his cottage-scenes beguile
                    His cares and pains.

'Some, bounded to a district-space,
Explore at large man's infant race,
To mark the embryotic trace
                    Of rustic bard;
And careful note each op'ning grace,
                    A guide and guard.

[1] Than soldiers, politicians, bards, or sages.—Ed.

'Of these am I—COILA my name;
And this district[1] as mine I claim,
Where once the Campbells,[2] chiefs of fame,
    Held ruling pow'r:
I mark'd thy embryo-tuneful flame,
    Thy natal hour.

'With future hope I oft would gaze,
Fond, on thy little early ways,
Thy rudely-caroll'd, chiming phrase,
    In uncouth rhymes,—
Fired at the simple artless lays
    Of other times.

'I saw thee seek the sounding shore,
Delighted with the dashing roar;
Or when the North his fleecy store
    Drove thro' the sky,
I saw grim Nature's visage hoar
    Struck thy young eye.

'Or when the deep green-mantled Earth
Warm-cherish'd ev'ry flow'ret's birth,
And joy and music pouring forth
    In ev'ry grove,
I saw thee eye the gen'ral mirth
    With boundless love.

'When ripen'd fields and azure skies
Call'd forth the reapers' rustling noise,
I saw thee leave their ev'ning joys,
    And lonely stalk,
To vent thy bosom's swelling rise
    In pensive walk.

'When youthful love, warm-blushing strong,
Keen-shivering shot thy nerves along,
Those accents, grateful to thy tongue,
    Th' adorèd Name,
I taught thee how to pour in song,
    To soothe thy flame.

[1] Kyle.   [2] Of Loudon.

'I saw thy pulse's maddening play
Wild send thee pleasure's devious way,
Misled by fancy's meteor ray,
    By passion driven;
But yet the light that led astray
    Was light from Heaven.

'I taught thy manners-painting strains,
The loves, the ways of simple swains,
Till now, o'er all my wide domains
    Thy fame extends;
And some, the pride of COILA's plains,
    Become thy friends.

'Thou canst not learn, nor can I show,
To paint with Thomson's landscape-glow;
Or wake the bosom-melting throe
    With Shenstone's art;
Or pour with Gray the moving flow
    Warm on the heart.

'Yet all beneath th' unrivall'd rose
The lowly daisy sweetly blows;
Tho' large the forest's monarch throws
    His army shade,
Yet green the juicy hawthorn grows
    Adown the glade.

'Then never murmur nor repine;
Strive in thy humble sphere to shine;
And trust me, not Potosi's mine,
    Nor king's regard,
Can give a bliss o'ermatching thine,
    A rustic Bard.

'To give my counsels all in one,
Thy tuneful flame still careful fan;
Preserve the dignity of Man,
    With soul erect;
And trust the Universal Plan
    Will all protect.

'And wear thou this': She solemn said,
And bound the holly round my head:
The polish'd leaves and berries red
              Did rustling play;
And, like a passing thought, she fled
              In light away.

II. THE SELKIRK GRACE[1]

I was impelled to include this over-famous Grace before meat by the following incident. A Scottish friend and colleague of mine recently found himself host at a business dinner party in London. He thought it would be a good thing to give his guests the benefit of a Grace, but, as the company was heterogeneous, he was in some difficulty as to the form of Grace. Not the usual gabble of pre- and post-Reformation Latin customary in the halls of Oxford and Cambridge colleges, not the solemn, heartfelt piety of Presbyterian thankfulness, and most certainly not the traditional Catholic form would suit this voracious, impatient gathering composed of two Scots, one Anglo-Irish of the one-time Protestant ascendancy, one learned Jewish friend of Scotland educated in Edinburgh and one successful English novelist. The Selkirk Grace supplied the answer. What an example of the wisdom of the Scots that Robert Burns was able to foresee the occasion and provide for it!

The Grace

Some hae meat and canna eat
And some wad eat that want it.
But we hae meat, and we can eat;
And sae the Lord be thankit.

---

[1] *Burns' Poetical Works*, Oxford, p. 297.

Sir Walter Scott

This, the largest of our literary figures, has all but defeated us. How would the compiler of an anthology on the wisdom of the English deal with Shakespeare? Difficult though his task would be we think it likely to be easier than ours when faced with the enormous bulk of Scott's work in poetry and prose, his letters and his journals, his recorded sayings, actions and behaviour, his life, his greatest creation—himself.

Shakespeare's divine gift of combining beauty and wisdom or truth in an imperishable line illuminates in flash after flash nearly all his plays and most of his verse. The only real difficulty in quoting Shakespeare is to know when to stop, what to leave out—a question that in the compiling of this anthology has given no bother, and only occasional distress.

Something more than the problem of what to leave out does arise with Scott, and that is the sheer question of space; indeed, it arises so largely as to be incapable of solution. You can, without doing damage to your subject or your conscience, chip bits off Shakespeare for the reason that he himself has already half-chipped them off for you. That huge bulk of genius which was Walter Scott, that mass of inspired writing and bad writing, of endless curiosity and vitality expended sometimes on high matters, sometimes on trivial, of deep feeling, of Scottish patriotism (ever so slightly clouded by the necessity forced upon him by his time of being a North Briton as well as a Scot), of an all but unclouded generosity, of a near all-time world record in sheer goodness (goodness, not sanctity), of . . . well, of so many other things, is unchippable. He is a lump of marble the size of Ben Nevis with some of the faults of that mountain in him and considerably more beauty. The only way in this book to cope with the Walter Scott space-problem would be to discover all of him; and that no one has even done.

This is not chauvinism. In saying that the only proper way to discover the wisdom of Scott is to discover all of him, the writer does not, of course, maintain that he was a greater author, a greater genius, a greater man, a greater anything else you can think of than Shakespeare, Cervantes, Beethoven, Homer or (the nearest analogy to him) Goethe or any nonsense of that sort. It is only that the wisdom of Scott the Scotsman as well as the wisdom of Scott the human being so much and so widely, perhaps even diffusely, pervades nearly everything he wrote, said and did that it is a hopeless task to anthologise his wise and inspired sense.

Take but one example. As much pernicious rot on both sides has been written about the time of the Covenanting wars in the seventeenth century as about any period in Scottish history. In one work of imaginative art, *Old Mortality*, Scott has really 'said it,' said once and for all nearly all that we need to know about what really animated our country at that time. The historian here and there may be able to pick him up on inaccuracies of fact, even of injustices to the individuals who made history, but in this great novel the soul of Scotland at that time lives again. It is the wisdom, the wise genius of Scott who could see and feel what it was like to be on both sides of that now dusty but still blood-stained conflict which has evoked this soul. How Scottish! The pun is deliberate. We cannot think of any other great writer of another nation who displays so remarkably the width of vision which Scott did in *Old Mortality*. Yet what is one to do with the book? Its effect is *en masse*; to quote from it is futile. Willingly we would have reprinted the whole of *Old Mortality* here, but even this is impossible.

Not recklessly then, but deliberately and thoughtfully, at random we have selected a few extracts out of Scott's writings. We have chosen them not to display carefully varied facets of his wisdom but merely gleams of it, gleams from that glancing sunlit river as it flows upon its tumultuous mountain course towards the sea. With regret we have chosen nothing, save a few aphorisms, from the novels. There were indeed great scenes clamant to be used. But they were too well known, and, torn from their context, what wisdom have they? We have chosen only a few lines of verse, one celebrated piece of polemics, one great but not well-known story and some fragments. For references from the novels we have given only the chapters. Other sources are more exactly noted.

THE PASSIONATE ANTITHESIS

The dichotomy in the Scottish soul, that dichotomy that separates caution, restraint and a reluctance to give oneself away from the equally Scottish love of abandonment, has seldom been more happily, never more melodiously expressed than in the two fragments of verse printed below. 'Lucy Ashton's Song' comes from the third chapter of *The Bride of the Lammermoors*. This whole novel, by the way, was dictated by Scott when he was almost unconscious with the pain of a protracted but temporary illness. When he came to correct the proofs he could recall nothing of the story. The novel and these lines of verse sprang from his sub-consciousness.

The four well-known lines hereunder called 'Answer' have an odd history. They head Chapter XXXIV of *Old Mortality* where Scott merely describes them as 'anonymous.' There was a good deal of speculation as to where they came from which, at the end of last century, resolved itself into the belief that Scott was himself the author. Recently, however, it was discovered that the lines had appeared in an ephemeral publication called *The Edinburgh Bee* in 1791, the author being one of whom little is known.

In 1791 Scott was twenty. It is now certain that Scott's extraordinarily retentive memory had enabled him to hold the lines in his head until 1815, the year of *Old Mortality*'s publication, but that at that time he could not remember their source and did his best with 'Anonymous.' He certainly did not wish to imply they were his own.

It doesn't really matter. 'Sound, sound the clarion' represents one side of Scott's attitude to life. He used it prominently in one of his greatest novels, and if it hadn't been for him we should never have heard of it. These two fragments represent in any event a characteristic Scottish antithesis.

Scottish or not, they were first coupled under the headings we have given them in *The Oxford Book of English Verse* (Nos. 544 and 545). Credit where credit is due. It was Sir Arthur Quiller Couch who publicly noted this antithesis. We therefore give, as immediate references for these lines, those from his celebrated 'English' anthology while referring above to their first sources.

Lucy Ashton's Song

Look not thou on beauty's charming;
Sit thou still when kings are arming;
Taste not when the wine-cup glistens;
Speak not when the people listens;
Stop thine ear against the singer;
From the red gold keep thy finger;
Vacant heart and hand and eye,
Easy live and quiet die.

Answer

Sound, sound the clarion, fill the fife!
To all the sensual world proclaim,
One crowded hour of glorious life
Is worth an age without a name.

MALACHI MALAGROWTHER

Like most great men Scott is often enlisted in any cause which the writer or speaker happens to believe in. In Scotland Burns is perhaps the outstanding conscript of this kind. He has been put forward as a Jacobite and a Jacobin, a revolutionary and a couthy supporter of the established order as praised on Conservative platforms. His Bacchic songs have been piously sung by earnest Scottish topers in public toping places, while, incredible though it may seem, his admission of a weak stomach for liquor has enabled teetotallers to enrol him under their banner. It is quite possible that someone somewhere has held him up as a model of chastity or that someone else has claimed him as an eighteenth-century forerunner of the Empire League of Loyalists or the British Fascists.

Scott's large, many-sided genius and nature makes him highly susceptible to this treatment. He is, of course, recognised as a Scottish patriot, but there are plenty of people ready to point out the undoubted fact that he was also, at times, something of a North Briton. In his circumstances and his time this was unavoidable, but his deeper and more truly national side was always breaking through, and not only in the speech of the creatures of his imagination. Sometimes contemporary events would stir his indignation for Scotland's declining state.

We ask our southern readers to accept not as an 'Aberdeen joke' but as a fact that the proposal of the London government in 1826 to abolish the Scottish banknote would have inflicted hardships on Scotland and have hurt Scottish pride. This is the kind of proposal that could pass through Westminster today with no more than a timid and unnoticed cheep from some Scottish back-bencher. In Scott's day his powerful pen was more potent. As a result of his 'Malachi Malagrowther' letters to the *Edinburgh Weekly Journal*[1] this measure was defeated and today we still have our Scottish banknotes.

In these 'Malachi Malagrowther' letters Scott touched upon the general subject of the treatment of Scottish matters in London. This provoked from the egregious John Wilson Croker some priggish comments. Scott replied in a letter containing the well-known sentence: 'But if you unScotch us you will find us damned mischievous Englishmen.' Here is an extract from Malachi Malagrowther—Scott's pseudonym for the first appearance of these letters.

Malachi Malagrowther Speaks

But though this amicable footing exists between the public of each nation, and such individuals of the other as may come into communication with them, and may God long continue it—yet, I must own, the conduct of England towards Scotland as a kingdom, whose crown was first united to theirs by our giving *them* a King, and whose dearest national rights were surrendered to them by an incorporating Union, has not been of late such as we were entitled to expect.

There has arisen gradually, on the part of England, a desire of engrossing the exclusive management of Scottish affairs, evinced by a number of circumstances, trifling in themselves, but forming a curious chain of proof when assembled together; many of which intimate a purpose to abate us, like old Lear, of our train, and to accustom us to submit to petty slights and mortifications, too petty perhaps individually to afford subject of serious complaint, but which, while they tend to lower us in our own eyes, seem to lay the foundation for fresh usurpations, of which this mediated measure may be an example.

This difference of treatment, and of estimation, exhibited towards *individuals* of the Scottish nation, and to the *nation itself* as an aggregate, seems at first sight an inconsistency. Does a Scotchman approach

[1] *Miscellaneous Prose Works of Walter Scott*, A. & C. Black, pp. 725–55.

London with some pretension to character as a Preacher, a Philosopher, a Poet, an Economist, or an Orator, he finds a welcome and all-hail, which sometimes surprises those he has left on the northern side of the Tweed, little aware, perhaps, of the paragon who had emigrated, till they heard the acclamations attending his reception—Does a gentleman of private fortune take the same route, he finds a ready and voluntary admission into the class of society for which he is fitted by rank and condition—Is the visitor one of the numerous class who wander for the chance of improving his fortunes, his national character as a Scotsman is supposed to imply the desirable qualities of information, prudence, steadiness, moral and religious feeling, and he obtains even a preference among the Southern employers, who want confidential clerks, land-stewards, head-gardeners, or fit persons to occupy any similar situation, in which the quality of trustworthiness is demanded.

But, on the other hand, if the English statesman has a point of great or lesser consequence to settle with Scotland *as a country*, we find him and his friends at once seized with a jealous, tenacious, wrangling, overbearing humour, and that they not only insist upon conducting the whole matter according to their own will, but are by no means so accessible to the pleas of reason, justice, and humanity, as might be expected from persons in other cases so wise and liberal. We cease at once to be the Northern Athenians, according to the slang of the day— the moral and virtuous people, who are practically and individually esteemed worthy of especial confidence. We have become the caterpillars of the island, instead of its pillars. We seem to be, in their opinion, once more transmuted into the Scots described by Churchill— a sharp sharking race, whose wisdom is cunning, and whose public spirit consists only in an illiberal nationality, inclining us, by every possible exertion of craft, to obtain advantage at the expense of England.

CANOBIE DICK

Scott delighted in the collection not only of old ballads but of traditional Scottish stories which he would re-tell in his own unmistakable manner. In many of these there is a moral or a warning or a piece of wisdom which comes to the reader (or in older times the listener) all the more forcefully for appearing at the end of a gripping and sometimes supernatural tale.

The story of Canobie Dick is one of Scott's finest achievements in this kind.[1] He tells it splendidly and reserves a dry exposition of the

[1] Appendix to the General Preface of *The Waverley Novels*, Border Edition, pp. 43, 44.

S

moral—a true piece of Scottish wisdom—until the last sentence of comment.

Now, it chanced many years since, that there lived on the Borders a jolly, rattling horse-cowper, who was remarkable for a reckless and fearless temper, which made him much admired, and a little dreaded, amongst his neighbours. One moonlight night, as he rode over Bowden Moor, on the west side of the Eildon Hills, the scene of Thomas the Rhymer's prophecies, and often mentioned in his story, having a brace of horses along with him which he had not been able to dispose of, he met a man of venerable appearance and singularly-antique dress, who, to his great surprise, asked the price of his horses, and began to chaffer with him on the subject. To Canobie Dick, for so shall we call our Border dealer, a chap was a chap, and he would have sold a horse to the devil himself, without minding his cloven hoof, and would have probably cheated Old Nick into the bargain. The stranger paid the price they agreed on, and all that puzzled Dick in the transaction was, that the gold which he received was in unicorns, bonnet-pieces, and other ancient coins, which would have been invaluable to collectors, but were rather troublesome in modern currency. It was gold, however, and therefore Dick contrived to get better value for the coin than he perhaps gave to his customer. By the command of so good a merchant, he brought horses to the same spot more than once; the purchaser only stipulating that he should always come by night, and alone. I do not know whether it was from mere curiosity, or whether some hope of gain mixed with it; but after Dick had sold several horses in this way, he began to complain that dry bargains were unlucky, and to hint, that since his chap must live in the neighbourhood, he ought, in the courtesy of dealing, to treat him to half a mutchkin.

'You may see my dwelling if you will,' said the stranger; 'but if you lose courage at what you see there, you will rue it all your life.'

'Dick, however, laughed the warning to scorn; and having alighted to secure his horse, he followed the stranger up a narrow footpath, which led them up the hills to the singular eminence stuck betwixt the most southern and the centre peaks, and called, from its resemblance to such an animal in its form, the Lucken Hare. At the foot of this eminence, which is almost as famous for witch-meetings as the neighbouring windmill of Kippilaw, Dick was somewhat startled to observe that his conductor entered the hillside by a passage or cavern, of which he himself, though well acquainted with the spot, had never seen or heard.

'You may still return,' said his guide, looking ominously back upon him; but Dick scorned to show the white feather, and on they went. They entered a very long range of stables; in every stall stood a coal-black horse; by every horse lay a knight in coal-black armour, with a drawn sword in his hand; but all were as silent, hoof and limb, as if they had been cut out of marble. A great number of torches lent a gloomy lustre to the hall, which, like those of the Caliph Vathek, was of large dimensions. At the upper end, however, they at length arrived, where a sword and horn lay on an antique table.

'He that shall sound that horn and draw that sword,' said the stranger, who now intimated that he was the famous Thomas of Ercildoun, 'shall, if his heart fail him not, be king over all broad Britain. So speaks the tongue that cannot lie. But all depends on courage, and much on your taking the sword or the horn first.'

'Dick was much disposed to take the sword, but his bold spirit was quailed by the supernatural terrors of the hall, and he thought to unsheath the sword first might be construed into defiance, and give offence to the powers of the mountain. He took the bugle with a trembling hand, and blew a feeble note, but loud enough to produce a terrible answer. Thunder rolled in stunning peals through the immense hall; horses and men started to life; the steeds snorted, stamped, grinded their bits, and tossed on high their heads; the warriors sprung to their feet, clashed their armour, and brandished their swords. Dick's terror was extreme at seeing the whole army, which had been so lately silent as the grave, in uproar, and about to rush on him. He dropped the horn, and made a feeble attempt to seize the enchanted sword; but at the same moment a voice pronounced aloud the mysterious words—

'Wo to the coward, that ever he was born,
Who did not draw the sword before he blew the horn!'

At the same time a whirlwind of irresistible fury howled through the long hall, bore the unfortunate horse-jockey clear out of the mouth of the cavern, and precipitated him over a steep bank of loose stones, where the shepherds found him the next morning, with just breath sufficient to tell his fearful tale, after concluding which, he expired.

... It would be in vain to ask what was the original of the tradition. The choice between the horn and sword may, perhaps, include as a moral, that it is foolhardy to awaken danger before we have arms in our hands to resist it.

MISCELLANEOUS

Scott was always throwing off memorable or worth-while or wise remarks either through the mouths of his characters or in the introductions to his novels. They are so profuse that even our hardihood does not allow us to put forward a representative collection. Here, however, are a few, very few classic sayings or views of Scott's appearing in his fiction or in his notes upon his fiction.

They come from the subjects of the law, the Scottish character and literature. I make no comment save to draw the reader's attention to the last quotation of all, the one from the introduction to the *Fair Maid of Perth* on 'Vulgar incredulity.'

The Law

'A lawyer without history or literature is a mechanic, a mere working mason; if he possesses some knowledge of these, he may venture to call himself an architect.'[1]

'I have now satisfied myself, that if our profession sees more of human folly and human roguery than others, it is because we witness them acting in that channel in which they can most freely vent themselves. In civilised society, law is the chimney through which all that smoke discharges itself that used to circulate through the whole house, and put every one's eyes out—no wonder, therefore, that the vent itself should sometimes get a little sooty.'[2]

'I have kend the Law this mony a year, and mony a thrawart job I hae had wi' her first and last; but the auld jaud is no sae ill as that comes to—I aye fand her bark waur than her bite.'[3]

'Hout, there's nae great skill needed; just put a lighted peat on the end of a spear, or hayfork, or siclike, and blaw a horn, and cry the gathering-word, and then it's lawful to follow gear into England, and recover it by the strong hand, or to take gear frae some other Englishman, providing ye lift nae mair than's been lifted frae you. That's the auld Border law, made at Dundrennan, in the days of the Black Douglas. Deil ane need doubt it. It's as clear as the sun.'[4]

'I don't see, after all, why you should not have your lawsuits too, and your feuds in the Court of Session, as well as your forefathers had their manslaughters and fire-raisings.'

'Very natural, to be sure, sir. We wad just take the auld gate as readily, if it werena for the law. And as the law binds us, the law

---

[1] *Guy Mannering*, Chapter 37.   [2] *Ibid.*, Chapter 39.
[3] *Heart of Midlothian*, Chapter 13.   [4] *The Black Dwarf*, Chapter 7.

should loose us. Besides, a man's aye the better thought o' in our country for having been afore the feifteen.'[1]

The Scottish Character

'But fare ye weel—fare ye weel, for ever and a day; and, if you quarrel wi' a Scot again, man, say as mickle ill o' himsell as ye like, but say nane of his patron or of his countrymen, or it will scarce be your flat cap that will keep your lang lugs from the sharp abridgement of a Highland whinger, man.'[2]

Perhaps one ought to be actually a Scotchman to conceive how ardently, under all distinctions of rank and situation, they feel their mutual connexion with each other as natives of the same country. There are, I believe, more associations common to the inhabitants of a rude and wild, than of a well-cultivated and fertile country; their ancestors have more seldom changed their place of residence; their mutual recollection of remarkable objects is more accurate; the high and the low are more interested in each other's welfare; the feelings of kindred and relationship are more widely extended, and, in a word, the bonds of patriotic affection, always honourable even when a little too exclusively strained, have more influence on men's feelings and actions.[3]

The Scots and the English

He had to walk about two miles, a labour he undertook with the greatest pleasure, in order to secure to his kinsman the sale of some articles of his trade, though it is probable he would not have given him sixpence to treat him to a quart of ale. The good-will of an Englishman would have displayed itself in a manner exactly the reverse.[4]

Literature

No man of sense in any rank of life, is, or ought to be, above accepting a just recompense for his time, and a reasonable share of the capital which owes its very existence to his exertions. When Czar Peter wrought in the trenches, he took the pay of a common soldier; and nobles, statesmen, and divines, the most distinguished of their time, have not scorned to square accounts with their bookseller. But no man of honour, genius, or spirit, would make the mere love of gain the chief, far less the only, purpose of his labours. For myself, I am

[1] *Guy Mannering*, Chapter 38.
[2] *Fortunes of Nigel*, Chapter 9.
[3] *Heart of Midlothian*, Chapter 36.
[4] *Rob Roy*, Chapter 14.

not displeased to find the game a winning one; yet, while I pleased the public, I should probably continue it merely for the pleasure of playing; for I have felt as strongly as most folks that love of composition, which is perhaps the strongest of all instincts, driving the author to the pen, the painter to the pallet, often without either the chance of fame or the prospect of reward. Perhaps I have said too much of this.

'I have but one thing more to hint—the world say you will run yourself out.'

'The world say true; and what then? When they dance no longer, I will no longer pipe! and I shall not want flappers enough to remind me of the apoplexy.'[1]

Cant again, my dear son—there is lime in this sack too—nothing but sophistication in this world! I do say it, in spite of Adam Smith and his followers, that a successful author is a productive labourer, and that his works constitute as effectual a part of the public wealth as that which is created by any other manufacture. If a new commodity, having an actually intrinsic and commercial value, be the result of the operation, why are the author's bales of books to be esteemed a less profitable part of the public stock than the goods of any other manufacturer? I speak with reference to the diffusion of the wealth arising to the public, and the degree of industry which even such a trifling work as the present must stimulate and reward before the volumes leave the publisher's shop. Without me it could not exist, and to this extent I am a benefactor to the country. As for my own emolument, it is won by my toil, and I account myself answerable to Heaven only for the mode in which I expend it. The candid may hope it is not all dedicated to selfish purposes; and without much pretensions to merit in him who disburses it, a part may 'wander, Heaven-directed, to the poor.'[2]

To confess to you the truth, the works and passages in which I have succeeded have uniformly been written with the greatest rapidity; and when I have seen some of these placed in opposition with others, and commended as more highly finished, I could appeal to pen and standish, that the parts in which I have come feebly off were by much the more laboured. Besides, I doubt the beneficial effect of too much delay, both on account of the author and the public. A man should strike while the iron is hot, and hoist sail while the wind is fair. If a successful author keep not the stage, another instantly takes his ground. If a writer lie by for ten years ere he produces a second work, he is

[1] *Fortunes of Nigel,* Introductory Epistle.   [2] *Ibid.*

superseded by others; or if the age is so poor of genius that this does not happen, his own reputation becomes his greatest obstacle. The public will expect the new work to be ten times better than its predecessor; the author will expect it should be ten times more popular, and 'tis a hundred to ten that both are disappointed.[1]

Vulgar Incredulity

We talk of a credulous vulgarity without recollecting that there is a vulgar incredulity which, in historical matters, as well as in those of religion, finds it easier to doubt than to examine, and endeavours to assume the credit of an *esprit de corps* by denying whatever happens to be beyond the very limited comprehension of the sceptic.[2]

[1] *Fortunes of Nigel*, Introductory Epistle.
[2] *The Fair Maid of Perth*, Introduction.

Thomas Carlyle

The trouble with Carlyle is that some of what men looked upon as his greatest wisdom in his time, and even later, is now out of fashion or downright disliked.

Nevertheless Carlyle's influence, the memory of him, is still most potent. The reason for this lies in his character, his genius for historical perception and evocation, and in his extraordinary and individual style which, except when he is parodying himself, is irresistible—whether you like that style or don't. But, in the main, it is the character of the man that so strongly survives. He looked like a 'character,' spoke like a 'character,' wrote and thought like a 'character,' yet it is doubtful if there was any affectation in him. He was therefore much more than a 'character.'

It is probably his strong character, allied, of course, to his genius, that makes the English still so highly conscious of him. There was a time when Carlyle was the idol of the more serious-minded Lowland Scot who, as the nineteenth century darkened over Scottish independence, saw him as the rugged representative of the indestructible Scottish genius. Today Carlyle is not so highly regarded in his native country as he was. The younger and more ardent Scots are questing after newer gods.

In England, however, if the literary journals are any guide, Carlyle remains more constantly in men's minds. People are always writing new lives or appreciations of him and paying tribute to his influence. He has been subjected to literary psycho-analysis and even to a posthumous diagnosis by a physician. The English can't get him out of their heads. They pay more attention to him than to Scott, Burns and Hume put together (Boswell, and for different reasons, is another matter). Carlyle, South of the Border, is *the* writing Scot.

Let us not be ungenerous about this. The man's genius has much to do with it, so has his genuine character; but the fact that he was, be it repeated, without conscious affectation a 'character' leaves its influence. The phrase 'the Sage of Chelsea' was not invented, nor does it still live for nothing. The bearded, cloaked figure musing silently, yet (to the inner ear), audibly in a 'Scotch accent' still wanders through the Whistlerian fogs that come up from the river to steal along Cheyne Row. He belongs to what remains of Chelsea, as does Harry Lauder to what remains of the music halls of London.

Carlyle was very much a Scotsman with some of our faults, and with many of our virtues which he discovered in an excellent degree. He did not (and who is to blame him considering the century in which he lived) make the mistake of Scott, Burns and Hume of living in Scotland. Though indeed he tried to stay there, he eventually had to come south to London; and that large-hearted Imperial city, as she then was, took him to herself and made him her own as she has made so many other foreigners. London, vast though she may be, does not forget her more distinguished characteristic children, especially if they are not Londoners.

It seemed better to choose here from Carlyle's enormous output two large extracts rather than a number of shorter ones. It seemed a pity to cut more than was essential these long and sustained passages. If, then, the amount quoted from him below appears unusually large this is not because he is essentially more important than certain other Scottish writers who have received briefer treatment here. We begin with the longest extract, his fine and moving tribute to his father. It illustrates a point we would wish to make in the wisdom of the Scots.

MY FATHER

The mother, the female image, has, as has appeared, been a familiar and recurring theme in the Scottish mind. No less important is the paternal theme. It was implicit in Barbour's *Bruce* and in other extracts but never explicit. Here, in his tribute to his own father, Carlyle is speaking for more than himself and speaking openly as well as finely. It will be observed how, in this deeply-felt passage, Carlyle sheds his extravagances of style. Incidentally this verbal portrait of his presents a fine picture of a wise old Scot which should, irrespective of its author, have a place in any anthology on the wisdom of the Scots.[1] We give it plenty of space.

On Tuesday, Jan 26 1832 I received tidings that my dear and worthy father had departed out of this world. He was called away by a death apparently of the mildest on Sunday morning about six. . . .

In several respects, I consider my Father as one of the most interesting men I have known. He was a man of perhaps *the* very largest natural endowment of any it has been my lot to converse with: none of us will ever forget that bold glowing style of his, flowing free from the untutored Soul; full of metaphors (though he knew not what a metaphor was), with all manner of potent words (which he appropriated and applied with a *surprising* accuracy, you often could not guess whence); brief, energetic; and which I should say conveyed the most perfect picture, definite, clear not in ambitious *colours* but in full *white* sunlight, of all the dialects I have ever listened to. Nothing did I ever hear him undertake to render visible, which did not become almost ocularly so. Never shall we again hear such speech as that was: the whole district knew of it; and laughed joyfully over it, not knowing how otherwise to express the feeling it gave them. Emphatic I have

[1] Thomas Carlyle, *Reminiscences*, ed. J. A. Froude, Longmans, Green, Vol. I, pp. 7–66.

heard him beyond all men. In anger he had no need of oaths; his words were like sharp arrows that smote into the very heart. The fault was that he exaggerated (which tendency I also inherit); yet only in description and for the sake chiefly of *humorous* effect: he was a man of rigid, even scrupulous veracity; I have often heard him turn back, when he thought his strong words were misleading, and correct them into mensurative accuracy. *Ach, und dies alles ist hin!*

I call him a natural man; singularly free from all manner of affectation: he was among the last of the true men, which Scotland (on the old system) produced, or can produce; a man healthy in body and in mind; fearing God, and diligently working in God's Earth with contentment, hope and unwearied resolution. *He* was never visited with Doubt; the old Theorem of the Universe was sufficient for him, and he worked well in it, and in all senses *successfully* and wisely as few now can do; so quick is the motion of Transition becoming: the new generation almost to a man must make 'their Belly their God,' and alas even find *that* an empty one. Thus curiously enough, and blessedly, *he* stood a true man on the verge of the Old; while his son stands here lovingly surveying him on the verge of the New, and sees the possibility of also being true there. God make the possibility, blessed possibility, into a reality!

A virtue he had which I should learn to imitate. *He never spoke of what was disagreeable and past.* I have often wondered and admired at this. The thing that he had nothing to *do* with, he did nothing with. This was a *healthy* mind. In like manner, I have seen him always when we young ones (half roguishly, and provokingly without doubt) were perhaps repeating sayings of his, sit as if he did not hear us at all: never once did I know him utter a word (only once that I remember of give a look) in such a case.

Another virtue, the example of which has passed strongly into me, was his settled placid indifference to the clamours or the murmurs of Public Opinion. For the judgment of those that had no right or power to judge him, he seemed simply to care nothing at all. He very rarely *spoke* of despising such things, he contented himself with altogether disregarding them. Hollow babble it was; for him a thing as Fichte said 'that did not exist,' *das gar nicht existirte*. There was something truly great in this; the very perfection of it hid from you the extent of the attainment.

Or rather let me call it a new phasis of the *health* which in mind as in body was conspicuous in him. Like a healthy man, he wanted *only* to get along with his Task; whatsoever could not forward him in this (and how could Public Opinion and much else of the like sort do it?) was of no moment to him, was not there for him.

This great maxim of Philosophy he had gathered by the teaching of nature alone: That man was created to work, not to speculate, or feel, or dream. Accordingly he set his whole heart thitherwards: he did work wisely and unweariedly (*ohne Hast aber ohne Rast*), and perhaps *performed* more (with the tools he had) than any man I now know. It should have made me sadder than it did to hear the young ones sometimes complaining of his slow punctuality and thoroughness: he would leave nothing till it was *done*. Alas! the age of Substance and Solidity is gone (for the time); that of Show and hollow Superficiality (in all senses) is in full course——

And yet he was a man of open sense; wonderfully so. I could have entertained him for days talking of *any* matter interesting to man. He delighted to hear of *all* things that were worth talking of; the mode of living men had, the mode of working, their opinions, virtues, whole spiritual and temporal environment. It is some two years ago (in summer) since I entertained him highly (he was hoeing turnips and perhaps I helped him) with an account of the character and manner of existence of Francis Jeffrey. Another evening he enjoyed (probably it was on that very visit) with the heartiest relish my description of the people (I think) of Turkey. The Chinese had astonished him much: in some Magazine (from Little's of Cressfield) he had got a sketch of *Macartney's Embassy*, the memory of which never left him. Adam Smith's *Wealth of Nations*, greatly as it lay out of his course, he had also fallen in with; and admired, and understood and remembered,— so far as he had any business with it.—I once wrote him about my being in Smithfield Market (seven years ago); of my seeing St. Paul's; both things interested him heartily, and dwelt with him. I had hoped to tell him much, much of what I saw in this second visit; and that many a long cheerful talk would have given us both some sunny hours: but *es konnte nimmer seyn!*—Patience! Hope!

At the same time he had the most entire and open contempt for all idle tattle, what he called 'clatter.' *Any* talk that had meaning in it he could listen to: what had *no* meaning in it, above all, what seemed false, he absolutely could and would not hear; but abruptly turned aside from it, or if that might not suit, with the besom of destruction swept it far away from him. Long may we remember his 'I don't believe thee'; his tongue-paralysing, cold, indifferent 'Hah!'—I should say of him, as I did of our Sister whom we lost, that he seldom or never spoke except actually to convey an idea. Measured by quantity

of words, he was a talker of fully average copiousness; by extent of
meaning communicated, he was the most copious I have listened to.
How, in few sentences, he would sketch you off an entire Biography,
an entire Object or Transaction: keen, clear, rugged, genuine, completely rounded in! His words came direct from the heart, by the
inspiration of the moment: 'It is no idle tale,' said he to some laughing
rustics, while stating in his strong way some complaint against them;
and their laughter died into silence. Dear good Father! there looked
honesty through those clear earnest eyes; a sincerity that compelled
belief and regard. 'Moffat!' said he one day to an incorrigible reaper,
'thou has every feature of a bad shearer: high, and rough, and little
on't. Thou maun *alter* thy figure or slant the bog'—pointing to the
man's road homewards.—

He was irascible, choleric, and we all dreaded his wrath. Yet passion
never mastered him, or maddened him; it rather inspired him with
new vehemence of insight, and more piercing emphasis of wisdom.
It must have been a bold man that did not quail before that face, when
glowing with indignation, grounded (for so it ever was) on the sense
of right, and in resistance of wrong. More than once has he lifted up
his strong voice in Tax Courts and the like before 'the Gentlemen'
(what he knew of Highest among men), and rending asunder official
sophistries, thundered even into their deaf ears the indignant sentence
of natural justice, to the conviction of all.—Oh why did we laugh at
these things while we loved them! There is a tragic greatness and
sacredness in them now.

I can call my Father a brave man (*ein Tapferer*). Man's face he did
not fear; God he always feared: his Reverence, I think, was considerably mixed with Fear. Yet not slavish Fear; rather Awe, as of
unutterable Depths of Silence, through which flickered a trembling
Hope. How he used to speak of Death (especially in late years) or
rather to be silent, and *look* of it! There was no feeling in him here
that he cared to hide: he trembled at the really terrible; the mock-
terrible he cared nought for.—That last act of his Life; when in the
last agony, with the thick ghastly vapours of Death rising round him
to choke him, he burst through and called with a man's voice on the
great God to have mercy on him: that was like the epitome and concluding summary of his whole Life. God gave him strength to wrestle
with the King of Terrors, and as it were even then to prevail. All his
strength came from God, and ever sought new nourishment there.
God be thanked for it.

Let me not mourn that my Father's Force is all spent, that his

Valour was no longer. Has it not gained the victory? Let me imitate him rather; let his courageous heart beat anew in me, that when oppression and opposition unjustly threaten, I too may rise with his spirit to front them and subdue them.

On the whole, ought I not to rejoice that God was pleased to give me such a Father; that from earliest years, I had the example of a real Man (of God's own making) continually before me? Let me learn of *him*; let me 'write my Books as he built his Houses, and walk as blamelessly through this shadow-world'—(if God so will), to rejoin him at last. Amen!—Alas! such is the *mis*-education of these days, it is only among what are called the *un*educated classes (those educated by experience) that you can look for *a man*. Even among these, such a sight is growing daily rarer. My Father, in several respects, has not, that I can think of, left his fellow. *Ultimus Romanorum!* Perhaps among Scottish Peasants what Samuel Johnson was among English Authors. I have a sacred pride in my Peasant Father, and would not exchange him even now for any King known to me. Gold, and the guinea-stamp; the Man, and the Clothes of the Man! Let me thank God for that greatest of blessings, and strive to live worthily of it. . . .

The more I reflect on it, the more must I admire how completely Nature had taught him; how completely he was devoted to his work, to the Task of his Life; and content to let *all* pass by unheeded that had not relation to this. It is a singular fact, for example, that though a man of such openness and clearness, he had never, I believe, read three pages of *Burns's Poems*. Not even when all about him became noisy and enthusiastic (I the loudest) on that matter did he feel it worth while to renew his investigation of it, or once turn his face towards it. The Poetry *he* liked (he did not call it Poetry) was Truth and the Wisdom of Reality. Burns indeed could have done nothing for him. As high a Greatness hung over his world, as over that of Burns (the ever-present greatness of the Infinite itself): neither was he like Burns called to rebel against the world, but to labour patiently at his Task there; 'uniting the Possible with the Necessary' to bring out the *Real* (wherein also lay an Ideal). Burns could not have in any way strengthened him in this course; and therefore was for him a pheno-menon merely. Nay Rumour had been so busy with Burns, and Destiny and his own Desert had in very deed so marred his name, that the good rather avoided him. Yet it was not with aversion that my Father regarded Burns; at worst with indifference and neglect. I have heard him speak of once seeing him: standing in 'Rob Scott's Smithy' (at Ecclefechan, no doubt superintending some work) he heard one say, 'There is the Poet Burns'; he went out to look, and saw a man with boots on, like a well-dressed farmer, walking down the village on the opposite side of the burn. This was all the relation these two men ever had: they were very nearly coevals.—I know Robert Burns, and I knew my Father; yet were you to ask me which had the greater natural faculty I might perhaps actually pause before replying! Burns had an infinitely wider Education; my Father a far wholesomer: besides the one was a man of Musical Utterance, the other wholly a man of Action, even with Speech subservient thereto. Never, of all the men I have seen, has one come personally in my way in whom the Endowment from Nature and the Arena from Fortune were so utterly out of all proportion. I have said this often; and partly *know* it. As a man of Speculation (had Culture ever unfolded him) he must have gone wild and desperate as Burns: but he was a man of Conduct, and Work keeps all right. What strange shapeable creatures we are. . . .

One Macleod, 'Sandy Macleod,' a wandering pensioner invalided out of some Highland Regiment (who had served in America,—I must think with General Wolfe) had strayed to Brownknowe with his old wife, and taken a Cottage of my Grandfather. He, with his wild foreign legends, and strange half-idiotic half-genial ways, was a great figure with the young ones; and I think acted not a little on their character, least of any, however, on my Father, whose early turn for the *practical* and real, made him more heedless of Macleod and his vagaries. The old Pensioner had quaint sayings, not without significance: of a lacrymose complaining man, for example, he said (or perhaps to him) 'He might be thankful he was not in Purgatory.' The quaint fashion of speaking, assumed for humour, and most noticeable in my uncle Frank, least or hardly at all in my Father,—was no doubt partly derived from this old wanderer, who was much about their house, working for his rent and so forth; and was partly laughed at partly wondered at by the young ones.—Tinkers also, nestling in out-houses, melting pot-metal, and with rude feuds and warfare, often came upon the scene. These with passing Highland Drovers were perhaps their only visitors. . . .

I can remember his carrying me across Mein Water, over a pool some few yards below where the present Meinfoot Bridge stands. Perhaps I was in my fifth year. He was going to Luce I think to ask after some Joiner. It was the loveliest summer evening I recollect. My memory dawns (or grows light) at the first aspect of the stream, of the pool spanned by a wooden bow, without railing, and a single plank broad. He lifted me against his thigh with his right hand, and walked careless along till we were over. My face was turned rather downwards, I looked into the deep clear water, and its reflected skies, with terror yet with confidence that he could save me. Directly after, I, light of heart, asked of him what these 'little black things' were that I seemed sometimes to *create* by rubbing the palms of my hands together, and can at this moment (the mind having been doubtless excited by the past peril) remember that I described them in these words: 'like penny-rows' (rolls) 'but far less.' He explained it wholly to me: 'my hands were not *clean*.' He was very kind, and I loved him. All around this is Dusk, or Night, before and after.—It is not my *earliest* recollection, not even of him. My earliest of all is a mad passion of rage at my elder Brother John (on a visit to us likely from his grandfather's); in which my Father too figures though dimly, as a kind of cheerful comforter and soother. I had broken my little brown stool, by madly throwing it at my brother; and felt for perhaps the first time, the united pangs of Loss and of Remorse. I was perhaps hardly more than two years old; but can get no one to fix the date for me, though all is still quite legible for myself, with many of its features. I remember the first 'new half-pence' (brought from Dumfries by my Father and Mother for Alick and me); and words that my Uncle John said about it: this seems later (in 1799 ?), and might be ascertained. Backwards beyond all, are dim *ruddy* images, of deeper and deeper brown shade into the dark beginnings of being.

I remember, perhaps in my fifth year, his teaching me Arithmetical things: especially how to *divide* (of my Letters taught me by my Mother, I have no recollection whatever; of reading scarcely any): he said, 'This is the *divider* (divisor), this' etc., and gave me a quite clear notion how to do. My Mother said I would forget it all; to which he answered: Not so much as they that have never learned it.—Five years or so after, he said to me once: 'Tom, I do not grudge thy schooling, now when thy Uncle Frank owns thee to be a better Arithmetician than himself.'—

He took me down to Annan Academy on the Whitsunday morning, 1806; I trotting at his side in the way alluded to in *Teufelsdrockh*. It was a bright morning, and to me full of moment; of fluttering boundless Hopes, saddened by parting with Mother, with Home; and which afterwards were cruelly disappointed. He called once or twice in the grand schoolroom, as he chanced to have business at Annan: once sat down by me (as the master was out), and asked whether I was all well. The boys did not laugh (as I feared), perhaps durst not.

He was *always* GENEROUS to me in my school expenses; never by grudging look or word did he give me any pain. With a noble faith he launched me forth into a world which himself had never been permitted to visit: let me study to act worthily of him there.

He wrote to me duly and affectionately while I was at College; nothing that was good for me did he fail with his best ability to provide: his simple true counsels and fatherly admonitions have now first attained their fit sacredness of meaning: pity for me if they be thrown away.—

His tolerance for me, his trust in me was great. When I declined going forward into the Church (though his heart was set upon it), he respected my scruples, my volition, and patiently let me have my way. In after years, when I had peremptorily ceased from being a School-master, though he inwardly disapproved of the step as imprudent; and saw me, in successive summers, lingering beside him in sickliness of body and mind, without outlook towards any good, he had the forbearance to say at worst nothing, never once to whisper discontent with me. If my dear Mother, with the trustfulness of a Mother's heart, ministered to all my woes, outward and inward, and ever against hope kept prophesying good,—he, with whom I communicated far less, who could not approve my schemes, did nothing that was not kind and fatherly: his roof was my shelter, which a word from him (in those sour days of wounded vanity) would have deprived me of; he patiently let me have my way; helping where he could, where he could not help never hindering.—When hope again dawned for me, how hearty was his joy, yet how silent! I have been a happy Son.—

On my first return from College (in the Spring 1810) I met him in the 'Langlands Road,' walking out to try whether he would not happen to see me coming. He had a red plaid about him; was recovering from a fit of sickness (his first severe one), and there welcomed me back. It was a bright April day: *where* is it *now*?—

The great world-revolutions send in their disturbing billows to the remotest creek; and the overthrow of thrones more slowly overturns also the households of the lowly. Nevertheless in all cases the wise man adjusts himself: even in these times, the hand of the diligent maketh rich. My Father had seen the American War, the French Revolution, the rise and fall of Napoleon. The last arrested him strongly: in the Russian Campaign we bought a London Newspaper, which I read aloud to a little circle thrice weekly. He was struck with Napoleon, and would say and look pregnant things about him: empires won, and empires lost (while *his* little household held together); and now it was all vanished like a tavern brawl!—For the rest, he never meddled with Politics: he was not there to govern, but to be governed; could still *live*, and therefore did not *revolt*. I have heard him say in late years, with an impressiveness which all his perceptions carried with them: 'that the lot of a poor man was growing worse and worse; that the world could not and would not last as it was; but mighty changes, of which none saw the end, were on the way.' To him, as one about to take his departure, the whole was but of secondary moment: he was looking towards 'a city that *had* foundations.'—

In the 'dear years' (1799 and 1800), when the oatmeal was as high as ten shillings a stone, he had noticed the labourers (I have heard him tell) retire each separately to a brook, and there *drink* instead of dining,—without complaint; anxious only to hide it.—

At Langholm he once saw a heap of smuggled Tobacco publicly burnt. Dragoons were ranged round it with drawn swords; some old women stretched through their old withered arms to snatch a little of it, and the dragoons did not hinder them.—A natural artist!

The largest sum he ever earned in one year, I think, was £100; by the building of Cressfield House.

He wisely quitted the Mason trade, at the time when the character of it had changed; when universal Poverty and Vanity made *show* and *cheapness* (here as everywhere) be preferred to Substance; when as he said emphatically honest trade 'was done.' He became Farmer (of a wet clayey spot called Mainhill) in 1815; that so 'he might keep all his family about him'; struggled with his old valour, and here too prevailed. Two ears of corn are now in many places growing where he found only one: unworthy or little worthy men for the time reap the benefit; but it was a benefit done to God's Earth, and God's Mankind will year after year get the good of it.

In his contention with an unjust or perhaps only a mistaken Landlord, he behaved with prudent resolution; not like a vain braggart but like a practically brave man. It was I that innocently (by my settlement at Hoddam Hill) had involved him in it. I must admire now his *silence*, while we were all so loud and vituperative: he spoke *nothing* on that matter, except only what had practical meaning in it, and in a practical tone. His answers to unjust proposals, meanwhile, were resolute and ever-memorable for their emphasis: 'I *will* not do it,' said he once; 'I will rather go to Jerusalem, seeking farms, and die without finding one.'—'We can live without Sharpe,' said he once in my hearing (such a thing only *once*) 'and the whole Sharpe creation.'—On getting to Scotsbrig, the rest of us all triumphed; not he: he let the matter

T

stand on its own feet; was *there* also, not to talk but to work. He even addressed a conciliatory letter to General Sharpe (which I saw right to *write* for him, since he judged prudence better than pride): but it produced no result,—except indeed the ascertainment that none could be produced; which itself was one.—

When he first entered our house at Craigenputtock he said in his slow emphatic way, with a certain rustic dignity to my wife (I had entered introducing him): 'I am grown an *old fellow*' (never can we forget the pathetic slow earnestness of these two words) 'I am grown an old fellow; and wished to see ye all once more while I yet have opportunity.' Jane was greatly struck with him; and still further opened my eyes to the treasure I possessed in a Father.—

The last thing I gave him was a cake of Cavendish Tobacco sent down by Alick about this time twelvemonth. Through life I had given him very little; having little to give: he needed little, and from me expected nothing. Thou who wouldst give, give quickly: in the grave thy loved one can receive no kindness.—I had once bought him a pair of silver spectacles; at receipt of which and the letter that accompanied them (John told me) he was very glad, and nigh weeping. 'What I gave I have.' He read with these spectacles till his last days; and no doubt sometimes thought of me in using them.—

The last time I saw him was about the first of August last, a few days before departing hither. He was very kind, seemed prouder of me than ever. What he had never done the like of before, he said, on hearing me express something which he admired: 'Man, it's surely a pity that thou should sit yonder, with nothing but the Eye of Omniscience to see thee; and thou with such a gift to speak.' His eyes were sparkling mildly, with a kind of deliberate joy.——Strangely too he offered me on one of those mornings (knowing that I was poor) 'two sovereigns' which he had of his own; and pressed them on my acceptance. They were lying in his Desk, none knew of them: he seemed really anxious and desirous that I should take them; should take his little hoard, his *all* that he had to give. I said jokingly afterwards that surely he was *fey*. So it has proved.

I shall now no more behold my dear Father with these bodily eyes. With him a whole three-score-and-ten years of the Past has doubly died for me; it is as if a new leaf in the great Book of Time were turned over. Strange Time! Endless Time, or of which I see neither end nor beginning! All rushes on; man follows man; his life is as a Tale that has been told. Yet under Time does there not lie Eternity? Perhaps my Father, all that essentially *was* my Father *is* even now near me, with

me. Both he and I are with God. Perhaps, if it so please God, we shall
in some higher state of being meet one another, recognise one another:
as it is written, 'we shall be for ever with God!' The possibility, nay
(in some way) the certainty of perennial existence daily grows plainer
to me. 'The essence of whatever was, is, or shall be, even now *is*.'
God is great; God is good: His will be done, for it will be right!—

As it is, I can think peaceably of the Departed Loved. All that was
earthly harsh sinful in our relation has fallen away; all that was holy
in it remains. I can see my dear Father's Life in some measure as the
sunk pillar on which mine was to rise and be built; the waters of Time
have now swelled up round his (as they will round mine); I can *see*
it (all transfigured) though I *touch* it no longer. I might almost say his
spirit seems to have entered into me (so clearly do I discern and love
him); I seem to myself only the continuation, and *second volume* of
my Father.—These days that I have spent thinking of him, and of
his end, are the peaceablest, the only Sabbath I have had in London.
One other of the universal destinies of man has overtaken me. Thank
Heaven, I know and have known what it is to be a *Son*; to *love* a Father,
as spirit can love spirit. God give me to live to my Father's honour,
and to His!—And now beloved Father farewell, for the last time in
this world of shadows! In the world of Realities may the great Father
again bring us together in perfect holiness, and perfect love! Amen!

GEORGE FOX'S LEATHER SUIT

In *Sartor Resartus* Carlyle made his reply to the philosophy of Dandyism
which in the earlier half of the nineteenth century seriously occupied
certain literary talents. There is something a little comical, but also
something far more remarkable in the idea of the impoverished and then
apparently unsuccessful peasant Scot in lonely Craigenputtock sitting
down to reply to the ideas generated by Brummell, Dorsay and Bulwer
in the fashionable circles of London. But, of course, *Sartor* is far more
than a mere riposte to Dandyism.

It is a profession of faith in 'believing Radicalism.' The operative
word is believing. In *Sartor* Carlyle spoke for more than himself, for
more than an inspired son of the Scottish peasantry protesting against
the fopperies of a southern metropolis still partly in the eighteenth
century and partly in the new age of the new wealth. He spoke for
more even than his native land of Scotland, he spoke for the creed of
radicalism which was to animate so many of the best minds of all Britain
when Britain was bulging with wealth and power. Do any young men
read *Sartor* today when Britain is no longer bulging? They ought to.
For whether Britain bulges again or is merely content to accept the

opiate of never having 'had it so good,' young people might learn with
interest and perhaps with profit news of the spirit that animated their
great grandparents.

Here is Carlyle's celebrated passage upon George Fox (the antithesis
of the Dandy) with his suit of leather.[1] It is a noble passage in which
his style, already beginning to be explosive and thunderous, does not
obscure his lightning and his light. He begins by introducing his
imaginary Teufelsdrockh, and then lets the Professor speak for himself.

Neither, in so capricious inexpressible a Work as this of the Professor's, can our course now more than formerly be straightforward,
step by step, but at best leap by leap. Significant Indications stand
out here and there; which for the critical eye, that looks both widely
and narrowly, shape themselves into some ground-scheme of a Whole:
to select these with judgement, so that a leap from one to the other
be possible, and . . . by chaining them together, a passable Bridge be
effected: this, as heretofore, continues our only method. Among such
light-spots the following floating in much wild matter about
Perfectibility has seemed worth clutching at.

'Perhaps the most remarkable incident in Modern History,' says
Teufelsdrockh, 'is not the Diet of Worms, still less the Battle of
Austerlitz, Waterloo, Peterloo, or any other Battle; but an incident
passed carelessly over by most Historians, and treated with some
degree of ridicule by others: namely, George Fox's making to himself
a suit of Leather. This man, the first of the Quakers, and by trade a
Shoemaker, was one of those, to whom, under ruder or purer form,
the Divine Idea of the Universe is pleased to manifest itself; and,
across all the hulls of Ignorance and earthly Degradation, shine through,
in unspeakable Awfulness, unspeakable Beauty, on their souls: who
therefore are rightly accounted Prophets, God-possessed; or even
Gods, as in some periods it has chanced. Sitting in his stall; working on
tanned hides, amid pincers, paste-horns, rosin, swine-bristles, and a
nameless flood of rubbish, this youth had, nevertheless, a Living Spirit
belonging to him; also an antique Inspired Volume, through which, as
through a window, it could look upwards, and discern its celestial Home.
The task of a daily pair of shoes, coupled even with some prospect of
victuals, and an honourable Mastership in Cordwainery, and perhaps
the post of Thirdborough in his hundred, as the crown of long faithful
sewing,—was nowise satisfaction enough to such a mind: but ever
amid the boring and hammering comes tones from that far country,
came Splendours and Terrors; for this poor Cordwainer, as we said,

[1] Centenary Edition, Vol. I, pp. 166, 169.

was a Man; and the Temple of Immensity, wherein as Man he had been sent to minister, was full of holy mystery to him.

'The Clergy of the neighbourhood, the ordained Watchers and Interpreters of that same holy mystery, listened with unaffected tedium to his consultations, and advised him, as the solution of such doubts, to "drink beer and dance with the girls." Blind leaders of the blind! For what end were their tithes levied and eaten; for what were their shovel-hats scooped-out, and their surplices and cassock-aprons girt-on; and such a church-repairing, and chaffering, and organing, and other racketing, held over that spot of God's earth,—if Man were but a Patent Digester, and the Belly with its adjuncts the grand Reality? Fox turned from them, with tears and a sacred scorn, back to his Leather-parings and his Bible. Mountains of encumbrance, higher than Ætna, had been heaped over that Spirit: but it was a Spirit, and would not lie buried there. Through long days and nights of silent agony, it struggled and wrestled, with a man's force, to be free: how its prison-mountains heaved and swayed tumultuously, as the giant spirit shook them to this hand and that, and, emerged into the light of Heaven! That Leicester shoe-shop, had men known it, was a holier place than any Vatican or Loretto-shrine.—"So bandaged, and hampered, and hemmed in," groaned he, "with thousand requisitions, obligations, straps, tatters, and tagrags, I can neither see nor move: not my own am I, but the World's; and Time flies fast, and Heaven is high, and Hell is deep; Man! bethink thee, if thou hast power of Thought! Why not; what binds me here? Want, want!— Ha, of what? Will all the shoe-wages under the Moon ferry me across into that far Land of Light? Only Meditation can, and devout Prayer to God. I will to the woods: the hollow of a tree will lodge me, wild-berries feed me; and for Clothes, cannot I stitch myself one perennial suit of Leather!"

'Historical Oil-painting,' continued Teufelsdrockh, 'is one of the Arts I never practised; therefore shall I not decide whether this subject were easy of execution on the canvas. Yet often has it seemed to me as if such first outflashing of man's Freewill, to lighten, more and more into Day, the Chaotic Night that threatened to engulf him in its hindrances and its horrors, were properly the only grandeur there is in History. Let some living Angelo or Rosa, with seeing eye and understanding heart, picture George Fox on that morning, when he spreads-out his cutting-board for the last time, and cuts cowhides by unwonted patterns, and stitches them together into one continuous all-including Case, the farewell service of his awl! Stitch away, thou noble Fox: every prick of that little instrument is pricking into the heart of Slavery, and World-worship, and the Mammon-god. Thy elbows jerk, as in strong swimmer-strokes, and every stroke is bearing thee across the Prison-ditch, within which Vanity holds her Workhouse and Ragfair, into lands of true Liberty; were the work done, there is in broad Europe one Free man, and thou art he!

'Thus from the lowest depth there is a path to the loftiest height; and for the Poor also a Gospel has been published. Surely if, as D'Alembert asserts, my illustrious namesake, Diogenes, was the greatest man of Antiquity, only that he wanted Decency, then by stronger reason is George Fox the greatest of the Moderns, and greater than Diogenes himself: for he too stands on the adamantine basis of his Manhood, casting aside all props and shoars; yet not, in half-savage Pride, undervaluing the Earth; valuing it rather, as a place to yield him warmth and food, he looks Heavenward from his Earth, and dwells in an element of Mercy and Worship, with a still Strength, such as the Cynic's Tub did nowise witness. Great, truly, was that Tub; a temple from which man's dignity and divinity was scornfully preached abroad: but greater is the Leather Hull, for the same sermon was preached there, and not in Scorn but in Love.'

Miscellaneous Proverbs and Sayings

The selection of proverbs and sayings for Part II of this book is cut to the bone. Though, in our lifetime, it has receded, the Scottish capacity for coining laconic sayings and compressions of wit and wisdom increased enormously in the last three centuries. Indeed, a hundred and fifty years ago, as we can see in the pages of Scott and Galt, the Scottish peasant and burgher was almost as much addicted to proverbs as was Sancho Panza. During the last century over five thousand of these were gathered together in various collections.

Sometimes they were humorous, often earthy, sometimes doomful and always with a national quality about them; one could go on drawing on them almost endlessly. In book-form, even when gathered together in not much more than half a dozen pages, they become a little tedious, as do the national sayings of all peoples. For all their force and humour and shock-effect, they tend to repeat themselves on a few themes. Moreover, their very national qualities of dryness, pithyness and laconic style do not make them appear at their best in print. They demand the quality of the Scots voice speaking them and the Scots face, humorous or doomful, behind that voice.

Everyone has his favourite among these Scottish sayings, and his choice usually differs from others. Some, for instance, would regard 'Facts are chiels that winna ding' as the quintessence of Scottish wisdom. Others of us think of it as no more than the kind of platitude a bank-manager utters when telling us about the state of our overdraft. It is impossible to give, in the space at our disposal, a selection of the proverbs that please most people. We have therefore made a short selection only from those that please us. We have chosen ten per cent of those available, i.e. fifty.

A few words on the sources are necessary in case any reader should wish to delve further into the history of these sayings. These words on the past collections of Scottish proverbs also give an opportunity to quote in the annotation and in the by-going some oddities of 'Scottish wisdom.'

Apart from the Maitland Folio MS. quoted in Part I the first collection of Scottish sayings was made by Archbishop Beaton of Glasgow just before the Reformation. No copies are now known to exist. Immediately after the Reformation David Fergusson, Minister of Dunfermline, gathered together *Scottish Proverbs* which may have drawn upon the Archbishop's store. In 1721 James Kelly made a valuable collection, but its worth is reduced by being cast in Anglicised Scots. Indeed, he called his book *A Complete Collection of Scottish Proverbs Made Intelligible to the English Reader*.

This spurred Allan Ramsay, the vernacular poet, to make his improved *A Collection of Scottish Proverbs*, in 1736. He pours scorn on Kelly's work as 'a late large work fou of errors in a style neither Scots nor

English.' He then goes on to a passage worth quoting as an example of 'Scottish wisdom' but in the guise of eighteenth-century 'Pastoral Tradition.'

'As naething helps our happiness mair than to hae the mind made up with right principles, I desire you, for the thriving and pleasure of you and yours, to use your een and lend your lugs to these *guid auld says*, that shine with wail'd sense, and will as lang as the world wags. Gar your bairns get them by heart; let them hae a place among your family books; and may never a window-sole through the country be without them. On a spare hour, when the day is clear, behind a rick, or on the green howm, draw the treasure frae your pouch and enjoy the pleasant companion. Ye happy herds, while your hirdsels are feeding on the flowery braes, you may eithly mak yoursels maisters of the hale ware! How usefou it will prove to you (wha hae sae few opportunities of common clattering) when you forgather with your friends at kirk or market, banquet or bridal! By your proficiency, you'll be able, in a proverbial way, to keep up the soul of a conversation, that is baith blythe and usefou.'

This sort of thing was being printed all over Europe at the time, but there is a certain interest and piquancy in seeing its appearance in Edinburgh just before the literati there were beginning their efforts to write like Englishmen and well before Burns had appeared in the capital.

In the nineteenth century three full and valuable collections appeared: *Scottish Proverbs*, by Andrew Henderson (1832); *The Proverbs of Scotland*, by Alexander Hislop (1862); and *Proverbs of Scotland*, by Andrew Cheviot (1896). Recently the Edinburgh University Press has put out privately an interesting set, *Proverbs in Scots*, gathered from antique sources.

It is Hislop and Henderson's scholarly and zestful researches that we have found most useful. Hislop was in 1862 writing at a time when many of his four thousand five hundred proverbs were still (but only just still) in the popular mouth. Scottish speech was still uncorrupted by television, the radio, films and yellow journalism, which last must have begun its influence by the time Cheviot's book was out. The Education Act of the seventies and the consequent rise of the popular journalism of the nineties solely in English—of a sort—were beginning their work.

Hislop, moreover, published his book before the era of 'quaint' Scottish humour designed for export. Such humour is based upon the idea of a pitiable national meanness and was much exploited by the talents of that remarkable music-hall artist Sir Harry Lauder. It was also based upon the cringing provincialism of the equally talented 'Kailyard' school of Scottish authors who hawked their unctuous but highly saleable national humility about Fleet Street in the capital of England. There is nothing of this in Hislop's book. It is a genuine farewell (if conscious farewell). There is about it the ring of Silver Latin, the agreeable taste of a *deoch an doris*, a last drink offered to the guest before leaving— literally 'a drink at the door.'

Henderson's less scholarly work is not a farewell (for he had no reason to suppose that the Scottish proverbs were dying out in his day), and it is composed with more gusto. He gathered his sayings where he could find them, and he often found them living. He does not scorn 'indecencies' and indeed gives them a special part in his collection to themselves. His work contains a characteristic long preface by the 'Sheriff-Clerk poet' William Motherwell.

It is amusing to read now and note, nearly a hundred and thirty years later, how Motherwell's native and national love of Scots earthiness could not help breaking through his carefully acquired pedantic pomposity. But even when it did break through he could not help expressing it pompously. Here is the legal poet in a characteristic passage worthy of inclusion as a kind of curiosity of Scottish wisdom in the early nineteenth century.

'It has been a common error with the paraemiographers of this fastidious age, to purge their collections so far as their sense of conventional delicacy reaches, of all impureness of expression. We are not partial to obscenity of any description, but as honest students of human nature, and national character, we cannot sympathise in this affected regard for the purity of morals, or rather of written language, which the verbal refinements of a particular day seek to enforce. A clean tongue and a foul stomach, an open brow and a false heart, are not unfrequently found united—*nulla fronte fides*. But the cleanness of the one, or the openness of the other, does not alter the nature of that of which they should be as true an index as the shadow of the dial spike is of the sun's course, upon the graduated scale of time. Besides these revolting and unrefined illustrations, gathered as they for the most part are from the commonest, as they may be the most mortifying infirmities or offices of nature, are in themselves often more pungent, quaint, ludicrous, and striking, than those which are derived from a more elevated stock of ideas. As illustrative of the domestic habits, civil economy, and living speech of a people, they are frequently invaluable. Why should mere types be more disgusting than the things themselves? This shrinking from ourselves—from a fair exposition of our own nature and habits, is, according to our notions, utterly contemptible. It is only a vicious device to trick the soul of its integrity, and to divert our moral feelings from their right channels, that this circumlocutory horror of indecency in colloquial discourse has been invented. To wrap nasty ideas up in clean linen, is one sure sign of a degenerate and emasculate age. A spade is a spade all the world over, and is so understood, however it may be expressed. And they that have eaten the cow, and worry at its rump, or cry salt, like the souter, after swallowing the hide, only betray a fastidiousness of ear, which is as unphilosophical as it is ridiculous, and positively injurious to right thinking and pure morals.'

For all his fine language how Motherwell must have enjoyed the more scatological passages in the Scottish novelist Smollett who was still, in the 1830s, very popular.

And now at last for the brief selection of the proverbs themselves. They come mostly from Hislop and Henderson, some from other traditional sources, and some we have overheard ourselves in our profession as author in Scotland. We have marked their origin in each case. The reader may note that some proverbs are international or are, at least, shared between the English and the Scots. We have included these when the Scottish version has a particular interest.

A' things help quo' the wren when she pished in the sea.[1]

A blate [timid] cat maks a prood moose.[2]
  More character in this, surely, than in 'When the cat's away the mice will play.'

A cock's aye crouse on his ain midden heid.[3]
  A variant of English and other sayings, but more forceful in Scots. The English, indeed, have adopted the word midden.

Ane eagle taks na midges.[4]

A drunken man deid never of unseld [hunger].[5]
  It is true that heavy drinkers tend to lose their appetites, but this is unlikely to be the origin of this rather oblique proverb which we include simply because it sounds good.

A sorrowfu' heart's aye dry.[6]
  An unusually kindly saying to excuse widows who take to the bottle to drown their sorrows.

A Scotch mist will weet an Englishman tae the skin.[7]

Bachelors' wives an' auld maids' bairns are aye weel bred.[8]

Bastard broods are aye prood.[9]

By biting an' scarting the cat was got wi' kittens.[10]
  And in a like manner is many a Scots bairn begot. That is why they are so hardy.

[1] Henderson.	[2] Cheviot.	[3] Hislop.	[4] Henderson.
[5] Traditional.	[6–9] Hislop.	[10] Henderson.	

Better a toom [empty] hoose nor an ill tennant.[1]

An excuse offered by one who has unwittingly broken wind in company. Sometimes the saying is used by a tactful host to set a flatulent guest at ease. There is an equivalent saying in popular English usage, but the use of the word toom *(now almost fallen into desuetude) and the jingle and alliteration—*toom *and* tennant—*of the rhyme proclaim its Scottish origin. We have also overheard, as a proclamation of national independence, 'As lang as I live I shall fart by my ain fireside.'*

Courts tae the toon an' whures tae the window.[2]

Dinna gut your fish till ye get them.[3]

An international proverb, but, in our fish-surrounded, fish-swarming country, a Scottish version.

Dirt bodes luck.[4]

There are many proverbs in Scots tolerant of dirt. We shall quote at least one other similar saying below. Though Motherwell (who wrote the introduction to Henderson's work) did not mind homely obscene sayings he took a poor view of the old-time Scots kindly attitude towards dirt, especially as shown in proverbs. He was strongly anti-Catholic (doubting if Archbishop Beaton's collection was any good—if indeed it existed at all) and anti-French. He endeavours to excuse our ancestors by saying: 'We suspect the filthy domestic habits of the Scots were not improved by their long intercourse with the French, certainly the nastiest of civilised people.'

Dinna lee for want o' news.[5]

Do as the lasses do—say No, but tak it.[6]

Internationally national.

Eagles flee alane, but sheep herd together.[7]

Faint heart ne'er won fair ladie.[8]

It may surprise some readers to learn that the derivation of this is Scottish. But it is unquestionably out of a ballad from our side of the Border. It appears in Jock o' the Side *(Child, 187. B. 20. 2).*

Fair hair may hae foul roots.[9]

An old saying with an oddly modern application as anyone who observes the 'bleached blondes' of our age may note.

Far awa fowls hae fine feathers.[10]

Scots who stay at home, even if they succeed, are not much thought of.

Fiddlers, dogs and flesh-flies come aye tae the feast unca'd.[11]

A gaun fit's aye getting.[12]

An active, moving man will always do well.

---

[1] Traditional.   [2] Henderson.   [3] Hislop.   [4] Henderson.
[5-6] Hislop.   [7] Henderson.   [8] Old Ballad.   [9-12] Hislop.

God send us siller [money] for they're little thocht o' that want it.[1]

God send ye mair sense an' me mair siller.[2]

He's like a bagpipe, ne'er heard till his wame's fu.[3]

He that shames let him be shent.[4]
One of the oldest and best of Scots sayings of which we are justly proud. It means 'Let him that shames, or tells tales of his neighbour, be destroyed himself.'

Love and light winna hide.[5]

My tongue's no under your belt.[6]
From the Gaelic, meaning 'I'm not at your mercy.'

Naething tae be done in haste but gripping fleas.[7]
A patently authentic and admirable Scots saying. We have often heard it quoted but only once used. It was spoken quite naturally in conversation by an artist replying to the sneering and inaccurate innuendoes of some literary or dramatic critic attending the Edinburgh Festival.

Near's my sark [shirt] but nearer's my skin.[8]
Some friends and relations are indeed near to me but I (my skin) am nearest to myself.

O' a' sorrows a fu' sorrow's the best.[9]
This disagreeable saying refers to the death of a friend who leaves a good legacy.

Our sowens [pottage made of dust of oatmeal] are ill sour'd, ill seil'd, ill sauted, ill sodden, thin an' little o' them. Ye may stay a' night, but ye may gang hame if ye like. It's weel kenn'd your faither's son was ne'er a scambler.[10]
We include this extraordinary authentic and characteristic saying because of its length. It is fairly entitled to rank as the second longest proverb on record, the first being the German one beginning 'Folk say there is a lack of four people on earth,' etc. Kelly says that 'this was a speech of a country-woman of mine to a guest she would have gladly got rid of, which being so oddly expressed became a proverb.'

Poets and painters are aye poor.[11]
True enough, but it appears only in Henderson. He was an amateur painter and his friend Motherwell set up to be a poet. Still, no one else outside Scotland, as far as we know, has said it.

Quick at meal, quick at wark.[12]
And quickly in your grave.

[1-2] Hislop.	[3] Henderson.	[4-5] Hislop.	[6] Cheviot.
[7-10] Hislop.	[11] Henderson.	[12] Hislop.	

She lookit at the moon, but lichtet in the midden.[1]
Young women who boast of a fine match often land in the mire.

Silence and thocht hurt nae man.[2]
One of our most notable platitudes.

Silence grips the mouse.[3]
One of our most poetic statements; 'grips' here means catches.

Sins and debts are aye mair than we think them.[4]

Soon eneuch if weel eneuch.[6]

Soon ripe soon rotten.[7]

Sorrow's sib to [a relation of] a'body.[8]
True enough and often enough expressed, but here well expressed.

Spit on a stane an' a' will be wat at last.[9]
A more personal, therefore more characteristic way of saying that the dripping drop will wear away the stone.

Still waters rin deep.[5]
This is now, of course, an international saying, but we adapted it early and memorably:

> 'Tweed said to Till,
> "What gars ye rin sae still?"
> Till said to Tweed,
> "Though ye rin sae wi' speed
> An' I rin slaw,
> Where ye droon ae man,
> I dron twa." '

Tak a hair o' the dog that bit you.[10]
We all use this saying in various forms throughout the English-speaking world, but it is interesting to note that Hislop says that it had long been established in its Scots form. The Romans, however, were before us all: 'SIMILIA SIMILIBUS CURANTUR.'

The clartier [the more dirty] the cosier.[11]
See note on page 299, 'Dirt bodes luck.' This saying was used by Scott, who put it into the mouth of a fishwife in The Antiquary. *It is still in common use, and is sometimes put forward by a host as an excuse for the disarray of his room which (so he says) he has not had time to clean up. The fact that this neat old saying has lingered on in all classes of Scottish society is noteworthy. Scottish domestic economy has been much influenced by the Dutch (one of the cleanest people in Europe), but we also have other and Celtic strains in our blood which are at war with imported Hollands.*

[1-10] Hislop.   [11] Henderson.

Whisky does not mix with Bols gin, and it is unlikely that we shall ever lose the saying 'The clartier the cosier.'

The deil's no' sae ill as he's ca'd.[1]

This, one of the many familiar and sometimes affectionate sayings about the Devil in Scots, was used by Walter Scott in The Heart of Midlothian, *who put it into the mouth of Saddletree.*

The mair mischief the better sport.[2]

An old and characteristic Scottish saying. It was uttered and made famous by Lord Lovat in 1747 at his execution when he heard that the scaffolding for the spectators of his death had collapsed and killed many.

Wha burns rags will want a winding sheet.[3]

A characteristic combination of the economical and the macabre.

'Wha's he tae be a. . . .' [anything mildly distinguished you can think of, a provost, a town councillor, an oncoming lawyer, an artist, an actor, a creator of beauty, even a writer, a journalist or a compiler of anthologies] '*I* kent his faither.'[4]

This, regrettable though it be to have to admit it, is one of the commonest of everyday sayings in Scotland, and is, possibly, nineteenth century in origin. The implication is that the individual you are discussing has no right to aspire to any distinction. WHY? Because you (humble and decent person that you are) were acquainted with his equally humble father. Why, then, should he aspire higher? Why indeed? Who is he to think that he has any right to get out of the common decent ruck we all belong to? . . . I kent his faither.

It was left to the Germans to coin the unpleasing word schadenfreude: *it was left to the Scots to think of and repeat this common saying.*

Ye'll get your kail through the reek.[5]

You will receive an ill welcome from your wife when you get home late or because you have displeased her in other ways, i.e. you will get your dinner burnt and clouded with smoke for having kept her waiting. This is still very much in common usage amongst all classes, even those who have normally dropped speaking Scots. Our women still rule the home roost. And we pay them the tribute in the old tongue.

[1-3] Hislop.   [4-5] Common saying.

Robert Louis Stevenson

The number of books written 'entirely about' and 'largely about' Robert Louis Stevenson is now at least five hundred and thirty-five[1]—five hundred and five too many. This is not meant to denigrate our compatriot and fellow-citizen of Edinburgh. His peculiar charm and talent, amounting at times to something more than talent, can be as attractive as ever. His personality is pertinaciously long-living. The writer of these notes feels that with the exceptions of Wilde and Sidney Smith he would relish a talk with R. L. S. more than with any other English-speaking conversationalist in the nineteenth century. He would rather have met Scott, but that is a different matter from conversation.

All this admitted, it is absurd that there should be more books about R. L. S. than about Scott, Hume, Boswell, Dunbar, indeed about any other Scottish author with the possible exception of Burns, whose international fame in translation makes it impossible to compute the number of works 'about him.' The fact remains, however, that there has been this enormous flood of Stevensonian literature; and I do not propose to add much further to it in the way of comment, save what is pertinent to the theme.

If anyone had thought of putting out a work called *The Wisdom of R. L. S.* fifty years ago it might have made something more than a 'slim volume.' His reputation then was at the high noon of its respectability; and the faint but alluring shadow of his youthful and alleged low amours in Edinburgh had not yet been cast by the truffle-nosed industry of American literary thesis-writers. It would have contained sizeable extracts from his essays and travel-books, some of his more consciously literary letters, possibly some of his devotional essays in 'non-sectarian' prayer and the like; and would have formed a pious memorial built by pious editorial hands.

All that is now a thing of the past, the 'fragrant' but not regretted past. Stevenson today is neither widely idolised nor meanly denigrated. His peculiar charm (one most potent on his fellow-citizens), his felicity of expression and his remarkable power as a story-teller have secured his position, his modest yet world-recognised position. But wherein does his Scottish wisdom, in the context of this anthology, lie?

His observation of the Scottish character is wise. His devotion to the feminine ideal springs remotely from the same ethereal wisdom that we claim animated Thomas of Ercildoun. His dramatic perception of the dichotomy of man's nature, of good and evil, contained inextricably

[1] These facts are from the Catalogue of a Collection of Works by and about Robert Louis Stevenson formed by Edwin J. Beinecke, compiled by George L. Mackay, Yale University Press, Vol. II. The catalogue goes as far as 1952. I have added to the number there given those biographies and studies of Stevenson which have to my knowledge been published since that date. There may be more.

warring in one person is universal wisdom but was highly Scottishly expressed. How pleasant it would be to present to the reader his love of woman and his deep perception of the Scottish character in his portrait of the fifty-year-old Kirstie Elliott from *Weir of Hermiston*, how agreeable to remind the same reader that his study of good and evil, his 'Shilling Shocker,' as he called it, his *Jekyll and Hyde*, contains some still memorable passages! But there is no space.

There is space, however, to divagate briefly upon the origins of *The Strange Case of Dr. Jekyll and Mr. Hyde*; for this is relevant to our purpose and has bearing upon the single-linked quotations from Stevenson's works that we are going to make.

Jekyll and Hyde was the result of a nightmare which he had when recovering from fever, and it bears the undoubted marks of an outburst from his subconscious. Officially the scene of the story is London, but everyone knows that it is really Edinburgh. His native city gave him the true atmosphere, the true background for his dream.

It is worth pausing for a moment to consider this important fact in relation to Stevenson. The dramatic contrasts in the Scottish scene between drab dourness and great beauty, in the Scottish character between loyalty and treachery, tenderness and brutality, good and evil, have had their effect on Scottish writing, thought and wisdom. These effects have been implicit in much that is printed in this anthology. In Stevenson, the mid-Victorian Stevenson, their effects become patently explicit; and the reason for this is that his boyhood and youth were passed in that extraordinary city whose true character nearly everyone now conveniently forgets—mid-Victorian Edinburgh.

Edinburgh in the second half of the nineteenth century displayed, in stone and in human behaviour, contrast in its most dramatic form. As yet unencumbered and uninsulted by the disgusting growth of modern subtopia, the grey and splendid classical severities of the Augustan New Town faced in theatrical antithesis the romantic and rotting heights of the Old Town. Rarely in human memory has there been outwardly so respectable a community as that which lived in the New Town. Seldom has the spell of an historic old city fallen so quickly into so squalid a slum as did Edinburgh's Old Town; and those who lived in it with a truly Scottish power of abandonment adopted slum life with gusto.

The two towns lived cheek by jowl. But even that hackneyed simile is not quite correct. In the mews and small back streets of the New Town there lived communities in as great a state of squalor as did any in the heights of the Old Town. It is said that these sore spots within the body of the impressive New Town had been deliberately encouraged after the French Revolution. The respectable and rich did not like the idea of *all* the poor people living on the top of a rock from which they might descend in time of trouble.

Low life, too, in mid- and late-Victorian Edinburgh, was sensational, fruity, full of conscious and flaunting sin; and, it was obvious for those who wished to find it, to an extent that is today scarcely credible. There were more tolerated brothels in the capital of Scotland than in all the

growing and much larger city of Glasgow. They were more in evidence
and much easier of access than in London. This was very much not the
city of such sugary and unreal romances as those modern views of
Victorian Edinburgh *Marigold* and *Lady from Edinburgh*. Yet it *was*
the city in which the noble renunciation of the 'Disruption' of the
Kirk had but recently taken place—truly a City of Evil and Good.

Those who doubt the fruity nature of Edinburgh's low life in mid-
Victorian times are referred to the 'Murthly Case' (Stuart *v*. Wilson
or Robertson Session Papers for 1874–5). This case, presided over
in the initial stages by a Judge who was the grand-uncle of the author
of these notes, is scarcely remembered nowadays save in legal circles
(and then only late at night). In its time it was celebrated, and really
took the lid off Bacchic and venereal Victorian Edinburgh.

Much ink has been spilt on paper, mostly in America, in speculating
how far the youthful R. L. S. worshipped at these squalid Edinburgh
temples of Venus and Morpheus so close as almost to be contiguous to
his own Heriot Row. The answer is probably very little; but no one
knows now, and it doesn't matter very much.

What is clear is that Stevenson must have been aware of this fantastic
dichotomy in his native city, and it must have affected his youthful
imaginative mind. He must have known that the real piquancy of the
situation lay in the fact that the New Town was not entirely, or even
largely, occupied by Dr. Jekylls. No one better than 'Robert Lewis'
was conscious of the decent godly people in the great majority who
were apparently quite unaware of the squalor and the evil (the evil
apart from prostitution) that lay all around them. Hence *The Strange
Case of Dr. Jekyll and Mr. Hyde*. I have always thought it significant
that the 'Murthly Case' burst upon a horrified Edinburgh in 1874, the
very year in which Stevenson was admitted a member of the Faculty of
Advocates (was called to the Bar as it would be described in England)
and when Parliament House was resounding with the case.

The eternal puzzle of the evil and the good personality inhabiting the
same body, or animating closely related members of the same family,
fascinated Stevenson. Being a Scot, and an Edinburgh man, he saw
this puzzle in its dramatically Scottish form. *Jekyll and Hyde*, his best-
known study of the drama, is, we insist, an Edinburgh story. He also
played around with the Edinburgh theme of the respectable burglar,
Deacon Brodie. His finest character study, of Lord Weir of Hermiston,
is, too, a study in opposing elements incarnate in one piece of flesh.

And that brings us to the conjoined extracts we intend to give from
Stevenson's work. They are the portrait of Lord Hermiston and the
account of his scene of judgment with his son Archie Weir.

THE SCOTTISH JUDGE

Stevenson's unfinished masterpiece *Weir of Hermiston* was written in
a state of inspired homesickness for Scotland and Edinburgh from the
South Seas and in the last year of his life. Though separated by

U

'the thick of the world' from the people and the scenes of his childhood he never saw them more clearly, never expressed his vision of them more poignantly.

Lord Weir of Hermiston is his greatest creation. It is based upon Braxfield, the so-called 'hanging Judge' of the late eighteenth century, and it mirrors the popular view of the great Senator as a harsh unyielding moralist, yet coarse of a coarseness seldom found outside of Scotland. It is a fine example of Stevenson's power of portraying two contradictory elements in one person. It also shows Stevenson's shrinking horror of that stern paternalism which was on the other side of the Scottish nature to that which he possessed.

There are some who libellously maintain that Hermiston is a portrait of Stevenson's own father and that the clash between Archie and Hermiston is a recollection of domestic disputes at 17 Heriot Row. It is not worth wasting much ink in disputing this. Thomas Stevenson was a humane, kindly, decent, God-fearing man whom R. L. S. fundamentally loved dearly. He had his differences with him, but in the end they were forgotten. He did, however, remember other harshly paternalistic Scots from the days of his youth. They were repugnant to him; but it is a mark of his powers of perception as well as a writer that, in this last work of his, he could pay tribute also to their antique Roman qualities. Here is Scottish wisdom.

Literary style is not primarily the concern of this anthology, but it is difficult to resist drawing the reader's attention to the paragraph containing the words: 'On he went up the great bare staircase of his duty, uncheered and undepressed.' On that sentence alone Stevenson qualifies for an anthology on the wisdom of the Scots.

My Lord Justice-Clerk was known to many; the man Adam Weir perhaps to none.[1] He had nothing to explain or to conceal; he sufficed wholly and silently to himself; and that part of our nature which goes out (too often with false coin) to acquire glory or love, seemed in him to be omitted. He did not try to be loved, he did not care to be; it is probable the very thought of it was a stranger to his mind. He was an admired lawyer, a highly unpopular judge; and he looked down upon those who were his inferiors in either distinction, who were lawyers of less grasp or judges not so much detested. In all the rest of his days and doings, not one trace of vanity appeared; and he went on through life with a mechanical movement, as of the unconscious, that was almost august.

He saw little of his son. In the childish maladies with which the boy was troubled, he would make daily inquiries and daily pay him a visit, entering the sick-room with a facetious and appalling countenance, letting off a few perfunctory jests, and going again swiftly, to

[1] *Weir of Hermiston*, Chapter II.

the patient's relief. Once, a court holiday falling opportunely, my lord had his carriage, and drove the child himself to Hermiston, the customary place of convalescence. It is conceivable he had been more than usually anxious, for that journey always remained in Archie's memory as a thing apart, his father having related to him from beginning to end, and with much detail, three authentic murder cases. Archie went the usual round of other Edinburgh boys, the high school and the college; and Hermiston looked on, or rather looked away, with scarce an affectation of interest in his progress. Daily, indeed, upon a signal after dinner, he was brought in, given nuts and a glass of port, regarded sardonically, sarcastically questioned. 'Well, sir, and what have you done with your book today?' my lord might begin, and set him posers in law Latin. To a child just stumbling into Corderius, Papinian and Paul proved quite invincible. But papa had memory of no other. He was not harsh to the little scholar, having a vast fund of patience learned upon the bench, and was at no pains whether to conceal or to express his disappointment. 'Well, ye have a long jaunt before ye yet!' he might observe, yawning, and fall back on his own thoughts (as like as not) until the time came for separation, and my lord would take the decanter and the glass, and be off to the back chamber looking on the Meadows, where he toiled on his cases till the hours were small. There was no 'fuller man' on the bench; his memory was marvellous, though wholly legal; if he had to 'advise' extempore, none did it better; yet there was none who more earnestly prepared. As he thus watched in the night, or sat at table and forgot the presence of his son, no doubt but he tasted deeply of recondite pleasures. To be wholly devoted to some intellectual exercise is to have succeeded in life; and perhaps only in law and the higher mathematics may this devotion be maintained, suffice to itself without reaction, and find continual rewards without excitement. This atmosphere of his father's sterling industry was the best of Archie's education. Assuredly it did not attract him; assuredly it rather rebutted and depressed. Yet it was still present, unobserved like the ticking of a clock, an arid ideal, a tasteless stimulant in the boy's life.

But Hermiston was not all of one piece. He was, besides, a mighty toper; he could sit at wine until the day dawned, and pass directly from the table to the bench with a steady hand and a clear head. Beyond the third bottle, he showed the plebeian in a larger print; the low, gross accent, the low, foul mirth, grew broader and commoner; he became less formidable, and infinitely more disgusting. Now, the boy had inherited from Jean Rutherford a shivering delicacy, unequally mated with potential violence. In the playing-fields, and amongst his own companions, he repaid a coarse expression with a blow; at his father's table (when the time came for him to join these revels) he turned pale and sickened in silence. . . .

The boy was without confidant or friend. Serious and eager, he came through school and college, and moved among a crowd of the indifferent, in the seclusion of his shyness. He grew up handsome, with an open, speaking countenance, with graceful, youthful ways; he was clever, he took prizes, he shone in the Speculative Society. It should seem he must become the centre of a crowd of friends; but something that was in part the delicacy of his mother, in part the austerity of his father, held him aloof from all. It is a fact, and a strange one, that among his contemporaries Hermiston's son was thought to be a chip of the old block. 'You're a friend of Archie Weir's?' said one to Frank Innes; and Innes replied, with his usual flippancy and more than his usual insight: 'I know Weir, but I never met Archie.' No one had met Archie, a malady most incident to only sons. He flew his private signal, and none heeded it; it seemed he was abroad in a world from which the very hope of intimacy was banished; and he looked round about him on the concourse of his fellow-students, and forward to the trivial days and acquaintances that were to come, without hope or interest.

As time went on, the tough and rough old sinner felt himself drawn to the son of his loins and sole continuator of his new family, with softnesses of sentiment that he could hardly credit and was wholly impotent to express. With a face, voice, and manner trained through forty years to terrify and repel, Rhadamanthus may be great, but he will scarce be engaging. It is a fact that he tried to propitiate Archie, but a fact that cannot be too lightly taken; the attempt was so inconspicuously made, the failure so stoically supported. Sympathy is not due to these steadfast iron natures. If he failed to gain his son's friendship, or even his son's toleration, on he went up the great, bare staircase of his duty, uncheered and undepressed. There might have been more pleasure in his relations with Archie, so much he may have recognised at moments; but pleasure was a by-product of the singular chemistry of life, which only fools expected.

An idea of Archie's attitude, since we are all grown up and have forgotten the days of our youth, it is more difficult to convey. He made no attempt whatsoever to understand the man with whom he dined and breakfasted. Parsimony of pain, glut of pleasure, these are the two alternating ends of youth; and Archie was of the parsimonious. The wind blew cold out of a certain quarter—he turned his back upon it; stayed as little as was possible in his father's presence; and when there, averted his eyes as much as was decent from his father's face. The lamp shone for many hundred days upon these two at table— my lord, ruddy, gloomy, and unreverent; Archie with a potential brightness that was always dimmed and veiled in that society; and there were not, perhaps in Christendom, two men more radically strangers. The father, with a grand simplicity, either spoke of what interested himself, or maintained an unaffected silence. The son turned in his head for some topic that should be quite safe, that would spare him fresh evidence either of my lord's inherent grossness or of the innocence of his inhumanity; treading gingerly the ways of inter- course, like a lady gathering up her skirts in a by-path. If he made a mistake, and my lord began to abound in matter of offence, Archie drew himself up, his brow grew dark, his share of the talk expired; but my lord would faithfully and cheerfully continue to pour out the worst of himself before his silent and offended son.

'Well, it's a poor hert that never rejoices!' he would say, at the conclusion of such a nightmare interview. 'But I must get to my plew-stilts.' And he would seclude himself as usual in his back room, and Archie go forth into the night and the city quivering with animosity and scorn.

AN OLD MAN WHO APPROVES OF CAPITAL PUNISHMENT

Here is the scene between Father and Son. It has been the subject of much Stevensonian comment, but we can say one new thing about it here.

The late Albert Camus, whose untimely death in 1960 deprived France of one of her brightest literary lights, has one internationally famous novel. *The Plague* won him the *Prix des Critiques* in 1947 and has been widely translated. It contains an extraordinarily powerful passage in French either consciously or unconsciously derived from this scene printed below. The situation is the same. A sensitive youth is horrified to perceive the relentlessness with which his strict father, who is also a prosecutor, pursues a criminal. Stevenson's Scottish wisdom in imagination has had its posthumous effect upon European wisdom in imagination. There can be no doubt that Stevenson's great scene from *Weir* flowered again in the French language more than fifty years later. It is a scene of universal application, but was projected into Scotland from the South Seas.

For a moment Hermiston warmed his hands at the fire, presenting his back to Archie; then suddenly disclosed on him the terrors of the Hanging Face.[1]

'What's this I hear of ye?' he asked.

There was no answer possible to Archie.

'I'll have to tell ye, then,' pursued Hermiston. 'It seems ye've been skirling against the father that begot ye, and one of his Maijesty's Judges in this land; and that in the public street, and while an order of the Court was being executit. Forbye which, it would appear that ye've been airing your opeenions in a Coallege Debatin' Society'; he paused a moment: and then, with extraordinary bitterness, added: 'Ye damned eediot.'

'I had meant to tell you,' stammered Archie. 'I see you are well informed.'

'Muckle obleeged to ye,' said his lordship, and took his usual seat. 'And so you disapprove of Caapital Punishment?' he added.

'I am sorry, sir, I do,' said Archie.

'I am sorry, too,' said his lordship. 'And now, if you please, we shall approach this business with a little more parteecularity. I hear that at the hanging of Duncan Jopp—and, man! ye had a fine client there—in the middle of all the riff-raff of the ceety, ye thought fit to cry out, "This is a damned murder, and my gorge rises at the man that haangit him."'

'No, sir, these were not my words,' cried Archie.

'What were yer words, then?' asked the Judge.

'I believe I said, "I denounce it as a murder!"' said the son. 'I beg your pardon—a God-defying murder. I have no wish to conceal the truth,' he added, and looked his father for a moment in the face.

'God, it would only need that of it next!' cried Hermiston. 'There was nothing about your gorge rising, then?'

'That was afterwards, my lord, as I was leaving the Speculative. I said I had been to see the miserable creature hanged, and my gorge rose at it.'

'Did ye, though?' said Hermiston. 'And I suppose ye knew who haangit him?'

'I was present at the trial, I ought to tell you that, I ought to explain. I ask your pardon beforehand for any expression that may seem undutiful. The position in which I stand is wretched,' said the unhappy hero, now fairly face to face with the business he had chosen. 'I have

[1] *Weir of Hermiston*, Chapter III.

been reading some of your cases. I was present when Jopp was tried. It was a hideous business. Father, it was a hideous thing! Grant he was vile, why should you hunt him with a vileness equal to his own? It was done with glee—that is the word—you did it with glee; and I looked on, God help me! with horror.'

'You're a young gentleman that doesna approve of Caapital Punishment,' said Hermiston. 'Weel, I'm an auld man that does. I was glad to get Jopp haangit, and what for would I pretend I wasna? You're all for honesty, it seems; you couldn't even steik your mouth on the public street. What for should I steik mines upon the bench, the King's officer, bearing the sword, a dreid to evil-doers, as I was from the beginning, and as I will be to the end! Mair than enough of it! Heedious! I never gave twa thoughts to heediousness, I have no call to be bonny. I'm a man that gets through with my day's business, and let that suffice.'

The ring of sarcasm had died out of his voice as he went on; the plain words became invested with some of the dignity of the Justice-seat.

'It would be telling you if you could say as much,' the speaker resumed. 'But ye cannot. Ye've been reading some of my cases, ye say. But it was not for the law in them, it was to spy out your faither's nakedness, a fine employment in a son. You're splairging; you're running at lairge in life like a wild nowt. It's impossible you should think any longer of coming to the Bar. You're not fit for it; no splairger is. And another thing: son of mines or no son of mines, you have flung fylement in public on one of the Senators of the Coallege of Justice, and I would make it my business to see that ye were never admitted there yourself. There is a kind of decency to be observit. Then comes the next of it—what am I to do with ye next? Ye'll have to find some kind of a trade, for I'll never support ye in idleset. What do ye fancy ye'll be fit for? The pulpit? Na, they could never get diveenity into that bloackhead. Him that the law of man whammles is no likely to do muckle better by the law of God. What would ye make of hell? Wouldna your gorge rise at that? Na, there's no room for splairgers under the fower quarters of John Calvin. What else is there? Speak up. Have ye got nothing of your own?'

'Father, let me go to the Peninsula,' said Archie. 'That's all I'm fit for—to fight.'

'All? quo' he!' returned the Judge. 'And it would be enough too, if I thought it. But I'll never trust ye so near the French, you that's so Frenchifeed.'

'You do me injustice there, sir,' said Archie. 'I am loyal; I will not boast; but any interest I may have ever felt in the French——'

'Have ye been so loyal to me?' interrupted his father. There came no reply.

'I think not,' continued Hermiston. 'And I would send no man to be a servant of the King, God bless him! that has proved such a shauchling son to his own faither. You can splairge here on Edinburgh street, and where's the hairm? It doesna play buff to me! And if there were twenty thousand eediots like yourself, sorrow a Duncan Jopp would hang the fewer. But there's no splairging possible in a camp; and if you were to go to it, you would find out for yourself whether Lord Well'n'ton approves of caapital punishment or not. You a sodger!' he cried, with a sudden burst of scorn. 'Ye auld wife, the sodgers would bray at ye like cuddies!'

As at the drawing of a curtain, Archie was aware of some illogicality in his position, and stood abashed. He had a strong impression, besides, of the essential valour of the old gentleman before him, how conveyed it would be hard to say.

'Well, have ye no other proposeetion?' said my lord again.

'You have taken this so calmly, sir, that I cannot but stand ashamed,' began Archie.

'I'm nearer voamiting, though, than you would fancy,' said my lord.

The blood rose to Archie's brow.

'I beg your pardon, I should have said that you had accepted my affront. . . . I admit it was an affront; I did not think to apologise, but I do, I ask your pardon; it will not be so again, I pass you my word of honour. . . . I should have said that I admired your magnanimity with—this—offender,' Archie concluded with a gulp.

'I have no other son, ye see,' said Hermiston. 'A bonny one I have gotten! But I must just do the best I can wi' him, and what am I to do? If ye had been younger, I would have wheepit ye for this rideeculous exhibeetion. The way it is, I have just to grin and bear. But one thing is to be clearly understood. As a faither, I must grin and bear it; but if I had been the Lord Advocate instead of the Lord Justice-Clerk, son or no son, Mr. Erchibald Weir would have been in a jyle the night.'

Archie was now dominated. Lord Hermiston was coarse and cruel; and yet the son was aware of a bloomless nobility, an ungracious abnegation of the man's self in the man's office. At every word, this sense of the greatness of Lord Hermiston's spirit struck more home; and along with it that of his own impotence, who had struck—and perhaps basely struck—at his own father, and not reached so far as to have even nettled him.

'I place myself in your hands without reserve,' he said.

'That's the first sensible word I've had of ye the night,' said Hermiston. 'I can tell ye, that would have been the end of it, the one way or the other; but it's better ye should come there yourself, than what I would have had to hirstle ye. Well, by my way of it—and my way is the best—there's just the one thing it's possible that ye might be with decency, and that's a laird. Ye'll be out of hairm's way at the least of it. If ye have to rowt, ye can rowt amang the kye; and the maist feck of the caapital punishment ye're like to come across'll be guddling trouts. Now, I'm for no idle lairdies; every man has to work, if it's only at peddling ballants; to work, or to be wheepit, or to be haangit. If I set ye down at Hermiston, I'll have to see you work that place the way it has never been workit yet; ye must ken about the sheep like a herd; ye must be my grieve there, and I'll see that I gain by ye. Is that understood?'

'I will do my best,' said Archie.

'Well, then, I'll send Kirstie word the morn, and ye can go yourself the day after,' said Hermiston. 'And just try to be less of an eediot!' he concluded, with a freezing smile, and turned immediately to the papers on his desk.

Today

The genius of the Scottish people has always been opposed by one quality, one thing particularly inimical to it—mediocrity. When that genius has triumphed it has done so individually and in the face of mediocrity. When mediocrity does get a grip upon the people of Scotland its effects are particularly mischievous—because inimical to their true spirit.

The story of Scotland's achievements in thought, in dreaming, in poetry, in writing, in wisdom and in the action that may come from these things is the story of men individually, originally, yet with the national spirit animating them, triumphing over, scorning out of existence one thing—mediocrity. The true Scot of history and tradition may have had many bad qualities, but he was never a mediocrity. Not one name mentioned in this large anthology of wisdom, even of those whom we have held up for dislike or qualified praise, is the name of a mediocrity.

Yet today the curse of Scotland is not, as is commonly supposed, whisky or the nine of diamonds, or even after-dinner public speaking, but mediocrity. It is particularly pernicious and prevalent with us because essentially so unlike us. How has this come about? There are a number of reasons, but most of them stem from something that happened two hundred and fifty-three years ago.

The consent to the Act of Union in 1707 was the most mediocre thing that the rulers of Scotland ever did. This is not the place in which to bandy about political arguments. It is enough to state that the action was a compromise, therefore repugnant to the Scottish genius, and was mediocre. If we had resisted the Union the results might or might not, in your view, have been disastrous. If we had surrendered completely and had become Scotlandshire, a northern extension of England, the action might have been tragic, but neither course would have been mediocre. There is nothing mediocre in suicide or in a determination to live. But about the most mediocre thing you can do is to sell yourself slowly out of existence and be cheated even of your pieces of silver in doing so.

Ever since 1707 the spirit of mediocrity in Scotland has grown and spread.[1] Deep down in men's hearts there is the knowledge that this is unnatural to them, and it is this knowledge that is responsible for those

---

[1] It is remarkable how in the act of writing these notes, examples often leap to hand. A few weeks ago the Earl of Home's statement in the House of Lords at Westminster that 'publicity free' thrilled his Scottish blood fell pat into our hands as we were writing about David Hume and John Home. This morning (October 10, 1960) a gallant and popular literary Scottish soldier has written a letter to the leading Scottish journal, defending the policy of 'sitting on the fence.' We have never seen the policy of mediocre thinking more bluntly, more powerfully or better expressed. The iron of the fence would seem, from his posture, to have entered into his soul. It could only happen in Scotland.

gaucheries which display what we now call the Scottish inferiority complex. It is lamentable.

And yet, as anyone who glances back at the pages of this collection, covering the years since 1707, will see, the individual spirit of Scotland has time and again broken through. Was there ever a less mediocre man and philosopher than David Hume, a less ordinary oddity of a genius than Boswell, a poet more purely himself than Burns, an author more luminously and individually eminent than Scott? And there have been others whose words we have not quoted here, whose names we have not even mentioned. A gaggle of politicians huddling together to sign a document in Edinburgh two hundred and fifty-three years ago could not entirely quench the spirit of a nation, but they could do a great deal to encumber and depress it.

As far as writing, as far as the expression of true Scottish wisdom in print was concerned, the nadir of that depression was reached about the beginning of this century. Stevenson, the last author quoted here, had died in 1894 in the South Seas, and it had seemed that it was only the fact of his exile that could produce from him the most authentically Scottish work he ever achieved—his unfinished *Weir of Hermiston*. Those left behind did not carry on the task.

Since then there has been a revival. One sombre novel in the first decade of the century, George Douglas's *The House with the Green Shutters*, had the authentic ring, so had John Davidson's poetry. But it was after the First World War that the true stirring began to be felt. Mostly it was in verse, in Scots and in English, but its effects were felt in prose, in fiction and in imaginative writing. It is now nearly forty years since it was derided as a passing post-war literary cult, but, under various names (some of them quite inappropriate), it has remained obstinately news, obstinately alive. Men, young, middle-aged and elderly, have been writing and speaking with the authentic voice of Scotland. The quality has been varied, but such of it as has held the field has not been mediocre. It has at least been positive and individual.

From this group of writers we choose for selection here only one. He is unquestionably the most important, as he was unquestionably also the originator of the movement, C. M. Grieve who, in verse, writes under the name of Hugh MacDiarmid. He is Scotland's greatest living poet and one of the greatest and most individual our country has produced.

We refrain from the delicate task of choosing from the works of those younger than he whom he has inspired, but we precede a selection from Grieve with two samples of the work of two men older than he who owe nothing to his way of writing yet who have been inspired by the authentic voice of Scotland. For both of these men Grieve has an admiration and affection, one died twenty-four years ago, the other happily is still with us—R. B. Cunninghame Graham and Compton Mackenzie.

It may surprise some readers South of the Border that we should put forward in this purely Scottish anthology two well-known writers sometimes thought of as English (one of them partly Spanish) or at the most 'British.' In fact, as will be shown, both are intensely and consciously Scottish. Both have written prolifically on subjects little to do with Scotland, but Scotland has haunted them, has been at the back of much of their writing. That writing is strongly individual. The one was born two years after Stevenson, the other, at the time of writing, is rising seventy-nine. These two friends of Grieve, whose manner of writing is so unlike his, provide a link with the past yet are of today. It is for that reason that they are included with him under the heading of 'Today.'

No sooner written than another heading occurs to us. To the Romans the word mediocre was far from pejorative; indeed, in Horace's *auream quisquis mediocritatem diligit* the meaning is complimentary. All the same, 'mediocre' in our modern sense has its uses; and there is no other word that takes the place of 'mediocrity.' Unfortunately, as a result of the mixed history of its origin and present use, it has no perfect antonym; even Roget is defeated.

Linguistically 'extreme' fills the bill, but again the word has acquired in some circles a reprehensible meaning. The respectable mass of mediocrity which forms the most of modern Scotland regards the word 'extremist' with dislike and alarm. It is always used about an opponent to imply contempt and inflict damage.

It is precisely because of this that we use it here—and to imply praise. Cunninghame Graham, Compton Mackenzie and Christopher Grieve have all been called 'extremists'; and so they have been. In differing ways they have been extreme, yet eventually to the same purpose. This concluding chapter, then, about three Scottish friends might well bear the title 'Extremes Meet'—not only in infinity but here, even in modern Scotland.

CUNNINGHAME GRAHAM

Robert Bontine Cunninghame Graham was the most aristocratic man of any nation that I[1] have met in any land. I recall with photographic intensity of detail the first occasion I saw him and heard his voice.

I was a very young man scraping some kind of a living upon the fringes of literary journalism in London, which city I did not know well, having come there fairly recently from Scotland by way of France. Some distinguished printing press or something of the kind had just been opened, and all the writers, publishers, agents and professionals of literature had been invited to celebrate it. My job was to write a paragraph about it somewhere, and I remember wondering what there would be left to say when I had occupied space by giving no more than a list of the famous people present—and so recognisably present.

Then Cunninghame Graham came into the large and opulently furnished room. Immediately the life and the distinction seemed to drain out of everyone else. This old man of seventy-five made all the

---

[1] As this recollection of Cunninghame Graham is a purely personal one, it seemed to me ridiculous to continue here the 'we' style: I lapse again, with some relief, into the first person singular.—M. McL.

other notabilities at once appear not only undistinguished but unreal.
It was an extraordinary thing to observe. It was as if the figure out of
an old painting had stepped out of its frame and had moved among the
rest of us, to reduce us to dummies.

I met him briefly and in less crowded circumstances two or three
times again before he died in 1936. Always he produced the same effect;
the nearer he got to death the more vivid did he appear, the more unreal
did he render those around him.

Cunninghame Graham's appearance, manner, personality and achievements have been so often and so well described that the image of him
is even yet fairly clear in the popular mind. I add here only what is to
our purpose.

He was a Scottish laird of three-quarters pure Scottish descent and
one-quarter Spanish hidalgo. At times he said he felt more Spanish
than anything else, but in moments of stress or deep feeling, as he
admitted, the Scot in him overruled all other strains. He was one of the
most uncommon men one could meet, yet he had more, far more, than
his share of common humanity. This laird in Queen Victoria's reign
was one of the foremost champions of the oppressed working classes
of the period and was sent to prison in 1887 for taking part in a Trafalgar
Square demonstration of marchers.

Though the scene of his then highly left-wing activities was London,
he never put himself forward as an Englishman. One of his strongest
early devotions was to the Irish leader Charles Stewart Parnell, and
even then he repelled the description of British. As he grew older, and
particularly after the First World War, he became associated with the
cause of political Scottish Nationalism, and under that banner very
nearly became elected as Lord Rector of Glasgow University.

He wrote and spoke about Scotland, but it is not from these utterances
that we have made our single selection. Nor have we included his famous
Scottish short story *Beattock for Moffat*; it has been reprinted too often.

We print here, with the kind permission of his executors and publishers, the beginning of his story *Success*.[1] It has nothing to do with
Scotland. Indeed, at the time of its publication at the turn of the century,
it flew clean in the face of the accepted mediocre Scottish view about
the value of Success. The mere fact that such a Scotsman at such a time
could write such a story shows that the unquenchable spirit of an older
Scotland was not dead. Here it is without further comment.

Success

Success, which touches nothing that it does not vulgarise, should be
its own reward. In fact, rewards of any kind are but vulgarities.

We applaud successful folk, and straight forget them, as we do ballet-
dancers, actors, and orators. They strut their little hour, and then are

[1] From *Rodeo*. A Collection of Tales, by R. B. Cunninghame Graham
(Heinemann), pp. 417-19.

relegated to peerages, to baronetcies, to books of landed gentry, and the like.

Quick triumphs make short public memories. Triumph itself only endures the time the triumphal car sways through the street. Your nine days' wonder is a sort of five-legged calf, or a two-headed nightingale, and of the nature of a calculating boy—a seven months' prodigy, born out of time to his own undoing and a mere wonderment for gaping dullards who dislocate their jaws in ecstasy of admiration and then start out to seek new idols to adore. We feel that, after all, the successful man is fortune's wanton, and that good luck and he have but been equal to two common men. Poverty, many can endure with dignity. Success, how few can carry off, even with decency and without baring their innermost infirmities before the public gaze.

Caricatures in bronze and marble, and titles made ridiculous by their exotic style we shower upon all those who have succeeded, in war, in literature, or art; we give them money, and for a season no African Lucullus in Park Lane can dine without them. Then having given we feel that we have paid for service rendered, and generally withhold respect.

For those who fail, for those who have sunk still battling beneath the muddy waves of life, we keep our love, and that curiosity about their lives which makes their memories green when the cheap gold is dusted over, which once we gave success.

How few successful men are interesting! Hannibal, Alcibiades, with Raleigh, Mithridates, and Napoleon, who would compare them for a moment with their mere conquerors?

The unlucky Stuarts, from the first poet king slain at the ball play, to the poor mildewed Cardinal of York, with all their faults, they leave the stolid Georges millions of miles behind, sunk in their pudding and prosperity. The prosperous Elizabeth, after a life of honours, unwillingly surrendering her cosmetics up to death in a state bed, and Mary laying her head upon the block at Fotheringay after the nine and forty years of failure of her life (failure except of love), how many million miles, unfathomable seas, and sierras upon sierras separate them?

And so of nations, causes and events. Nations there are as interesting in decadence, as others in their ten-percentish apogee are dull and commonplace. Causes, lost almost from the beginning of the world, but hardly yet despaired of, as the long struggle betwixt rich and poor, which dullards think eternal, but which will one day be resolved, either by the absorption of the rich into the legions of the poor, or vice versa, still remain interesting, and will do so whilst the unequal combat yet endures.

Causes gone out of vogue, which have become almost as ludicrous as is a hat from Paris of ten years ago; causes which hang in monumental mockery quite out of fashion, as that of Poland, still are more interesting than is the struggle between the English and the German, which shall sell gin and gun-powder to negroes on the Coast.

Even events long passed, and which right-thinking men have years ago dismissed to gather dust in the waste spaces of their minds, may interest or repel according as they may make for failure or success.

Failure alone can interest speculative minds. Success is for the millions of the working world, who see the engine in eight hours arrive in Edinburgh from London, and marvel at the last improvement in its wheels. The real interest in the matter being the forgotten efforts of some alchemist who, with the majesty of law ever awake to burn him as a witch, with the hoarse laughter of the practical and business men still ringing in his ears, made his rude model of a steam engine, and perhaps lost his eyesight when it burst.

COMPTON MACKENZIE

The one selection we make from Sir Compton Mackenzie's enormous, varied and fruitful output is drawn from his address to the students of Glasgow University when he was installed as their Lord Rector in 1932.[1] We use the word 'their' to enforce the point that in the Scottish Universities the Lord Rector is the students' representative on the University Court and is chairman of it; he is elected by them. Mackenzie was the first Scottish Nationalist ever to be elected Lord Rector by the students of any one of our four ancient universities; there has been one since; and, just before Mackenzie, Cunninghame Graham had narrowly missed election. As will be seen below in the text, Compton Mackenzie refers with admiration to the illustrious failure of his friend and predecessor as candidate. It is this that gives us a link with the previous extract from 'that old cavalier, the defeated candidate.'

But it is not merely because of the convenience of the link that we have chosen extracts from this Rectorial address. Throughout his earlier, southern and wandering life the fact of Scotland and of his Scottish descent had haunted Compton Mackenzie; you may perceive evidence of this in his first work even and remotely in *Sinister Street*. From the late 1920s he has lived for the most part, and latterly entirely, in Scotland. He has written and spoken much about Scotland in differing moods, varying from deep seriousness through affection to satire and

[1] Address by Compton Mackenzie on his installation as Rector. Jackson Wylie, Glasgow, pp. 6 and 23–30.

even good-humoured farce. Never in our opinion has he spoken or
written on this subject more effectively, more explicitly or more from
his heart than on this occasion in 1932.

Three years and three months ago to this very day I was waiting
in the lounge of an Edinburgh hotel to hear the result of the previous
Rectorial. I had allowed myself to hope for a vote sufficiently conspicuous to impress itself upon what was seeming at that time—three
years and three months ago—the scepticism or apathy of the country.
When that old cavalier, the defeated candidate, came into the lounge,
holding between his fingers like a lace handkerchief the telegram from
Glasgow which told how high he stood, a pale regretful dream of mine
haunting the lost battlefields of our race was in that moment by a
single gesture of contemporary youth magically endowed with
pulsating life. If you will stop to consider the acute condition of self-
consciousness to which the Scottish nation has been reduced by that
experiment and adventure of yours, three years and three months
ago today, I believe you will acquit that last sentence of rhetorical
inflation. . . .

Compton Mackenzie then spoke of the political atmosphere in which
he had grown up; he described his conversion to the ideal of small
nations and, in particular, of the idea of the small nation of Scotland.
He spoke of his return to Scotland, and ended thus:

You are luckier than I am, my constituents. You have not to return
to Scotland: you are there. And you have not had to maintain your
faith through the shifting and deceptive colours of a dream, waking
from it only in middle-age to behold the white and clear and stedfast
dawn. You are young at that awakening. There is at this moment
sitting in one or other of these halls a student who when ten trienniums
shall have passed will stand where I stand now, and be triumphant
in the golden noon of his country's new life. But that country can live
only by the fullness with which every individual man and woman
begins now to live with it, and for it, and by it. The measure of such
a fullness will be the ruthlessness with which you expel the incomplete
group-selves that are being formed by the spirit of the time and
replace them at whatever the cost to your material comfort with the
true and perfectible selves of the individual man and woman. We
now alive in Scotland, though not necessarily therefore living, are
offered the grace of sharing in the rebirth of a nation. That mysterious
gift of Divine life which is continually being granted to individuals
has hitherto eluded the analysis of any psychologist. We are familiar

with, and with familiarity often contemptuous of, the phenomenon of religious conversion. We know that in many cases it is an hysterical phase of adolescent growth. Yet when we have disposed of a hundred cases there will be found one of which we cannot dispose and of which we cannot deny the permanence and fruitfulness. Among the constant characteristics of all genuine conversions is the subject's suddenly heightened sense of ordinary life and an immensely wider perception of its richness. In a single instant of revelation he is made aware of the immortal substance of things; but his secret remains incommunicable. The phenomenon of conversion, though usually accorded a religious significance, is not peculiar to religion. An artist may pass through a mental state analogous to conversion in the first moment of an imaginative conception, and when he does we call it 'inspiration.' I have seen the phenomenon of conversion among those who have been wakened to a sudden comprehension of what true nationalism is. They are changed by some mystical experience, and in loving their country they love their fellow-countrymen. It is such a love which alone can justify the reformer. Too many attempts at reformation have been made either in a spirit of hate and destructiveness or, what is ultimately more deadly, in a spirit of constructive utility. Desire the good of your fellow-men, but desire it because you love them, not because a well-fed, well-clad, well-housed creature will be an economic asset to the state. Many of you present are filled with ambition to re-create a nation; but your immediate and predominant duty is to re-create yourselves, for only in re-creating yourselves will you re-create that nation. . . .

When the Roman Empire broke up and Europe was ravaged by horde upon horde of barbarians from the East, almost the only light that shone forth into the bloodstained darkness shone from Erin and from the holy Western Isles of Alba. It may be that once again beside the Atlantic the souls of men will save themselves, and in saving themselves save the soul of man. It may be that this task is the supreme destiny of the Celtic race. I cannot but think that the rise of nationalism primarily in Glasgow is of tremendous significance to the potential force and endurance of the movement, for, though we must acclaim Edinburgh as the capital, the stern and masculine parent, Glasgow is the metropolis—the mother city. No other city is so representative of the whole country, and what is true of Glasgow is true of Glasgow University. Every criticism which is levelled against it may be levelled against Scotland itself. The virtues, faults, hopes, fears, ambitions, and dreams of the country as a whole are more completely expressed

X

in this University than anywhere. Its very position in the midst of a crashing industrial turmoil and yet always within sound of the two voices of liberty, the voice of the sea and the voice of the hills, is a prefigurative symbol of our country's future.

A few weeks ago upon the Campsie Fells I gazed down at Glasgow. From a mass of dark cloud the sun, himself obscured from where I stood, sloped his golden ladders into that rain-washed city, which lay with all her spires and chimneys, with all her towers and tenements and sparkling roofs, like a vision of heavenly habitations. I have looked down over Athens. I have looked down over Rome. With beauty unparagoned the glory and the grandeur of the past have been spread before my eyes; but in that sight of Glasgow something was added which neither Rome nor Athens could give—the glory and the grandeur of the future, and the beating heart of a nation.

CHRISTOPHER MURRAY GRIEVE

(Hugh MacDiarmid)

The first and most important thing to say about Christopher Grieve, poet, writer, visionary, controversialist, rebel, and most kindly friend to so many in Scotland today, is this. If it had not been for him, none of the younger and few of the elder writers of any note in Scotland now would be writing as they are. This is not to say that they are writing in imitation of him, but merely that they are writing as they are because of him and his achievements. On this we are here in Scotland unanimous.

The phrase 'the Scottish Literary Renaissance' has been tarnished by over-use, misuse and misunderstanding. It has certainly been mis-understood in England. In so far as it retains its meaning—and it does for us—it would be safe to say that this renaissance would not have had its form, certainly not its impetus, and possibly might not have occurred without C. M. Grieve. It is true that in the uneasy period between the wars someone else might have come along to speak for Scotland, but if so the effect would have been different. At any rate, no one else did come along before Grieve.

By his genius and by his achievements in the 1920s and '30s, he created a conception of Scottish poetry and what has to be done in it. Many poets today in Scotland, whose manner and form are quite different from his, are writing under the original influence of his verse and within the scope of his conception. He has also had his influence on prose-writers who have never attempted a line of verse in their lives but who feel his impetus. As a man, too, his integrity, his single-minded, courageous and arduous devotion to the idea of Scotland as a nation within the nations of the world (a nationalist who is an internationalist), he has acted as an inspiration on many of his countrymen and country-women who have no literary pretensions at all.

Of course he has hostile, sometimes bitterly hostile, critics among the Mandarins as well as the Philistines. It is, in a sense, almost a tribute to him that most of these critics have either not read his poetry or, if they have looked at it, have no idea what it is all about. His personality is so strong that it enables people who have not read a line of his verse or who have made no attempt to understand it, to object to it in principle. The mediocre are repelled by him instinctively and can thoroughly dislike him with their eyes shut and their fingers stuffed into their ears.

Of course he has said silly things in public, and particularly on public platforms (so would most of us if we had had to endure the opposition he has faced). Of course he has blotted his copy-book in behaviour and convention (that is partly what copy-books are for), and he has sometimes been wantonly rude, though I cannot recollect that he has ever done anyone a real unkindness or a malicious service (of how many men of letters could one say this?) and I have known him for thirty years.[1] Of course he has his affectations and minor absurdities. Of course we could forgive him these things on account of what he has given us in his poetry; but what is remarkable, as all his friends and most of his large acquaintance will testify, is that we could forgive them just for himself alone. His good humour, his generosity of temper, particularly towards the young, his courage and unshaken patriotic integrity far outweigh those faults of his which are so readily seized upon by those who are against him.

He was born in 1892 in what would then have been called humble circumstances in the town of Langholm, very close to the English border. Indeed, it is a sign of his intense preoccupation with his national and racial roots that he has been known to say that if he had been born six miles farther south he would have become an English nationalist poet. This he might well have done, but the one thing he would never have been was a British poet.

He received a good modest country and Edinburgh education of the kind then open to a youth of his circumstances; but his considerable learning in literature he acquired for himself by his voracious reading from early boyhood. It was not until the 1920s, when he was just in his thirties, that he made his impact as a Scottish poet speaking *for*, not just about, Scotland. It was an impact that was immediately felt by all lively minds in his own country, but passed utterly unrecognised by the entrenched ranks of academic mediocrity. The officials and the Mandarins (such as they were) of Scottish literature paid little or but scornful attention to him.[2] It was left to *The Times Literary Supplement*,

[1] As this is a paragraph of personal experience and opinion I have once again lapsed into the first person singular.—M. McL.

[2] It is fair to add that a few eminent Scots in England, or those who had been educated in England, such as John Buchan, did recognise his talents early.

four hundred miles to the south, to say this of his first volume of Scots lyrics:

'He writes in the faith without which there can be no conquest; the belief that Scotland has still something to say to the imagination of mankind, something that she alone among the nations can say, and can say only in her native tongue.'

This was English criticism at its best and most generous.
Even farther south, Professor Denis Saurat exclaimed in *Marsyas*:

'Il faut que MacDiarmid prenne la place de Burns. Ce serait une calamité. Mais, comme Burns a commencé quelque chose de nouveau, MacDiarmid commence quelque chose de nouveau; par conséquent quelque chose qui n'est pas Burns. Et qui cependant est écossais, mais qui, en même temps, est européen. Burns n'etait européen que par ses platitudes.'

But in Scotland, with a very few honourable exceptions, no one of the slightest academic importance paid the slightest attention to him.
Until the 1930s he continued his struggle to express the idea of Scotland in the language of Scottish poetry. He had his ardent followers, but they could do little to help him to earn a livelihood. He never compromised, never wavered; but eventually it seemed that the blank wall of Scottish mediocrity had become too much for him; he had a complete collapse in health.
He was forty-three or forty-four and, as it happily turned out, that collapse was the curable *crise de la quarantaine* which George Bernard Shaw used to insist is almost an obligatory experience for men of high talent in the forties. He emerged from this experience curiously serene; and his serenity has lasted and grown as he has become old. Though Scotland may, in parts, have quarrelled with him, he has never quarrelled with Scotland: he loves her too well.
He did, however, almost abandon the all too strenuous and exciting practice of Scots lyric poetry and expressed his philosophy in free English verse. It is impossible to compress that philosophy here. Let us simply say that he is as intensely nationalist as ever, but sees the future of Scotland against the background of humanity. He is a strongly forward-looking man, and he differs from many nationalists in that there is not, and never has been, in his nationalism any weakening nostalgia for the past.
He has been much recognised in Eastern Europe, and it is perhaps natural for him to see the future of humanity developing along the lines of the Communist philosophy. While he doubtless has his reservations about the regimes of the Communist countries as at present conducted, he is a Communist and looks forward with serenity to the contribution Scotland can offer to a Communist world.
There are so many qualifications one could make about such a statement that I think it best for me to assume the personal role again and speak of but one which I have personally noticed. Grieve is the only

Communist I have known with whom it is possible to discuss religion rationally. The reason is simple. As anyone who reads him attentively will note, he knows what religion is about. He had not accepted at their face value the party *clichés* about religion. He has a fair knowledge of the rudiments of Catholic theology, and has in my presence expressed a genial, if guarded, appreciation for that faith. I do not for one moment believe that this is merely politeness. Chris Grieve has never been rude to me, but he has never (except for the exercise of a rather old-fashioned courtesy) gone out of his way to be polite to me.

We print below, with as few comments as possible, extracts from his poetry. The first is from his most powerful poem in Scots and of his first period. The last extracts are from his latter period and are in English.

A Drunk Man Looks at the Thistle

A Drunk Man was published in 1926 and was a powerful departure from the earlier lyricism in Scots. It is a tough poem that was, when it came out, not easy to grasp.[1] It is now clear what Grieve was getting at, but it remains difficult to quote from. Grieve's thought is *extensive*, and he must be read *extensively*, but we have done our best with our selections.

A drunk man, having taken enormous quantities of whisky, falls into a ditch and, *in aqua vitae veritas*, perceives a vision of Scotland. From this we have chosen one little snatch from the end of the poem which sums up very well his doctrine of Scotland and the infinite. Unless we can see Scotland properly we cannot be truly international, and unless we are international we cannot see Scotland. That is indeed what is wrong with us now.

This first extract is the climax of the work right at its end. It is full of irony, and ironical abuse. 'Mercy o' Gode, I canna thole wi' sic an orra mob to roll.' You would scarcely believe that that is the beginning of a passage which is to end with the great statement 'A Scottish poet maun assume the burden o' his people's doom.' This is precisely what Grieve was doing in his thirties; hence his collapse in his forties, and hence his present reward.

> Whatever Scotland is to me,
> Be it aye pairt o' a' men see
> O' Earth and o' Eternity.

---

[1] *A Drunk Man looks at the Thistle* (Blackwood, Edinburgh, 1926) came out shortly after T. S. Eliot's *The Waste Land*. Comparisons on grounds of idiom and style have been made. The two works are, however, fundamentally utterly unlike. *The Waste Land* is a defeatist work, a work, so it seems to us, redolent of the consciousness of sexual decline. *A Drunk Man* is not a defeatist poem. It is tough and unmistakably masculine with not a sniff of impotence in it.

Wha winna hide their heids in't till
It seems the haill o' Space to fill,
As 'twere an unsurmounted hill.

He canna Scotland see wha yet
Canna see the Infinite,
And Scotland in true scale to it. . . .

And as I looked I saw them a',
A' the Scots baith big and sma',
That e'er the braith o' life did draw.

'Mercy o' Gode, I canna ^athole   ^abear
Wi' sic an ^aorra mob to roll.'   ^aodd
—'Wheesht! It's for the guid o' your soul.'

'But what's the meanin', what's the sense?'
—'Men shift but by experience.
'Twixt Scots there is nae difference.

'They canna learn, sae canna move,
But stick for aye to their auld groove
—The only race in History who've

'Bidden in the same category
Frae stert to present o' their story,
And deem their ignorance their glory.

'The mair they differ, mair the same.
The wheel can whummle a' but them,
—They ca' their obstinacy "Hame,"

'And "Puir Auld Scotland" bleat wi' pride.
And wi' their minds made up to bide
A thorn in a' the wide world's side.

'There ha'e been Scots wha ha'e ha'en thochts,
They're strewn through maist o' the various lots
—Sic traitors are nae langer Scots!'

'But in this huge ineducable
Heterogeneous hotch and rabble,
Why am *I* condemned to squabble?'

'A Scottish poet maun assume
The burden o' his people's doom,
And dee to brak' their livin' tomb.

'Mony ha'e tried, but a' ha'e failed.
Their sacrifice has nocht availed.
Upon the thistle they're impaled.

'You maun choose but gin ye'd see
Anither category ye
Maun tine your nationality.'

And I look at a' the random
Band the wheel leaves whaur it fand 'em.
                              'Auch, to Hell,
I'll tak' it to avizandum. . . .'

O wae's me on the weary wheel,
And fain I'd understand them!

And blessin' on the weary wheel,
Whaurever it may land them! . . .

From the Later Poetry

The last selections are from Grieve's poetry written in English and since the 1930s. It is all in irregular metre and those who are antagonistic to it would say that it is merely prose chopped up into bits. There is no space to argue that point here. If those who find their attention caught by these selections which we have with difficulty made here will take the trouble to read further in Grieve they will find that the range of his mind in this later medium of his is intensely poetic, if often intellectually poetic. There are *clichés* and unfortunate phrases here and there, but such minor imperfections are soon forgiven by anyone who takes the trouble to steep himself in this truly Scottish, yet truly world-ranging poetry.

(1) FROM 'LUCKY POET'

This beautiful yet meticulously detailed extract[1] should surely appeal to anyone who approaches it with an unbiased mind. 'Our Scotland small?' he exclaims and then, with the aid of his botanical knowledge, goes on to show how smallness in its infinite detail is infinitely large.

Scotland small? Our multiform, our infinite Scotland *small*?
Only as a patch of hillside may be a cliché corner
To a fool who cries 'Nothing but heather!' where in September
    another
Sitting there and resting and gazing round
Sees not only the heather but blaeberries
With bright green leaves and leaves already turned scarlet,
Hiding ripe blue berries; and amongst the sage-green leaves
Of the bog-myrtle the golden flowers of the tormentil shining;
And on the small bare places, where the little Blackface sheep
Found grazing, milkworts blue as summer skies;
And down in neglected peat-hags, not worked
Within living memory, sphagnum moss in pastel shades
Of yellow, green, and pink; sundew and butterwort
Waiting with wide-open sticky leaves for their tiny winged prey;
And nodding harebells vying in their colour
With the blue butterfles that poise themselves delicately upon
    them,
And stunted rowan with harsh dry leaves of glorious colour.
'Nothing but heather!'—How marvellously descriptive! And
    incomplete!

(2) FROM 'IN MEMORIAM JAMES JOYCE'

This[2] has a less direct and clear appeal. We include it to show the undoubted mystical element in the poet's character which he here proclaims in his own fashion. He believes that there is an ultimate harmony of which we can get no more than the kind of intuition of which he here speaks.

While as a Scottish Borderer
I still take an unholy delight

[1] *Lucky Poet*, by Hugh MacDiarmid, p. 252. Methuen.
[2] *In Memoriam James Joyce*, by Hugh MacDiarmid, p. 98. Wm. Maclellan, Glasgow.

(Like the man who could not be a good philosopher
Because cheerfulness was always breaking in)
In occasional ascholic invasions
Of the autotelic,
Yet, continually tempering my judgment
With new understanding,
Not denying the autonomy of new work
Even as I declare its human value,
I know that in the final artistic
—The highest human—vision
There is neither good nor evil,
Better nor worse,
But only the harmony
Of that which is,
The pure phenomen
Abiding in the eternal radiance.

The vision is in no sense dynamic or prophetic.
It is a vision of understanding, not creation;
Of some vast wisdom deepening into twilight,
The glimmering light of intuition
Fading into mental complication;
Typical perhaps of the kind of psychism
That breaks out at the end of a dispensation,
But it is not the 'scream of Juno's peacock.' . . .

(3) FROM 'LUCKY POET'

In the hope of giving something which would show the unity of this
kind of poetry which he personally has created we have printed nearly
all of one long poem. It is the third of his *Direadh* ('climbing') poems.[1]

It would be possible to say a great deal about this extraordinary poem.
We confine ourselves to the following comments. From the image of
the dove flying into the cleft of the rock the poet sees his country flying
back into his own heart for refuge. This is a long way from the Drunk
Man's 'A Scottish poet maun assume the burden o' his people's doom,'
but it is the outcome of it. It is an astonishingly novel idea and one full of
splendid hope on which to end this anthology. In this poem Christopher
Grieve, as nowhere else, looks to the future of Scotland and of mankind
with serene confidence. He looks with the poet's eye but also according
to his own wisdom which is a part of the wisdom of his country today.

[1] *Lucky Poet*, pp. 300–5.

*'So, in the sudden sight of the sun, has man stopped, blinded, paralysed
and afraid?'*

I am reft to the innermost heart
Of my country now,
History's final verdict upon it,
The changeless element in all its change,
Reified like the woman I love.

Here in this simple place of clean rock and crystal water,
With something of the cold purity of ice in its appearance,
Inhuman and yet friendly,
Undecorated by nature or by man
And yet with a subtle and unchanging beauty
Which seems the antithesis of every form of art.

Here near the summit of Sgurr Alasdair
The air is very still and warm.

The Outer Isles look as though
They were cut out of black paper
And stuck on a brilliant silver background,
(Even as I have seen the snow-capped ridges of Hayes Peninsula
Stand out stark and clear in the pellucid Arctic atmosphere
Or, after a wild and foggy night, in the dawn
Seen the jagged line of the Tierra del Fuego cliffs
Looking for all the world as if they were cut out of tin,
Extending gaunt and desolate),
The western sea and sky undivided by horizon,
So dazzling is the sun
And its glass image in the sea.
The Cuillin peaks seem miniature
And nearer than is natural
And they move like liquid ripples
In the molten breath
Of the corries which divide them.
I light my pipe and the match burns steadily
Without the shielding of my hands,
The flame hardly visible in the intensity of light
Which drenches the mountain top.

TODAY   331

I lie here like the cool and gracious greenery
Of the water-crowfoot leafage, streaming
In the roping crystalline currents,
And set all about on its upper surface
With flecks of snow blossom that, on closer looking,
Shows a dust of gold.
The blossoms are fragile to the touch
And yet possess such strength and elasticity
That they issue from the submergence of a long spate
Without appreciable hurt—indeed, the whole plant
Displays marvellous endurance in maintaining
A rooting during the raging winter torrents.
Our rivers would lose much if the snowy blossom
And green waving leafage of the water-crowfoot
Were absent—aye, and be barer of trout too!
And so it is with the treasures of the Gaelic genius
So little regarded in Scotland today.
Yet emerging unscathed from their long submergence
Impregnably rooted in the most monstrous torrents
—The cataracting centuries cannot rive them away—
And productive of endless practical good,
Even to people unaware of their existence,
In the most seemingly-unlikely connections. . . .

It is easy here to accept the fact
That that which the 'wisdom' of the past
And the standards of the complacent elderly rulers
Of most of the world today regard
As the most fixed and eternal verities—
The class state, the church,
The old-fashioned family and home,
Private property, rich and poor,
'Human nature' (today meaning mainly
The private-profit motive), their own race,
Their Heaven and their 'immortal soul,'
Is all patently evanescent,
Even as we know our fossil chemical accumulations
Of energy in coal, peat, oil, lignite and the rest
Are but ephemeral, a transitory blaze
Even on the small time-scale of civilized man,
And that running water, though eminently convenient and practicable

For the present, will give us a mere trickle
Of the energy we shall demand in the future.

And suddenly the flight of a bird reminds me
Of how I once went out towards sunset in a boat
Off the rocky coast of Wigtownshire
And of my glimpse of the first rock-pigeon I saw.
It darted across one of the steep gullies
At the bottom of which our boat lay rocking
On the dark green water—and vanished into safety
In a coign of the opposite wall
Before a shot could be fired.
It swerved in the air,
As though doubtful of its way,
Then with a glad swoop of certainty
It sped forward, turned upward,
And disappeared into some invisible cranny
Below the overhanging brow of the cliff.

There was such speed, such grace, such happy confidence of refuge
    in that swoop
That it struck me with the vividness of a personal experience.
For an instant I seemed to see into the bird's mind
And to thrill with its own exhilaration of assured safety.
Why should this be? It was as though
I had seen the same occurrence,
Or some part of it, before.

Then I knew. Into the back of my mind had come
The first line of the loveliest chorus in *Hippolytus*,
That in which the Troezenian women,
Sympathising with the unhappy Phaedra,
Who is so soon to die by her own hand,
Sing of their yearning to fly away from the palace
Whose sunny terraces are haunted by misery and impending doom.
They long to escape with the flight of the sea-birds
To the distant Adriatic and the cypress-fringed waters of Eridanus
Or to the fabulous Hesperides,
Where beside the dark-blue ocean
Grow the celestial apple-trees.

It is the same emotion as filled the Hebrew poet
Who cried: 'O for the wings of a dove,
That I might flee away and be at rest.'
'Ηλιβάτοις ὑπὸ κευθμῶσι γενοίμαν.[1]

The untranslatable word in that line
Is the ὑπό.[2] It includes more
Than a single word of English can contain.
Up-in-under: so had the pigeon
Flown to its refuge in 'the steep hiding-places,'
So must Euripides have seen a sea-bird
Dart to its nest in the cliffs of Attica.
For an instant, sitting in that swaying boat
Under the red rocks, while the sunset ebbed down the sky
And the water lapped quietly at my side,
I again felt the mind of the poet reaching out
Across the centuries to touch mine. . . .

So every loveliness Scotland has ever known,
Or will know, flies into me now,
Out of the perilous night of English stupidity,
As I lie brooding on the fact
That 'perchance the best chance
Of reproducing the ancient Greek temperament
Would be to cross the Scots with the Chinese.'
The glory of Greece is imminent again to me here
With the complete justification his sense of it
In Germany—his participation in that great awakening
Taking the form of an imaginative reliving,
On behalf of his people, of the glory of Athens—
Lacked in Hölderlin. I see all things
In a cosmic or historical perspective too.
Love of country, in me, is love of a new order.
In Greece I also find the clue
To the mission of the poet

[1] Eur., *Hipp.*, 732.
[2] It is a favourite sneer of those who dislike Grieve's work to say that he chucks about quotations from languages with which he is not quite familiar. Perhaps he sometimes does. But he has an extraordinary instinct for looking up the right quotation and right reference. This is a poetic rather than pedantic gift. He has here, for instance, *perceived* the meaning of the word perfectly. And he has pounced upon the quality of the word ὑπό perfectly and poetically.

Who reveals to the people
The nature of their gods,
The instrument whereby his countrymen
Become conscious of the powers on whom they depend
And of whom they are the children,
Knowing, in himself, the urgency of the divine creativeness of Nature
And most responsive to its workings in the general world. . . .

So Scotland darts into the towering wall of my heart
And finds refuge now. I give
My beloved peace, and her swoop has recalled
That first day when my human love and I,
Warmed and exhilarated by the sunny air,
Put on our skis and began
A zigzag track up the steep ascent.
There was no sound but the faint hiss and crush
Of the close-packed snow, shifting under our weight.
The cloudless bowl of the sky
Burned a deep gentian. In the hushed, empty world
Where nothing moved but ourselves,
Our bodies grew more consciously alive.
I felt each steady beat of my heart.
The drawing and holding of my breath
Took on a strange significance.
Nor was I merely conscious of myself.
I began to be equally aware of my love;
Her little physical habits
Sinking into my mind
Held the same importance as my own. . . .

I am with Alba—with Deirdre—now
As a lover is with his sweetheart when they know
That personal love has never been a willing and efficient slave
To the needs of reproduction, that to make
Considerations of reproduction dictate the expression of personal love
Not infrequently destroys the individual at his spiritual core,
(Thus 'eugenic marriages' cannot as a whole
Be successful so far as the parents are concerned,
While to make personal love master over reproduction
Under conditions of civilisation is to degrade
The germ plasm of the future generations,

And to compromise between these two policies
Is to cripple both spirit and germ),
And accept the only solution—unyoke the two,
Sunder the fetters that from time immemorial
Have made them so nearly inseparable,
And let each go its own best way,
Fulfilling its already distinct function,
An emancipation the physical means for which
Are now known for the first time in history!

Let what can be shaken, be shaken,
And the unshakable remain.
The Inaccessible Pinnacle is not inaccessible.

So does Alba surpass the warriors
As a graceful ash surpasses a thorn,
Or the deer who moves sprinkled with the dewfall
Is far above all other beasts
—Its horns glittering to Heaven itself.

These lines of the living poet C. M. Grieve might well end this anthology and without comment. A coincidence appeared, however, which is so significant that it does not seem purely fortuitous. Part I of this book ended in *The Cherry and the Slae* with the youth attaining and climbing the impossible tree of his desire. Part II ends with the noble statement that 'The Inaccessible Pinnacle is not inaccessible' and with the comparison of Alba to the deer 'Its horns glittering to Heaven itself.'

I did not design this. The book under its own impetus moved to these two endings. It was inevitable; for herein lies the true wisdom of the Scots.